AFRICAN VISIONS

AFRICAN VISIONS

Literary Images, Political Change, and Social Struggle in Contemporary Africa

Edited by
Cheryl B. Mwaria, Silvia Federici,
and Joseph McLaren

Prepared under the auspices of Hofstra University

PRAEGER

Westport, Connecticut
London

The Library of Congress has catalogued the hardcover edition as follows:

African visions : literary images, political change, and social struggle in contemporary
Africa / edited by Cheryl B. Mwaria, Silvia Federici, and Joseph McLaren; prepared under the auspices
of Hofstra University
     p. cm.—(Contributions in Afro-American and African studies, ISSN 0069–9624 ; no. 197)
     Includes bibliographical references and index.
     ISBN 0–313–31045–9 (alk. paper)
     1. Africa—Civilization—20th century. 2. Africa—Social conditions—1960– 3. African
literature—20th century—History and criticism. 4. Politics and
literature—Africa—History—20th century. 5. Africa, Sub-Saharan—Civilization—20th
century. 6. Africa, Sub-Saharan—Social conditions—1960– 7. Africa,
Sub-Saharan—Literatures—History and criticism. 8. Politics and literature—Africa,
Sub-Saharan—History—20th century. I. Mwaria, Cheryl Benoit, 1948– II.
Federici, Silvia. III. McLaren, Joseph. IV. Hofstra University. V. Series.
DT14.A37434 2000
960.3'1—dc21   99–043520

British Library Cataloguing in Publication Data is available.

A hardcover edition of *African Visions* is available from Greenwood Press,
an imprint of Greenwood Publishing Group, Inc.
Contributions in Afro-American and African Studies, number 197;
(ISBN 0–313–31045–9)

Library of Congress Catalog Card Number: 99–043520
ISBN: 0–275–97102–3

First published in 2000

Praeger Publishers, 88 Post Road West, Westport, CT 06881
An imprint of Greenwood Publishing Group, Inc.
www.praeger.com

Printed in the United States of America

The paper used in this book complies with the
Permanent Paper Standard issued by the National
Information Standards Organization (Z39.48–1984).

10 9 8 7 6 5 4 3 2 1

To the Memory of
Ken Saro-Wiwa
and to the peoples of Africa

Contents

Part II: Literature, Social Change and Culture

Acknowledgments

This volume collects a series of essays, some of which were originally presented at the Africa 2000 conference that was held at Hofstra University on October 12 through 14, 1995. The conference was dedicated to the struggle of the Ogoni people and to Ken Saro-Wiwa, who was executed in Port Harcourt (Nigeria) on November 5 of the same year.

The conference, sponsored by the Hofstra Cultural Center, brought together scholars, political activists, and artists to discuss the future of Africa at a very crucial moment in the continent's history. The present volume completes the task with the incorporation of new materials directly bearing on the discussion.

African Visions was made possible from its inception by the assistance provided by the Hofstra Cultural Center, the cooperation of the Hofstra Africana Studies Committee, as well as the financial help given by the Dalton School and Hofstra University to whom we owe our deepest gratitude. We want to also thank here the many colleagues that have helped in the process. In particular, we thank Athelene A. Collins-Prince, Judy M. D'Angio, and Rob Leonard.

Introduction

Cheryl B. Mwaria

What can be said of Africa at the dawn of the twenty-first century? The answers are both complex and varied. The colonial division of Africa has given rise to fifty-four countries each of which is multiethnic, multilingual, multicultural, and multireligious. Though this has often been perceived as the core of Africa's problems, it may well be seen as its strength. The invented national memories and uniformities designed to chronicle the teleological march of African cultures, economies, and polities from 'tradition' to 'modernity' to paraphrase Paul Zeleza (1997: 19) are being replaced by new voices of change and resistance without the facile optimism of President Clinton's remarks during his 1998 visit to the continent and without the hopelessness and despair of earlier critics. The question raised by Basil Davidson at the beginning of the postcolonial era, "Whither Africa?" is still valid. It is against this background of unprecedented change, symbolized most graphically by the fall of apartheid, that this book examines the current crises, new forms of resistance, and proffered paths of reconstruction in Africa at the dawn of the twenty-first century.

This volume opens with the words of South African poet and activist Dennis Brutus. His poem, *"What Is the Soul of Africa?"* captures the spirit of this volume, and his chapter, "Africa 2000: In the New Global Context" was based on his keynote address, which opened the conference out of which this volume grew. Brutus focuses our attention on the devastating consequences of structural adjustment policies, particularly for Africa, policies that still have not been adequately addressed, even given President Clinton's momentous visit, and raises the call for change. Brutus asserts, "It is crucial, in this context, that we do not accept the current academic wisdom which pretends that there are no choices or alternatives. . . . Alternatives exist. A crucial condition is that African countries begin to cooperate with each other on a regional basis, so that they are no longer forced to be dependent on the global structures and agencies that today are trying to dictate Africa's political and economic course. If this can happen, then a better, more promising future can be envisaged."

Africa has, for too long, been seen through a myopic lens, which has depicted the continent as both helpless and hopeless. Media portrayals of the AIDS pandemic, starvation, "tribal wars," political corruption, and chronic dependence on external aid have resulted in what Bourenane (1992) has termed "afro-pessimism," discussion that apportions blame entirely to Africans themselves, since it is largely supported by the powers that be, by groups opposed to the regimes in power, including experts of international bodies responsible for finance and development. While there is no doubt that the interplay of geography and capitalism have placed a heavy burden on Africa resulting in unprecedented inequalities of income, the unpaid and unpayable debts of many African governments have not forced them, during the last two decades of the twentieth century, into bankruptcy. Instead they have been forced into accepting the devastating structural adjustment policies of the World Bank and the International Monetary Fund as Brutus asserts.

These policies have stripped countries of the ability to invest in the development of sound infrastructures, particularly in health and education, and have resulted in the brutal repression of ordinary citizens struggling to make ends meet. On the local level too, there has been repression. The cold war both ushered and nurtured a number of dictatorships in postcolonial Africa, military and civilian, whose leaders squandered their countries wealth while amassing personal fortunes. While some of the most notorious, Mobutu Sese Seku in the former Zaire, Banda in Malawi, and Abache of Nigeria have departed, others such as Moi of Kenya remain in power.

The postcolonial history of Africa, therefore, has tended to be analyzed from two different perspectives: on the one hand there are those who argue that colonial capitalist intervention did not destroy the specificity of African cultures and, consequently, that modern inequality and corruption existing in Africa must be laid squarely at the feet of Africans themselves, or at the very least, be seen as an outcome of precolonial social structures. This thinking is typical of those who attribute modern political conflict to "tribalism" rather than to more complex external factors. On the other hand, there are those who acknowledge that the political institutions characterizing African states after independence were imposed by former colonizers who continue to play an active and direct role in African political processes, the complexities of which often mask external efforts to maintain or increase political and economic hegemony of these same neocolonialists.

François Ngolet's chapter, "Democratization and Interventionism in Francophone Sub-Saharan Africa," is of the latter mode. Ngolet argues that France still plays a major role in state building in Francophone Africa, an argument underscored by France's notable support for corrupt allies including those responsible for the genocide in Rwanda, Banda in Malawi, Eyadema in Togo, and its prolonged support of Mobutu Sese Seko in Zaire. Ngolet, however, goes further to examine the post-cold war climate of economic competition between France and the United States, wherein the U.S. has begun to seriously challenge France's interests while the efforts of Africans themselves to shape their political future during the democratization process hangs in the balance.

Diane Ciekawy's chapter, "Mijikenda Perspectives on Religious Freedom and Cultural Rights," provides ethnographic support for the argument that African cultural values, as An Na'im and Deng assert "embody ethical, moral, spiritual, and religious norms that are similar or are identical to the overall goals of legitimizing and promoting universal human rights and ideals" (1990: 1). Though the notion of human rights for Africans was historically considered an oxymoron by centuries of slavers, colonial exploiters, and dictators, Ciekawy argues that the syncretic belief systems held by the Mijikenda and other indigenous African peoples emphasize tolerance and are compatible with many statements made in con-temporary human rights, cultural rights, and religious rights literature. The failure of many contemporary human right activists to recognize this, she opines, can be attributed to the socially embedded (as opposed to abstract) nature of rights and obligations in African cultures. Nevertheless, Ciekawy documents the ways in which a precolonial Mijikenda institution, the *kaya,* continues to operate in Kenya influencing local political affairs and, like other such indigenous institutions, can make a significant contribution to the reemergence of African civil societies.

Although the colonial state, as Paul Zeleza (1997: 19) has opined, despite its pretensions as a civilizing force, did little to promote education, African student activism played a critical role in the anticolonial struggle in virtually every African country. This is even more surprising given the fact that during the colonial period African students in higher education comprised a minority, often educated abroad, who were expected at the end of colonialism to become the future leaders of peoples from whom they had often become distanced physically, linguistically, economically, and even culturally. In other words, they were an educated elite.

The postcolonial explosion of education at all levels in Africa marked an attempt to break away from colonial forms of education, which were designed to serve colonial capitalism and fend off the nationalist fervor of the masses. These universities were both few in number and dominated by expatriates. A university education was a passport to state administration and virtual guaranteed upward mobility and employment, student activism as a result tended to be limited in scope and generally supportive of the state.

More important, the state continued to loom "large in all discussions of academic freedom in Africa, because African universities, except the ancient Islamic and modern Christian Universities, were founded, financed, and controlled by the state" (Zeleza 1997: 19). The plight of institutions of higher education in Africa, and the role of student activism within them under the terms of structural adjustment policies is addressed from varying perspectives by several of the essays in this volume. Silvia Federici's chapter, "The New African Student Movement," examines African student activism in the wake of structural adjustment policies that have devastated higher education in Africa. In it she argues that "the main difference between the new student movement and those that have preceded it concerns its changed class character, as determined by the status of university students as a social group, and their future economic and political destination." On both counts she argues, "It is clear that African students have been proletarianized." Federici focuses attention on the underreported pan-African student struggle as a continuum with students in various parts of the world to challenge a corporate agenda to reshape education to fit their narrow interests. It is a struggle within which African students have paid the heaviest costs, including loss of life, while the world looks elsewhere.

In "Academic Pursuits under the Link," Karim F. Hirji provides a personal account, as a member of the Faculty of Medicine of the University of Dar Es Salaam, of the fragmentation of university life and the subsequent "intellectual atrophy" that it brings. Hirji argues that increasing dependence on foreign support has resulted in the vast expansion of higher-education facilities in Tanzania, on the one hand, "but these institutions sprang up as appendages of the government or parastatal bureaucracy," which in turn, has led to them having little if any "impact on its respective social or economic sector." Indeed, Hirji notes, "In some cases the growth of the educational arm went hand in hand with the deterioration of the sector it was to serve." Waste, corruption, and the misallocation of resources are not restricted to Tanzania or even Africa, they have been evident in the "developed" world as well. What is particularly disturbing in Africa is the stifling of creativity and initiative in education and educational research that has resulted in the failure to address the most pressing problems facing its people, problems that Hirji believes can successfully be addressed with cooperation and courage.

George Caffentzis's chapter, "The International Intellectual Property Regime and the Enclosure of African Knowledge, reiterates Hirji's argument that African universities have been undermined by targeted short-term funding on the part of external (foreign) agencies of select departments or programs. Caffentzis focuses on a novel area: seed and pharmaceutical patents that transnational corporations have appropriated by "plundering the knowledge and terrain of people living in the most biologically diverse parts of the planet," tropical rain forests. By allowing only the patenting of final products, rather than production processes, the World Trade Organization favors the most technologically advanced and costly processes over more labor-intensive ones. Without support of domestic academic institutions, Caffentzis asserts, transnational corporations easily trampled farmer's rights with respect to plant breeding while weakening "the ability of African countries to enforce measures that would protect Africa's knowledge, traditional or otherwise." The short-term, contracted projects favored by First World donor agencies, corporations and governments ("LINKS," in Hirji's terminology) reap profits while rendering African universities mere "intellectual plantations." African universities are, as these three essays assert, once again at the forefront of the struggle to resist encroachment in favor of true intellectual collaboration.

Public health issues in Africa remain a primary concern at the dawn of the twenty-first century. Given the failure of colonial administrations to develop the infrastructure of African societies, rapid population growth, environmental degradation, and the subsequent emergence of postcolonial dictatorships followed by stringent structural adjustment policies, it is no wonder that Africa lags behind the developed and much of the developing world in terms of public health. Nowhere can this be seen more dramatically than in the arena of the AIDS pandemic, which according to recent estimates inflicts one in four African men, women, and children in those areas of the continent most heavily hit. Research in the spread of AIDS in Africa has tended to portray Africans as promiscuous and ignorant while ignoring or minimizing the link between poverty and disease transmission. Advances in treatment, and in the understanding of the transmission of the virus from mother to child have led to dramatic reductions in transmission rates in the United States, but in Africa, apologists have argued such treatment is prohibitively expensive and impractical despite the fact that in some areas, including South Africa, up to 40 percent of pregnant women are HIV positive.

Ida Susser's cutting-edge chapter, "Women and AIDS in Southern Africa: A Report from the Field," demonstrates the wealth of grassroots interest and knowledge about AIDS characteristic of African women who also expressed an eagerness to try new methods of "safe sex." It should be noted that these data contradict the often repeated media presentation of such women as both ignorant and apathetic. The real barrier to decreasing the spread of the AIDS epidemic, Susser asserts, is poverty. Conversely, as her informants opine, the best method for preventing HIV is to provide work for women.

The close of the twentieth century has witnessed the struggle for social change in many arenas, increasingly located in urban settings. Contemporary African cities for the most part are characterized by problems confronting urban centers the world over—pressures of population, poverty, pollution, and general inability to maintain and expand infrastructures laid down long ago and inadequate to the rapidly increasing demands of ever expanding populations. What distinguishes urban centers in many African countries is the fact that despite these problems they still offer vastly more opportunities than the rural hinterlands comprising most of the continent.

This is due in part to disparate development policies of colonial administrations to plan disperse urban centers. Political corruption, crippling debt and draconian restrictions imposed by the International Monetary Fund and the World Bank have only exacerbated the problem. Habibeh Rahim's chapter, "A Vision of the Past as a Beacon for the Future: The Application of the Fatimid Ideals in the City of Cairo," examines Cairo, one of the oldest cities in Africa, and contrasts the Fatimid ideals practiced by its founders with the realties of the modern city. In so doing, she raises the question of whether it is possible to reshape and revamp an aging, antiquated megalopolis not only with physical changes of the built environment but also with philosophical and ideological transformations that may facilitate its dynamic participation in world events.

In answering the question, she examines issues not only of trade and commerce but issues of social welfare, justice, gender relations, and cross-communal patronage as well.

A new wave of African emigration has emerged in the late twentieth century in response to growing inequalities and shifting sands of current world politics and economies. In what Manuel Castells (1996: 379) has called the informational age of capitalism, the "informational/global economy is organized around command control centers able to coordinate, innovate, and manage the intertwined activities of networks of firms." In so doing, a new class of professional elites has emerged, connected by instantaneous flows, while common people remain outside the network to cope with growing inequalities, the polarization of wealth differentials and new patterns of labor exploitation. Under these conditions, what is political consciousness? What kinds of social networks do common people rely upon? Steven Colatrella's chapter, "Structural Adjustment and the African Diaspora in Italy," focuses on the characteristics of African immigrants living and working in the Veneto region of northeast Italy. These immigrants fleeing pressures created by structural adjustment programs in their countries of origin have formed social networks which facilitate political mobilization in their country of arrival and yet must resist becoming subordinated to global forces, such as organized crime, international planning institutions, and state policies. We see here once again the contribution of Africans to national histories and working-class movements beyond Africa.

The second part of this volume opens with Maina Kīnyattī's poem, *"The Monstrous Instrument"* as a reminder of the power of the pen and the influence of writers in Africa and, indeed, everywhere. In assessing the position of the African writer, Ngũgĩ wa Thiong'o (1988: 102) has argued:

The lot of the writer in a neo-colonial state will be harder and not easier. His choice? It seems to me that the African writer . . . who opts for becoming an integral part of the African revolution has no choice but of aligning himself with the people: their economic, political and cultural struggle for survival. In that situation he will have to confront the languages spoken by the people in whose service he has put his pen.

Ngũgĩ's chapter in this volume, "African Languages and Global Culture in the Twenty-first Century," reiterates this theme. There are over one thousand languages spoken in Africa. While most of these languages are in no immediate danger of extinction, being spoken by anywhere from a few hundred to a million people, the advent of colonialism introduced a form of linguistic hegemony which has placed African languages and cultures at a disadvantage. In the face of increasing globalization of culture through technological development, Ngũgĩ asserts there will also be a countermovement of localization, "a sense of looking for identity and place in the global community." Africa, he argues, has been robbed of languages in a literal and figurative sense.

Further, Ngũgĩ asserts: "Just as the working person in Africa produces gold from mines, coffee, and tea leaves, exports to the Western world, in the same way at the level of languages, he or she produces proverbs and songs, drawing upon those songs to create this other identity which is important. Ngûgî opines that while the world has been enriched by Africa, the reverse is not true. Looking forward to the next century he argues that "one of the areas that needs important and urgent attention is the decolonization of that one most basic means of imagination and most basic means of naming the world, that is, languages." What Ngûgî is arguing here is that African languages at the very least be used on par with European and Asian ones, in so doing, African peoples will be returned to the creative center in the area of not only language, but of literature, culture, and hopefully economic and political organization as well. This then is the main challenge to writers and scholars.

The dawn of the twenty-first century is a momentous period in terms of African cultural and political identity. F. Odun Balogun's chapter, "Hybridity, Neo-universalist Cultural Theory, and the Comparative Study of Black Literatures," focuses on the interventions of four interrelated approaches of black intellectuals to multiculturalism: Kwame Anthony Appiah's *In My Father's House: Africa in the Philosophy of Culture* (1992), Paul Gilroy's *The Black Atlantic: Modernity and Double Consciousness (1993)* Mole Kete Asante's 1989 revised edition of *Afrocentricity*, and Ngûgî wa Thiongo's *Moving the Center: The Struggle for Cultural Freedoms* (1993). In questioning the philosophies of these four differing approaches to multiculturalism, Balogun sheds light upon their implications for the "textual analysis of African and African American literatures as separate entities, but more especially as comparable cultural phenomena." The debate here revolves around the cultural manifestation of identity in terms of ethnicity, nationality, class, and gender, as well as the appropriate modes of socioeconomic and political cooperation and development. Nancy Topping Bazin takes up the question of gender, identity and political direction in her chapter. "White Women, Black Revolutionaries: Sex and Politics in Four Novels by Nadine Gordimer." Bazin's analysis focuses on a critical question, raised by Gordimer, for a liberated South Africa, "Where do whites fit in?"

Alamin M. Mazrui's chapter, "Socialist Oriented Literature in Post-Colonial Africa: Retrospective and Prospective, addresses the question of the direction of socialist inspired writing in post-colonial Africa and the foundation of this literature as well. Mazrui analyzes the contrasting predictions of two African writers: Udenta O. Udenta who argues that "African literature is deemed to be on a progressive path from its apologist beginnings through intermediate liberationist, negationist and critical stages, to a final revolutionary, Marxist peak" and that of Jack O. Ogembo who in focusing on the developments in Kenya's literary scene views what he calls post-Ngûgî fiction as moving away from the kinds of political concerns that normally sustain the growth of socialist inspired literature, in favor of narrower themes like corruption, rural-urban tensions, and cultural conflicts.

Mazrui argues that "the struggle for political pluralism in Africa is leading to a decline of neonationalism. At the same time, however, that struggle seems to be leading to a rising ethnonationalism. This focus in the politics of pluralism may, in turn, promote greater use of indigenous African languages in writing African literature, including socialist inspired literature." Mazrui believes that the economic realities in Africa seem to be leading to both social restratification and linguistic restratification. In a somewhat contrasting view from that of Ngûgî, Mazrui points to a proliferation of journals and other literature in ethnic-bound languages, which has accompanied the democratic tide of the nineties. At the same time he views English consolidating itself, "especially in the urban areas—the fertile ground of socialist inspired literature." This English is, he argues, increasingly being Africanized and is likely to serve as the medium of the "educated underclass" from whose ranks a new socialist inspired literature may eventually arise.

Joseph McLaren's chapter "The Nigerian Novel in English: Trends and Prospects," examines the predicament of politically committed Nigerian novelists brought about by both the repression imposed by the military who control Nigeria, and the restrictions imposed by structural adjustment policies which have severely curtailed publishing opportunities. Nigerian writers committed to protest are faced with the dilemma of living in exile, as has Nobel laureate, Wole Soyinka, or facing imprisonment and possibly death, as in the case of Ken Saro-Wiwa who was executed by the Abacha regime shortly after this conference and to whom this volume is dedicated. McLaren argues that in situations where the state is oppressive, committed writers often couch political protest in popular forms. Literary survival is dependent on reaching the broadest possible audience, which, McLaren asserts, primarily seeks entertainment through popular themes. This has led many Nigerian writers, particularly those who produce novels in English, to exploit a variety of mediums, including the publication of serialized novels in the popular press, the use of television, and the production of plays. Although Nigeria is believed to have more than forty booksellers and publishers, their productivity is questionable. Furthermore, as McLaren points out, the development of internal publishing is crucial if writers are to avoid having their agendas set by outsiders, a situation which may ultimately deny Africans their own voice. Nevertheless as McLaren opines, there is still a role for external publishers to play in promoting Nigerian writers "if these houses are willing to take risks associated with literary production in Nigeria, and if they are to expand their publication of works by writers in exile in the West and elsewhere."

As in the case in Nigeria, politically committed writers in Algeria are increasingly faced with the choice of exile, or faced with the threat of death. Soraya Mekerta's chapter, "Writing in and out of Algeria, Writing Algeria, Today," examines this dilemma, particularly from the standpoint of women writers in Algeria. Focusing on the work of Afsa Zinai-Koudil, Letifa Ben Mansour, and others, Mekerta examines the mechanics of fear, noting that in contemporary Algeria, "everything can be potentially distorted, look suspicious, and become abnormal, justifying in turn, the abnormal." If Algeria is ever to acknowledge that it is a pluralistic society, if it's leadership is ever to be forced to protect the rights of all of its citizens, women included, writers must not be silent. This takes acts of courage, the courage to "keep on standing up, to speak and shout, to write, to create, to organize to protest, to denounce, to dare, to hope, to imagine, to live." Mekerta reiterates the power of the pen by reminding us that "the bodies of those who stand or die serve as marks, that is, as evidence that an important activity is going on and consists in writing in and out of Algeria, writing Algeria."

Oussena Alidou Dioula's chapter, "Popular Hausa Drama in Niger and the Politics of Its Appropriation," explores traditional Hausa drama prior to colonization that set the stage for the emergence of the modern Hausa popular theater. Alidou focuses on *Wasan kara-kara*, a form of public satire or parody of prominent leaders in Hausa society. The objective of this art form was to do more than merely entertain. According to Alidou, it was to give the common people the opportunity to express their assessment of the sociopolitical performance of the society's leadership through the parody. With the advent of colonialism, new elements in the form of linguistic transformations were added to this popular theater as French and "broken" French were used to reflect the new power dynamics operating within Hausa culture. During the colonial period, asserts Alidou, the internal class dialectic characteristic of traditional *Wasan kara-kara* is transformed into a "popular" national symbol of resistance, and *Wasan kara-kara/ gujiya* is born as the major artistic tool of contestation. Alidou traces changes in this art form through independence when it is used as a political tool to denounce Dioro Hamani's regime, which called for the development of an alternative, *Wasan Kwaykoyo*, ostensibly for the sake of national unity, but actually to facilitate the censorship of *Wasan kara-kara*. Alidou contends that for Hausa drama to once again assume a genuine and active role in the process of democratization, it must regain its traditional role of dialectically engaging both its producers, the masses, and the ruling classes to reflect on the conditions of the cultural struggles both within and outside without any attempt to control.

Loren Kruger's chapter, "Developmental Pleasures: Education, Entertainment, and Popular Literacy in South Africa," explores the emergence, in the wake of the victory over apartheid, of "patchwork of popular cultures—a variety of forms, practices and habits of consumption—in contradictory relation to ongoing grassroots struggle, regional, national, and international mass media, and the pleasures and pitfalls of modernity." Among these is the comic, or graphic short story, which has emerged as a bridge, straddling the boundaries between formal and informal communication, pleasure and instruction, word and image. As such it has been an effective tool for the development of literacy, particularly among those whose education was disrupted by a decade and a half of social turmoil. Kruger examined the work of the Storyteller Group and Story Circle as part of a number of projects in post apartheid South Africa that depart in a number of ways from the culture for development paradigm. These groups use both oral transmission and live performance to reflect the specific concerns of both rural and urban communities while demonstrating their necessary interaction. More important, Kruger argues that these cultural projects acknowledge that the "lives of their audiences and interlocutors, even in areas like the former Bantustans, are shaped in positive, as well as negative ways, by the pleasures of mass mediated representations of popular recreation, as well as those of local recreation."

Donald Morales's chapter, "Postapartheid Drama" presents a review of recent plays by South Africans, both black and white. In it, he raises the oft-repeated question of whether art will remain tied to politics in the new South Africa. Morales argues that there has to be a compromise between acknowledging the past and developing new themes or "politics will consume all of South Africa along with its artists. If not, their record of literature will be of period works that mark a decade but do not reveal a generation or culture." While one may not entirely agree with Morales, it is a relief to be able to ponder the question.

REFERENCES

An Na'im, Abdullahi and Deng, Francis. Introduction. In *Human Rights in Africa: Cross Cultural Perspectives*. Washington, DC: The Brookings Institution, 1990.

Bourenane, N. "Prospects For Africa for an Alternative Approach to the Dominant Afroessimism." In *30 Years of Independence in Africa: The Lost Decades?* Ed. Peter Anyang' Nyongo, Nairobi: Academic Science Publishers, 1992, 47–61.

Castells, Manuel. *The Rise of the Network Society*. Oxford: Blackwell, 1996.

Davidson, Basil. *Which Way Africa?* Middlesex , England: Penguin, 1964.

Ngûgî wa Thiong'o, "Writing against Neo-colonialism." In *Criticism and Ideology: Second African Writers' Conference, Stockholm 1986. Ed. Kirsten Holst Petersen, Uppsala: Scandinavian Institute of African Studies, 1988, 92–103.*

Zeleza, Paul Tiyambe. "Academic Freedom in the North and South: An African Perspective." *Academe* (November–December 1997): 16–21.

Part I
Social Movements

Poem: "What Is the Soul of Africa?"
by
Dennis Brutus

What is the soul of Africa?
What is it?
Is there a soul of Africa?
Is it simply that we have
contrived to be what humans are
while everywhere humanity
was being deformed?
and in the new age of man
this lunatic unsublunary age
is it still valuable to be man?
to assert the old humanities?

1

Africa 2000: In the New Global Context

Dennis Brutus

As we are preparing to enter the third millennium, Africa is undergoing major developments in a new global context. A new political and economic agenda is being designed for the continent, that will deeply affect the life of the African people far beyond the year 2000. What are the contents of this agenda, their implications, and some of the possibilities which they open?

Since the end of the cold war, a new vision of the world has taken shape. This is based on the fact that we live today in a unipolar world, dominated by only one superpower. The end of the conflict between capitalism and socialism has so changed the global political landscape that Francis Fukuyama has even suggested that we are witnessing "the end of history" (Fukuyama 1992). According to Fukuyama, we are moving toward a world whose major trends and patterns can be expected to remain essentially unchanged politically and economically. It is a world where power will always be in the hands of those who now possess it and the powerless will continue to remain so, a world, most important, where the rich will get richer, and the poor will get poorer. This, today, is the new orthodoxy that politicians as well as academics are spreading through the world.

This new trend has been promoted by World Bank and the International Monetary Fund (IMF), according to guidelines that were established in 1944, at the Bretton Woods Conference, in New Hampshire, when policies were devised to create a world where the type of political and economic disruptions brought about by the World War II would no longer occur. These two institutions recently celebrated their fiftieth anniversary. Perhaps what they were also celebrating is the fact that they now seem to be capable of imposing on the populations of the planet the agenda that issued from Bretton Woods, that until now they have been unable to realize, due to the existence of a conflictual world in which the two dominant powers had nuclear missiles turned against each other.

Glimpses of this agenda, particularly as it affects Africa and other "less developed" countries, can be caught from a statement made in 1992 by Lawrence Summers, who was then chief economist of the World Bank and is now deputy secretary of the Treasury in the Clinton Administration. In an internal memo leaked, however, to the press, Summers proposed that the toxic waste of the "First World" be shipped to the countries of the "Third World." His argument was that the Third World had more space for such waste and the cost of treating the diseases that nuclear waste may produce is much lower in these countries ("Let Them Eat Pollution" 1992).

Summer's views are typical of the perspective embraced by those who are shaping World Bank policies. The Bank has been arguing that the causes of Africa's economic bankruptcy are the corruption and inefficiency of its political class and its wasteful governmental spending, including that for education. What Africa needs, according to the World Bank is not more educated people–professionals, people with managerial skills–but rather more people who have "practical" skills, that is, people who can work at service counters or in the service industry. "Capacity," not education, is the key word in this context, and the World Bank has appointed itself as the agency equipped to provide it, as we learn from a document they have published in 1991 titled "Africa Capacity Building Initiative" (Committee for Academic Freedom in Africa 1994; World Bank 1991).

What the World Bank has recommended are massive cuts both in the education budgets of African countries, cuts reaching 50 percent of the spending for universities (for buildings, for salaries of staff and teachers) and cuts in the number of the students admitted. The supporting argument is that instead of training doctors, engineers, dentists, lawyers, Africa's higher-education institutions should train people to work in industry.

What we see at work here is a strategy that Paul Johnson, a writer for the *New York Times Magazine,* described in an article titled "Colonialism's Back and Not a Moment Too Soon" (Johnson 1993). In this article, Johnson made three points: (1) African countries are economically bankrupt; (2) they have discovered that they cannot govern themselves; and (3) African countries are now asking the colonial powers to return to run them. As unbelievable as these claims may seem, they now express the position of the two Bretton Woods institutions, as they are extending their hegemony over Africa and other "less-developed" regions of the planet.

One of the central mechanisms by which this recolonization process is carried out is the loans system. Significantly, none of the countries that have received loans from the World Bank have seen their economies improve. Quite the opposite. All are in a far worse economic position and far more indebted, than they were prior to taking those loans. Zimbabwe, for instance, is now diverting 30 percent of its gross national product to the repayment of the loans it has taken from the World Bank.

Once the loan is taken, paying it back is a back-breaking matter, a staggering cost for the economy of the borrowing country. But this is only a part of the problem. Even more pernicious is the fact that, in making the loan, the World

Bank dictates how the money is to be spent, which is specified through a whole set of "conditionalities." One of them is the drastic reduction of public spending for education that, in some cases, is cut by as much as 50 percent. Other conditions include equally devastating cuts in the number of civil servants; and massive currency devaluations, that have dramatically diminished the purchasing power of the African people, while at the same time dramatically increasing the cost of imported products.

This policy goes by the name of structural adjustment program). It is interesting to note, however, that in the case of South Africa, which is still struggling to obtain a loan from the World Bank, the policy is referred to as a "rationalization" program. The implication is that there is something quite irrational that needs to be corrected, with the number of professional, students, and teachers who are present in African universities today. The World Bank is also insisting that South Africa should remove any legislation in support of a minimum wage. The existence of a minimum wage is seen as a major flaw, as the World Bank believes that there should be no limits to how far down wages are to be depressed. In addition, the South African government, under Mandela, is being asked to promise that it will not allow workers to strike.

The end result of structural adjustment is, in all cases, a country even more bankrupt, more unable to repay its loans, and more immiserated, as its currency is devalued, its services are gutted, and its agricultural sector is turned upside down to produce cash crops for export rather than food for the people's subsistence. This has been the case of Zimbabwe, where the World Bank has persuaded the government to shift production from food crops like maize, which are geared to local consumption, to an export crop like tobacco. Not surprising, malnutrition has grown, and infant mortality, for children below the age of one, has doubled.

It is hardly imaginable that anyone could knowingly devise such a ruthless, heartless system, entirely devoted to increasing profit and absolutely indifferent to its human cost. This, however, is the system that is shaping life in Africa today, and it is the system that we must challenge.

It is crucial, in this context, that we do not accept the current academic wisdom that pretends that there are no choices or alternatives. This is a position that, these days, one often hears rehearsed also in South Africa. The group of people who embrace it calls itself TINA, which means exactly that *There Is No Alternative*. But we have to challenge the assumption that structural adjustment is inevitably Africa's way to the future.

Alternatives exist. A crucial condition is that African countries begin to co-operate with each other on a regional basis, so that they are no longer forced to be dependent on the global structures and agencies that today are trying to dictate Africa's political and economic course. If this can happen, then a better, more promising future can be envisaged.

What is certain is that we cannot accept the prospect of a world where the majority continues to become poorer and poorer, while a few individuals continue to amass incredible riches. This is what the people in Africa or, better, people all over the planet, are saying. Last week, while the World Bank was celebrating its fiftieth birthday, there were demonstrators in the streets of Washington, declaring that "fifty years are enough!" They were part of a powerful campaign that has been mobilizing across the United States and other countries and that carries this name: "50 Years Is Enough?" Along the same lines, during the summit of the G-7 in Halifax, Nova Scotia, earlier this year, three thousand people gathered in the streets protesting the G-7's global agenda. Among them were the homeless, women who are fighting against discrimination, and teenagers who know that there are no jobs for them and who have no hope for the future.

They all understood what structural adjustment involves, and not just in the Third World, for this program is being carried out not only in Africa, Asia, and South America but also in Canada and the United States. Both in Washington and Halifax people recognized that there is a link between the recolonization of Africa and other parts of the Third World and the attack on workers' social and economic rights in the metropoles. They recognized the increasing homogenization of global rule, as the multinational companies and the multinational financial agencies like the World Bank and IMF are increasingly taking over the economies of every country in the world. Most important, they recognized that the struggle for self-determination and human welfare must be a globally coordinated project. The future will decide whether or not this project can be realized. But there can be no doubt that the answer to this question will determine the course of African history in the twenty-first century.

REFERENCES

Committee for Academic Freedom in Africa. (1994). "The World Bank's African Capacity Building Initiative: A Critique," *CAFA Newsletter, 6* (Spring), 14–19.

Fukuyama, Francis. (1992). *The End of History and the Last Man.* New York: Free Press.

Johnson, Paul. (1993, April 18). "Colonialism's Back—And Not A Moment Too Soon." *New York Times Magazine,* 22.

"Let Them Eat Pollution" (excerpt from a letter written by the chief economist of the World Bank). (1992). *The Economist, 322,* 66.

World Bank. (1991). *The African Capacity Building Initiative: Toward Improved Policy Analysis and Development Management.* Washington, DC: Author.

2

The International Intellectual Property Regime and the Enclosure of African Knowledge

C. George Caffentzis

> We must be firm in naming names and telling our trading partners
> that we will act if they harbor pirates, counterfeiters, or permit
> infringements to go unpunished—Ira S. Shapiro, General Counsel,
> Office of the U.S. Trade. (U.S. Senate Committee on Finance 1993)

> The question must again be asked: to which workers ought the
> (unevenly) developed productive forces belong? Which workers'
> wages should be determined by them? Those of the area where
> these forces are located? Those of the branch of production or
> the enterprise that possess them? (Emmanuel 1972)

The motivations behind the structural adjustment policy the World Bank has
imposed on African universities are by now the object of a large debate
(Committee for Academic Freedom in Africa 1991, 1995, 1996; Seidman and
Anang 1992). Inevitably, one of the questions that scholars and activists have
asked is why the World Bank has been unwilling to reconsider this policy,
despite the fact that it undermines one of the main achievements of postcolonial
Africa—the creation, in one generation, of a university system virtually
exnihilo—and despite the fact that its pernicious consequences have for some
time been evident. In addition, why has the World Bank forced many universities
to practically grind to a halt (as in the case of Nigeria and the former Zaire) or to
survive by relying on foreign "donors" and, in the process, loose any
semblance of independence (as in the case of Tanzania and Uganda)? Why
has it assisted the most massive brain drain witnessed in Africa, since the slave
trade, and why has it ignored the endless violations of students' and teachers' rights
that the adjustment policies have cost?

This situation seems even more puzzling given that the World Bank has
persistently stressed the importance of knowledge for "developing" countries,

and presents education as a *sine qua non* condition for the "wealth of nations." Why, then, this contradiction?

Among the explanations offered, the most convincing makes reference to (1) the "recolonization" of the Third World, which has been carried on by the transnational corporations (TNCs), with the assistance of the World Bank and International Monetary Fund (and now the World Trade Organization [WTO]); and (2) the new international division of labor that has followed from it (Federici 1997). According to this view, the dismantling of African education is part of a process aimed to restore the "metropoles" to their role of "heads" of the world economic system—those who take the managerial lead, make decisions for the world economy and produce the standard cultural models—while most regions of the Third World, beginning with Africa, are being returned to their colonial role as providers of raw materials and "cheap" labor for the international market. In other words, according to this perspective, we witness an attempt to redivide and centralize world economic functions, with the First World aiming again to play the "mind," and forcing the Third World back into its colonial role as the "body" or "hand" of the empire. The World Bank's hosannas in praise of knowledge would be, in this context, a further example of that double talk for which the Bank's hired intellectuals have become so famous.

As convincing as it is, I propose that this analysis does not cover an important aspect of the World Bank's strategy for education in Africa. This is the fact that the defunding of Africa's higher-education systems, and their consequent loss of independence are functional to the success of the policy of intellectual property rights, enforced, since the early 1980s, by the TNCs and the United States government, with the assistance of the World Bank. In this article, I argue that the "adjustment" of African universities is not only intended to limit the Africans' access to knowledge. It is also intende to expropriate Africans of the knowledge that they have accumulated over the centuries, and to restore an unequal exchange that is even more pernicious than the one that prevailed in the colonial and postcolonial periods, since it forces African countries to pay an exorbitant price even for the acquisition of the very knowledge from which they have been expropriated. It is to this process that I give the name of the "enclosure of African knowledge."

INTELLECTUAL PROPERTY RIGHTS AND
A NEW UNEQUAL EXCHANGE

The institution of "intellectual property rights" is in essence a policy by which pharmaceutical, agricultural, biogenetic, and computer software TNCs are allowed to privatize, enclose, and assert their exclusive monopoly over the cultural wealth of the planet—so that no shred of information and knowledge can "ideally" be acquired without passing through a monetary exchange, and without a toll being paid by the purchasers to these companies (Fowler 1995; Jussawalla

1992; Shand 1994; Shiva 1994; Watkins 1992).

This may not seem a new process, given that the commercialization of knowledge has historically been an integral component of capitalist development and is a structural imperative in a capitalist society where everything must be subordinated to the cash nexus (Long 1991). However, trade in "intellectual property"—patents, copyrights, trademarks—has intensified in the recent past. With the simultaneous introduction of computer software, biogenetically manipulated seeds and pharmaceuticals, video and sound recordings, and the new importance acquired by international name-brand recognition, intellectual commodities have become one of the lifelines of world trade. For instance, the export of computer software (that, in real terms, involves permission to use the software programs and not the discs they are inscribed on) reached $95 billion in 1995, with the U.S. firms being the dominant suppliers, shipping 75 percent in 1993. Intellectual property is now the main surplus sector in the U.S. balance of trade, and, not surprisingly, it is defended with the same viciousness with which the British protected the opium trade in China.

World trade tribunals and a world trade police have been instituted, managed by the WTO, through the trade-related intellectual property clauses of the Uruguay Round of General Agreement on Tariffs and Trade (GATT), that stipulate its right to intervene at the slightest sign of a violation of the companies' "intellectual property rights" (Dawkins 1994). Worse yet, the U.S. Congress has also given the companies a hand, through the trade legislation Special 301, which foresees stiff retaliatory measures—such as trade boycotts— against governments found guilty of violating the U.S. companies' intellectual property rights (U.S. Senate Committee on Finance 1993).

The ascendance of this intellectual property regime has been very costly to producers and consumers of science, art and culture throughout the planet, with the meting out of lengthy jail sentences to individuals, and the imposition of collective punishment for wayward nations.

As I will argue, this process is assisted and legitimized by the defunding and deactivation of the institutions of higher learning in the Third World, particularly in Africa. First, however, it must be stressed that the very countries that, from the viewpoint of the world market, seem to have "no inventions for sale" and no intellectual property exports, are increasingly the sources of the products that the U.S. and European seed and biogenetic companies are selling as their inventions. It goes without saying that these same countries have nothing to gain under the current WTO "intellectual property" regime (Richardson and Gaisford 1996).

The bulk of the seed and pharmaceutical patents that the TNCs have introduced in recent years have been appropriated by plundering the knowledge and terrain of people living in the most biologically diverse areas of the planet: the tropical rain forests (Shiva 1995). Countries like Brazil, India, China, Tanzania, Ivory Coast, and the Philippines (Wilson 1992: 262–263) are the main areas of operation of the TNCs, in their effort to monopolize knowledge and establish their property rights over biological species. They are the biodiversity "hot spots" of the planet, that is, the areas with the highest concentration of unique species and the greatest danger of species extinction.

The traditional knowledge possessed by indigenous peoples in these hot spots has become a prized asset as demonstrated by the World Bank's new interest in it, that has already generated a new classic in bad faith, Ismail Serageldin's speech to the World Bank–sponsored two-day conference on traditional knowledge and sustainable development held in September 1993 (the proceedings of the conference were published in Davis and Ebbe (1995).

On this occasion, after decades of financing projects that physically and culturally destroyed indigenous peoples (e.g., the Chixoy Massacre in Guatemala) (Majot 1996/1997), Serageldin treated its audience of "indigenous experts" to a new rhetoric of "empowerment," replete with quotes from Aime Cesaire:

Indeed, we have to recognize that, by and large, everywhere in the world indigenous peoples have been victimized in the name of "progress." They have been persecuted by that which should have empowered. They have been oppressed by that which should have liberated. We must recognize that the post-colonial independence of many states has not translated into respect for the individual rights of indigenous peoples or indigenous communities . . . As Aime Cesaire said, "The universal is enriched by all its various particularisms." Empowerment and recognition of the rights of people to be themselves do not lead to disintegration into many cultural groups. . . . To the exponents of that broader society who speak with a certain degree of arrogance of the modernism and advancement that they contribute, I think we should remind them of the precarious reality of the human condition in most of these societies, the vulnerability of unskilled labor, the soul-destroying impact of poverty and homelessness, and the ease with which the rich and powerful subvert law enforcement to their own ends. (Davis and Ebbe 1995: 31)

We can be sure, however, that once these peoples' expertise in classifying the biodiversity of the tropical forests is acquired and all their "secrets" are revealed and appropriated, they too will meet the fate typical of indigenous people in World Bank's projects—possibly through a resettlement plan.

It is within this framework that we have now to reconsider the World Bank's policy toward education in Africa. At the most minimal level, it is clear that the collapse of Africa's hgher education systems allows the TNCs and the international financial agencies, like the World Bank, to present themselves, in the eyes of the world, as the centers best equipped and, consequently, best entitled, to protect, preserve, and control the cultural wealth of the continent, whatever form it may take (from agricultural seeds to "cultural property," such as archaeological sites, to pharmaceutical substances to be discovered through the exploration of Africa's forests) (World Bank 1992).

The ability of the TNCs to obtain licenses and legitimacy for "bioprospecting" relies, above all, on the general impoverishment of the African countries, that in the wake of liberalization must literally sell their birthrights (Tripp 1993). The disabling of the universities gives a powerful contribution to this process, as it weakens the ability of African countries to enforce measures that would protect Africa's knowledge, "traditional" or otherwise. Thus, ironically, just at the time when the dynamism of African knowledge is being recognized and the importance of "local," "situated" knowledge is being given a new episte-mological stature (Braidotti *et al.* 1994; Guyer 1996; Harding 1986), the World Bank is undermining any institutional basis for its protection.

In addition to legitimizing intellectual property rights, the structural adjustment of African universities helps to reduce the TNCs' costs of research and production, by making available to them a rich pool of cheap intellectual labor, and research facilities in the African higher-learning institutions. (There is parallel here with what is taking place with the Russian computer scientists, who are similarly being hired for a pittance, in this case by U.S. software companies, after the destruction of the Russian universities).

The recruitment occurs through the funding of select universities' departments, or programs that are allowed to survive, with the injection of short-term, task-oriented funds to pay for the personnel that is to help with bio-prospecting work or that is to provide a liaison with local communities and give the project a veneer of local/indigenous input.

Much gene hunting and gene plundering is now conducted in this fashion, with only those segments of the African universities being revitalized that can be used as intellectual plantations, where workers are expected to survive on short-term, contract-work projects, issuing from First World "donors" agencies, governments, and the TNCs themselves, which reap immense profits in the process. In other words, much of current research by pharmaceutical or agricultural companies consists of the "looting" of the medical and agricultural knowledge of Third World peoples.

The attack on African universities has had two other major consequences. First, it has undermined their ability to develop, on the basis of local/national research, cheaper products than those marketed by the TNCs. It has also subverted their capacity to protect "farmers rights" from external exploitation.

The WTO property rights regime allows the patenting of final products (the DNA-specified seed or the chemically defined pharmaceutical substance) rather than the patenting of production processes. Consequently, anyone wishing to utilize the processes leading to those products must pay fees to the patents' holder. This means that a Third World research institution would not be allowed to produce, by means of a different, low-tech, low-cost process, an ingredient present in a product patented by a U.S. company without paying fees to that company; nor could a Third World government allow a local company to patent it (Prashad 1994). That is why U.S.-based firms have fought a hard war against process-based patenting laws, and favored, instead, product-based laws. Product-patenting most often gives monopoly rights to the most technologically costly production process. Thus, any breakthrough replacing a high-tech process with a more labor-intensive one would be nullified, as the producer would have to pay a licence fee to the high-tech patent owner (Watkins 1992: 37–38).

Along the same lines, the rights of farmers living in the villages, fields and forests of Africa are more easily trampled upon, without the protection coming from the presence of a domestic academic institution, or branch of government capable of standing up to the TNCs (Brush 1992). This is what happened in the Uruguay Round of GATT (which led to the creation of the WTO), in the context of the debates over patent rights. The "plant breeders"—read, the TNCs—were unambiguously privileged over the farmers, who were thus deprived of their "comparative advantage," and prevented from putting it at the service of new agricultural technology (Dawkins 1994: 7).

This defeat of the African farmers' rights is directly related to the weakness of the universities that should be in charge of the conservation and exploration of their countries' wealthy biodiversity, and the protection of local knowledge. Calestous Juma suggested this much in the late 1980s:

By granting farmers' rights, African countries would also be asserting property rights over material that is in their territories and would therefore strengthen their capacity to bargain with potential users for other forms of compensation. They, for example, may require that the information and technical knowledge arising from the use of genetic material collected from the continent for breeding be exchanged freely with African scientists as a way of building local capability in related fields. (Juma 1989: 234)

Attempting, then, some general conclusion from this scenario, we can say that the weakening of the African universities is more than a means to devalue the workforce and to curtail Africa's political autonomy. It is also a means of intensifying the exploitation of the continent in a total and enduring way, by expropriating it of the capacity to reproduce itself materially and culturally.

Undermining university research, or allowing it to continue in a fragmented and dependent manner, under the direction of donors' programs and at the service of foreign TNCs, increases the expropriation of the continent's wealth, since it prevents Africans from devising local products, cheaper and more fit for local needs. It also forces them to pay exorbitant costs for commodities that have to be imported from abroad and which in many cases are—ironically or, better perhaps, tragically—made out of information robbed from local farmers or healers. By virtue of the peculiar working of the world market, in the transfer from the hands of Africans to those of the TNCs, the same products acquire a much higher value than they previously had, even though their use value may have remained unchanged. This is because the TNCs high-wage and high-tech work environment is more capital intensive than the low-wage, low-tech work of indigenous knowers in diverse African bioregions; and the value of intellectual property is not determined by its "use value."

More generally, the intellectual property regime has contributed to a situation in which the African people (but this situation is not confined to Africa) are forced to pay in order to use their own knowledge; as the products now patented by the TNCs are often nothing more than "high-tech" versions of a seed, plant part, chemical or drug that can only be found in the same "low-tech, low-wage" country that now has to pay for it.

Also, firms producing in the country of origin of a particular seed, plant part, chemical or drug, must pay a license fee to a foreign TNC patent holder, even though the use of the product was discovered by indigenous people of that very same country. Thus, the unequal exchange, first defined for nonintellectual products by Arghiri Emmanuel in the 1960s (Emmanuel 1972), could not be more complete and more perverse than it is in this new form.

This situation has sparked off a movement in the Third World to demand that either the patenting of life forms be abrogated or that intellectual property protection be extended to indigenous "farmers," to the peoples whose knowledge was used in creating a new lifeform, or to Third World countries whose territories are home to the species in question (Brush 1992). These claims, however, have had no impact on the WTO, whose primary goal is to expand the hegemony of the commodity form.

As this chapter suggests, one front for this struggle is education. This means that university struggles have an important bearing on the resistance to the WTO/U.S. intellectual property regime. Intellectual workers in the physical and social sciences, as well as artists and historians, could play a major role in the defense of local knowledge. This perhaps is one further reason why they have come so severely under attack from international agencies like the World Bank. Independent faculties and universities could, in fact, go a long way to ensure that the universities are not used as launching pads for bioprivateering.

REFERENCES

Braidotti, R., Charkiewicz, E., Hausler, S., and Wieringa, S. 1994. *Women, the Environment and Sustainable Development: Towards a Theoretical Synthesis.* London: Zed Books.

Brush, Stephen B. 1992. "Farmers' Rights and Genetic Conservation in Traditional Farming Systems," *World Development, 20* (11), 1617–1630.

Committee for Academic Freedom in Africa. 1991. *Cafa Newsletter, 2* (Fall), 2-12.

_____. 1995. *Cafa Newsletter, 9* (Fall), 8-13.

_____. 1996. *Cafa Newsletter, 11* (Fall), 5-8.

Davis, Shelton, and Ebbe, Katrinka (Eds.). 1995. *Traditional Knowledge and Sustainable Development: Proceedings of a Conference Held at the World Bank.* Washington, DC: World Bank.

Dawkins, Kristin. 1994. *NAFTA, GATT and the World Trade Organization: The Emerging New World Order.* Westfield, NJ: Open Magazine Pamphlet Series.

Emmanuel, Arghiri. 1972. (1969 1st ed.). *Unequal Exchange: A Study of the Imperialism of Trade.* New York: Monthly Review Press.

Federici, Silvia. 1997. "African Universities in the Globalization of Higher Education." Unpublished manuscript.

Fowler, Cary. 1995. "Biotechnology, Patents and the Third World." In Vandana Shiva and Ingunn Mosser (Eds.), *Biopolitics: A Feminist and Ecological Reader on Biotechnology*. London: Zed Books, 214-225.

Guyer, Jane I. 1996. "Traditions of Inventions in Equatorial Africa." *African Studies Review, 39* (3) 1–28.

Harding, S. 1986. *The Science Question in Feminism*. Ithaca, NY: Cornell University Press.

Juma, Calestous. 1989. *The Gene Hunters: Biotechnology and the Scramble for Seeds*. Princeton, NJ: Princeton University Press.

Jussawalla, Meheroo. 1992. *The Economics of Intellectual Property in a World without Frontiers: A Study of Computer Software*. Westport, CT: Greenwood.

Long, Pamela O. 1991. "Invention, Authorship, 'Intellectual Property,' and the Origin of Patents: Notes Toward a Conceptual History." *Technology and Culture, 32,* 846–84.

Majot, Juliette. 1996/1997. "Bank Acknowledges Chixoy Massacre, Hedges on Responsibility." *Bank-Check Quarterly, 16,* 3.

Prashad, Vijay. 1994. "Contract Labor: The Latest Stage of Illiberal Capitalism." *Monthly Review, 46,* 5 (October), 19-26.

Perelman, Michael. 1991. *Information, Social Relations and the Economics of High Technology*. New York: St. Martin' Press.

Richardson, R. Stephen, and Gaisford, James D. 1966. "North-South Disputes Over the Protection of Intellectual Property." *Canadian Journal of Economics, 29,* Special Issue Part 2 (April), S376-S381.

Seidman, Ann, and Anang, Frederick (Eds.). 1992. *Twenty-first Century Africa: Towards a New Vision of Sustainable Development*. (Trenton, NJ: Africa World Press.

Shand, Hope. 1994. "Patenting the Planet." *Multinational Monitor, 15,* 6 (June), 9-13.

Shiva, Vandana. 1994. "The Seed and the Earth: Biotechnology and the Colonization of Regeneration." In Vandana Shiva (Ed.), *Close to Home: Women Reconnect Ecology, Health and Development Worldwide*. Philadelphia: New Society Press.

_____. 1995. "Biotechnological Development and the Conservation of Biodiversity." In Vandana Shiva and Ingunn Mosser (Eds.), *Biopolitics: A Feminist and Ecological Reader on Biotechnology*. London: Zed Books, 193-213.

Shiva, Vandana, and Moser, Ingunn (Eds). 1995. *Biopolitics: A Feminist and Ecological Reader on Biotechnology*. London: Zed Books, 32.

Tripp, Robert. 1993. "Invisible Hands, Indigenous Knowledge and Inevitable Fads: Challenges to Public Sector Agricultural Research in Ghana." *World Development, 21* (12), 2003–2016.

U.S. Senate Committee on Finance. 1993. *Special 301 and the Fight against Trade Piracy*. Washington, DC: U.S. Government Printing Office.

Watkins, Kevin. 1992. "GATT and the Third World: Fixing the Rules." *Race and Class, 34* (1), 23–40.

Wilson, Edward O. 1992. *The Diversity of Life*. Cambridge, MA: Belknap Press.

World Bank. 1992. *The World Bank and the Environment*. Washington, DC: World Bank.

_____. 1994. *Higher Education: The Lessons of Experience*. Washington, DC: World Bank.

3

Mijikenda Perspectives on Freedom, Culture and Human "Rights"

Diane Ciekawy

In *Human Rights in Africa: Cross Cultural Perspectives,* the editors Abdullahi An Na'im and Francis Deng make three major contributions to the international human rights project.[1] The first concerns the claim that "African cultural values embody ethical, moral, spiritual and religious norms that are similar or are identical to the overall goals of legitimizing and promoting universal human rights ideals" (An Na'im and Deng 1990:1). By presenting African cultures and examples, An Na'im and Deng acknowledge the importance of Africa's rich philosophical traditions, and thus situate African societies at the forefront of human rights research. In so doing, they contribute to the development of broad cross-cultural understandings about humanity and justice that can be used to create international support for human rights. Broad support for the international human rights project will ideally mean that in "Africa 2000" state leaders will be less able to claim legitimacy for human rights violations.[2]

The second major contribution of An Na'im and Deng's volume is in its presentation of rich, well-documented ethnographic material from African societies that had not been analyzed previously in terms of human rights issues. Not only is this material relevant to the international human rights project, but it has instructive significance for other societies and provides new human rights models. The third contribution lies in its inclusion of material based on well-researched ethnographic sources that serves to familiarize readers with the perspectives and critical thoughts of people who have experienced human rights violations. The value of presenting these perspectives and thoughts is not commonly acknowledged in the literature on international law and human rights, which largely confines witness contributions to descriptive information about specific cases that can be used in legal or social science analysis. The inclusion of their voices and views represents an important step in creating the kind of diversity within the human rights project that will make it truly international.

Using these three contributions to human rights research as a guide, this work examines Mijikenda perspectives on freedom, culture, and human "rights" that closely correspond to what are conventionally recognized as Western notions of religious and cultural rights. It explores some of the problems Mijikenda face in their attempt to conduct practices based on Mijikenda tradition, the thoughts Mijikenda have about these problems, and some of the philosophical and ethical arguments Mijikenda raise against government interference. The perspective is drawn from senior Mijikenda men of a secret society whom I have known since 1984 and visited over the course of five periods of research in coastal Kenya.[3]

These senior men have lived their lives in ways similar to other Mijikenda men of their age, but have adopted a particular kind of philosophy and practice. Either through personal predilection or encouragement from lineage members, these men studied seven to fifteen years to become members of the secret society generally referred to today as the *kaya*. Mijikenda consult *kaya* elders in order to diagnose and treat problems in their relations with the supernatural world, to judge domestic or neighborhood disputes, and to conduct religious rituals that restore health and harmony to Mijikenda life.

I initially consulted these elders as authorities on aspects of Mijikenda life and history, but often sought their company because their discussions were so interesting and challenging to me personally. Partly because of their training which emphasizes skilled debate (*malau*), and partly because of a selection process that favors elaborate linguistic skills, these men tend to be gregarious and intellectually curious. Accustomed to the role of counselor and teacher in their work, they seemed to view their discussions with me similarly. There were occasional exceptions, when they asked me to explain what I knew about events in world history or geography. What was of particular delight to me was their evaluation of my ideas through a process of intense questioning and demands for clarification and illustration; their explanation to me displayed the same rigor.

The Mijikenda are a people comprised of nine closely related subgroups that share a common language and history (Parkin 1972; Spear 1978). Most of my work has taken place in the administrative Locations of Rabai, Ruruma, and Kambe-Ribe,[4] where approximately 98 percent of the residents claim Mijikenda identity (Ciekawy 1992b). The Locations are situated on a ridge running parallel to the coast, about ten to fifteen miles from the city of Mombasa. Most Mijikenda speak both Kiswahili and their subgroup dialect of Kimijikenda.[5]

A BRIEF MIJIKENDA HISTORY

Until the second half of the eighteenth century, each Mijikenda subgroup lived in a fortified forested area known as a *kaya*, constructed for defense against the raids of pastoralists and slave traders. Progressive advancement in the age-set system entailed induction into secret societies that offered members status and social power. The senior men of the male age-set system participated in a discussion and decision-making institution called the *kambi*. As Mijikenda began to construct dispersed settlements outside the *kaya* after 1880 (Spear 1978), clan and lineage elders largely replaced the authority of the *kambi* in everyday life, although many of the religious, legal and political practices of the secret societies continued in modified forms. The area of original forest settlement, containing special places used by secret society members to conduct rituals, continues to be called the *kaya*.

The post*kambi* organization of clan and lineage elders had little time to solidify before British colonial authorities entered Mijikenda areas and began to create administrative centers. In Rabai the first administrative center was established in the early 1900s, which was soon followed by the construction of the Native Tribunal Court. The Native Tribunal Court was composed of two to five elders chosen by colonial authorities to decide cases in accordance with what colonists referred to as "customary law," the interpretation of indigenous (or folk) law by colonial agents, simplified for the purpose of administrative expedience (Moore 1986). Mijikenda continued to rely on their own legal traditions to construct informal clan, lineage, and neighborhood councils (Ciekawy 1992b). Councils continue today, but their independence from administrative power varies from one Location to another.

Unlike many of the communities in central Kenya, Mijikenda of Southern Division were largely able to resist permanent wage labor until the 1940s and 1950s. The relative abundance of land, adequate subsistence agriculture, and the sale of a variety of agricultural commodities such as palm wine, copra, fruits, and grain provided Mijikenda with most of their subsistence needs until the 1960s (Parkin 1972, Ciekawy 1988). Due to the persistence of low prices for coconut products internationally, and increased interest in services and commodities only available through cash purchases, Mijikenda increasingly sought out wage employment rather than depend on the sale of agricultural commodities. Opportunities in education and employment in the late 1950s and early 1960s were largely restricted to younger men, which contributed to generational conflict in Mijikenda lineages and households (Ciekawy 1992b).

Along with new modes of access to economic power were changes in the structure of political power; the young and educated took control of political party organizations and occupied positions of leadership in District Councils and Parliament. These positions, and the acquisition of state resources that accompanied them, further consolidated the power of this new elite (Ciekawy 1992b, Caruso 1992). By the 1970s membership in the new elite was directly tied to support for the Kenya African National Union (KANU), the single political party. Over the past thirty years political and economic differentiation in Mijikenda communities has been primarily structured according to a person's relationship to state administrative institutions, KANU, and the national political economy.

Other avenues for political power within Mijikenda communities exist through participation in healing activities and other rituals designed to improve the quality of Mijikenda life. Both *kaya* elders and a group of independent ritual specialists called *aganga* (sing *muganga*) perform activities that diagnose and cure problems through their ability to communicate with supernatural agents. Where strong *kaya*-based secret society organizatiions still exist, such as among Aravahi and Agiriama, *kaya* elders maintain exclusive influence in some areas of ritual concerned with crop fertility and epidemics (Ciekawy 1992a).

Mijikenda do not employ a single term like "religion" to describe the ideas and practices surrounding their relationship to the supernatural. Their characteristic ways of communicating with supernatural agents blend together with other forms of received wisdom, or tradition, to which the Kiswahili words *desturi, tabia,* and *adabu* refer. What some scholars call religion is for Mijikenda simply an aspect of *desturi za Mijikenda* (Mijikenda tradition) that is an encompassing way of life, transmitted through a heritage of understanding and lived practice.

Those who know the language of Kiswahili might wonder why Mijikenda do not use the Kiswahili word for religion (*dini*) to describe Mijikenda ideas and practices. One reason is that *dini* carries some of the same conceptual biases as Western notions of religion or faith: it refers almost exclusively to major world religions such as Islam or Christianity. Mijikenda adopted this concept and usage of *dini* in Kiswahili, which for them does not refer to their own *desturi* or *tabia*.

It is impossible to estimate how many Mijikenda are Moslems or Christians. What is more important about Mijikenda life is that these religious identifications are not mutually exclusive. Both Islamic and Christian identifications are compatible with Mijikenda identity and the observation of Mijikenda *desturi*. Among Mijikenda there is a great deal of respect and tolerance for ideas associated with other religions.[6] Some Mijikenda maintain that they have been actively engaged in the ideas and practices of each tradition at different times in their lives and have not cared to repudiate any one of them. Further evidence of the high degree of diversity in religious experience and tolerance of other religious perspectives can be found through an examination of the religious identifications of the members of any one lineage or household. Different lineage or household members may primarily identify with any of three religious orientations, without causing discomfort or disharmony within the social unit. Young people often make the decision to convert independently, without asking permission from an older family member and without fear that a family member will disapprove of their choice. Mijikenda individuals therefore often have a multiple religious orientation that may or may not be syncretic.

THE IDENTITY AND WORK OF *KAYA* ELDERS

Today the male Mijikenda secret society is popularly known as the *kaya*, as is the sacred forest where secret society members conduct meetings and rituals. In Kimijikenda the secret society members are commonly referred to as *azhere a kaya* (elders of the *kaya*), and in English, *kaya* elders.[7] Membership requires initiation into a primary secret society, with the option of progressing to higher ranks. *Kaya* elders' abilities are shaped by their training and their participation in meetings that require oratorical skills, philosophical debate (*malau*), knowledge of philosophy and tradition, and the ability to enact particular rituals. Like many other elders, they are experienced judges and arbiters in legal councils, but their skills are enhanced by greater knowledge of Mijikenda philosophy and tradition, and they alone maintain esoteric power derived from the ability to mediate relationships between Mijikenda and supernatural agents. According to Parkin (1991), both *kaya* elders and the sacred forest are central to Mijikenda identity, but are understood or imagined differently in ways that reflect the changing lifestyles of Mijikenda people.

Kaya elders' views are not formally represented in public meetings organized by government administrators (*barazas*). In regional and national fora, *kaya* elders occasionally receive publicity when politicians "borrow" their legitimacy by incorporating them or references to them into their speeches (Ciekawy 1992a). The individual wealth of *kaya* elders varies, and some *kaya* elders who are regular consultants in legal councils or maintain a healing practice have a moderately high income.

When speaking about the equality of discussion and decision making processes in elder's councils and in *kaya* institutions, *kaya* elders do not mention the influence of hierarchy and status differentials. The fact that women and youth are not members of their organization is absent from their portrayal of how the *kaya* guards Mijikenda interests and serves as an emissary for the Mijikenda to various supernatural entities. But their claim that, in comparison to the political institutions of the Kenyan state, their organization is more interested in the welfare of common people, is better organized, and is more egalitarian, certainly cannot be faulted.

Most *kaya* elders' political thought has been influenced by debates and issues that were prominent during the time of independence in the late 1950s and 1960s, such as the nature of representative government, the importance of freedoms guaranteed by the constitution, the value of political pluralism and multi-partyism, and the comparison of regionalist (Majimbo) and centralist government structures. Mijikenda and members of other small ethnic groups were concerned that the larger and more powerful ethnic groups such as the Kikuyu would dominate coastal economic and political life. This problem still preoccupies Mijikenda today, enforced by over twenty-five years of economic exploitation by national elites and party members from outside the region.

Mijikenda were devout supporters of the Mijikenda politician R. G. Ngala, who was the leader of the Kenya African Democratic Union (KADU) party and major advocate of regionalism (Majimboism). KADU and Kenya African National Union (KANU) were the central competing political parties during the time of Independence, and when KANU won, Ngala was pressured to dismantle KADU and join KANU. The concept of a regionalist system of government and the Majimbo constitution created by R. G. Ngala remains one part of Kenya's political heritage of which Mijikenda are proud. When multiparty politics returned to Kenya in the 1990s, Mijikenda renewed discussion on the concept of regionalism and adapted it to address contemporary issues.

A HISTORY OF ADMINISTRATIVE
INTERVENTION IN MIJIKENDA *DESTURI*

The postcolonial situation for rural Mijikenda includes the continuation of policing practices and the application of laws from the colonial era that constrain their ability to follow Mijikenda *desturi* (Ciekawy 1997a, 1997b). At the Kenya Coast these laws and policing practices affect people who follow aspects of precolonial African *desturi* more than those who follow practices prescribed by Christian and Islamic religious orientations. State laws intended to protect religious rights have little practical applicability. One of the most glaring examples is the Witchcraft Act of Kenya, created in the 1920s by the colonial administration (Mutungi 1977). It was one of the first documents that defined particular rituals and traditional practices as punishable by law (Ciekawy 1997b), and served to demonize African culture (Ciekawy 1999). Given the high degree of continuity from the colonial to the postcolonial era, it is perhaps not surprising that today in the Laws of Kenya, the Witchcraft Act exists virtually unchanged.[8] Other legal practices that continue from the colonial era include the right of chiefs and District Officers to limit the number and types of *ngoma* (dance and musical celebrations) Mijikenda can perform. This practice is supported by the legal requirement for Mijikenda to obtain permits for *ngoma* from the chief of their Location, and is included in the provisions of the Public Assembly Act and the Chief's Authority Act, created during colonial times.[9]

Policing has provided a direct way for the colonial and postcolonial administrations to shape Mijikenda religious practice and political action (Ciekawy 1989, 1997a, 1997b, 1999).[10] The postcolonial administration has been particularly successful in developing policing as a form of domination that can be used by KANU, the main political party, to penetrate the lives of Mijikenda and insure KANU political hegemony (Ciekawy 1997a). In the process, Mijikenda people are denied the freedoms of association, assembly, and religion.[11] Human rights activists and scholars have waged an extensive campaign to publicize the abrogation of these freedoms, and have even influenced some changes in the Kenyan Constitution, but these abrogations continue through deeply institutionalized administrative practices.

In order to conduct Mijikenda rituals and collective ceremonies, Mijikenda must obtain permits and can be subjected to degrading inquiries and surveillance by administrative agents. Failure to comply with administrative demands can result in more investigations, police searches, arrest, legal charges and involvement in a court case. Mijikenda often attempt to avoid some of the more harmful and extensive forms of policing by paying direct bribes or keeping up with what are euphemistically known as *harambee,* or public development, donations to chiefs and subchiefs.

MIJIKENDA PERSPECTIVES ON
FREEDOM AND CULTURE

I did not seek out *kaya* elders with the explicit intention of conversing with them about religious freedom, problems in their relationship with government agents, or human rights. Since they were local historians and intellectuals, I consulted them often about matters pertaining to other projects. The idea to initiate discussions with *kaya* elders about their views on the policing practices I described above, and their ideas about it's affect on Mijikenda religious practice, occurred to me in 1991 during a discussion in which one *kaya* elder declared: "We have not yet tasted the fruits of *uhuru.*" I had heard middle-aged and older Mijikenda make this statement before, and I was familiar with variations of it from my readings on Kenyan history. A similar phrase, "not yet *uhuru"* was the title of Oginga Odinga's book written just after independence, where he criticized the neocolonial policies of the Kenyatta regime. *Uhuru* is the Kiswahili word for freedom or independence, and symbolizes the many freedoms and benefits that colonized peoples expected to experience after Independence. With this phrase, the elder not only indicated his agreement with Oginga Odinga's assessment of the Kenyatta government, but suggested that Kenyans were still suffering from the effects of colonialism.

During this particular discussion, *kaya* elders elaborated on the theme of *uhuru,* describing the freedoms they enjoyed and those they lacked. Their greatest concern was a variety of "harassments" and "interferences" from chiefs and police encountered in daily life. One elder continued, "With *Uhuru,* we expected that such frustrations would be gone . . . but instead, we find the same and new ones." Some *kaya* elders added that they thought that before Independence there was less "frustration" and "interference" from administrative agents.[12]

After this discussion, I began regularly to ask *kaya* elders questions about the freedoms they thought all people should have and the problems they encountered from administrative agents who frustrated their attempt to exercise freedom in their own lives. These discussions were popular and lively. *Kaya* elders allowed me to take notes and ask questions, and often asked me to provide my opinion or information about world events, politics, or history.

Mijikenda do not have a tradition of separating out the responsibilities Mijikenda have to one another from the responsibilities the state has to them. Furthermore, the state is not the same kind of abstract entity that it is for Westerners. Mijikenda usually address issues concerning the state by examining the actions of people who represent it: chiefs, subchiefs, district officers, and police. The motivations and actions of chiefs and subchiefs most concerned the *kaya* elders I knew.

Kaya elders often expressed alarm about the effect of government interference on *desturi*. One elder stated "there is no freedom to follow *desturi*," and continued to explain how Mijikenda attempts to practice *desturi* were thwarted by government officials. I asked if all people should be free to practice their group's *desturi*. The elders responded that this freedom should exist for all people, even children, and that preventing someone "was not justice" (*si haki*) and constituted a moral wrong (*uwongo*). Some of the elders concluded that changes were needed to diminish the power of administrative agents, particularly chiefs, on matters related to *desturi*.

Kaya elders were quick to point out that administrative authorities do not harass people who go regularly to the Mosque or practice Christian religious rituals in church on Sundays, and do not require them to obtain permits from their chiefs. They also observed that during public state ceremonies administrators do not provide *kaya* elders with the same degree of respect as Christian and Muslim leaders. Many Mijikenda also know that this prejudice reflects a wider attitude held by non-Mijikenda that associates Mijikenda *desturi* with backwardness, but find that it is nearly impossible to challenge directly.

In my attempt to understand more fully their ideas about the problem or injustice created by the inability to easily practice *desturi*, I asked the elders to elaborate on concepts of freedom and the constraint of freedom. The most common term and metaphor *kaya* elders used to conceptualize all of the problems from administrative agents described above is derived from the experience of colonialism. It is the Kiswahili term *ubeberu*, which can be translated as "colonialism" or "in the manner of colonialism." They employed this word primarily to characterize a system and set of attitudes developed by colonists during the colonial era, but in use among some administrators and politicians today. In everyday discussion *ubeberu* can be used to characterize a relationship of unequal power or describe any situation where one person or group takes advantage of another.

Kaya elders dwelled on the theme of administrative agents using common people and benefiting at the common person's expense, as they did during colonialism and the time of slavery. The elders agreed that the Kiswahili verb *kutumiwa*, which literally means "to be used" more concretely described human exploitation. The Mijikenda's long history of residence at the coast placed them in situations where they witnessed the inhumanity of slavery (*utumwa*) and were themselves its victims when Swahili took them as "pawns" during seasons of poor agricultural production to work off food loans (Spear 1978). Occasionally Swahili broke their agreement with Mijikenda and sold Mijikenda pawns, historical events that Mijikenda still hold in active cultural memory. This memory also serves to articulate contemporary concerns about Mijikenda political and economic exploitation by members of other ethnic groups and through the policies of the central government.

Returning to the topic of *uhuru, kaya* elders reflected on their hope in the 1960s that many of the freedoms lost during colonialism would be restored. They argued that Mijikenda *utamaduni* (philosophy) maintains the equality of all adult human beings, thereby providing a foundation for human freedom. They cautioned that freedom did come with restraints, for adults often had to control children who did not understand Mijikenda *desturi* and their obligations to others, and even elders and people in positions of power sometimes required correction by other adults or a council of elders. No one, they argued, was exempt from proper standards of human conduct or could be allowed to act in ways that harmed other human beings. The languages of Kimijikenda and Kiswahili can express moral unacceptability in different ways. The expression, "(it) is not human" or "(it) is not in the manner or way of humans" (*si binadamu* in Kiswahili, and *si chidamu* in Kimijikenda) is commonly used to convey the immorality of a particular act. Individuals can also be described as inhuman with the Kiswahili phrase "*fulani si mutu*" (literally, the person is not human), an evaluation made frequently of administrative agents.

Some *kaya* elders lamented the impossibility of examining administrators' and politicians' behavior in an elders' council, asserting that better leadership and a check on the excessive use of power would result if such scrutiny were possible. One major advantage of the *kaya* as a governing body, they maintained, was that its large membership prevented one person's excesses from harming others. Unlike the institutions of the current Kenya government, they commented, *kaya* institutions had procedures for correcting and improving the behavior of its leaders.

Kaya elders also stressed that a public examination of or pronouncement about a person's behavior should be treated with respect and a great deal of thought, which was why Mijikenda elders councils were composed of experienced men. They also insisted that a person's behavior be considered in view of the relationships and pressures affecting him or her, whether or not a person acted "with a good heart" (*roho mudzo* in Kimijikenda), and whether the person is or is not generally a "good person," (*mutu mudzo* in Kimijikenda). Having a "bad heart" (*roho muvya*) or spoiled heart (*roho muevi*) would be an unequivocal statement of immorality, and would require social rehabilitatiion.

Two *kaya* elders noted that the actions of people in positions of traditional Mijikenda authority, or other legitimate leaders, could be evaluated differently from those of common people. The verb *kufanya sawa*, which means literally "to act equally, evenly, or fairly" could refer to the action of any person, but when considering if a person with authority has decided well, or properly, Mijikenda might use the verb *kufuata sheria* (to follow law). Usage would depend on the context, the relationship between persons, and the social expectations for each person,[13] but it is commonly applied when the authoritative standards under consideration involve Islamic Law or state law. It is interesting that by phrasing an inquiry in terms of whether or not the authority figure followed law, issues of equality and fairness, and the character of the authority figure become obscure. *Kaya* elders insisted that chiefs, subchiefs, police, District Officers and District Commissioners were not examples of the important authorities described above, and were subject to the same forms of evaluation as common people.

In the literature on human rights there has been much discussion of the differences between local or indigenous concepts and those formed from a Western legal tradition. Acknowledging that a Western liberal tradition positing an individual person's ability to make a claim against the state is not a universal concept, many human rights scholars stress the importance of focusing instead on comparable concepts of humanity and justice. An Na'im and Deng (1990) argue that important similarities exist among all cultural traditions. Wiredu (1990) is particularly concerned that interest in difference does not obscure similarity, and advocates focusing instead on the concept of human dignity rather than human rights.

Like people in many African societies, Mijikenda do not view humanity, justice, and accountability in ways that directly translate into Western human rights discourse. The closest term that approximates "right" is the Kiswahili word *haki,* glossed as a privilege, claim, or right held by a person in a particular circumstance, or a legitimate decision by a person in position of authority such as the supreme being or a king. "My right" can be expressed by the phrase *haki yangu.* Mijikenda rarely speak of "rights" in the abstract, for the concept *haki* only acquires meaning in social relationships and specific situations, but can readily give their opinion about whether a particular behavior is or is not *haki*, and a detailed analysis of the obligations of the particular persons toward one another. In the earlier example where *kaya* elders used the pharase *si haki* to refer to policing practices, they not only conveyed the idea that government interference in *desturi* was "not justice" and "not correct," but they also indicated that a serious moral breach had taken place that conflicted with higher philosophical and ethical principles.

CONCLUSIONS

Throughout this work *kaya* elders presented concepts and principles concerned with human dignity and showed how their perspectives derived from or were consistent with aspects of Mijikenda *desturi. Kaya* elders' perspectives can be compared with those of many other peoples around the world who voice concern about domination and constraints on freedom, and wish to improve conditions for all of humanity. Although the language of international human rights does not distinguish among some essential social realities that make up the Mijikenda world, and although in Kimijikenda and Kiswahili there are no direct collaries for the concepts "religion" and "right," *kaya* elders make unmistakable statements about freedom, the importance of cultural expression, justice and human accountability that have universal relevance.

Kaya elders argue that certain freedoms, or what some people might call liberties, exist for all human beings and that state agents should not interfere with them. They understand this freedom to include culture, which they conceptualize as *desturi*. The terms "interference" and "harassemnt" they employ to describe the abrogation of freedom, and use metaphors of colonialism and slavery to describe their situation. *Kaya* elders conclude that the violation of their freedom to practice *desturi* is not correct, or just.

This exploration of Mijikenda perspectives illustrates the value of examining cultural traditions that have not previously influenced research on human rights. Both unique and universal aspects of the perspectives provided by *kaya* elders can contribute to discussion on human rights, and failure to include such voices is to reproduce the silencing processes of the Kenyan state and the legacy of colonialism. If the international human rights project is conceived as an on-going debate that will sustain many arguments about standardizing and creating universal norms, it will require wide documentation of culturally-derived understandings of human freedom, cultural freedom, justice and accountability that draw from the perspectives of peoples seldom heard in international arenas.

NOTES

I acknowledge helpful comments and criticisms from Willy Mutunga, Alamin Mazrui, Jira Katembe and Bruce Owens.

1. The international human rights project is conceived as a broad initiative to develop universal human rights standards that will be accepted by all states.

2. Often in opposition to universalism is extreme cultural relativism, which holds that because each culture has its own values and practices, anthropologists should not make value judgments about the differences between cultures. The concept was once thought to be a corrective to ethnocentrism but now poses some difficulties for the construction of international human rights standards.

3. I have worked closely with three Mijikenda subgroups, the Aravahi, Akambe, and Arihe. Most of the material on which this work is based comes from discussions with *kaya* elders in 1991 and 1993, some of which has been published in Ciekawy 1997a. I gratefully acknowledge financial support from the Fulbright Hays Doctoral Dissertation Abroad Program, the National Science Foundation, The Wenner-Gren Foundation for Anthropological Research, the MacArthur Foundation, the Bowdoin College Faculty Research Fund and the Ohio University Research Committee.

4. A Location is an administrative unit created by the colonial administration. In areas of Mijikenda settlement, Location boundaries were based on administrators' ideas of the land area each subgroup occupied.

5. My reference to languages does not use appellations common in most academic texts. I rely on appellations from the Swahili language in order to distinguish the language of a group of people from their ethnic group name. In the language of Kiswahili the prefix "ki" before the name of a group of people designates the language of that group of people. Thus, Kimijikenda refers to the Mijikenda language and Kiswahili refers to the Swahili language.

6. There is some exception to the practice of religious tolerance in families that have a long association with Christian organizations such as the Rabai Methodist Church and the Ribe Methodist Church. Such families spoke openly of the superiority of their religion and condemned "African" practices that were historically condemned by European missionaries.

7. In precolonial times initiated men would be referred to more specifically according to their age grade status, rather than *kaya* elders, and the proper name of the governing body composed of the highest age grade would be referred to as the *kambi*.

8. The Witchcraft Act, Cap. 25 contained t en sections which prohibited: pretending to exercise witchcraft, supplying advice or articles for witchcraft with intent to injure, using witchcraft medicine with intent to injure, the possession of charms, accusing persons with witchcraft, the attempt to discern crime with witchcraft, and a chief permitting the practice of witchcraft. The Witchcraft Act also permitted the District Commissioner to order persons practicing witchcraft to reside in a specific place, and to deport or restrict a person previously convicted of the Witchcraft Act.

9. The Native Authority Ordinance, Cap. 128, called the Chief's Authority Act under the independent Kenya Government, gives chiefs the power to issue orders at the beginning of the year which are then approved by the District Commissioner and the District Court in order to be made legal. This Act gives chiefs power over activities that are not specifically detailed in the Laws of Kenya. In the late 1990s, President Moi acted to change aspects of the Kenyan Constitution that concerned this Act, but all indications are that in the rural areas of the Kenya coast, policing policies on the ground have not correspondingly transformed.

10. Administrators throughout the colonial and postcolonial periods acknowlledged the potential in any public gathering for organized protest and challenge to the state, which presents the most obvious need for surveillance. Coastal administrators are well aware that one of the first challenges to the colonial government came from the Giriama War of 1914, when a medicine woman named Mektilili led the Giriama subgroup of the Mijikenda to revolt against the colonial authorities (Brantley 1981). In the 1950s and 1960s the administration again feared the spread of anticolonial sentiment that drew inspiration from religious life. Mau Mau organizations were active up-country, and at the coast, witchcraft detection organizations and acts of social banditry were tied to emerging political party organizations and the issue of squatter land rights (Ciekawy 1988, 1992b; Caruso 1992).

11. Refer to Mutunga (1990) and Kibwana (1990) for more extensive discussions of the protection of these freedoms in The Laws of Kenya.

12. Comparative statements like this one are difficult to interpret because they are so general and cover a wide range of historical experiences. In view of the other research I have conducted on coercion from chiefs and British colonial officials during the colonial era, I would generally not conclude that conditions during the colonial era were better. Research shows that forms of policing changed considerably over time and varied greatly in accordance with the character of chiefs. *Kaya* elders' comparative statements can perhaps also be understood to convey how unethical, unacceptable and extreme they considered their policing situation to be.

13. I am grateful to Jira Katembe and Aamin Mazrui for providing some insights on the uses of these words among speakers of Kiswahili and Kimijikenda.

REFERENCES

An Na'im, Abdullahi, and Deng, Francis. 1990. "Introduction." In Abdullahi An Na'im and Francis Deng (Eds.), *Human Rights in Africa: Cross Cultural Perspectives.* Washington, DC: The Brookings Institution.

Brantley, Cynthia. 1981. *The Giriama and Colonial Resistance in Kenya 1800-1920.* Berkeley: University of California Press.

Caruso, Joseph. 1992. *The Social Basis of Anti-Colonial Politics Among the Mijikenda of the Kenya Coast, 1929-1963: A Case Study of Kilifi District.* Ph.D. Dissertation, Columbia University.

Ciekawy, Diane. 1999. "Witchcraft in Statecraft: Five Technologies of Power in Colonial and Postcolonial Coastal Kenya," *African Studies Review,* 42 (2): 237–249.

_____. 1997a. "Human Rights and State Power on the Kenya Coast: A Mijikenda Perspective on Universalism and Relativism," *Humanity and Society,* 21 (2): 130–47.

_____. 1997b. "Policing Religious Practice in Coastal Kenya," *Political and Legal Anthropology Review,* 20 (1): 62–72.

_____. 1992a. *Political Imagination and the Discourse of Democracy in Coastal Kenya.* Paper presented at the Annual Meetings of the American Anthropological Association, November, San Francisco.

_____. 1992b. *Witchcraft Eradication as Political Process in Kilifi District, Kenya, 1955-1988.* Ph.D. Dissertation, Columbia University.

_____. 1989. *Witchcraft and Administration in Coastal Kenya, 1955–1967.* Paper presented at the Annual Meetings of the African Studies Association, November 9–12, Atlanta.

_____. 1988. "Land Tenure Reform in Kenya's Southern Kilifi District, 1955–1987," *East African Journal of Rural Development,* 18: 164–180.

Kibwana, Kivutha. 1990. *Fundamental Rights and Freedoms in Kenya.* Nairobi: Oxford University Press.

Moore, Sallie Falk. 1986. *Social Facts and Fabrications:* "Customary" *Law on Kilamanjaro, 1880–1980.* Cambridge: Cambridge University Press.

Mutungi, Onesmus. 1977. *The Legal Aspects of Witchcraft in East Africa.* Nairobi: East African Literature Bureau.

Mutunga, Willy. 1990. *The Rights of an Arrested and an Accused Person.* Nairobi: Oxford University Press.

Parkin, David. 1972. *Palms, Wine and Witnesses.* San Francisco: Chandler.

_____. 1991. *The Sacred Void: Spatial Images of Work and Ritual Among the Giriama of Kenya.* Cambridge: Cambridge University Press.

Spear, Thomas. 1978. *The Kaya Complex.* Nairobi: Kenya Literature Bureau.

Wiredu, Kwasi. 1990. "An Akan Perspective on Human Rights." In Abdullahi An Na'im and Francis Deng (Eds.), *Human Rights in Africa: Cross Cultural Perspectives,* 240–251. Washington, DC: The Brookings Institution.

4

Structural Adjustment and the African Diaspora in Italy

Steven Colatrella

From the fifteenth to the nineteenth century, millions of Africans were forcibly abducted and transported across the Atlantic as slaves, to live and work and die, producing the key commodities—sugar, tobacco, cotton—of the early phases of capitalist development. In the process they transformed the cultures and languages, as well as political histories of four continents and laid the basis for the pan-African movements of modern times, while contributing greatly to national histories and working-class movements in lands to which they and their ancestors had been transported.

Today large numbers of Africans are once again in movement across the planet, as part of a worldwide migration flow both between countries of the south, and from the south to the wealthier areas of North America and Europe. This chapter discusses the characteristics of the African immigrants living and working in Italy. It is based on a field research carried out between 1994 and 1997 in the Veneto region of northeast Italy, which is part of the so-called Third Italy, an area known for small-scale industrial production for the world market. The chapter argues that African and other immigrants in the region link the experiences of structural adjustment in their countries of origin with themes of flexible production in the north of Italy; further, it sees immigrant transnational communities and social networks as a form of organization that seeks to resolve the pressures created by structural adjustment and makes possible political mobilization in the countries of arrival, in this case, Italy. These networks are in turn under pressure to surrender their autonomy to worldwide forces including organized crime, international financial-planning institutions, and states that seek to subordinate immigrant networks to their own objectives. Since the research conducted included other communities beyond those from African countries, I will at times refer to these as well, though the focus in this chapter is on the African experiences.

STRUCTURAL ADJUSTMENT AND MIGRATION TO ITALY

An examination of the regions of origin of immigrant workers in the Veneto region of Italy reveals a close relationship between the migrants and the effects of structural adjustment programs (SAPs) imposed in their various countries of origin. To understand the migration process, and the presence of these diverse nationalities in Italy, we must examine the regions of origin of the migrants, and the social transformations that in part led to the migrations. To do so requires that we look at forms of work, changes in social policy and land use, cuts in social services.

At the base of the migrations we find expropriation—from small landholdings; communal land rights and usages; stable or guaranteed employment; small, petty trade; subsidies to basic consumption goods. In investigating the social transformations in Ghana, Senegal, and Nigeria, we open questions of proletarianization and forms of resistance.

Taking only those groups that are more numerous in the Veneto, we find that their family histories are linked to forms of work impacted by SAPs and that the timing of their migration is linked to cycles of SAPs, the resistance to them, and to the movements of certain commodity prices. Most of the Ghanaians are children of cocoa farmers and market women, and many were themselves cocoa farmers before migrating. Almost two-thirds, twenty-six of the forty-one Ghanaians interviewed reported having parents or brothers and sisters who had been cocoa farmers, and fourteen described their mothers or sisters as market traders. Another five had themselves farmed cocoa before migrating.

The overwhelming majority of Senegalese in Veneto come from the peanut-producing regions of central Senegal, especially near the holy Muslim city of Touba. No fewer than thirty-four of the forty-seven interviewed reported being the children of peanut farmers, or 72 percent of all respondents. All Senegalese respondents were Wolof, and all were Mouride Muslims, largely reflecting both the ethnic and religious composition of the Senegalese population in Italy as a whole. Of the eighteen Nigerians interviewed, all but one were originally from a crescent of southern Nigeria running along Highways A 122 and A 2 from Owo to the Port Harcourt region, a center of oil production. Eleven described their mothers as market traders or businesswomen. In order to understand these experiences, we must see what migration has to do with export production. Ghana (cocoa), Senegal (groundnuts) and Nigeria (oil) are all highly dependent on the sale of one single commodity. The southern and central zones of these West African countries, which previously received migrants to work in these industries, are now the zones of migrant origin. Capital has begun to abandon its dependence on small farmers and traders for certain commodities, and to develop agribusiness on a larger scale in such regions, making these workers available as labor power in the cities or the richer countries.

GHANA

In Ghana, cocoa accounts for more than 60 percent of the total export earnings, and the SAP program, lauded as an International Monetary Fund (IMF) show-case, has brought about both a considerable increase in cocoa production, and a serious crisis in agriculture. Domestic food production plummeted and food imports rose 400 percent in the decade up to 1984 (only about 20 percent of the arable land is under cultivation).[1] Greater emphasis on export cocoa production has meant a further dependence on the world market for cocoa prices, something that is utterly outside the control of the Ghanaian farmers.

Further, a significant concentration of holdings has occurred under the SAP in the cocoa sector, which combined with the collapse of urban real wages also resulting from currency devaluations caused by the IMF plan, has led to the decision to emigrate for thousands of Ghanaians.

Based on a somewhat reckless frontier approach to extensive farming of cocoa—the average life of a cocoa farm is about forty or fifty years—Ghana was able to maintain a price advantage on the world market after independence. Most production was by smallholders with some share-cropping.[2] Structural adjustment has led to a crisis of land ownership and a concentration of wealth in cocoa production, and has increased inequality among traders, which disproportionately affects Ghanaian women. The volume of Ghana's cocoa exports rose from 1983 to 1988 by more than 70 percent.[3] But the world market price of cocoa has fallen during the subsequent period. For a country deriving 70 percent of its export earnings by the early 1990s from cocoa, this meant serious damage to the social fabric involved in cocoa production. Yet these results followed logically from the entire approach of the structural adjustment program. For, as Mihevc charges, the IMF and World Bank policy of encouraging the revival of cocoa production was based on the idea that Ghana could increase overall cocoa production without having any impact on the world price of cocoa.[4] In keeping with the neoliberal world market policies that the bank and the IMF espouse, production of export crops was encouraged in many countries at the same time.

Thus, world production increased by up to 7 percent, while consumption rose only 2 percent from the mid-1980s to the mid-1990s.[5] Ghanaian farmers, despite receiving a higher nominal price in devalued *cedis*, have been receiving an increasingly lower percentage of the wealth that they have produced. But this migration is not merely a response to declining regional income *per se*. For the results of structural adjustment for cocoa production, as well as for small scale trade in West Africa, have been to increase inequality and concentrate landholdings and market control. Landholdings in cocoa and agricultural export earnings are increasingly concentrated in a few hands; thus, by the mid-1990s, the top 7 percent of Ghana's cocoa producers owned almost half of all cocoa producing land, while 70 percent of cocoa producers farmed less than six acres.[6]

Therefore, while cocoa has been highly favored over food production all along by the IMF-World Bank economic program, only a small group of cocoa farmers have benefited from the latter. A study of one region revealed that only 32 percent of cocoa farmers received 94 percent of all gross income, leaving the remaining 6 percent for the other 68 percent of farmers.[7] Cocoa farmers constitute 18 percent of all agricultural households in Ghana, but it is the minority of this minority who have reaped the benefits of the SAP, while the majority of Ghanaians have experienced a decline in their living conditions and perhaps, just as importantly, a rending of the social fabric due to rising inequality, and the loss of control over subsistence.

Thus, food production has been driven into a deep crisis in Ghana throughout the SAP period. This is due to the unswerving commitment of the structural adjustment program to favor cocoa production over food production, even though the devaluations of the *cedi*, while not helping exports, raise the prices of food imports. Small-scale food producers have increasingly lost the competition over land use to large scale cocoa production.

The SAP has impacted women and children disproportionally. It is a long-standing West African practice for women to market their own produce to earn some income and meet their children's needs. One-third of the Ghanaians interviewed for this study described their mothers or sisters as market traders. This category of worker, often linked to subsistence food production and a cocoa-growing household, is also in deep crisis as a result of the SAP. Recent studies have found an increasing inequality between rich and poor traders, and the movement of many small traders into other fields in order to survive. The Ghanaian community in the Veneto is accordingly characterized by one of the highest percentages of women of any immigrant group. Subsistence itself has become difficult for many Ghanaians as a direct result of SAP policies—not only the favoring of cocoa over food and the devaluation of the *cedi*, but also the ecological destruction wrought by timber exports (in addition to the deforestation due to extensive cocoa production), and the cuts in public employment insisted upon by the international financial agencies.

The structural adjustment program has promoted the export of timber, speeding up the destruction of the country's forest cover. As a result, timber exports have increased both in volume and in value, rising from $16 million at the start of the SAP in 1983, to $99 million in 1988.[8] Deforestation, already a serious problem due to the extension of cocoa farming, has reached disastrous proportions. Between 1981 and 1985, the annual rate of deforestation was 1.3 percent, and some estimates indicate that this rate has more recently risen to over 2 percent per year.[9] Some estimates claim that by the year 2000, the forest cover will be completely removed.

Deforestation has had a serious impact upon living standards in Ghana. Not only does it contribute to soil erosion, drought, and regional climate change, conditions which Kojo Sebastian Amanor verified in his study of the Volta Lake region.[10] This deforestation has worsened the food crisis, because 75 percent of Ghanaians depend on wild game for protein, a food source which is, in turn, dependent on the existence of the forest.[11]

For women, this also means a loss of income from the harvesting of food, fuel and medicine from the forest. Ironically, a substantial part of the export of wood arrives in the Veneto as raw material for the important furniture industry. In 1995, Ghana exported 8,630 tons of wood to the Veneto, at a value of 19 billion Italian lire, or about $12 million—a sum equal to 75 percent of the entire 1983 (pre-SAP) revenue of Ghanaian timber exports. The Veneto's wood furniture exports totaled 2.5 trillion lire, or about $1.7 billion.[12]

Though Ghanaian workers in the Veneto are more heavily represented in tanneries and foundry work, four of the Ghanaians interviewed, or roughly 10 percent, worked in the furniture industry in the province of Vicenza. So we see that Nkrumah's hope that Ghanaian workers could increasingly process the raw materials produced in their own country has perhaps come to pass, but in the factories and workshops of the Veneto!

Among Ghanaians in Italy, any access to income is made available to a large extended family, a practice common to the African migrant communities in Italy. One Ghanaian man told me, "When you ask me how many brothers and sisters I have, that's one thing, but when you ask how many people are in my family, it's about one thousand." An average of 15 people are estimated to be dependent on the wages of a single Ghanaian wage earner.

While nearly all of the Ghanaians interviewed responded that finding work was their main motivation for emigrating, seven, or about one-sixth, specifically added that helping their family with money problems was a reason for emigration, though the number sending remittances to their family in Ghana approaches 100 percent. One Ghanaian man told me that his job as a furniture upholsterer had not provided enough pay to live and work in Ghana. Another said he had emigrated to try to find a life, describing the conditions in Ghana as very troubled. Yet another described his motivation to emigrate as "so much low pay in Ghana after the devaluation, that I had to come to work in Italy."

After the expulsion of Ghanaian immigrants from Nigeria, and following the SAP policies, emigration to other destinations increasingly appeared as a survival strategy, not only for the individual migrants, but for entire families and households remaining in Ghana. Indeed, at least 20 percent of the Ghanaians interviewed had lived somewhere else before coming to Italy, five of them reported having previously worked in Nigeria.

After ten years of structural adjustment, Ghana's foreign debt had risen from $1.6 billion in 1983 to $4.2 billion in 1992, and during that same period no less than two million Ghanaians, almost one-fifth of the entire population, had emigrated to other countries. Many found their way to Italy, where, after a sojourn in the underground, underdeveloped economies of the south of the country, they moved north by word of mouth and arrived at the factories of the Veneto province of Vicenza, one of the world's leading export zones, exporting more annually than all of Greece.

NIGERIA

Nearly all of the Nigerians interviewed reported coming from southern Nigeria, with the largest concentration coming from the Port Harcourt region, center of Nigeria's oil industry. The Nigerian immigration to Italy is related to four specific developments linking Nigeria with the outside world. One is the growth of organized crime within Nigeria; another is the repressive quality of the Nigerian military government, that so far has successfully resisted every attempt to replace it. Several of the Nigerians interviewed specifically mentioned the political situation in their country as a reason for emigrating.

One man said that the political situation was his motivation for emigrating, while another responded that he had left Nigeria to seek greater political freedom. One Nigerian factory worker told me, "when the political situation changes in my country, that is when I will consider going back." One man summed up the situation eloquently: "Nigeria is bad, man," he told me. The third factor linked to the Nigerian immigration to Italy is the rise and fall of oil prices and their social impact. Everyone of the Nigerians interviewed had arrived since 1985, the year of the coup d'etat, that brought the military government of General Babangida to power, just after Babangida's predecessor had rejected the draconian terms of a $2 billion IMF structural adjustment loan (a 50 percent devaluation, a rise in the local price of gasoline, and the opening up to trade and foreign investment).

The first major flow of Nigerians took place between 1987 and 1989, with the majority of interviewees arriving in that period. This followed the oil price collapse of early 1986, which ended the 1970s era oil boom that had provided the resources for the building of a social infrastructure, hospitals, schools and universities (such as the University of Calabar), while at the same time, driving local subsistence agriculture, fishing and trade activity into crisis.

Professor Silvia Federici has described the impact of the Mobil Oil refinery on the Atlantic Coast near the junction with the Qua River as ruining the local fishing industry and eliminating an important local source of protein. Land use patterns have also been severely disrupted, not only by oil spills onto crop land, but also by the absolute priority given by law to land use by oil interests, including the right to immediately take possession of land even before allowing for the harvesting of crops in the field.[13]

The lowering of oil prices dealt a devastating blow to a region already economically disoriented by the dominance of oil. Many local businesses were dependent indirectly on the oil industry or at least on the circulation of the wealth and social spending generated by oil production and the revenue which came from it. Thus, thirteen of the nineteen Nigerian respondents in this study described themselves as small business people, or traders, before migrating. More than half had families with a background in agriculture. The fourth horseman of the Nigerian diaspora is the SAP that was imposed in early 1986, after the Babangida coup and the oil price drop.

These factors, the military government, the oil price fall and the SAP, as well as the subsequent migration, are all different facets of the same process of expropriation. In this sense, Nigeria shares the general fate of the oil exporting countries.[14]

By the late 1980s, with the migration to Italy already established, the devaluations of the Nigerian naira had in effect tripled the foreign debt in local currency.[15] Privatizations of land and the elimination of subsidies on fertilizers and other agricultural inputs, and the encouragement of agribusiness continued the pressure on the local rural economy.[16] The massive prodemocracy movement in Nigeria in the early to mid-1990s, including a three-month-long national general strike, failed to remove the increasingly repressive military government.

Several interviewees mentioned the execution of Ken Saro-Wiwa in November 1995 as an example of why going home was not yet a possibility. Since, as we have seen, most of the Nigerians in Italy seem to have come from the Niger River Delta region, they would not be unaware of the Ogoni struggle, nor of the effects of oil multinationals on the local economy and environment. Saro-Wiwa called Nigeria a modern slave state and its rulers indigenous colonizer.[17] Yet the repression in Nigeria serves a program of privatization and wholesale theft of public wealth, and causes a deterioration in Nigerian living conditions, that has taken a similar form to that in other countries undergoing structural adjustment.

SENEGAL

The Senegalese in Italy are almost all Mouride Muslims. The Mourides are a Sufi Muslim Brotherhood founded in 1886 by Amadu Bamba (d.1927), based on reverence for and service to the marabout teachers and leaders, and on a theology that glorifies work.[18] They are the predominant religious affiliation among the Wolof, who constitute the overwhelming majority of the Senegalese immigrants in Europe. Ottavia Schmidt di Friedberg estimates that 90 percent of the Senegalese in Italy are Wolof, and cites social workers' estimates that this group constitutes at least two-thirds of all Senegalese in Italy.[19] Of the forty-seven Senegalese interviewed for this study, thirty-five reported being from the area around the city of Touba. Eight others, including six who claimed the region near Dakar as their home, were from outside this region, while the remaining four were from an area bounded by Thies, Touba, and Louga. Forty of the forty-seven listed peanut growing as one of their family's main occupations.

The Mourides have long been central to peanut production, the main export crop of Senegal (accounting for over a fourth of the national total, and over two-thirds in the largest producing regions). It was the Brotherhood, and its ability to mobilize large scale labor power that enabled the French colonialists to institute peanut production over a wide zone of the Senegalese interior.[20]

The acceptance of Amadu Bamba's leadership by Shaykh Ibra Fall, a former warrior, led many of the former ruling class to accept the Mouride organization as a replacement for the social fabric that had been ripped apart by French rule and the export economy. For ex-slaves, the Brotherhood expressed dignity and salvation through agricultural labor. It provided the protection and blessing by the Sufi leader, and it held the attraction of a social bond that was reciprocal and protective, and less exploitative than the previous Wolof system. The French authorities were at first concerned about the potential threat posed by such a movement, which by 1912, already counted at least eighty-thousand members,[21] and they exiled Amadu Bamba twice. But after the start of the First World War, they came to see the potential usefulness of the Marabout hierarchy, that could guarantee peanut production and even military recruitment in wartime. The Brotherhood was afterwards encouraged by the French colonial government.[22] By the late 1950s, the Mourides accounted for about one-eighth of the Senegalese population, and one-fourth of peanut production.[23]

Mouride organization is both hierarchical and reciprocal, with unquestioning submission to the will and teachings of the Sufi master, in exchange for his blessing (*baraka*) and material aid, the basis of both social organization and ideology. One part of the *talibs'* (member or student) obligation to the Marabout is a type of *corvé* labor called *Tukket*, that involves work, usually on Wednesdays, on the Sufi master's fields.[24] The *dara*, then, is both the main historical means of Mouride colonization and settlement, and the main organization of collective labor. It is, therefore, the main means of Marabout enrichment as well. For the Sufi leaders, after Senegalese independence, had become among the largest landholders and richest individuals in the country.[25]

After independence, the Senegalese ruling Socialist Party developed an unwritten alliance with the Marabout leaders of the Brotherhood, based on peanut export. In recent years, however, the relationship has been strained, with the Mouride cultivation practices criticized for soil exhaustion and deforestation, as well as for their concentration of holdings of national land and commercial interests. The material basis of this break was a SAP implemented with extraordinary rapidity in 1984, that cut government subsidies to crucial agricultural inputs such as fertilizers, essential to sustain the groundnut monoculture. As international terms of trade for peanuts worsened, the government was willing to listen to the IMF and World Bank. One of the SAPs goals was to increase export production—primarily peanuts, despite the country's excessive dependence on this product, and the ecological damage already done.

The SAP further encouraged the rise of agribusiness for agricultural export production, exacerbating the already serious food shortages and therefore driving up imports. [26] But for many small farmers, the loss of the fertilizer subsidies for a cash crop that exhausts the soil, was the final blow. Abdoulaye Ndiaye writes,

Senegalese farmers were unprepared to do without the agricultural inputs . . . that had been provided by the state. With the government out of the seed distribution business, farmers were left on their own for obtaining key inputs. Given their low income levels, the challenge has been difficult, if not impossible to meet.

For the entire agricultural sector, the use of fertilizer, which averaged 100,000 tons per year before the policy-reform program started, declined to less than 25,000 tons in 1989. Fertilizer subsidies were eliminated, leading to a five-fold price increase. . . . Of the 1,700 collection points established for peanut commercialization identified in 1984, only 750 remained by 1988—1989.[27]

This crisis of peanut farming is directly responsible for the collective choice of migration by Mouride members. The main historian of the Brotherhood writes, "Agrarian crisis in northern Senegal has prompted beleaguered Mouride disciples to seek economic salvation in the town."[28] One interviewee explained to me that the capital city of Dakar had grown to become a very large city due to the migration of people fleeing the peanut-agricultural crisis, but that in Dakar there was not enough work for everyone. Others said that they had migrated from Senegal due to a natural disaster, referring to the lack of rain. But this natural disaster, in large part resulting from long-term deforest- ation leading to drought, was greatly worsened by the farmers' inability to use fertilizer to revitalize the earth, and by the changed marketing policies of the government cited above. One said earlier, "I worked just fine in Senegal. But things failed in 1982, the politics and economics changed, everything changed."

This migration, first to the cities of Senegal, and the subsequent growth of Mouride commercial activity, is the background to the international migration, first to France and more recently to Italy. As a result, the Mourides have become an international commercial network stretching from the West Side of Manhattan to Italy to Dakar. At the same time, the Brotherhood becomes the basis of community for migrant men who spend years in the country of arrival, traveling home for a month or two every couple of years.[29] Whereas the Ghanaian communities usually consist of married couples and even their children (though they usually have large extended families dependent on their remittances), the Senegalese community in Italy is 90 percent male, of whom virtually all have wives and children in Senegal, who depend on the remittances sent from men working in Italian factories.

Migrant Networks and Mobilization in Italy

In July 1984, Pap Khouma arrived at the airport in Rome from Dakar. He had heard, in Senegal, from others who had been to Italy, of a city called Riccione, on the coast of Emilia-Romagna. He had the address of a cousin of a Senegalese friend he had met while working as a street vendor to European tourists in Abidjan, in the Ivory Coast.

Speaking no Italian upon arrival, he luckily ran into another Senegalese at the airport who helped him get directions to Riccione, over two hundred miles from Rome and who bought his train ticket. Finding that the friend's cousin no longer lived at the apartment in Riccione, he was helped by the other Senegalese residents of the apartment who brought him to a second apartment where another group of Senegalese promptly agreed to let him stay; as he put it in his autobiography, "The guys don't ask me about anything."[30] Later, they warned him against going out alone to get to know the city, since street selling was not legal, and they were all without work permits.

The autobiography of Pap Khouma, *Io venditore di elefanti*, (I, seller of elephants) is one of the very few pieces of immigrant literature yet to come out of the immigrant experience in Italy. In the story of his arrival in Italy, and his initiation into the craft of street vending, we find many themes which are increasingly characteristic of migrant organization, and of how the world labor market is being shaped by migrant activity. Virtually every moment of Pap Khouma's migration process was lived out within the organizational possibilities of a Mouride-Wolof social network.

From the decision to migrate, to the choice of destinations, from work to housing, from how to defend oneself when up against the law, to with whom and how to socialize, from whether to stay abroad, to how to bring or send money or gifts to the family in Senegal, the loose but active network of contacts, information and mutual aid laid the basis for his life options and choices. He began to consider emigrating for the first time in November 1979, being fed up with conditions in Senegal:

In Senegal there are a lot of people who go all around without doing anything. Walking along the white streets of Dakar is the national pastime. My country, divided by caste, is poor. It's always getting poorer, because after ten years of drought, the cultivation of peanuts went into crisis. Other countries produce them, and the prices went down. There is a socialist government in Senegal. I never really understood why it's called socialist. ... To protest is the second national pastime. . ... In the villages, corruption is widespread. If money arrives, whoever's on the side of the government, pockets it.[31] In this context, emigration is widely viewed as both a personal solution to escape such a situation, and as a collective strategy for changing one's conditions.

Pap Khouma also noted:

Africa is poorly governed. Too many profiteers. You can study and work, but it doesn't change, because those in control aren't disposed to concede you a little bit of space. So people have to leave there. Only those who manage to escape, who manage to reach Europe have hope. Only a few have work. Everyone depends on them. Because of this you can't return: if you return, you go alone and join the many who live on the work of the few. The job I have, for me, there couldn't be anything more. I must remain in Europe.[32]

Since migration is seen as participation in a collective strategy, the choice of migration is expected to be taken in conjunction with others. Informal community leadership in Wolof society, still a largely illiterate population, is linked to the social relations of an oral culture. Elders known as *griot*, storytellers who are able to memorize the entire histories of the family lines of entire villages, are still very widely respected, and the oral exchange of life histories and of information and experience remains a vital institution in Senegal. "Every old person who dies is a library that burns," one Wolof man told Valerio Belotti.[33]

Thus, choices as to immigrant destination are made in the context of ancient community institutions, but based upon a contemporary diaspora that allows for possible destinations as diverse as the Ivory Coast, Morocco, the United States, Germany, France, Italy and Saudi Arabia, taking into account their varying conditions. In Abidjan, Paris, and various cities in Italy, Pap Khouma regularly found a group of Senegalese with whom he could stay for at least some period of time, with whom he could eat, and who helped him look for work and housing, to obtain the goods—usually on credit—to be sold on the street, even on occasion to take the rap when the police arrived so as to protect those whose position was more vulnerable if arrested or deported.

Such experience suggests the creation of worldwide networks of communication, information, resource, distribution and cultural and religious affiliation. Such networks, in one form or another, increasingly common to migrant communities from diverse parts of the world, would seem to be a working class answer to globalization. That is, given the increasingly global nature of markets, of the exchange of goods and services, raw materials, money and capital, such networks make survival possible for communities impacted by these developments. Further, migrant communities interact with these forces on the basis of at least partial autonomy, rather than as the atomized individuals who make up the *homo economicus* of neoclassical and neoliberal imagination. These social networks, as Professor Nestor Rodriguez has argued in the case of Mexican migration, constitute transnational migrant communities. Such communities autonomously arrange for employment opportunities, meet other needs such as housing or health care, sustain family and community relations, organize religious and cultural practices, develop political and other associations, and mobilize the transfer of resources across political state boundaries.[34] They are a form of social order improvised from the previously existing social relations in the country of origin, and transformed into a new set of social relations capable of sustaining the lives of the individuals and communities in the country of origin.

An astounding percentage of the immigrants interviewed for this study had lived in countries other than Italy and their own country of origin, and an even greater number had relatives in at least one other country. Of the forty-one Moroccans, for instance, twenty-seven had relatives in third countries. Among the Senegalese interviewed, third countries where they had lived included Mauritania, France, Algeria, and the Ivory Coast. Countries where they had relatives living included Central Africa, Spain, Portugal, the United States and France. All told, just under half, twenty-three of the forty-seven interviewed, reported having relatives in third countries, while twenty of the forty-seven had themselves lived in a country other than Italy and Senegal. Eighteen of the forty-seven had relatives in Italy. One Senegalese man had lived in fourteen different countries throughout the Middle East, North and Sub-Saharan Africa and Europe. Many immigrants in Italy had previously worked in the Gulf States of the Middle East.

We may say, therefore, that the present day migration represents a vast circulation of experience across many countries of destination. In countries like Senegal, Nigeria, Ghana or Morocco, migration decisions are made within the context of the whole family or of the community relations. The more the migration network expands, the more information is available on work and other conditions in each possible destination and, as in the case of Pap Khouma, such factors may be taken into account to influence the choice of destination. This is a decision usually taken together with others.

There is considerable evidence that migrant social networks, like those of the European migration to the United States at the start of the twentieth century, are able to largely control employment within firms, workplaces, industries and sectors of the economy. In terms of the individual migrant's opportunities, this appears in the form of aid in finding work. Fourteen of the forty-seven Senegalese interviewed said that they had found work with the help of friends or relatives already employed at the same workplace. A majority of the Ghanaians, twenty-two of forty-one, said that they had found their jobs through friends or relatives.

Employment patterns for Ghanaians reflect the influence of these social networks in job finding. Eighteen of the Ghanaians interviewed using a questionnaire indicated that forty-four percent worked in tanneries. The rest of those employed were divided between plastics (4), furniture (4), foundries (4), machine tools (3), soldering (4) and food production (2).

Ghanaian social networks and community life in Italy are heavily church oriented. Twenty-one of the questionnaire based interviews with Ghanaians revealed membership in the evangelical Pentacostal Assembly of God church, that has a predominantly Ghanaian congregation in Vicenza, and a predominantly Nigerian congregation in Padua. Two Ghanaians were Jehovah's Witnesses, and two belonged to the Khalik Catholic association that helped them find their factory jobs. The Assembly of God minister in Vicenza had himself worked in a tannery. Many Ghanaians reported spending their spare time in Church activities, reading the Bible at home, attending Church services on Sunday, or associating primarily with other Church members.

Entry into Italy essentially takes two forms: arrival by boat or, much more commonly, air, at first legally with a tourist or religious pilgrim's visa, or illegally, usually by boat or across the mountains and forests of Slovenia by land. In the first group of cases, the cost involved is merely the normal price of a plane ticket from Dakar, Lagos, Casablanca or Manila, to Rome, Palermo, Naples, or Milan. In the second case, a worldwide network transporting human cargo has grown up, occasionally making headlines in U.S. or European newspapers but more often remaining in the shadows.

The first and legal method of entry, of course, is legal only for tourism, since technically Italy's borders are closed to new immigration as part of Italy's adherence to the Schengen accords. Since the end of an amnesty program in the spring of 1996, no new work permits are to be given out, at least in theory, essentially criminalizing all those who did not take advantage of the last amnesty, and all those who have arrived since then; this includes many who arrived at first with legal visas and then remained without a resident permit, as did Pap Khouma. Flights leave twice a week from Dakar to Rome on the main Italian airline, and the cost is around 2 million lire, or U.S. $1,250.

Many immigrants raise this sum either through loans from family or other community members, or by first emigrating to another country—the Ivory Coast or Mauritania in the case of West Africans, the Middle East in the case of some Arab workers, then saving up the cost of plane fare to Europe or the United States. The ability to make use of the most advanced means of transportation is also fundamental to both the mobility of migration networks—to rapidly change residence or take advantage of work opportunities as conditions change—and to the ability of migrant communities to remain in close contact. Most of the Senegalese workers in Veneto return home every two years for several months. Along with reduced long-distance telephone rates—there are several Nigerian businesses in Padua which specialize in this service—modern means of transportation and communication make possible much more extended and frequent contact among the various geographical parts of the worldwide web of migrant communities.

At the other end of the spectrum of migration are the various criminal organizations that often use previously established roads of drugs or weapons smuggling to also ship people. This practice has given rise to various methods of illegal transportation of persons across borders. It is necessary however, to distinguish between two phenomena that, though they can overlap, are also somewhat distinct.

The first is the illegal shipment of willing immigrants who have paid exorbitant fees to arrive because of their desperation to find a means of entry into Europe. The second is the either forced transportation of unwilling persons, through kidnapping, debt repayment default, sale of children by their parents for debt or lack of subsistence, false promises of work opportunities, or other coercive methods. The first usually involves payment for the passage into Europe in advance by the migrant, their family, or a third party. The latter usually involves the migrant working under unfree conditions directly for the network that has coerced them into leaving home.

Italy being a long peninsula, bordering across the Mediterranean with Morocco and Tunisia, and sitting on the ex–cold war border between East and West Europe at a time of instability in Yugoslavia and Albania, is a site of perhaps daily attempts to enter surreptitiously. One widely used road runs from China and Pakistan through Moscow where the Russian mafia manages transport, usually through Bucharest, into the ex-Yugoslavia or Albania, or to Tunisia, or even Greece, and then by boat on to the southern Italian beaches or ports by night.[35] Passages from Tunisia to Italy by smugglers cost between five hundred and two thousand dollars. The Italian mafia utilizes big motor cruisers, that are faster than most national coast guard ships, and fit up to fifty people per voyage.

Comparisons of the current labor market and the slave trade are not solely hyperbole. For along with the growth of privateering in the transport of workers willing, even desperate to enter Europe, comes the rise, or better, the return, of practices that strikingly resemble the methods by which enslaved Africans, and kidnapped or press-ganged Europeans and shanghaied Asians were transported in previous migrations. As in the United States in recent years, a disturbingly large number of stories involving the coerced transportation of workers from their homes, and their exploitation in unpaid or unfree conditions, has come to light in Italy during the 1990s.

Such stories involve a variety of national networks. At one time or another, Chinese, Albanian, Romanian, Russian, Yugoslav, Nigerian, and Nigerien networks have been charged with the forced transportation of workers. In most cases women were forced to work in Italy as prostitutes, drug dealers and even factory workers.

In July 1995, Stella, a twenty-one year old woman from a village near the Niger capital of Niamey was approached by a young man who told her, "In Italy, there's work in the factories or as a domestic. We can advance you 50 million lire ($32,000) for expenses, which you can repay gradually when you start to get paid." She was then brought by plane to Russia, then by train across Europe to Padua. By the time she had been convinced by a Catholic volunteer service worker named Franco to take advantage of an amnesty program, obtain a legal permit, live with his family and work for his artisan shop, Stella had repaid thirty-five million of the fifty million lire loan. But the organization in Padua, headed by a matriarch named Kate, threatened to kill Stella or her family in Niger, if the rest was not repaid, something that was largely impossible on legal wages. Stella had made four million lire a month as a prostitute (U.S. $2,500), or well over double average factory wages, and nearly five times domestic workers' wages. She had paid Kate 1.5 million lire per month for room and board.[36]

When they manage to remain autonomous, migrant networks have provided the organization needed for subsistence strategies, such as the extraordinary worldwide Mouride trade network in which women travel as far as New York and Istanbul to purchase goods, that Senegalese men then sell on street corners, piazzas and beaches across Italy.[37]

These networks also provided the information and collective decision-making necessary to carry through one of the more striking aspects of the migration experience in Italy. This is an internal migration by hundreds of thousands of international immigrants from the south of the country to the north, as entire communities reject the precarious and often illegal work conditions that characterize Italy's Mezzogiorno for the steady work—industrial and domestic—to be found in the central and northeast regions of the country.

The networks have also proven capable of organized mass mobilization. In the town of Villa Literno, outside Naples, about three hundred immigrants of various nationalities created a sort of shanty town in order to be near the fields they work picking tomatoes. Their conditions, which included low pay, no health or other benefits (there was no hospital within thirty kilometers), and long hours at precarious, seasonal and back-breaking work in the hot climate of Campania, came to light after a South African man, Jerry Essan Masslo was murdered in August 1989.[38]

The murder of Masslo, however, dramatically changed the political situation of immigrants in Italy. Various immigrant communities in many cities protested, a number of antiracist groups were formed and public opinion, for a very brief moment, was shocked and sympathetic to immigrant conditions and the danger of a growing climate of racism. Masslo's death is often cited as the trigger for the passage of Law 39 (1990), usually called the Martelli Law, that improved the legal conditions of immigrants in the country and allowed for the legalization of many thousands.[39] On October 7, 1989, hundreds of thousands of people marched on Rome against racism and called for a multicultural society, the first demonstration of its kind in Italy.

In the wake of these protests, immigrant associations grew rapidly. By the end of 1991, there were over three hundred officially registered immigrant organizations, some based on one nationality, some with pan-immigrant membership bases, and yet others including Italian members also.[40] These organizations variously described their objectives as defending the immigrants' culture of origin, winning social integration into Italian society, and changing Italian public opinion regarding immigration. Overall membership is hard to determine, nevertheless a conservative estimate would place the number of immigrants joining or forming associations in the tens of thousands during the period of a few years.[41]

From this time on, the labor unions began to take more of an interest in immigrant affairs, to collaborate with immigrant associations on campaigns involving racism, housing, and workplace issues.[42] The unions, especially the left-oriented Confederazione Generale Italiana del Lavoro (CGIL), also began to recruit immigrant staff members for the first time.[43] To be sure, unions continue to show reluctance to make demands, when negotiating contracts, relating to the specific needs of immigrants regarding housing, health care, or racism in the workplace.[44] But their generally favorable attitude to immigration and equal rights, their efforts to organize immigrants, however inadequate, and their sponsorship of large national demonstrations, have helped to demarginalize immigrant organizing efforts with respect to the larger working-class movement in Italy.

Given a perennial housing shortage in Italy, combined with discriminatory renting policies, it is not surprising that it was over urban housing conditions that the most militant and spontaneous immigrant protest grew from 1989 to 1990. What is surprising is that the protests showed as great a degree of unity and cooperation among the many different nationalities as they did.

All over Italy, immigrants of different national origins together occupied public housing projects, abandoned buildings, municipal offices, city-owned edifices, train stations, and churches, either directly appropriating these spaces for at least temporary lodging, or demanding that housing be made available. By May 1990, at least two hundred immigrant men of various nationalities had essentially made the train station in Vicenza, Veneto's most industrial city, their nightly lodging. Housing occupations and protests were particularly hard-fought in Bologna and Padua. In Padua, a grouping of informal networks and formal associations came together to organize the occupation of various municipal offices, public structures, housing projects and the train station, fighting with the police against eviction on several occasions.

This struggle involved Moroccans, Nigerians, Eritreans, Senegales, and Tunisians joined together in an effort to gain access to both housing and respect in a city, that had, up to that time, not recognized in any public way the presence of immigrants.[45]

Other protests continued to take place as well. In Bologna, Senegalese street vendors fought the police for the right to use public space to make a living throughout 1990 and 1991. In Venice, the mayor announced publicly to street vendors, "the police won't stop you," citing commercial aggression on the part of the West towards the immigrants' countries of origin. In Brescia, in early 1992, immigrants held demonstrations demanding that more legal resident permits be given to those who remained without official documents.

The immigrant movement of 1989 to 1990 yielded results. Access to at least some housing was won in many cities, and in other occupations received *de facto* legitimation from the authorities. Immigrants, in some cities, won the right to sell on the street, and in general, the right to be treated in a manner consistent with human dignity. One of their main gains was a significant change in Italy's legal system of immigration. The Martelli Law both signaled Italy's compliance with the requirements of the Schengen Accords, by offici-ally allowing for systematic legal border control, and represented, with regard to immigrants already within Italy, one of the more advanced pieces of legislation in the history of the Italian nation-state.

A more repressive piece of immigrant legislation, decreed in November 1995, was repealed a year later after ongoing immigrant protests. Increasingly, immigrants have joined labor unions to defend their workplace rights against employers' efforts to take advantage of their labor market position. Fourteen of the forty-one Ghanaians interviewed reported being union members, or just over one-third, as were about half of the Senegalese.

Immigrant workers also participate in collective actions as union members along with their organizations. Hundreds marched along with Italian workers in 1997 in a demonstration in Rome as part of the metal mechanic's (machine tool, automobile, and other metal industries) contract negotiations.

At times, African workers bring to such struggles their own knowledge of how to conduct collective action, and can provide criticisms of the limits of class unity manifested by even the Italian workers, who are well known among western industrial workers for their militance. Indeed, one Nigerian metal mechanic, criticizing his Italian coworkers' behavior during a recent national metal mechanics' strike, told me:

The Italian situation is not like the strikes I know in Nigeria, where the union decides to stay out of the job for one week, and it is a general thing, everybody accepts it. Sometimes I believe the workers have divided might. Like the experience I had in my factory. The unity is not there. Some might decide to work at strike time. Some decide to prolong their job more than the hour of the strike if a machine has broken down. So, they are missing the unity they should have, if they want to get what they want. That is what I could comment.[46]

In this case, the speaker had experience of the militant union conflicts in Nigeria. Admittedly, other political cultures, such as the Senegalese workers' background in the Touba-based Mouride network, eschew collective action, and stress deference to authority. However, Senegalese workers in Veneto seem willing to unionize once they find themselves in legal industrial work. In this case, a remarkable transformation of the cultural possibilities of Mouride Islam seems to take place. The experience of how to organize together, indeed, the very network of organization used, is derived from the Mouride Brotherhood's training in cooperation and community solidarity, and union meetings with Mouride workers often resemble the question and answer format used in Koranic schools. Yet the experience of industrial work, and of waged work, of cooperative labor and class conflict, has altered the substance of their collective efforts, and it is possible that the presence of Senegalese in union federations in Italy represents a weakening of the hold of the Sufi hierarchy on the now industrial workers. But it seemingly also means that the continued interest in their religious community does not preclude working-class organization.

The combination of immigrant associational strength, and the general tone of the local political culture has worked also at the level of immigrant representation recently bringing about a watershed in the history of immigrant political participation in Italy. In both Padua and Vicenza, in the spring of 1997, immigrants elected a council of representatives that would advise the city council on immigrant affairs and elect a representative to take a non-voting seat on the city council—a concession to immigrant pressure by city councils. The results were successful beyond the estimates of optimistic participants. In early March 1997, two-hundred and twenty-seven immigrants attended a two-day assembly and elected representatives of several nationalities, with a Nigerian, an Iranian, a Moroccan, and a Ghanaian winning the top numbers of votes. In Padua, on May 25, there was an even more impressive turnout. In an election held at the Office of Social Intervention, on a narrow street in the medieval historic center of Padua, over eight hundred immigrants of dozens of nationalities showed up. At the first assembly of immigrant representation held two weeks later, a Senegalese man was overwhelmingly voted the council's president and representative to city council meetings. In both cases, voting seems to have crossed national and ethnic lines, revealing a greater potential unity.

Once again, after centuries, Africans are circulating their experiences around the planet in conjunction with transformations of world capitalism. Once again, they are playing important roles in transforming the composition of the planet's working class and its political cultures.

NOTES

1. Kojo Arthur, *Ghana's Food Crisis: Alternative Perspectives Africa Research and Publications Project Inc.* Working Paper No. 16, 1983, 3.

2. Ibid., 46, 90; John Mihevc, *The Market Tells Them So: The World Bank and Economic Fundamentalism in Africa.* (London: Zed Books, 1995), 160–161.

3 . Ross Hammond and Lisa McGowan, "Ghana: The World Bank's Sham Showcase," in Kevin Danaher, ed., *50 Years is Enough: The Case against the World Bank and the International Monetary Fund* (Boston: South End Press, 1994), 80.

4. Ibid., 56.

5. Hammond and McGowan, "Ghana," 80.

6. Ibid.

7. Mihevc, "Market," 161.

8. Hammond and McGowan, "Ghana," 81.

9. Ibid., 82.

10. Kojo Sebastian Amanor, *The New Frontier: Farmers' Response to Land Degradation—A West African Study.* (London: Zed Books, 1994), 193.

11. Hammond and McGowan, "Ghana" 81–82; Amanor, "New Frontier," 33; Unione Regionale delle Camere di Commercio Industria Artigianato e Agricoltura del Veneto, Fascicolo di aggiornamento alla relazione sulla situazione del Veneto nel 1995. Import/ Export 1993–1995 Venice. 1996, 236. Ghana exported 8,630 tons of wood to Veneto in 1995, valued at U.S. $13 million, the entire rest of its exports to the Veneto consisted of about U.S. $500,000 in agricultural and forest products, and U.S. $2,000 in machine parts.

12. I have derived these figures from Unione Regionale Delle Camere di Commercio, Industria, Artigianato e Agricoltura del Veneto, Fascicolo di Aggiornamento alla Relazione sulla Situazione del Veneto nel 1995 Import/Export 1993–1995. Venice 1996, 46–47 and 236–237; this volume is the Veneto Chamber of Commerce's official statistical analysis of all Veneto import and export trade.

13. Federici, Silvia. "Development and Underdevelopment in Nigeria" in Midnight Notes Collective ed., *Midnight Oil: Work, Energy, War 1973–1992* (New York: Autonomedia, 1992), 87–89.

14. For a fuller analysis see Midnight Notes Collective ed., *Midnight Oil, Work, Energy, War. 1973-1992.* (New York: Autonomedia, 1992).

15. Zuwaqhu A. Bonat and Yahaya A. Abdullahi, "The World Bank, the IMF and Nigeria's Rural Economy, " in Bade Onimode, ed., *The IMF, the World Bank and the African Debt.* (London: Zed Books, 1989), 164.

16. Ibid., 166.

17. Ken Saro-Wiwa, *A Month and a Day,* (London: Penguin, 1995) 7.

18. See, among others, Abdoulaye-Bara Diop, *La Société Wolof.* (Karthala: Paris 1977), which stresses the hierarchy and inequality of Mouride social organization; L. Behrman, *Muslim Brotherhoods and Politics in Senegal* (Cambridge, MA: Harvard University Press, 1970); Ira Lapidus, *A History of Islamic Societies* (New York: Cambridge University Press), 837–838; Donal B. Cruise O'Brien, *The Mourides of Senegal* (Oxford, England: Clarendon Press, 1971), and his "Charisma Comes to Town: Mouride Urbanization 1945–1986," as well as Christian Coulon, "Women, Islam and Baraka," both of which appear in Donal B. Cruise O'Brien and Christian Coulon, eds., *Charisma and Brotherhoods in African Islam* (Oxford, England: Clarendon Press, 1988).

19. Ottavia Schmidt di Friedberg, *Islam, solidarietá e lavoro: i muridi senegalesi in Italia* (Turin: Fondazione Agnelli, 1995), 96.

20. See Lapidus, "History"; O'Brien, *Mourides*, 246.

21. Lapidus, "History," 834.

22. Lapidus, "History," 835; O'Brien, *Mourides*, 14; Schmidt di Friedberg "Islam," xiv-xvi; Jean Suret-Canale, *French Colonialism in Tropical Africa. 1900-1945.* New York: Pica Press, 1971, 234.

23. O'Brien, *Mourides*, 216.

24. Ibid., Chapter 8.

25. Ibid., 217.

26. Abdoulaye Ndiaye, "Food for Thought: Senegal's Struggle with Structural Adjustment," in Danaher, ed., *50 Years Is Enough*, 85–86; Abdoulaye Bathily, "Senegal's Structural Adjustment Programme and Its Economic and Social Effects: The Political Economy of Regression," in Onimode, ed., *The IMF*, 130.

27. Abdoulaye Ndiaye, "Food," 86.

28. O'Brien, "Charisma," 135.

29. Ibid. Schmidt di Friedberg, *Islam*, 113-125.

30. Pap Khouma, *Io, Venditore di elefanti* (Milan: Garzanti, 1990), 25.

31. Ibid., 17.

32. Ibid.

33. Valerio Belotti, ed. *Voci da lontano: breve viaggio in quattro comunitá di immigrati che vivono e lavorano nel bassanese.* (Libreria TEMPOlibro Editrice, Bassano del Grappa, (1994), 23.

34. Nestor Rodriguez, "Battle for the Border: Autonomous Migration, Transnational Communities and the State," *Social Justice, 23* (5).

35. Antonio Nicaso and Lee Lamonthe, *Global Mafia: The New World Order of Organized Crime* (Toronto: Macmillan, 1995), 33–34; "Darkness Hides Migrant Flood into Italian Underworld," *Independent*, January 8, 1995.

36. "Io, schiava della mafia nera," *Il Gazzettino (Padua)*, November 15, 1996.

37. Ibid., 119–121; and Valerio Belotti, from research on vending on the beaches of Emilia-Romagna to be published: "Vendere in spiaggia: l'abusivismo commerciale nella Riviera emiliana-romagnola for Istituto Poster," (Vicenza, 1998).

38. See among others, Veugelers, 41; "Sindaco senza memoria," *Il Manifesto*, August 24, 1990.

39. Veugelers 41; see also Umberto Melotti, "International Migration in Europe: Social Projects and Political Cultures," in Tariq Modood and Pnina Werbner, eds., *The Politics of Multiculturalism in the New Europe* (London: Zed Books, 1997).

40. Ibid. "Immigrati: 300 associazioni in tutta Italia. Un primo identikit," *Il Manifesto*, January 30, 1992.

41. Ibid.

42. Ibid. "Sindaco senza memoria," *Il Manifesto,* August 24, 1990; Giovanni Mottura and Pietro Pinto, *Immigrazione e cambiamento sociale: strategie sindacali e lavoro straniero in Italia.* Rome: Casa Editrice EDIEFFE, 1996, 67.

43. Ibid.

44. John W. P. Veugelers, "Recent Immigration Politics in Italy: A Short Story," *West European Politics,* 17 (2) April 1994, 33-49.

45. Interview with Paul Ocoye, President of National Union of Nigerian Citizens in Italy, Padua, February, 1995; interview with Michele Fassina of Associazione Immigrati Extracomunitari of Padua, February 1995; interview with Mortes, Vicenza. December, 1995; "Milano, immigrati al rogo," *Il Manifesto,* May 11, 1990; "Vicenza offre lavoro, ma si dorme alla stazione," *Il Manifesto,* May 11, 1990; "Un tranquillo weekend di paura: A Castelvolturno fra 300 negri assediati," *L'Unitá,* April 30 1990; "Brescia: La spina nel fianco della Lega," January 1, 1992; "Padova: Per un pugno di letti," *Il Manifesto,* August 23, 1990; "Il comune di Bologna sgombera 300 immigrati" *Il Manifesto,* July 21, 1991; "Bologna: La giunta alla prova immigrati," *L'Unitá,* September 11, 1990; "Dramma casa immigrati: Moruzzi apre il dialogo." Bologna, supplemento *L'Unitá* September 13, 1990; Cacciati dai loro connazionali 6 immigrati sospettati di spaccio *L'Unitá,* May 1, 1990; "I neri all' assalto delle case, "*La Repubblica* (Bologna edition), September 11, 1990. As many of the dates of these newpaper articles indicate, some of these occupations were reported on only after eventual eviction by the police months after they had begun. I am indebted to Silvia Federici, Ferruccio Gambino, and Mariarosa Dalla Costa for providing me access to materials and newspaper clippings regarding the immigrant protests of 1989 to 1991.

46. Interview with F. December 27, 1996, Padua.

5

The New African Student Movement

Silvia Federici

"What meaning does independence have for you?" It was asked of students who were citizens of countries who had recently obtained independence. "Independence, very simply, is life itself," said a student from Gabon. "It is . . . the fulfillment of a nation; the free expression of its being," said one from Upper Volta. And "liberty to wish to live, liberty to wish to die," said a Cameroonian (Hanna and Hanna 1975b).

"Independence is meaningless and will elude us if it is not linked to our right to free education " (President of the National Union of Ghanaian Students).

WHY STUDENT STRUGGLES IN AFRICA?

It can be easily agreed that if we want to understand Africa's contemporary political reality, we must start from the struggles that people are making, for they express the tendencies operating in the social body, the existing possibilities, the proposed or imagined alternatives to the status quo. It is in this spirit that I look at the struggles that, over the last decade, African students have made, particularly in the universities, against the program of structural adjustment that has been imposed, since the mid-1980s, by the World Bank on their countries' economies and educational systems.[1] My purpose in doing so is first to demonstrate the existence of a new pan-African student movement, continuous in its political aspirations with the student activism that developed in the context of the anti-colonial struggle, and yet more radical in its challenge to the established political order.

Little is known about this movement in North America and Europe where, in the collective imagination, student activism remains associated with countries like France, the United States or China. Both the media and scholarly journals have generally ignored this topic. Between 1987 to present, for instance, the *Journal of Modern African Studies* has published only one essay on African students, despite its frequent coverage of the social impact of structural adjustment,[2] as for the *African Studies Review*, between 1991 and 1996, it has touched upon it only twice, once in the context of a recollection of Ngũgĩ wa Thiongo's student days at Makerere in the 1950s, and another time in an analysis of intergenerational conflict in the Cote d'Ivoire.[3] This contrasts with the situation in the 1970s, when the place of African students in the continent's political economy, and their contribution to development, were frequently an object of study for U.S. political scientists and sociologists. Whether this diminished interest is a reflection of the changed institutional approach, that prescribes a lesser political and economic role for African students than might have been expected two decades ago, is a matter of speculation. It is worthwhile, however, to mention a number of assumptions, shared by African political theorists, that similarly deemphasize African students' political potential.

I refer to the tendency, spread among African intellectuals, to question the contribution that students can make to liberation struggles and accentuate the obstacles standing in the way of their becoming effective agents of political change, namely, the transitory nature of their organizing, their lack of roots in any productive activity, their elite status, their pronness to opportunism and corporatism. Exemplary of this approach is a recent article by Bathily, Diouf, and Mbodj (1995) on the student movement in Senegal, which concludes that students cannot be trusted as political subjects, even though they may score significant moral and political victories, as Senegalese students did, in their confrontation with the government in the 1980s. According to the authors,

[The] intention of students to be involved in the life of their nation . . . does not take into account the fact that they are only in a transition, over which they have no control because they have no impact on the socio-economic stakes. So instead of being actors/initiators of this change, they have turned into mere artifacts of this evolution. (401)

Such an assessment may be a healthy reaction to earlier accounts, rooted in the colonial era, that pictured students unproblematically as a revolutionary vanguard and their countries' "natural leaders."[4] But the danger, in following the opposite course, is that of underestimating not only the novelty of the present African student movement, but also the importance of the ongoing struggles over African education and against Structural Adjustment, both from the viewpoint of Africa's future and the international liberation struggles.

In this context, a further objective of this article is to show that (1) while still a numerical minority, African students have undergone a process of proletarization in the wake of structural adjustment policies (SAPs) that places their concerns and struggles on a continuum with those of other workers;

(2) African student struggles against SAPs are an essential part of the resistance to the World Bank's takeover of African resources and decision making, a process that some have likened to an attempted recolonization; (3) African student struggles are also an integral part of the international movement against the escalating cost of education, which is putting schooling, almost at any level, out of reach for the majority of the people worldwide.

I conclude that the struggles of African students must be given more attention and support than they have received so far not only by grassroots activists but also by academics and students in North America. This applies, in particular, to those who are concerned with the ongoing structural adjustment of our own educational institutions and with the propagation of "African knowledge," that is, the knowledge produced on the African continent, whose existence and circulation are, in good measure, dependent on the success of struggles such as those which African students are fighting.

AFRICAN STUDENTS' ACTIVISM IN THE COLONIAL
AND THE POSTCOLONIAL PERIOD

Political activism has a long tradition among African students, dating back to the colonial period when their mobilization contributed to the creation of an anticolonial consciousness, at home and abroad. Exemplary is the case of the West African Student Union (WASU) formed in London in 1925, which became a training ground for Nigerian nationalists (Ayu 1986; Hanna, Hanna and Sauer 1975: 84; Segal 1963: 230). WASU denounced colonial racism, the practice of forced labor, the expropriation of communal lands, and the transfer of the surplus from Africa to the metropoles. On the occasion of the London Conference of 1941, it formulated a program that remains a model for decolonization today. Inspired by the international anticolonial struggle, WASU (among other things) called for the return of expropriated lands, for the abolition of monoculture and export crops, and the development of local food production (Ayu 1986). It also called for a society free from class divisions and for mass education at all stages, arguing that "mass education is the preparation of public opinion to appreciate current social changes" (Ayu 1986: 70–71).

WASU was not a unique case. Student activism is part of the anticolonial struggle in every African country—Ivory Coast, Guinea, Algeria, Rhodesia—and can certainly be credited with having contributed to the growth of the anticolonial movement. Student organizations were often the first political force to demand independence and chastize their leaders when they would seem ready to compromise on this question.[5] Nevertheless, in the 1940s and 1950, student activism was a restricted phenomenon. Africa had only a handful of secondary schools and universities (Hanna 1975a: 6–7),[6] thus, those who made it to a college were an absolute minority, who in most cases had to study abroad, often spending many years away from their countries.

Their physical distance from the struggles at home was compounded by the economic and social distance that speaking the master language, enjoying a relative affluence, and going to school, instead of performing manual labor, introduced between them and their compatriots. Most important, student activism was often the response of an educated elite to its marginalization within the colonial system, and it occurred in a context in which the leading sectors of international capital were preparing to come to terms with the end of colonialism and looked at formally educated Africans as the future rulers. Consequently, student activists and student organizations did not face the repression that workers and trade unions experienced, nor did they directly challenge the international power structure.

In the postcolonial period as well—that is, in the 1960s and 1970s—many factors contributed to limit the scope of African student struggles. The most important is the unique relation that the achievement of independence created between students and the state. For on the one side, the African states were vitally dependent on students to replace the empty spaces left by departing expatriates and saw the expansion of higher education as a key condition for economic development. Thus, everywhere, the African national state upheld education as a means of personal and national advancement, making of it the cement of a new "social contract." As for the students, in addition to benefiting from the opportunities this situation opened to them, they were reluctant to criticize governments that had often emerged from a process of struggle, that were still besieged by the ex-colonial powers, that had limited means to carry out the needed reforms and, as it were, were still "in the make." Thousands enthusiastically responded when asked to leave their classes and go to build roads in the early days after independence.[7]

The fact that university education was conceived as a port of entry into the state administration and as the pillar of national development, further strengthened the students' identification with the goals of the national state, and shaped their sense of identity, and their relation with other social groups. Being a university student in Africa in the 1960s and 1970s meant having a strong sense of one's self-importance; it also meant a guaranteed life of upward mobility and employment and the enjoyment of benefits from which the majority of Africans were excluded. All these factors discouraged oppositional politics[8] and tended to instill elitist attitudes that, on several occasions, saw students defending their privileges against governments bent on democratizing education.[9]

Student activism, however, did not cease after independence, and often played a crucial role in preventing the new African governments from capitulating to foreign interests. In Nigeria, for instance, student opposition was largely responsible for the cancellation of the Anglo-Nigerian Defense Pact of 1960 that was "designed to maintain Britain's strategic military interests and preserve Nigeria as a market for the British defense industry" (Ayu 1986: 80; Hanna 1975a: 2). In the Ivory Coast, students protested Houphouet-Boigny decision to invite Indo-Chinese rubber plantations to resettle in the country (Zolberg 1975: 114–115) and his support to France's policy in Algeria. Anti-imperialist mobilization by African students in this period included demonstra tions against the killing of Lumumba and the massacre at Sharpeville, Portuguese violence in Angola, Mozambique, Guinea Bissau, the Smith regime in Rhodesia, and the testing of Atomic bombs in the Sahara desert by France (Ayu 1986: 80–81).

As W. J. Hanna and J. L. Hanna have pointed out, "[A]s the countries of particular student groups achieved independence, attention has often turned to the issue of majority rule in those territories dominated by a white minority, and to neo-colonialism in the countries of independent Black and North Africa" (1975b: 53). Another issue that preoccupied African students after independence was "educational reform" above all the questions of Africanization and student participation in the administration of the university. By the late sixties, in Zaire, Senegal, Ethiopia, this was leading students into an open confrontation with the state that took a heavy toll in terms of the number of students killed and arrested (Hanna, Hanna, and Sauer 1975: 72–78).

Rarely, however, did students challenge the state's legitimacy, except when it openly usurped its powers,[10] or did challenge the state's definition of national development or address economic issues that were of concern to most workers.[11] From all these viewpoints, the new student movement that has developed in the 1980s in response to structural adjustment, represents a radical departure. This is not to say that African students today do not draw inspiration from the struggles of their predecessors.

In some countries like Nigeria, the history of past struggles is so much part of the students' sense of identity and imagination that, until recently at least, on all the campuses students have commemorated the killing of fourteen students in April 1978, during the Obasanjo regime, with a special "Solidarity Day," in which they participate in rallies and other activities evocative of the circumstances surrounding the killings.

AFRICAN STUDENTS AND STRUCTURAL ADJUSTMENT

The main difference between the new student movement and those that have preceded it concerns its changed class character, as determined by the status of university students as a social group, and their future economic and political destination. On both counts, it is clear that African students have been proletarianized.

First, by the early 1980s, the majority of university students were still drawn from the lower classes[12] and often came from poor families.[13] According to World Bank statistics, by 1986, 39 percent of the parents of African university students were farmers, and 21 percent were manual workers and traders, which makes the African university student body the one with the smallest percentage of white collar parents (40 percent) in the world (World Bank 1986:

62). This means that African university students have a direct experience of the conditions in which the bulk of the African population lives and identifies with its problems. Moreover, in the wake of structural adjustment, their own situation has dramatically deteriorated[14] due to the removal of tuition grants, the increased cost of studying, as well as the collapse of the standard of living in their communities. As is well known, the great majority of African students today have no money for food, books, accommodations or transport. They eat one meal a day (in Nigeria they call it "0-1-0, without," meaning zero breakfast, lunch without any meat, and zero supper). They sleep in overcrowded hostels where rooms fit for two now host up to fifteen people taking turns on the floor; some even sleep in the classrooms; they work in dilapidated buildings that are constantly subject to power and water shortages and where toilets are nonexistent. They have no educational materials, and they study with teachers who go to school when they can because they are too busy trying to survive, which they cannot do on a professor's salary sufficient, at best, to feed a family for a week.[15]

In addition, for the first time since independence, college students know that what awaits them at graduation is most likely unemployment or perhaps a job as a taxi driver. They know that the days when students could look at a university degree with the certainty that it would gain them financial security, and possibly a role in their countries' political life are gone, as demonstrated by the large number of those who, even with a degree, decide to emigrate to countries where all they can hope for is a blue-collar job.

This is not a conjunctural, but a structural, situation. For the World Bank's SAP, to which practically every African government has subscribed,[16] calls for a drastic reduction of higher education and the cut of all state subsidies to both the students and the universities. As George Caffentzis points out, "[T]his reduction (of the higher education system) is promoted in the name of higher efficiency and a more egalitarian distribution of educational resources. Yet the evidence provided and the guidelines prescribed raise serious doubts that these are the actual concerns. More likely, the World Bank's attempt to cut higher education stems from its bleak view of Africa's economic future, and its belief that African workers are destined for a long time to remain unskilled laborers" (Caffentzis 1991: 2).

Caffentzis is referring here to the fact that SAP in Africa pins the hopes for economic "recovery" (the rhetoric of "development" has now been discarded) on the continent's ability to attract foreign investment and its "comparative advantage" in the global market, and accordingly, demands the boosting of agricultural exports and the cheapening of African labor. SAP also transfers crucial aspects of economic planning and decision-making into the hands of international bodies, donors' "cartels," and non-governmental organizations. Thus, in more than one way, it reduces the need for a formally educated workforce, and for civil servants prepared to fill the different branches of the public sector, which, in fact, has been drastically downsized.[17] In other words, SAP is a reversal of the policies pursued, or promised by the African national states at independence, when "reconstruction" represented a commitment to build an autonomous road to development, and to improve the conditions of the African population.

This means that the prospects for higher education in Africa today are bleak both in the short and in the long run. The present trends point to the development of a two-tier system, where the majority of students will be destined to receive devalued degrees, from institutions that, for all practical purpose, are allowed to "fall apart," while a minority is groomed, through subventions by foreign "donors," to provide a small body of technocrats, attuned to the needs of foreign investors. As much is prescribed by the World Bank's Africa Capacity Building Initiative (Caffentzis 1994, World Bank 1991).[18]

What follows is that, far from being esteemed as future members of the African intellighentsia and the state, and being called upon to contribute to their countries' development, African university students today are seen as largely irrelevant to their countries' economic life, or are even considered an economic deficit from the viewpoint of a cost-benefit analysis of education. In other words, they are being totally devalorized, politically and economically. This situation, inevitably, has had a deep impact on their lives, their sense of identity and their politics.

Thus, African students today are different as political subjects from their peers in the period before and after independence. Not only has their loss of status, their devaluation, brought them closer to the concerns of other social groups—trade unions, market women, human rights groups, civil servants—with whom they frequently join in protest. Their struggles, even when they are in defense of their living conditions and the right to education, articulate a more general social interest, as they connect with the resistance to structural adjustment that mobilizes every sector of the African proletariat, and with the opposition to the restoration of a colonial division of labor that again condemns Africans to be the "hands" for decisions that others are making. Thus, in many ways, the battle that students are fighting, even when they are confronting the state on "bread-and-butter" issues such as housing, food, book and transport allowances, is a continuation of the battle for African self-determination. But today it is a battle that brings them directly in conflict with the international power structure, as represented by the World Bank, the IMF and the panoply of agencies, through which the ex-colonial powers and the United States are trying to assert their control over Africa's resources. For the very existence of a growing body of students, determined to have a voice in the decisions taken by their governments, and opposed to the sale of national assets, is an obstacle to the appropriation of their countries' wealth by transnational agencies and companies, justified now in the name of "adjustment," "free trade," and "intellectual property rights."[19]

Not surprising, African students are experiencing today the same type of repression that, in the past, was reserved for those whom Frantz Fanon described as the "wretched of the earth," and often engage in forms of struggles and tactics (riots, road blocks, burning of buildings) that are among the means of protest of the disenfranchised. Moreover, while in the past, with few exceptions, Africa student protest was episodic, today, in many countries, it has become endemic, continuing year after year, despite the frequent shutdowns of the universities, in what appears as a protracted warfare (see "Chronology of African Student Struggles" published in the CAFA Newsletter No. 10, Spring 1996).

A NEW PAN-AFRICAN STUDENT MOVEMENT

It is this broader political challenge combined with the commonality of student demands and the sameness of the forces that students are confronting that enable us to look at the present phase of student activism not as a set of separate struggles but as one pan-African student movement.

It is a movement that has no coordination across national borders and, nevertheless, is remarkably unified in its motives and objectives.[20] As stated in a recent newsletter of the Committee for Academic Freedom in Africa (No. 10, Spring 1996: 8), "No to tuition fees," "No to starving while studying," "No to cuts in books, stationary, transport allowances," and "No to SAP and the recolonization of Africa" are slogans that have appeared on every campus from Lusaka to Cairo, in the 1980s and 1990s, providing the deepest bond among students who are often seen as irremediably divided on ethnic and religious grounds.

Student struggles against SAP and its consequences for education have varied in correspondence with the different ways in which the programs have been implemented. In francophone Africa, student anti-SAP activism escalated after January 1994, when the CFA *(Communauté Financière Africaine)* franc was devalued, and the full impact of adjustment was felt. However, already by 1989, 90 percent of the strikes and boycotts on African campuses were called to protest the introduction of tuition fees, delays in the payments of grants and allowances, and the poor conditions of housing, food, and the means of instruction. Protests have also been organized in support of teachers and workers' strikes, to obtain the release of jailed students, or their reinstatement when expelled from school, to demand the removal of the police or the army from campus premises and the unbanning of student unions, to denounce the lack of employment prospects after graduation and the authoritarism of the state and the university administration.[21]

In several countries, moreover, the mobilization around student welfare has expanded into a broader political confrontation. In 1989 in Zimbabwe, the frustration of the students over the government's plans to increase their fees sparked off a wave of demonstrations against the government's corruption and revolutionary pretenses (Cheater 1991). In Ghana, student protest against the cutbacks in the funding for education has strengthened the opposition to Jerry Rawlings (Kraus 1991; Yeebo 1991); in Sudan, it has merged with the struggle against the Islamization of education (Hamad 1995; Leatherbee and Osman 1993).

In no country has students' resistance to structural adjustment been more organized and defiant than in Nigeria, where, since the late 1980s, almost every year it has escalated into a national crisis (Jega 1994; Mustapha 1996). It is worth remembering here that Nigerian students began paying the price of "adjustment" even before the program was introduced in the country. For there is good reason to believe that the motive behind the infamous "ABU massacre" that occurred at the University of Ahmadu Bello (Zaria) on May 23, 1986, was the preempting of student opposition to an agreement with the World Bank and the IMF.

On that day, a week after representatives of the World Bank had arrived in the country to finalize the SAP agreement, anti-riot policemen attacked the campus of Ahmadu Bello University in response to a peaceful demonstration, unleashing what the media described as "an orgy of violence" (Agan 1986; ASUU 1986; ASUU, ABU Branch 1986; Olojede *et al*. 1986). By the end of the day, more than thirty students had been killed, scores had been wounded, and the National Association of Nigerian Students (NANS) had been banned, a clear indication that the Babangida government would not tolerate any dissent on such a sensitive issue. Nigerian students, however, have not been detracted by this horrendous show of force. Despite government repression, and the passing of two decrees in 1989 (Decree 47 and 49) curtailing unionism in tertiary schools and prohibiting students from demonstrating (Bako 1994: 160), they have continued to mobilize under the leadership of NANS, joining with workers, market women, and human rights organizations in a broad campaign against the government and SAP.

In 1988, for instance, students joined workers in a nationwide protest against the rise of gasoline prices. In 1989, in Benin, Lagos, Ibadan, and other cities, they took to the streets in what have become known as the anti-SAP riots (Mustapha 1996; "SAP Sparks Riots" 1989; Akinrinade *et al.* 1989), joined by unemployed youth, motorists, market women, and other proletarians, with whom they built barricades blocking the traffic for several hours. In Benin City, on this occasion, the students liberated 809 prisoners from jail; then took food from the jail's pantry and brought it to the nearby Central Hospital to feed the patients ("SAP Sparks Riots" 1989: 18). In 1990, the students were out again, all over the country, to protest a World Bank loan presumably designed to revamp higher education which they accused of undermining Nigeria's intellectual independence and commercializing university education (Bako, 1994: 165-167, Civil Liberties Organization 1990). In particular, the students rejected the loan's conditionalities that included:

a freeze on recruitment of all categories of staff, mandatory staff retrenchment, the introduction of fees . . . the procurement of 60 percent of equipment from manufacturers approved by the World Bank, the scrutinization of all curricula by the World Bank, and the mandatory importation of expatriate staff whose salaries were too heavily topped. (Bako 1994: 166–167)

In 1991, undaunted by the repression unleashed against its members, NANS launched a nine points ultimatum to Babangida, again demanding that SAP be eliminated and campus conditions improved. When the government failed to respond, it organized a nationwide boycott of classes in the course of which several students were killed, and many more were arrested; (Akani 1994: 67-90; Civil Liberties Organization 1991; Okorie 1991). In 1992, they joined the "Babangida must go" campaign, as part of a coalition against the failed transition to civilian rule and the electoral sham, again demonstrating their capacity to connect the students' struggle to a broader political interest. In the same year, students came out in support of the Academic Staff Union of Universities (ASUU) strike, on some campuses organizing defense groups to prevent the police from breaking the strike. Again, students were in the forefront of the protest against the murder of Ken Saro Wiwa and the other Ogoni leaders in 1995, declaring President Abacha persona non grata on their campuses.

Nigerian students have not been alone. Resistance to SAP, to dictatorial rule, and the defunding of higher education have been woven together in campus protest in practically every African country contributing to stall unpopular measures, as was the case in Senegal. On several campuses (e.g. in Tanzania and Nigeria) the anti-SAP protest has also brought students and teachers together, undermining one of the main taboos of campus life.

One of the positive results of the students' struggles is that they have helped demistify the campaign for "democratization," "popular participation" and "human rights" that has been launched by the United Nations as part of its rationalization of the African state. Like other forms of popular protest that the students have demonstrated is that no democracy is possible where people are denied the basic means of survival, and the possibility of being autonomous producers of knowledge.

How threatening is the challenge of students activism to the economic planning and the institutional arrangements prevailing in Africa today can be measured by the ferocity with which student protests have been, and continue to be repressed. It is no exaggeration to say that most African governments, in the 1980s and 1990s, have treated university students as if they were their countries' enemies and that campuses have been turned into war zones.

As in China, students have been ritually denounced as hooligans and a selfish lot, intent on preserving their privileges at the expense of the general well-being, and their protests have been treated accordingly as a problem of law and order. Consequently, in almost every country, student organizations have been banned and forced underground. Hundreds of students have been killed, many more have been savagely beaten, maimed, raped, in the course of demonstrations or commando-style police raids on campuses and student hostels, a frequent occurrence in African universities over the last decade. Thousands have been arrested, some being detained for long periods and subjected to many forms of torture and degrading treatment; as in the case of students arrested in the Ivory Coast, who were forced to lie down and stare at the sun or lick the blood from the wounds of other students (Dégni-Ségui 1996: 71–73). Thousands, again, have been expelled from all schools, and all have suffered because of the constant closing off of the campuses that, at times, stretches for almost a year. To this, we must add the growing militarization of the universities. Police intervention, and even the occupation of the campuses by security forces, are becoming matter of fact in many institutions, and so is the presence of intelligence officers and police informers in the classrooms.

Since the early 1990s, one aspect of the repression of student activism has been the appearance on the campuses of "secret cults" (Nigeria) and "self-defense groups" (Cameroon) (Ouendji 1996: 123–124). These are gangs of students heavily armed and clearly enjoying the connivance of the campus police who operate as vigilante groups with regard to student activists, breaking up meetings, harassing student leaders, and terrorizing the student population (Civil Liberties Organization 1991; Usen *et al.* 1990). (A more systematic means to destroy student activism has been adopted by the Sudanese government, that has created, in a very short time, twenty six new universities, while at the same time withdrawing all funding).

It is important to underscore that never has the attack on African students been denounced by international agencies like the World Bank, or the United Nations, not even when state repression has reached levels of unspeakable ferocity, as in the case of the punitive expedition conducted by the Zairian authorities, on the night of March 1990, against the students of Lubumbashi University, where more than 150 were brutally murdered. The World Bank, it seems, is all too aware that SAP cannot be applied to the schools without destroying many students' lives and violating academic free-dom, in the same way as it cannot be applied to the economic life of any country without destroying the livelihood of its workers. This is why it should not be surprising that its support for many of Africa's dictatorial regimes and their use of a "strong hand" in dealing with students has never wavered.

THE STUDENT MOVEMENT AS A MOVEMENT FIGHTING TO EXPAND ACCESS TO HIGHER EDUCATION

It is against this background that we should rethink the claim that African student struggles, even at present, have elitist and corporatist goals and only reflect the interests of a minority bent on preserving its privileges at the expense of the general well-being. This argument has for years now been routinely used by the World Bank and the African governments in order to justify their policy of cuts and repression. The evidence, however, is against it.

Not only (it is worthwhile remembering) in many African countries, university students often come from poor families. Even *prima facie* it is hard to identify as members of an elite young people who risk going to jail, or being killed, in order to obtain a book or transport allowance; who sleep ten in a room, taking turns on the floor, because they cannot afford to pay the accommodation fees; who go to class without food in their stomachs, eating only one meal a day, as it is happening today in nearly every country of Africa (Federici 1991, 1993a, 1993b).

Moreover, when students struggle to defend education as "an inalianable right" they are not fighting in defense of a privilege, or a corporatist interest, but against it. For the downsizing of the higher-education system, and the introduction of "cost-sharing" schemes, as demanded by structural adjustment are guaranteed to limit the entry to the universities to an elite as during the colonial period. It was precisely to democratize university education and to allow for recruitment on the basis of merit alone that African leaders like Nyerere (in 1965) abolished school fees (Barkan 1975: 13). Thus, those who chastize the student resistance to the cuts in university funds and student allowances as a sign of elitism are hypocritical, for there is no question that, in the absence of subsidies, only a minority of students coming from affluent families, or selected according to "donor" specifications, will be able to continue their studies. Furthermore, as already mentioned, the African students struggle against the adjustment of the universities goes to the core of the question of "self-determination." It challenges the World Banks' right to establish what the continent's educational needs must be, what should qualify as education, and to destroy educational systems that, for all their limits, represent an important achievement and national assets, which all Africans have paid and sacrificed for.

This is not to say that African university student bodies and organizations do not need to become more egalitarian. Being impoverished and often brutalized makes it possible for African university students to develop a class consciousness and rethink social change from the viewpoint of those at the bottom. But this is not an automatic process. In addition, student activism in Africa is still predominantly a male affair as demonstrated by the low presence of women in student organizations, particularly in decision-making positions, and by the students unions' demands, which rarely acknowledge that on campus as well women are subject to unique forms of pressure and discrimination.

This, undoubtedly, is one of the main obstacles the African student movement must overcome if it is to grow. For the battle for education is not going to be won unless those who fight it are committed to eliminate, rather than create or reproduce, social hierachies. From this viewpoint, there can be no doubt that the future of the African student movement is also closely tied to its ability to articulate an alternative vision of education to the one that was promoted in the post-independence period in the context of the politics of "national reconstruction and development."

This, however, does not diminish the importance of the present student struggles against SAP and for the right of education. For the campuses no less than the factories are places where students come together, socialize, where ethnic or religious divisions can be overcome, where information is gathered, processed, and circulated, where an understanding of the implications of national and international policies can be facilitated. Thus, if the universities are allowed to collapse, and if only those who are economically privileged have access to them, it will become even more difficult for Africans to make autonomous decisions concerning their educational systems, not to mention other political and economic issues. One wonders, for instance, whether a Nyerere would be allowed today by the World Bank to make Swahili the means of instruction in university education.

The struggles of African students against SAP appear even more essential considering that the same policies which they are fighting against are simultaneously being imposed on students practically all over the globe, and in response, an international student movement is growing against the escalating cost of tuitions, school budget cuts, and the growing commercialization of knowledge. In other words, the condition of African students does not represent an exception. One could not speak today, as J. Barkan did in 1975 of an "African pattern" differentiating African university students behavior from that of their peers in Europe or the United States, presumably motivated by a higher degree of "political idealism" (128–130). A comparison of student protest internationally over the last decade would show that the struggles of African students is on a continuum with that of students in Latin America, Asia, Australia, as well as Europe and the United States, that indeed we can speak today of an international student movement, and that Africa students are paying by far the heaviest cost for the effort this movement is making to reverse the corporate agenda by which education is being reshaped wordwide.

This implies that there is also a direct connection between the African student struggles and the struggles of students and teachers on our campuses. This, however, has not been recognized yet. Thus, it is still primarily human rights organizations (Africa Watch, Africa Rights) and The World University Service (WUS) that protest when African students or teachers are detained, tortured, or universities are closed. Few are the occasions in which North American teachers and activists have made their voice heard in their defense. Year after year, as African universities have collapsed and turned into war zones, the academic world in North America has been silent. Selectively, African universities have become the destination of American study abroad programs; but to this day, few American students and teachers have any idea of the reality of "college life" in most of the continent or, if they do, consider it necessary to take a strong position against it.

It is to be hoped that this will change. It is time that North American academics recognize that we, too, are implicated in the condition of African universities and not only as contributing taxpayers to the World Bank and IMF budgets. Although North American colleges may fair better in a word completely subsumed to a market logic, we still face a tremendous loss if we accept the high costs at which education must be purchased and the international hierarchies that are being built upon it.

NOTES

1. Structural adjustment both as a general economic program and in its specific application to higher education is a household name for students of international politics and economics and the object of a vast literature. I will only mention here the studies that are more directly concerned with the restructuring of university education and African student struggles in the 1980s and 1990s: Caffentzis (1991, 1994, 1995); Codesria (1996); Diouf and Mamdani (1994); Kraus (1991).

2. This essay is Daddieh (1988).

3. See Sicherman (1995) and Toungara (1995).

4. This attitude is satirized in *The Future Leaders*, a novel by Mwangi Ruheni (Heinemann 1973), quoted by Carol Sicherman (1995: 31). Writes Sicherman: "The 1958 Makerere commencement orator in Ruheni's novel, *The Future Leaders* praises the graduates in a premonitory fashion, calling them 'the future leaders of this country,' on whom depend 'the hopes of the peoples of the great territories of Uganda, Kenya and Tanganika'.... Not long after, the narrator dismisses the speech: 'How can they all be the future leaders? And who will do the work?'"

5. Guineans and Ivorian students, for instance, were openly critical of Sekou Toure's and Houphouet Boigny's ready acceptance of the *loi cadre* passed in June 1956, which established territorial autonomy in the territories of French West and Equatoria Africa. "[Sekou Toure's] willingness to cooperate with France was regarded as a betrayal of African nationalism by the more radical of the African intellighentsia, and he was attacked, from time to time, in the pages of the *Etudiant d'Afrique Noire*, the organ of the Federation of Students from Black Africa in France" (Segal 1963: 311).

6. "Only after the Second World War ended were universities established in many parts of Africa" (Hanna 1975a: 7). A University College was established at Ibadan in 1948, the University of Dakar was founded in 1950, the University of the Goald Coast (now University of Ghana) in 1948; the University of Lybia was established in 1955 (ibid.). There were no universities in Portuguese Africa until the early 1960s (Duffy 1963: 176–177).

7. I rely in part for this information on conversations I had with African students from countries who had recently achieved independence, in Paris in 1962 and 1963.

8. This has been overstressed by J. Barkan in his 1975 study of university students in Uganda, Tanzania, Ghana. On the basis of interviews he conducted on these countries' university campuses, Barkan concluded that African students were reluctant to take risks, still had too many opportunities to be able to afford the political

idealism displayed by students in Europe or the United States in the 1960s, and that little originality in economic or political life could be expected of them.

9. The most famous case, in this context, is the crisis that developed at the University of Dar es Salaam (Tanzania) in October 1966, when students confronted President Nyerere on the question of their participation in the National Service, a move which convinced Nyerere that university education was becoming a means of class differentiation. It was in response to this confrontation that he introduced his *Education for Self-Reliance* program (Barkan 1975: 13–20; Morrison 1976: 237ff.). Similar confrontations also occurred in Ghana, between Nkruma and the faculty and students of the University of Ghana at Legon (Barkan 1975: 22), and in Mozambique, where in 1967 Eduardo Mondlane "issued a White Paper" critical of those students who sought special privileges (de Bragança and Wallerstein 1982: 102–103, 107–114).

10. An example here is the mobilization of the Ghanaian students in 1977 against the Acheampong regime (Yeebo 1991: 108).

11. An exception to this tendency was the contribution by Nigerian students to the formation in the late 1970s of the Anti-Poverty Movement that became one of the rallying points for the democratic struggle in the last period of the Gowon regime. At the peak of the movement, around 1976, left-wing students joined with peasant organizations in the southwest of the country, and some went to live in rural areas to do agitational work in farming communities. (From Edwin Madunagu's "The Unmaking of Nigeria. A Refutation of Official History"). Two years later, in Nigeria, there was the first confrontation between students and the Obasanjo government about the cost of higher education, culminating in the "Ali Must Go" movement that took off after eleven students were killed in April, during clashes with the police in Lagos and Zaria.

12. Compare with the statistics gathered by J. Barkan in the mid-1970s that placed the percentage of students coming from a peasant background at 37 percent in Ghana, 54 percent in Tanzania, 50 percent in Uganda (Barkan 1975: 28). In his study, Barkan detected a tendency in the educational systems towards the emergence of a self-perpetuating educated class, more pronounced in a country like Ghana where the educational system had been in existence for more than a century (ibid.). However, the continuous expansion of university education through the early 1980s has guaranteed that the majority of students continue to come from the lower classes.

13. It is interesting, in this context, to read the extensive acknowledgments by which graduating Nigerian university students preface their dissertations to thank those who have made their degrees possible. They help dispell the myth that students are a privileged elite, as they demonstrate that very often an entire community has to come together and pool its resources for a student to be able to enter the university gates. It is also significant that in Nigeria the language of communication among university students, outside the classrooms, is not English but pidgin, the language of West Africa's urban proletariat.

14. On the students deteriorating standards of living, see above all *CAFA Newsletter* No. 10 (Spring 1996) and Codesria (1995).

15. Ibid. See also Hirji (this volume) and Jega (1994).

16. The main exception being South Africa where *apartheid* has functioned as a form of structural adjustment.

17. It is significant, in this context that, at a meeting in Harare with African Vice Chancellors in 1986, the World Bank representative went as far as suggesting that Africa has no need for universities. He was forced, however, to soften his position in

front of the resistance and outrage expressed by the African Vice Chancellors.

18. On the implications of the World Bank's "Africa Capacity Building Initiative," see Caffentzis (1994).

19. See, among others, Caffentzis (this volume).

20. There is, however, a remarkable circulation of experiences across borders due to the high circulation of African students from country to country.

21. *CAFA, 1993. CAFA Newsletter* No. 5 (fall).

REFERENCES

Agan, Iya. 1986. "Crisis on Nigerian Campuses." *Africa-Asia,* July 21, 46–47.

"The Agitated Student Front." 1989. West Africa, January 16–22, 49.

Akani, Christian Uche. 1994. *My Ordeal. A Prison Memoir of a Student Activist.* Port Harcourt: (Nigeria): Jeson Books.

Akinrinade, Soji et al. 1989. "Orgy of Violence." *Newswatch,* June 12, 10–19.

ASUU ABU Branch. 1986. *The Killings at ABU.* Zaria: Gaskiya Corporation Ltd.

ASUU. 1986. *ASUU and the 1986 Education Crisis in Nigeria.* Ibadan (Nigeria).

Ayu, Iyorchia D. 1986. *Essays in Popular Struggle.* Oguta (Nigeria): ZIM Publishers.

Bako, Sabo. 1994. "Education and Adjustment in Nigeria." In Mamadou Diouf and Mahmood Mamdani (Eds.), *Academic Freedom in Africa,* 150–155.

Barkan, Joel D. 1975. *An African Dilemma. University Students, Development and Politics in Ghana, Tanzania and Uganda.* London and Nairobi: Oxford University Press.

Bathily, Abdoulaye; Diouf, Mamadou; and Mbodj, Mohamed. 1995. "The Senegalese Student Movement from its Inception to 1989." In Mamhmood Mamdani and Ernest Wamba dia Wamba (Eds.), *African Studies in Social Movement and Democracy* 369–407.

de Bragança Aquino, and Wallerstein, Immanuel. 1982. *The African Liberation Reader: Vol. 1. The Anatomy of Colonialism.* London: Zed Books.

CAFA. 1993a. *CAFA Newsletter* No. 4 (Spring).

_____. 1993b. *CAFA Newsletter* No. 5 (Fall).

_____. 1996. *CAFA Newsletter* No. 10 (Spring).

_____. 1997. "Students Murdered in Kenya. What Can be Done?" *CAFA Newsletter* No. 12 (Spring) 7-8.

Caffentzis, George C. 1991. "The World Bank and Education in Africa." *CAFA Newsletter* No. 2 (Fall) 2-12.

_____. 1994. "The World Bank's African Capacity Building Initiative: A Critique." *CAFA Newsletter* No. 6 (Spring) 14-19.

_____. 1995. "The Fundamental Implications of the Debt Crisis for Social Reproduction in Africa." In Mariarosa Dalla Costa and Giovanna Franca Dalla Costa, (Eds.), *Paying the Price. Women and the Politics of International Economic Strategy.* London: Zed Books, 15–41.

"Chronology of African University Student Struggles: 1985–1995." 1996. *CAFA Newsletter* No. 10 (Spring) 8–19.

Cefkin, J. Leo. 1975. "Rhodesian University Students in National Politics." In W. J. Hanna et al., *University Students and African Politics,* 135-165.

Cheater, Angela. 1991. "The University of Zimbabwe: University, National University, State University, or Party University?" *African Affairs, 90,* 189–20.

Civil Liberties Organization. 1990. "The $120 Loan and Human Rights." *Liberty,*

1 (June) 1–3.

Civil Liberties Organization. 1991. *A Massive Crackdown on Student Activists in Nigeria.* Lagos (Nigeria): CLO.

Civil Liberties Organization and Committee for the Defense of Human Rights. 1991. *When Student Kills Student. Report on the Intra-students Clash of May 27, 1991 at the Obafemi Awolowo University, Ile-Ife.* Lagos (Nigeria): CLO.

Codesria. 1996. *The State of Academic Freedom in Africa 1995.* Dakar (Senegal): Codesria.

Daddieh, Cyril Kofie. 1988. "The Management of Educational Crises in Côte d' Ivoire." *Journal of Modern African Studies, 26* (4), 639–659.

Daniel, J.; de Vlaming, F.; Hartley, N.; and Nowak, M. (Eds.). 1993. *Academic Freedom. A Human Rights Report.* London: Zed Books with World University Service.

Daniel, John et al., (Eds.). 1995. *Academic Freedom 3. Education and Human Rights.* London: Zed Books and World University Service.

Dégni-Ségui, René. 1996. "Academic Freedom and University Autonomy in Côte d' Ivoire." In Codesria, *The State of Academic Freedom in Africa, 1995,* 57–80.

Diouf, Mamadou and Mamdani, Mahmood (Eds.). 1994. *Academic Freedom in Africa.* Dakar (Senegal): Codesria.

Duffy, James. 1963. *Portugal in Africa.* Baltimore: Penguin Books.

Fanon, Frantz. 1963. *The Wretched of the Earth.* New York: Grove Press.

Federici, Silvia. 1991. The Recolonization of African Education." *Association of Concerned Africa Scholars Bulletin,* 34.

_____. 1993a. "Academic Freedom in Africa." ACAS Policy Paper. ACAS *Bulletin* Nos. 38–39.

_____. 1993b. "The Economic Roots of the Repression of Academic Freedom in Africa." *CAFA Newsletter* No. 4 (Spring).

Hamad, Al-Zubeir Abdelhadi. 1995. "Sudan." In Daniel, John et al. (Eds.), *Academic Freedom 3. Education and Human Rights,* 68–88.

Hanna, William John. 1975a. "Students, Universities and Political Outcomes." In Hanna et al., *University Students and African Politics,* 1-22.

_____. 1975b. "Systemic Constraints and Individual Action." In Hanna et al., *University Students and African Politics,* 257-290.

Hanna, William John, et al. 1975. *University Students and African Politics.* New York : Holmes & Meier.

Hanna, William J., and Hanna, Judith L. 1975a. "Students as Elites." In Hanna et al., *University Students and African Politics,* 23-48.

Hanna, William J., and Hanna, Judith L. 1975b. "The Cynical Nationalists." In Hanna et al., *University Students and African Politics,* 49-70.

Hanna, William J., Hanna, Judith L., and Sauer, Vivian Z. 1975. "The Active Minority." In Hannah et al., *University Students and African Politics,* 71-102.

Human Rights Watch/Africa. 1996. *Behind the Red Line. Political Repression in Sudan.* New York: Human Rights Watch.

Jega, Attahiru M. 1994. *Nigerian Academics under Military Rule.* University of Stockholm. Report No. 1994: 3.

Kraus, John. 1991. "The Struggle over Structural Adjustment in Ghana." *Africa Today, 38* (4), 19–40.

Leatherbee, Lea, and Osman, Hibaaq. 1993. "Sudan." In Daniel, J. et al., *Academic Freedom,* 117–135.

Madunagu, Edwin. 1995. "The Unmaking of Nigeria. A Refutation of Official History." Unpublished Manuscript.

Mamdani, Mahmood. 1994. "The Intelligentsia, the State and Social Movements in Africa." In M. Diouf and M. Mamdani (Eds.), *Academic Freedom in Africa*, 247-261.

Mamdani, Mahmood, and Wamba dia Wamba, Ernest (Eds.). 1995. *African Studies in Social Movement and Democracy*. Dakar (Senegal): Codesria.

McKowen, Roberta E. 1975. "Kenya University Students and Politics." In Hanna et al., *University Students and African Politics*.

Morrison, David R. 1976. *Education and Politics in Africa. The Tanzanian Case*. Montreal: McGill–Queen's University Press.

Mustapha, Abdul Raufu. 1996. "The State of Academic Freedom in Nigeria." In Codesria, *The State of Academic Freedom in Africa 1995*, 103–120.

NANS. *Letter to All Mass Organizations*. June 17, 1992.

_____. 1992. *Solidarity. Organ of the* National Association of Nigerian Students (NANS) *2* (2).

Okorie, Emenike. 1991. "The Distrust Deepens." *The African Guardian. 14*, (January) 38–41.

Olojede, Dele. 1986. "Oh, God, Not Again!" *Newswatch* (Nigeria) June 9, 10–18.

Ouendji, Norbert N. 1996. "Cameroon: 'Mined' Campuses and Muzzled Staff." In Codesria, *The State of Academic Freedom in Africa 1995*, 121–132.

"Restive Campuses." 1992. *The African Guardian*, July 6.

Ruheni, Mwangi. 1973. *The Future Leaders*. Ibadan, London, Nairobi: Heinemann.

"SAP Sparks Riots." 1989. *Newswatch* (Nigeria) June 12.

Segal, Ronald. 1963. *African Profiles*. Hammondsworth (England): Penguin Books.

Sicherman, Carol. 1995. "Ngũgĩ's Colonial Education: The Subversion . . . of the African Mind." *African Studies Review, 38* (3), 11–35.

Sow, Christian and Fox, Ibrahim. 1996. "Guinea: Violations of the Rights of Students and Teachers." In Codesria, *The State of Academic Freedom in Africa 1995*, 143–148.

Toungara, Jeanne Maddox. 1995. "Generational Tensions in the Parti Démocratique de Côte d'Ivoire." *African Studies Review, 38* (2) (September), 11-38.

Usen, Anietie et al. 1990. "Reign of Terror." *Newswatch*, March 12, 14–19.

Woods, Dwayne. 1996. "The Politicization of Teachers' Associations in the Côte d' Ivoire." *African Studies Review, 39* (3) (December), 113-129.

World Bank. 1986. *Financing Education in Developing Countries*. Washington, DC: World Bank.

World Bank. 1991. *The African Capacity Building Initiative. Towards Improved Policy Analysis and Development Management*. Washington, DC: World Bank.

Yeebo, Zaya. 1991. *Ghana: The Struggle for Popular Power. Rawlings: Saviour or Demagogue*. London: New Beacon Books.

Zolberg, Aristide. 1975. "Political Generations in Conflict: The Ivory Coast Case." In Hanna et al., *University Students and African Politics*, 103-134.

6

Academic Pursuits Under the LINK

Karim F. Hirji

This chapter is based on my personal experiences in teaching and research at the Faculty of Medicine at the University of Dar es Salaam during the year 1989. Not that these are in any sense unique. Far from it; similar tales can be elicited from most members of the academic staff, be they in medicine, science, the social sciences, or law. What is uncommon, however, is a public articulation and discussion of issues emanating from them. At most, they may be the subject of gossip and gripe in one's intimate circle. But such experiences reflect the state of the university, and they need to be debated in the open if a way out of our present predicament is to be found.

In January 1989, after an absence of eight years from Tanzania, I took up my present position at the Faculty of Medicine. Upon reporting for duty, I was given an office and a teaching assignment. So I briskly strode down to the departmental office and asked for some stationery—nothing extravagant, just a pen, a pencil, and writing paper. The looks my request elicited constitute my first encounter with the LINK.

The head of the department patiently conveyed to me that the annual departmental budget for purchasing such items was inadequate. It had, in fact, been exhausted long ago. I protested that given my salary, which had a purchasing power of about fifty U.S. dollars, I could not be expected to provide these things myself. When I looked around the office, I did see a few usable items. Surely, there were some to spare here, I thought. At that moment, the LINK came to my rescue. The secretary, after being beckoned to do so, brought out one of the nicest notebooks I have ever seen from a drawer. On it was inscribed "Kollegieblock," together with other undecipherable characters. Notwithstanding, I cherished the book and used it with care for six months. I later gathered that this was one of a few left over from a Scandinavian funded research project. The pen and pencil, however, I had to find elsewhere. The department had a large supply of computer paper obtained from this and other LINKs. So it was suggested that in the future I should use that as writing material!

From then on, time after time, I have run across the LINK in all sorts of places, even in the toilet! Its all pervasive nature making it seem like an Orwellian Big Brother. I have learned that to progress one needs to be LINKed. If you march out of tune with it, you are only courting disaster. Those academicians blessed by the LINK smile radiantly and subsequently prosper, and those with a missing LINKage are perpetually enveloped by an aura of gloom.

Thanks to the LINK, our department has five microcomputers, a number of dot-matrix and laser printers, photocopiers, and a host of computer paraphernalia and supplies. But for almost the whole of 1989, the bread-and-butter items like pens, pencils, writing paper, rulers, and so on were in short supply, and mostly one had to fend for oneself. I say almost, because just a week before the year's end, each member of the department got a Christmas present comprising a writing pad, two red pens, and two blue pens. A week earlier some prominent LINK personalities had visited the place. Whether the gift was related to the visit or whether that was a simple coincidence is anyone's guess.

Whatever the facet of academic life at the Faculty of Medicine I look at, I see such anomalies. Can an academic institution discharge its responsibilities in such paradoxical circumstances? What kind of academic activities do they engender? What attitudes toward teaching and research does the presence of the LINK foster? Taking my experiences as the springboard, these are the issues I examine in this chapter. I start with teaching.

TEACHING

Biostatistics is a required first-year course for postgraduate students pursuing a master of tropical diseases control course, or a master of medicine program in one of the specialties like community health, microbiology, and internal medicine. This is what I was assigned to teach, albeit from the middle of the academic year. My class had ten enthusiastic students.

It seems trite to state that books are a necessary though not sufficient condition for effective learning. Societies where knowledge passes from generation to generation by the word of mouth are supposed to be found in historical works only. Today pupils in an elementary school also need books. But my students, most of whom had practiced medicine for some years, did not, among them, possess a single text on the subject, nor did they have much photocopied material. Some copying paper was available. But producing handouts for students was not among the priorities for its use. Consequently, in the initial months, a lot of class time was spent having students simply copy the essential parts of the course notes.

The current prices of books make the book allowance for students grossly inadequate. Asking the students to copy an important paper at their own expense can be done only rarely. It is a strain on their limited budget. The LINK has a role here too, as I soon found out. Some books had been ordered through the British LINK and were expected at any time. (A stipulation was that only books published in the United Kingdom could be purchased). These arrived a couple of months later. Some were kept in the offices of the lecturers and professors. The rest were sent to the library and put on special reserve. This offered some respite; however, by the start of next academic year, half of the books sent to the library had mysteriously vanished. By then I had learned my lesson, and through my own LINK I had secured a sufficient number of bound volumes of photo-copied material and salvaged seven copies of a book procured by the department. These were loaned out so that two students shared a copy of each item. I have also seen one lecturer use his LINK to provide books for students. This year therefore the class time can be devoted to discussing issues and concepts, rather than copying notes. What the situation will be next year is at the mercy of some LINK. These remarks apply not just to books but also to laboratory and other supplies needed to conduct preclinical and clinical training at a medical school. In all these dimensions, without the blessings of a LINK, students and teachers end up in dire circumstances, able to proceed only with great difficulty.

There are two categories of courses at the Faculty of Medicine. First, there are the regular courses listed in the university catalogue. The above remarks relate to such courses. Then there are the specially funded "short courses." I was involved in one such course a few months after my arrival. It was a short course on reproductive epidemiology. The participants were drawn from all over Africa and included local physicians. Though it was funded by the Rockefeller Foundation, it was organized and conducted by our department.

While lecturing for the short course, I continued to teach my regular class. Both were in the same building. The regular class was held in a ground-floor room that was never cleaned, where the students had to wipe off the dust from the chairs and tables at the start of the session, where I wrote on a worn-out blackboard and used a dirty rag to wipe it, where most window panes were broken and in which all sorts of debris, including old and rusted air-conditioning equipment, lay in the corners. The short course was held in a room just above it which had been recently built using German funding. This room was immaculate and sparkling clean with new furniture and with the latest teaching aides and a host of ceiling fans to ward off the tropical heat.

The short-course students had the books and supplies they needed. They also got decent meals, lodging, and transport as well as a hefty allowance. The instructors and course organizers also secured an allowance. My reward for the five or so lectures I gave in this course amounted to twice my regular monthly salary.

The support staff derived benefits from it as well. Thus the level of administrative efficiency associated with this course was an order of magnitude higher than that one would encounter from the same workers in the regular course of their duties.

From an academic point of view, however, I am of the opinion that such a course has little value. What the students get is a hodgepodge of topics. The basic motivation for participation, both among the instructors and students, is monetary and related more to travel opportunities than to anything else. But such courses secure the lion's share of attention and devotion. In turn, where the effort should really be invested, that is, in the training of regular postgraduate and undergraduate medical, dental, pharmacy and public health students, relative neglect and disinterest prevails.

For example, what can one make of a recent short course funded by Swedish Agency for Research and Economic Cooperation (SAREC) that was held at a splendid beach hotel? The aim was to teach word processing and other computer software to the academic and nonacademic staff including local secretaries. A secretary and the instructors flew over from Sweden to conduct it. Surely, there are qualified Tanzanians who could have done the job. Or was the purpose of the course to provide a tropical holiday for the instructors? They were paid allowances that can only be regarded as discriminatory when compared with that given to the Tanzanian participants, though the local organizers did manage to get a few more crumbs. The point is not that such courses should not be held. By all means, where there is a need, let us have them. But they can be organized on a rational basis. If organizations like SAREC want to assist, they must do it on terms in line with the academic and other needs and capabilities of the university.

If the large sums dissipated for the short courses were used to support the regular courses, in terms of additional teaching allowances for instructors, and books and supplies for students, they could help improve the quality of instruction substantially. The professors and lecturers would be encouraged to spend more time on pedagogic pursuits than on growing and marketing pineapples and eggs from their farms. They would also be around when the students need them. Or is it that international agencies like the Rockefeller Foundation or SAREC are somehow locked into supporting inconsequential courses of dubious academic value?

Some regular courses do receive special LINK funds. However, here one finds that a scant portion of these funds filters down to the students. The lecturers are unable to purchase course supplies from the funds; facilities available from them are monopolized by the coordinator; no meetings are held to discuss the utilization of the funds; and there is little accountability in relation to them. So even where LINK funds are available, they hardly impact the quality of teaching for these courses. An attitude of resignation and frustration therefore prevails among the students and concerned academic staff, with no one able to do anything to resolve the problems.

It is thus difficult to avoid concluding that in spite of the multitude of LINKs available to the faculty, the quality of the instruction imparted to the regular students leaves a lot to be desired.

Surely, this is one of the principal, though not the sole reason, behind the poor and declining performance of the students in the university examinations. That is an issue the faculty is currently grappling with, but no solution is in sight.

BOOKSTORE AND LIBRARY

The days when inexpensive textbooks and supplementary reference material were in abundant supply at the university bookstore seem so distant that most students do not know they ever existed. In the early seventies, with a book loan of about a thousand Tanzanian shillings, one could acquire the latest books recommended by the professors, obtain the stationery needed, get other books of interest, and still have money left over to purchase sundry items like alarm clocks. In those days, the students did not get their book allowance in cash. Instead, each student had an account at the university bookstore. This arrangement provided the bookstore with revolving capital. The cash book allowance given today is not necessarily used on books. It is insufficient, the books are not available, or there are other pressing needs toward which the money is diverted.

Years of mismanagement, among other things, have reduced the university bookstore into a position where it cannot compete with streethawkers. A book-seller operating in a dilapidated hut near the Kisutu market had better books on medicine and statistics. When I visited the bookshop, I was horrified to see the pathetic state it had stumbled into. What was once a first rate store with the latest books and journals on a diversity of disciplines was now a place where one could not find adequate material for a single one of all the academic degrees offered at the university. It was a place replete with paradoxes. For a particular course, there were abundant supplies of a specific book. This was a course that was connected to a special LINK. But then one would find not a single book for all the courses taught in a program bereft of a LINK.

The bookshop had, at a point in time, received a large grant through an exclusive LINK. But orders were not placed in time. Some items were ordered at the last minute. Many of these turned out to be not the ones needed. Coordination between academic departments and the book store hardly exists these days. Each department or faculty tries to find its own solution to the book shortage through cultivating its own LINK. One may thus come across a few departments well endowed with books and journals while others wallow in a state of intellectual famine.

In a university, the library should be an important resource for research and teaching material. The main campus library, though now it is only a shadow of its glorious past when it was among the best university libraries in

Africa, has managed to maintain a modicum of organization. Its repertoire of current journals is better than what I expected. A LINK, responsible management, and additional incentives offered to library staff, are the secrets behind its present condition.

The medical library, on the other hand, resembles a dusty museum more than anything else. For most medical specialties, the shelves are stocked with ancient material. This is compounded by the problem, alluded to above, of the disappearance of new material from the library. Here and there, one sees an exception; a valuable text or complete volumes of a key journal. Basic reference materials are also unavailable. For example, the library does not have complete recent volumes of *Index Medicus*, the basic bibliographic Bible for medicine! Previous volumes had been put in the main library by mistake, and nobody seemed to have missed them until I located them.

The second half of the twentieth century has witnessed an explosive growth of scientific and medical knowledge. With conditions like those described above, day by day, we are receding further and further from the frontiers of knowledge. Books and journals are a precious resource. The amount allocated for them in the internal budget is absolutely appalling. Could a part of what is wasted in the numerous unofficial trips with official vehicles be used for books? Could the Bank of Tazania spare more of the foreign exchange available through the International Monetary Fund to purchase books and educational material?

What current material the library has is provided by the generosity of a number of LINKs. But that does not amount to much. Now and then one sees a new journal. The library does have a computer, though it is not visible to the ordinary users. Whether they will ever benefit from it, in terms of being able to search computerized bibliographies and databases, is another question.

RESEARCH

Research and consultancy are the two areas where the LINK is omnipresent at the faculty level. A colleague recently said that if one cultivates proper LINKs with regards to such endeavors, one can "mine diamonds." Not every-one can aspire to be a globe-trotting consultant like some senior professors or heads of departments. (Some of these departments are effectively run by junior staff. I wonder at the quality of instruction and supervision imparted to the students). But everyone aspires to do research. And research generates data. When a researcher has gathered volumes of data, it is not uncommon for him or her to be at a loss as to how to interpret them. That is when he or she consults a statistician. Being one of a few statisticians at the faculty, I am regularly on call. Students, academic staff, and other researchers are constantly at my doorstep seeking advice on what to do with their data.

More often than not, they discover that they should have consulted a statistician prior to embarking upon the study. Either the design of the study or the type of data collected are found to be inappropriate to answer the questions posed. At this stage the medical researcher may decide to seek a second opinion that may render a more favorable diagnosis of the research effort, or he or she may desire a palliative exercise to be undertaken. Such an experience is common to statisticians in biomedical institutions the world over. At the Faculty of Medicine as well, I believe that a substantial proportion of the research effort is ill-conceived and badly executed, and the results erroneously interpreted. There are a few exceptions I will note later.

The research projects undertaken at the Faculty of Medicine fall into two groups: undergraduate and graduate student research and faculty research. That done by undergraduate students, whether in the form of collective or individual projects, is generally of no consequence. Not that the potential to do good work is lacking. Adequate preparation and guidance are the absent ingredients. I recall a request to accompany a class of undergraduate medical students on a weeklong project to evaluate the Essential Drugs Program in Kibaha. I asked the department concerned for a write up on the aims, design and implementation of the project. To my surprise, none was available; the best I could get was a hastily scribbled note on the issue.

The postgraduate students spend a year or more on dissertation work. They are better placed to conduct research. Primarily due to a lack of adequate supervision, many flounder for months in their efforts. By international standards, their research budget is meager, often less than the equivalent of two or three hundred U.S. dollars. Despite the plethora of obstacles they face, I find that some of them can, when properly guided, undertake sound research that is also relevant to the health needs of the nation, with amazing dedication and perseverance. The work I have seen by postgraduate students in pediatrics deserves high commendation.

On the other hand, there are the grandiose projects with senior faculty members as the principal investigators. These are funded by international organizations, and their budgets may run into tens of thousands of dollars. I find that the quality of such undertakings is inversely related to the size of the budget. When I read the grant proposals for some of these projects, I wonder how they were approved by the funding agencies. If a graduate student had brought such a proposal to me, I would have unceremoniously tossed it out of the window. Or is it that the LINK agencies have different standards for Third World nations? Given the paternalistic attitudes prevalent in these organizations, I would not be amazed if such was indeed the case. Sometimes it is also a case of you scratch my back, and I will scratch yours. These international institutions, to justify their existence to their domestic tax payers, need to show that they are aiding the poor of the world. In order to make up for their inability to assist those who truly need it, they end up funding projects from which they derive glowing reports from their local counterparts, and data of dubious quality to support their charitable claims.

To paraphrase P. J. Davis and R. Hersh, scientific research is of three types: (1) pure research, which results from the internal dynamics of the particular discipline; (2) applied research, which emanates as a response to particular problems in society, be that in engineering, medicine, agriculture, or education; and (3) rhetorical research, "which is neither pure nor applied, and whose sole consequence is to generate publications, reports and grant proposals filled with empty verbiage and pretentious obfuscation."[1] In the many years that I spent in the United States as a student at prominent universities and on their faculties, I came across instances of all three types of research. One would be amazed at the extent of time, energy and resources expended on rhetorical research at these world famous institutions.[2] But since my return to Tanzania, I have come across a new category of research, namely, pseudo research.

This effort camouflages itself as applied research. But the way in which it is designed and executed, and the quality of information generated by it, rule out any applicability of its conclusions. Hardly anything of scientific or policy value arises out of it. It is characterized by a paucity of even the scholarly sounding publications that are the hallmarks of rhetorical research. The report may, at most, decorate the pages of a conference proceeding, and its existence is forgotten even by the authors. The primary motivation why it is ever undertaken are the pecuniary interests of the investigators (if one may call them by that title) including the opportunities for international travel for shopping purposes. As a complement to the numerous research projects performed at the Faculty of Medicine, we have the multitude of conferences held there. One day it is the medical association, the next the public health association, then the surgeons follow, and so on.

From September to December this year, almost every other week a new blue and white banner was put up near the entrance of the hospital announcing one meeting or another. These are usually held under the sponsorship of a LINK. They have glossy folders and nicely printed material for the participants. But the quality of the papers presented generally reflects the questionable quality of research done at the Faculty of Medicine and by other research establishments.

The bulk of the papers presented by the faculty members at such conferences are either text book reviews of a subject, summaries of hospital case records, or results of surveys conducted on an *ad hoc* basis. Seldom does one see the results of a scientifically designed and executed investigation, and even more rare is to see a report about a research leading to a specific action being taken to resolve a problem. In the words of the editors of the *World Health Forum*: "The job of the researcher is not only to publish the results but also to start the process of decision-making. Thousands of research papers have, over the years, proved only to be of academic interest."[3]

Action based reports are indeed rare. At a recent meeting of the Tanzania Public Health Association, a presentation of one such project, namely the control of filariasis through the use of polystyrene beads in pit latrines, was given. The project was conducted in the Makunduchi area in Zanzibar. This was a fascinating exercise undertaken by British and Zanzibari scientists, and it was one that had enormous implications for control of vector borne diseases all over the country. The method is a relatively cheap but effective form of mosquito control, and its use would impact the transmission of other vector borne diseases as well. Not much publicity was given to it in the media. In Dar es Salaam, the project has ended up just as a show-piece project. I wonder if the officials in the Ministry of Health dream of implementing the project on a wider scale. Maybe they need LINK funds to travel to London to learn more about it!

Another concomitant development with the horde of research projects initiated at the faculty level is the computer boom currently in progress there. Many departments already have, or are in the process of getting microcomputers and related equipment. Other departments are vying for LINK funds to procure them. No doubt computers have a role to play in medical and public health research. But there is a widespread tendency to consider *scientific praxis* to be synonymous with the use of the latest gadgetry. The implications of the well known adage among computer scientists "garbage in, garbage out" seems to have been lost on researchers here. The quality of any research project is not necessarily improved simply by the fact that the data have been fed into a computer and the results printed out in a fancy format on a laser printer. In the case of a study with a faulty design, or conducted inappropriately, computer use may actually help to create a false impression. I have certainly seen a number of essentially faulty grant proposals or research reports printed in a glossy format.

In an environment where the tradition of scientific rigor is weak, computer use may help sustain unscientific practices. The training of physicians in most parts of the world does not inculcate a scientific attitude. Much of their training is memorization of a huge mass of information, and promotes reverence for authority.[4] In Third World countries this is compounded by a general absence of democratic traditions, of a spirit of critical inquiry in academia, and the presence of an attitude of political and social submissiveness. In such circumstances, an electronic gadget can more easily be used to camouflage the shortcomings of existing practices rather than to carry out fundamental changes, be they in the field of health, agriculture, industry or education.

It is also not realized that the use of a computer in itself may add errors to a study. For example, until recently, the practice of checking data in a computer file was virtually unheard of in our department. This is a department that has the largest number of computers compared to any other department at the Faculty of Medicine and that processes a large volume of data generated by the studies conducted by other departments as well. When we started checking the input data, we found that for some studies, what was on the forms and what was in the computer were two different things! When data are not checked for accuracy and consistency is not done at every stage of a research project, the validity of the study can be seriously compromised.

Computers are the academic status symbols of this era. Often one finds a powerful computer used exclusively for word processing. Could not an electronic typewriter with memory or a dedicated word processor, both of which are much less expensive, suffice? Often, computer accessories that are particularly suitable to our conditions are not in use. Given the unstable power supplies, one would think that cheap and reliable surge suppressors would be often used. But most computer users have not heard of such a thing. Instead they have or they need the expensive voltage stabilizer or uniterruptible power supply units. When continuous feed paper is so costly and not easy to obtain, one would think that printers would be fitted with cut sheet feeders. But hardly anyone knows about them.

A reason for this state of affairs is that more often than not the decision about what kind of equipment to acquire is not taken locally. Supplies are frequently dumped on us by a LINK, and we have to get by with what they have. Thus one department has Swedish equipment with all documentation in Swedish, another has Japanese equipment with the material in Japanese, and so on. Many things come without basic facilities for preventive maintenance like disk-drive cleaning kits and print-head cleaners, for example. They are used like Usafiri Dar es Salaam (UDA) buses, without preventive care, until they grind to a halt, and then a new LINK is sought. Even the elementary practice of making regular backup copies of the data on the hard disk drive is seldom practiced.

The use of computers is not a panacea for improving the quality of research at the Faculty of Medicine. First and foremost, what is needed is to inculcate a spirit of scientific inquiry that is both rigorous and critical. In pursuit of the truth, it would neither sacrifice professional and academic standards, nor would it compromise for the sake of personal or political expediency. In science it is not what anyone says that is the gospel truth. The credibility of a statement is gauged by the degree to which it conforms with what is revealed by experiment or observation. If computer use complements such process, than it can promote quality research that is relevant to the health needs of the country. But in absence of such an effort, computer use can at best only help transform pseudo research into rhetorical research. Further, the consolidation of scientific traditions to perform rigorous and relevant research, if it is to be sustained on a long term basis, has to be done by ourselves. The LINK is certainly not a substitute for that.

CONCLUDING REMARKS

Discussions with several lecturers and professors lead me to believe that the above remarks are pertinent for all faculties of the University of Dar es Salaam. Has academic life here always been like this? If not, what internal and external factors have led to the present situation? What has been the reaction of the academics when confronted with symptoms of intellectual atrophy? Is there a way out?

Given the cursory scope of this communication, it does not claim to have definitive answers to these fundamental questions. My purpose is to set the ball rolling and generate a debate. I give my views with the hope that they will provoke others to respond so that analyses based on firmer foundations and solid evidence can emerge. If the debate can generate a broad consensus on the basic causes and possible remedies for the academic ailments at our university, then hopefully it can lead to preventive and curative therapies to deal with them.

In the late 1960s and the early 1970s, when the faculties at the University of Dar es Salaam had been in existence for a decade or so, and the Faculty of Medicine had just been inaugurated on a firm footing, one could claim, with some justification, that a graduate from the university had received an education comparable to that from the best universities in the world. For example, a 1971 bachelor's degree graduate from the mathematics department, who had enrolled for advanced study at a prestigious Canadian university, wrote to me that he found most of the required courses there relatively easy as he had scaled a more arduous terrain in his undergraduate years. Scholars and students from many parts of Africa and the world came to teach or study at the University of Dar es Salaam. During those years a minor but significant trend to ensure that university instruction be more in line with the nation's requirements was also in evidence. Even though the departments in the university were set up with external assistance, qualified Tanzanians soon manned the upper echelons of the academia. They included prominent economists, lawyers, historians, chemists, surgeons, parasitologists, and so on.

Given this solid foundation, have the intervening two decades seen the quality of academic endeavor develop further? I have argued above, taking the Faculty of Medicine as an example, that today academic life is in the doldrums, and despite efforts to rescue it through the LINK, what was once a beacon of scholarship is now a place where intellectual mediocrity is rampant. But it would be inaccurate to single out the academics as those solely responsible for this state of affairs. What we see at the university in general, and at the Faculty of Medicine in particular, reflects the state of and trends in the broader Tanzanian society. The excessive dependence on the LINK evident among the faculty parallels national policies pursued over the past two decades that impaired the growth of an independent and strong economy. Despite its political ideology, the Tanzanian government has always pursued a vigorous policy of relying on foreign loans, grants and planners for most of its projects. Even in the heyday of political sloganeering about socialism and self-reliance, Tanzania was the highest per capita recipient of foreign funds in Africa. Projects like adult education or health education campaigns which could have been implemented with purely local effort were not undertaken without external backing.

Political leaders in Tanzania have, over the years, mastered the art of saying with a straight face exactly the opposite of what they do. While the government projects followed plans laid out by foreign consultants, we were supposed to be deciding over our own future. While the local university educated experts were referred to with derision as *wasomis* in their speeches, the foreign *wasomis* were being taken at their word. There was no systematic government policy to harness local intellectual resources at the university or elsewhere to promote national development. If anything, in practice, there was a significant discouragement of such efforts.

Over the past three decades, there has been a vast expansion of higher education facilities in Tanzania. New departments and faculties arose at the University of Dar es Salaam, the Faculty of Agriculture became a separate university, and many colleges and institutes were started around the country. The variety of advanced training available, at least formally, now rivals that found in any other African country. But these institutions sprang up as appendages of the governmental or parastatal bureaucracy.

Hardly any of them has had an notable impact on its respective social or economic sector. In some cases the growth of the educational arm went hand in hand with the deterioration of the sector it was to serve. Thus, the fact that Tanzania is among a few nations of Africa to have a Cooperative College has not implied that the cooperatives in the country are better managed than elsewhere; the fact that Tanzania is one of a handful to have a Transport Institute has not resulted in the bus or rail companies being run on a more efficient basis; the presence of the Ardhi Institute has not meant that land is used in a rational and planned manner; the presence of the Institute of Finance Management did not result in healthier financial institutions; the existence of the Social Welfare Training Institute did not lead to better services to the disadvantaged and the destitute, and so on. One can multiply such examples *ad infinitum* from health, education, agriculture and other sectors, and paint a similar picture with respect to the faculties of the two universities as well.

This suggests that in practice educational development has become an end unto itself, not related to social and economic development. For students, the acquisition of higher education has become a formal exercise. What one learns in the process is not applied at work, either because of its unsuitability to the local environment, or because of resistance towards absorption of innovative ideas. If what one has learned is in line with how things are currently done, then one can use the knowledge. If not, then it is of no use. The bureaucracy in Tanzania has little room for creativity. Fresh graduates from the university or other educational institutions have generally found themselves frustrated if they dared to suggest or implement any innovations at their place of work.

This negative political attitude on creativity and intellectual endeavor has impacted life within the university as well. The administrative arm has become stronger compared to the academic arm; the channeling of resources has favored those in the administration; democratic traditions have become weaker, and accountability has been reduced. (With the new vice chancellor, this trend may have been arrested somewhat). The quality and originality of research, its applicability to practical problems, or excellence in teaching were not, in practice, firmly adhered to as criteria for academic advancement. This was another factor that lead to the neglect of teaching and to the decline in research quality. This in turn has contributed to a stultification of academic life to the extent that these days, any exchange of ideas beyond the confines of the classroom has virtually ceased. (Unless, of course, it is in the context of a LINK sponsored conference!) For example, what was once a seminar and discussion room in the Community Medicine Building is now used by the staff to take a nap. The cupboards lining the walls are chock-full of moldy books and journals that have been untouched for years.

Together with a reduction of the overall government budget for education, the university budget has also declined in real terms. The departments without a LINK were reduced to an absolute state of penury. With mounting inflation, the salaries of the university staff have reached their present ridiculous proportions. In Tanzania today, what a professor earns is not far from the minimum wage in Kenya. I find it miraculous that in spite of the minuscule paycheck, some secretaries still type well, some workers do keep the toilets clean, and some lecturers give well-researched and thought-out lectures!

With the above said, what was the response of the academics towards the academic decline at the university? I feel that in general they reacted in a manner that only led to a further deterioration of the quality of the academic environment. When faced with institutional decline, they retreated inward and sought individual solutions to their problems. Many got involved in other income-generating projects with no relation to their professional work; others (like myself) sought refuge in higher-paying jobs abroad; others became globe-trotting consultants or conference attendees, always on the go; others kept churning out grant proposals by the month; and so on. Since, in most cases, economic gain was the primary motivation, academic standards were not upheld.[5] Dedicated teaching and quality research further suffered as a consequence of this search for personal salvation.[6]

Seeking the missing LINK became the sole preoccupation in academia. Both the leftists and rightists, conservatives and radicals, engineers or doctors, all looked beyond the national boundaries for a savior.[7] Even those who wrote papers critiquing foreign investments did so with foreign assistance. Life within the faculties became fragmented. Each department head cultivated and oversaw his own LINK. This became his or her mini empire, where, in most cases, he or she allocated the resources available according to his or her whims. I have noted that the distribution of benefits derived from a LINK, whether in terms of research funds or trips abroad, is not a topic on the agenda at what may otherwise appear to be a distinctly democratic departmental meeting. In such a situation planned aademic endeavors within the faculties are next to impossible, and the cohesion of the faculties or the departments melts away.

As one goes around the Faculty of Medicine, one wonders whether, about a hundred years after Karl Peters landed here, a second partition of Africa is in progress or not. The Dental School is run by the Finnish, the AIDS research programs by the Swedes, community health projects by the Germans, with the British, Italians, Danish, and so on; all having their exclusive spheres of influence. International exchange should be promoted in a university. I certainly favor it. However, when such an exchange is conducted solely in the framework of a donor-recipient relation, what is there to assure that it will be done on the basis of academic equality and mutual respect? One can only hope that the professors and heads of departments who sign the LINK agreements and control their resources are not the modern day chiefs resembling their historical counterparts who sold out their peoples for a pittance.

What is to be done? There are no simple answers to this simple but important question. But there are simple answers as to how to go about finding appropriate solutions. What we need to do is to take steps in a direction that will eventually lead us to them. These steps include a reaffirmation on the part of the academia of a commitment to uphold universal academic and ethical values, and to undertake collective and democratic endeavors, rather than individual and *ad hoc* ones, to resolve the problems facing us.

The academics should, as a group, reassert their commitment to seek the truth and advance the frontiers of knowledge while at the same time find ways and means of using their know-how to deal with the problems facing society. They should stress their commitment to pursue these values in the framework of democracy and respect for human dignity. They need to shed off their cloak of timidity and selfishness and be more audacious in the search for solutions to institutional and societal problems.

For example, the current misallocation of national resources whereby education and health account for about 5 percent of the governmental budget while the military gets more than 15 percent should come under the critical scrutiny of the academia. Does a poor country such as ours need guns and bullets more than medicines and books? The policy of paying starvation salaries to highly qualified personnel only promotes corruption, mismanagement, and brain drain, and needs to be thoroughly criticized.

Instead of seeking private and unethical solutions to such problems as the *Chakula cha Daktari*[8] practices rampant at the Faculty of Medicine, the academics should discuss and search for solutions to these problems in the open. At present, for example, a patient undergoing surgery at Muhimbili Hospital may be asked to pay an under-the-table fee that is small by international standards but large by local ones. This is inevitable when the monthly salary and allowance of a qualified surgeon does not exceed one hundred U.S. dollars. Everyone, including the government, is aware of such practices. But the politicians want to maintain their traditional stance of dignified hypocrisy. The academics should not. They should demand a more rational system of payment resulting in the delivery of efficient services to the patients.

For example, why not institute a system whereby, for every operation done, a surgeon is paid a reasonable fee directly. In return, the surgeon should be asked to undertake a required number of cases where the patient is unable to pay any fee. The academics at the Faculty of Medicine must declare themselves against the corruption and waste so rampant in the health sector. They should, for instance, put under a microscope and bring out into the open why and how urban malaria control projects faltered due to misappropriation of resources. Such an exercise has to go hand in hand with finding ways and means of improving the economic and working conditions of the nurses, medical and laboratory assistants, and doctors. The academics should scrutinize the performance of the Ministry of Health, and find out why, if the nation is supposed to have been in the forefront of the fight against disease for many years, the health of the typical person in Tanzania is so poor, and the medical services so primitive. How trustworthy are the statistics dished out by the Ministry of Health? Do they just paint a rosy picture of a worsening situation? Instead of incessantly clamoring for more research funds, the academics should perform well designed and executed research that can contribute to knowledge and assist in solving the problems found in the health sector. The LINK funds that are available should be utilized rationally and in a transparent manner for the benefit of all in the faculty.

The solutions to our predicament can emerge from collective and democratic efforts within departments, faculties and the university as a whole. They do not lie in mounting arbitrary expeditions to seek LINK funds. The University of Dar es Salaam can enter the twenty-first century as a shining center of scholarship only if the academics are prepared to commit themselves to addressing institutional and social problems without fear or favor.

The preceding sections constitute a stylistically edited version of an article that was published in 1990. As we approach the end of the millennium, does it still constitute an accurate portrayal of the academic environment in Tanzania? If not, what has changed?

I left the University of Dar es Salaam for the University of California at Los Angeles (UCLA) in January 1991. The move was motivated by a combination of financial, family and professional reasons. In sum, I was broke and frustrated. And so, I became fully LINKed. I went back to teach at the Faculty of Medicine for five months at the end of 1994. The place had a new name; now it was called the Muhimbili University College of Health Sciences (MUCHS). There were a few changes here and there. On the whole, however, I observed that what I had written earlier had not lost validity. From my communications with colleagues in Dar es Salaam, I gather that to this day, the LINK reigns supreme at MUCHS and the University of Dar es Salaam. Moreover, these institutions have yet to embark on the path of recovery from the academic afflictions described above.

In 1994, I found that the remuneration package for the academic staff had improved considerably. It allowed one to at least feed one' family without engaging in another income raising activity. Unfortunately, that did not mean that the lecturers and professors spent more effort on teaching. The more lucrative LINK related activities consumed most of their time. The status of the students, in terms of both the pedagogical and living environments, had, if anything, markedly declined. Basic academic integrity also seemed to have been compromised to an extent. I unearthed evidence of examination fraud on a wide scale but no one wanted to do, or did, anything about it. The library had more recent books and journals. But a huge pile of LINK donated material was dumped on a damp, musty floor and was in the process of rotting away. The administrators had refused to release overtime payment for the library staff and hence the neglect.

A couple of faculty members had published papers based on well designed and executed research relating to HIV infection. But a myopic outlook, and an inability or unwillingness to raise basic questions were more evident than before. The research agenda was not formulated through internal discussion. It was patterned on the priorities set by the LINK agencies. Money was available for research on population issues and AIDS but not for much else. No one seemed interested to research the patently vexing issue: why had the multitude of foreign-funded health projects in the past three decades either resulted in abysmally paltry gains or had failed miserably? Instead, the academicians were on the lookout for more LINK funds to do more of the same. Narrow-minded ethnic and regional rivalries had risen to prominence in the internal academic politics. Otherwise, intellectual and social apathy were the order of the day. Of course, there were more computers spread around the medical, dental, and public health schools. But more of the seriously ill hospital patients slept on the cold, hard floor as beds were unavailable. The hospital wards lacked basic supplies like gloves, bandages, syringes, anti-biotics, and pain medication.

Corruption and mismanagement were rampant. Notwithstanding, the LINK funds kept pouring in . In brief, what I saw at MUCHS was a microcosm of the trends in Tanzania as a whole. Abject poverty and misery were on the ascendence while a minority reaped the rewards of unbridled aggrandizement. We had multiparty democracy and many independent newspapers. But each had their own LINK, and none dared to raise any principled challenge to the external and internal economic overlords. Political conflicts revolved around personality issues, and the politicians vied with each other to better imple-ment the externally imposed agenda of complete take-over of the economy by the multinational corporations. That it led to mass unemployment and rapid deindustrialization appeared to be of no consequence to the guardians of public welfare.

What I have called the LINK in this chapter is but a complement of a more basic LINK, the economic domination of Tanzania and other African nations by the multinational corporations. The main aspects of this basic LINK include unequal terms of trade, exploitation of local labor and other re-sources, minimal or no local reinvestment of the profits, absence of protection for nascent local industries, high burden of debt, imposition by the World Bank and IMF of skewed economic priorities that only lead to more indebtedness, military exports, support for dictatorial and undemo-cratic regimes, and so on. An apt characterization of the LINK is modern day global imperialism led by the United States and economically enforced by the World Bank and IMF. Both types of LINKs complement one another. They should not be viewed in isolation. For example, a United States Agency for International Development (USAID) program to promote condom use, in order to prevent HIV infection, should be related to the economic agenda imposed on the Tanzanian government by Western agencies, because the latter leads to massive layoffs and promotes urban prostitution, and thus increases the HIV infection rate.

Some regard the LINK as a rescuer of Africa from its dire circumstances. Nothing can be farther from the truth. It is the LINK in its most basic form, and its relation to those who hold the reigns of power, that constitutes the central cause of the problems facing Africa. By keeping in power those who do not have the interests of the people at heart, the LINK undermines genuine democracy and the right of people to self-determination. It is the LINK that prevents Africa from embarking on sustained and sound programs to feed, house, and clothe its people. The charitable aspect of the LINK is at most a stopgap remedial measure to try to arrest a catastrophe. But the LINK itself contributes to the promotion of that condition. The LINK is not a novel entity. It has been with us throughout the post independence period. The forms have been changing. Previously we had the massive, foreign funded, multi-purpose development programs that led to nowhere, and now we have the same in a more targeted form.

The portrait I have painted with respect to the LINK is a systemic one. It is not simply caused by personal or moral shortfalls on the part of some individuals. In fact, there are well intentioned and dedicated persons on both sides of the coin. There are noble and diligent local university teachers and researchers from outside who do their utmost despite the many obstacles they face. They do get positive results here and there. But more often they end up in a blind alley, spent and disillusioned. It is the system that promotes anomalous individual behavior. And it is the system that needs a fundamental overhaul. The LINK as it is constituted at present is a basic feature of this system.

The tragedy is that the local elites in Tanzania and Africa have internalized the ideology of the LINK. Like the slave trading chiefs of yesteryears, they benefit by enforcing the will of imperialism on the people of the continent. But we also see valiant challenges to the LINK. This is a manifestation of the desire of the people of Africa to take their destiny into their own hands. In Zaire, the brutal Western-LINKed dictator is no more, although the road to liberation is still a long and confusing one. In Nigeria and Kenya, there are heroic efforts in this regard. In Tanzania, a day is bound to come when the people will, if only for the sake of their children, want to take control of their own lives. When that day comes, one can only hope that the students and faculty of the University of Dar es Salaam and MUCHS will not be found on the wrong side of the fence.

NOTES

1. P. J. Davis, and R. Hersh, *Descarte's Dream: The World According to Mathematics.* (Boston: Houghton Mifflin, 1986), 58–59.

2. Actually, there is quite a bit of outright fraudulent research done at various prominent biomedical establishments in the United States. For a documentation of such cases, consult issues of *Science* between 1987 and 1989, and W. Broad and N. Wade, *Betrayers of the Truth: Fraud and Deceit in the Halls of Science.* (New York: Simon & Schuster, 1982).

3. See *World Health Forum, 1* (9) (1988), 322.

4. S. J. Pocock, *Clinical Trials: A Practical Approach.* (New York: John Wiley & Sons, 1983), 246–247.

5. One way by which the academics claim to uphold academic standards is setting difficult examinations for students. But their strictness with students is in strange contrast to their lax evaluation of faculty research, publications and teaching.

6. See I.G. Shivji, "Professional Standards, Professional Ethics, Professional Conscience." *University of Dar es Salaam (UDASA) Newsletter/Forum 9* (1988), 3–9.

7. An interesting facet of the LINK is its ideological neutrality. Both ultra-conservatives and hot radicals benefit from it. In fact, some of the leftists I know have been using the LINK to purchase their jeans and underwear abroad since the early seventies.

8. A Swahili phrase, literally meaning "the doctor's food."

7

Democratization and Interventionism in Francophone Sub-Saharan Africa

François Ngolet

> France's economic (and political) role in Francophone Black Africa seems destined to decrease in importance in relation to that of other nations.
>
> Tony Chaffer

Two different methods have been used, over the last decade, to analyze the postcolonial history of Africa. The first interprets it in terms of local rationalities.[1] This approach has been popularized by Jean François Bayart, who has argued that in order to understand the functioning of African states we must focus on the internal dynamics of African societies. According to Bayart, capitalism did not destroy the specificity of African cultures; therefore, the relations of inequality and domination existing in modern African states should be seen as an outcome of precolonial social structures. For Bayart, the social and political dynamics of African societies today perpetuate their ancestral history in a modern form;[2] thus, it is the cultural and historical experiences of African people that can help us understand phenomena such as patrimonialism,[3] predatory states,[4] and the tensions between state and "civil society."[5] External factors, of course, are supposed to play a small role in the occurrence of these phenomena.

Without neglecting local factors, a contrasting approach is taken by Patrick Chabal.[6] For Chabal, the political institutions adopted by African states after independence were more or less imposed by the former colonizers, and there is nothing specifically African about current African politics. As this chapter shows, the situation of Francophone countries supports Chabal's argument. For example, France's military presence in Africa, after the cold war, has remained strong. In 1996, French troops intervened in the Central African Republic to repress a military mutiny threatening Ange Patasse's regime.[7] In 1994, important French military garrisons were active in Rwanda, before and after the massacres of the Tutsi by the Hutu.[8] In 1990, the French army again distinguished itself by helping to crush a popular rebellion in Gabon's Port Gentil to save the collapsing regime of Omar Bongo.[9]

France's presence in Francophone Africa has also had a deep impact on the "democratization process" that has proceeded in the region in the wake of the La Baule summit, held in France in 1989. This chapter analyses the different political trajectories adopted by Francophone countries after the La Baule summit. It shows that France still plays a major role in state building in Francophone Africa, even though, increasingly, the United States is challenging French hegemony in this part of the world, as the cold war ideological divide is being replaced by economic competition[10] between French and American interests.

. The U.S. penetration of the French *chasse gardee* (hunting grounds) in Africa has led to multiple diplomatic, economic and cultural tensions between the two countries. In 1994, for instance, under heavy American influence, France was forced by the World Bank and the International Monetary Fund (IMF) to accept the devaluation of the Franc (Communauté Fineneière Africaine) (CFA), a move that opened African markets to global economic competition, and facilitated the rise of new political perspectives. It is one of the conclusions of this chapter that the intrusion of the United States in Francophone Africa and the globalization of the economy after the General Agreement on Trade and Tariffs (GATT) agreements are dismantling the colonial pact between France and the Francophone African countries. As a consequence, these countries are finding themselves projected into a new historical situation, that is compelling them to renegotiate their political status.

A PLURALITY OF POLITICAL TRAJECTORIES

The election of François Mitterrand in 1981 and the nomination of pro Third World ministers such as foreign minister Claude Cheysson and cooperation minister Jean Pierre Cot raised the hopes of the African masses and intellectuals.[11] In a detailed African project published by the Socialist Party in 1981, a critique was presented of the

neo-colonial nature of French links with its former colonies in Africa, which led to a proposal to distribute French aid more widely and in particular to increase links with Anglophone and Lusophone Africa. The Franc zone was criticized for maintaining ties of a neo-colonial nature between France and its ex-colonies. Although no alternative was proposed, there was a promise of military intervention in Africa, a denunciation of a highly personalized relation cultivated by former president Giscard D'Estaing, and finally, the idea was put forward by Jean Pierre Cot that France should take a more prominent role on human rights in Africa.[12]

Mitterrand's liberal policy, however, created much anxiety among many African dictators who openly opposed this new political orientation. French business also saw this policy as a threat to their activities in Africa, and they began to pressure Mitterrand to adopt a more conservative approach.[13] It was not long before Mitterrand capitulated these requests; his political shift to the right being signalled by the resignation of Claude Cheysson and Jean Pierre Cot as ministers and the nomination of Mitterrand's son, Jean Christophe, ex-minister for African affairs. With this readjustment, Mitterrand assumed direct control over African matters. At the same time, Jean Claude Mantion a former director of the French Secret Services was placed in charge of security in the Central African Republic.[14] These political readjustments marked a turning point and shaped French African policy during the Mitterrand regime.

While steadily becoming more conservative, France's intervention in the politics of sub-Saharan Francophone African countries took a new turn after the fall of the Berlin Wall and the collapse of Communist regimes in Eastern Europe,[15] when alliances forged in the cold war period by Western powers began to loose their function and democratization, multipartism and human rights became rallying cries in Washington and other western halls of power. Thus, at a Franco-African summit held in 1990, in the city of La Baule in Southern France, President François Mitterrand urged African leaders to adopt democratic reforms promising a special financial reward, *conditionalité*, to the countries that would accomplish the transition.[16] A wave of political reforms immediately swept Francophone Africa and multipartism became a common trend. But the nature of these transitions was heavily influenced and distorted by French interests in the region.

Benin was the first country to adopt a multiparty system. In 1990, a national conference was called in Cotonou. It was a large forum consisting of political parties, professional organizations, religious groups, peasants and women's groups gathered to discuss the problems affecting the country.[17] Among the solutions proposed was the adoption of a new constitution. After President Mathieu Kerekou was stripped of his political power, elections were organized in 1991, and Nicephore Soglo became the first elected president in Benin since 1972.[18] This "democratic transition" occurred smoothly due to the fact that France secretly prevented Benin's former communist party from taking power. France also pressured the opposition leaders to adopt a more moderate profile, and even pressured the Catholic Church to act as a moderator during the national conference. For France, Benin's "democratic transition" became the best example for all Francophone countries in Africa.

The next country to opt for "democracy" was Mali. The first sign of the "transition" were the student demonstrations in Bamako in 1991. The students asked for a better education, for the disbursement of scholarships that had been promised but had never materialized, and for the liberalization of Moussa Traore's regime. When the Malian police fired on unarmed students, many of whom were killed, a climate of revolt spread across the country, leading to a *coup d' état* against Moussa Traore. The coup brought to power General Toumani Toure, who organized presidential elections that saw the victory of the archeologist Alpha

Omar Konare in 1992. Throughout these developments, the French influence was obvious behind the scenes, even though the "transition" seemed sparked off by local contradictions.[19] It was Charles Pasqua, France's interior minister, who advised General Toure to carry out the *coup d' état* in order to avoid chaos in the country.[20]

France's control over the "democratization" process was facilitated in Benin and Mali by the fact that both countries lost the support of the Soviet Union in the late 1980s. Gorbachev's decision to pull the Soviet Union out of its African zones of influence accelerated the fall of Mathieu Kerekou and Moussa Traore, enabling France in each case to direct political change in accordance with its interests, by choosing candidates, organizing elections and even instigating *coups d' état*.

In other Francophone countries, the "transition to democracy" followed different and unexpected trajectories, as the national conference formula[21] initiated by Benin became an instrument used by opposition parties to over-throw former leaders and threaten French interests.[22] Whenever this occurred, the fear of loosing control pushed France to adopt more aggressive tactics and become even more involved in the local political of Francophone countries.[23] As a result, in some countries the "democratic transition" even led to the restoration of authoritarian regimes, and paved the way to massacres and civil war.

A "controlled democracy" was established in Gabon when France's hegemony was challenged by the national conference held in Libreville in 1990. Following the same formula adopted by Benin, the Gabonese conference regrouped many civilian associations and became an arena for the criticism of the Omar Bongo regime and its French allies.[24] It also proposed a new political platform that would radically change the relations between Gabon and France. In addition to calling for multipartism, the conference called for multilateral cooperation between Gabon and other western powers; a move guaranteed to threaten France's interests and was introduced, in fact, by the opposition to break France's political influence and economic monopoly in the country. Immediately after the conference, however, the main opposition leader, Joseph Rendjambe was killed. In response, violent protests erupted in Libreville, Port-Gentil, and other cities across the country with Omar Bongo and France being accused of murder[25] because of their attempt to resist political change.

The French Consul and several oil company employees were also taken hostage by militants of the *Parti Gabonais du Progrès* (PGP) in Port-Gentil (they were later freed). The Gabonese and French authorities counter-attacked by sending troops to Libreville and Port-Gentil to repress the revolt.[26] The troops occupied the airport, communication facilities, and oil installations. Eighteen hundred of the twenty-five hundred French residents, including 180 of the 220 member staff of Elf-Gabon, the country's largest oil company, chose to depart by airlift, while Elf suspended operations for five days.

France, however, managed to reestablish communications between the Bongo regime and the leadership of the PGP, headed by Re-Ndjambe, and to diffuse the tension. It urged Bongo to proceed with the reforms worked out at the national conference of March and April 1990, and to reaffirm Bongo's power; it helped organize legislative elections the same year, that were won, by a slight majority, by the *Parti Democratique Gabonais*, which thus continued to control the government. France also got heavily involved in the preparation of the presidential elections held in December 1993. It contributed funds and personnel for conducting the national census, a prequisite for updating voter rolls and provided identity cards, indelible inks, and transparent urns.

Meanwhile, Charles Pasqua sent electoral experts to Gabon to help Bongo falsify the election results in many of its provinces. It was no secret that the presidential elections were to be won by Bongo.[27] Even before the end of the ballot counting, Omar Bongo declared himself the winner and sent troops into the streets of Libreville to prevent demonstrations. France's interests were saved. Later on, after the devaluation of the franc CFA in 1994, after the demonstrations that followed, and after many opposition leaders either went into hiding or fled the country, "democratic reforms" were introduced in Gabon; of course, strictly within the limits imposed by the Bongo regime and France.

A similar political evolution took place in Congo. In 1990, immediately after the national conference in Gabon, a national conference was organized in the Congolese capital of Brazzaville that was declared "sovereign" to stress that it was an independent constitutional body with executive powers. The conference stripped Denis Sassou Nguesso, a "protégé" of France of his power, amidst an unparalled criticism of his regime and of the *Parti Congolais du Travail* (PCT). Andre Milongo was designated as the head of the interim government and for a time exercised all powers, including the control of the armed forces, foreign affairs, and economic policy while the presidency, reduced to a figurehead position, was retained by Sassou.[28] Later presidential elections were organized, resulting in Pascal Lissouba's victory in 1992.

The next year witnessed the disintegration of social peace in Congo. The first crisis was an institutional one, officially due to the fact that Lissouba only allocated two ministerial seats to the PCT, leading to new political alliances in the assembly. The second crisis was apparently due to Lissouba's dissolution of the National Assembly and the opposition's resistance to this action. According to many observers, however, it was above all provoked by Lissouba's deal with the American oil company, Occidental Petroleum (Oxy).

Animated by a spirit of independence, and out of compliance with the International Monetary Fund (IMF), Congo could not acquire the external funds to pay the arrears on its salaries. It is in this context that Lissouba asked Oxy for $150 million; in exchange, the oil company was allowed to exploit half of the Congolese oil. With this deal, Oxy took a significant portion of business from Elf Aquitaine which previously had a total monopoly on Congo's oil franchises. This economic tension aggravated the political crisis in Congo—a crisis in which France was deeply involved, and that manifested itself in the form of ethnic cleansing, bringing the country to the brink of civil war. The threat of a military coup accompanied the political turmoil, and tensions only began to decline in 1994, when Pascal Lissouba reinstated Elf Aquitaine as the country's only oil explorer.[29]

Another African country where the "democratic transition" was controlled by France was Burkina Faso. After Sankara's death and Blaise Campaore's takeover, the country experienced a series of political assassinations during which two of the leaders of the revolution Henri Zongo and Jean-Baptiste Lingani were killed. Then in 1991, following the *La Baule* summit, "democracy" was introduced. Many political parties were created, but the opposition coalition boycotted the presidential elections to protest Campaore's manipulations. As the only candidate, inevitably Campaore was elected President. After rejecting the idea of having a national conference, he formed a government, co-opted some members of the opposition leaders, who were seen as a threat to French assets and political interests in Burkina Faso.

As one can see, external influence is still a determining factor in the post cold war politics of Francophone Africa. France has helped maintain Bongo's in power in Gabon, by pressuring opposition leaders to adopt a more moderate profile; French influence has been even more apparent in Congo where the future of democracy was linked to the interests of Elf Aquitaine. Similar concerns have dictated the fate of democracy in Burkina Faso. Wherever French interests were threatened, the democratization process has been derailed.

One further example is the case of Cameroon, where Paul Biya systemaically refused to organize a national conference and, instead, proceeded to jail lawyers, journalists and other members of opposition parties.[30] Then, in 1993, when a multiparty election that he had organized was won by the Anglo-phone[31] opposition leader Nfru Ndi, Biya rejected the results, despite the many demonstrations across the country and the revival of tensions between the Anglophone and the Francophone regions.[32] Nfru Ndi was thrown into prison. But negotiations between Biya and the opposition were encouraged by France, that secretly pressured the opposition leaders to moderate their political stand. French intervention ensured a new mandate for Biya, while helping to preserve French interests in Cameroon, which demanded (among other things) that a representative of the Anglophone community should not be elected.

French influence has also been evident in the Central African Republic, during the 1993 presidential elections. After providing the material support necessary for the voting, at the second round, in order to prevent Andre Kolingba from canceling the elections that were not going in his favor, France closed its embassy in Bangui. Then it openly endorsed Kolingba's opponent Ange-Felix Patasse, who won the elections.[33] The French involvement in the political affairs of the Central African Republic was again illustrated when twenty-four hundred French legionnaires, paratroopers and diverse military personnel intervened to repress a mutiny in The National Army that was threatening Patasse's regime.

France's determination to ensure the victory of a congenial candidate has been demonstrated in the Ivory Coast, where Henri Conan Bedie, former chairman of the National Assembly, and the constitutional successor of Houphouet Boigny, was elected president in 1991. After Houphouet Boigny's death, France endorsed Bedie instead of Alassane Ouattara, the prime minister suspected of being close to the World Bank and the IMF. As in Cameroon and the Central African Republic, also in the Ivory Coast, France helped manipulate the election results and used diplomatical pressure to bring to power a candidate of its choice.

In sum, France has controlled election results in Gabon, Congo, Burkina Faso, Cameroon, the Ivory Coast, and the Central African Republic. France has also intervened in Togo where in response to the attempted "democratization," the political situation even deteriorated, leading to the restoration of military dictatorship and the repression of the opposition leaders.[34] In Togo, a national conference was called in 1990 by the opposition parties; but Gnassingbe Eyadema, inspired by the Kerekou situation in Benin, intimidated the representatives who had participated in it and imprisoned Joseph Koffigoh, the prime minister appointed for the transitional period. The demonstrations that followed led to a French military intervention, officially described as a mission to protect French citizens. New presidential elections were organized in 1993 and were boycotted, however, by the opposition parties. All foreign observers recognized that they were not fair;[35] indeed, they were a political "masquerade" to legitimize and perpetuate Eyadema's regime, who predictably won the elections with a 96.5 percent of the vote. Since then, Eyadema has systematically repressed and intimidated its opponents turning its government into a classic dictatorial regime. The same type of authoritarian restoration has occurred in the Comoros Islands where an abortive coup incited a French military intervention that put into power Mohamed Caabi El Yachrountu (his government is now being challenged by Said Ali Mohamed who has created a rival government) and is in Zaire.

That "democratization" can become a vehicle for the restoration of dictatorship has been most evident in former Zaire. A national conference organized in Kinshasa in 1990 nominated as prime minister the opposition leader Etienne Tshisekede. But the latter could never exercise his functions as his nomination was rejected by President Mobuto Cese Seko. As social tensions mounted with demonstrations being organized across the country, a military rebellion exploded during which the French embassy in Kinshasa was attacked, and the ambassador killed.[36] Conflicts betwen Mobuto and Tshisekedi made the country ungovernable, and led to a situation of general chaos that lasted until 1994 when, in the wake of the massacre in Rwanda, Mubuto could play again the role of a regional leader, and a new prime minister, Kongo wa Dondo, was appointed. Once again, this turn of events was made possible by France's support for Mobuto, depicted in French eyes as the protector of Francophone interests against the encroaching influence in the region of the Anglophone world as represented by the Ugandan President Yuweri Museveni.[37]

France's need for a sure ally against the perceived Anglophone threat escalated after the Rwandese Patriotic Front (RPF) took control in Kigali. France holds tremendous responsibility for the attempted genocide of the Tutsi in Rwanda.[38] It is now proven that the Rwandan Armed Forces had been massively equipped and trained by France and that they had also been encouraged in their organization of a hostile "antisubversive" Huto militia—the *Interahamwe*—for the introduction of democracy as stated in the La Baule summit, had to be preceded by the "resolution of internal conflicts."

In Mali and Niger, the democratization process led to the brink of civil war when both countries were confronted with a rebellion of the Tuareg, a population who had been marginalized during both the colonial and post-colonial period. When democracy was placed on the agenda, the Tuareg rebels created two military opposition forces to fight for autonomy and independence: *The Front de Libération de l'Air et de L'Azawad* in Mali, and the *Front de Libération du Sahara* in Niger.[39] In May 1990, in Niger, a major military operation was launched against them, during which over four hundred rebels were massacred. The official report to the national conference that was being held in Nyamey admitted that during one attack, nineteen Tuaregs were summarily executed. The conference immediately dismissed and detained the officers involved, an action which led to the rebellion of one section of the army, and put pressure on the prime minister of the transition Tcheffou Amadou to remove his Tuareg minister of interior. This Tuareg crisis ultimately caused the whole cabinet to dissolve, and the two Tuareg ministers and other high state officials were relieved of their functions and detained. Today, negotiations between the government of Niger and the Coordination of Armed Resistance, representing the two Tuaregs guerilla movements have failed.[40]

In Mali as well, there has been constant fighting between the national army and the Tuaregs of the Azawad Front. In 1992, to try to resolve the conflict, negotiations were conducted between the Malian government and leaders of the Front. But the effort to develop the northern regions, the detouring of aid to the South, and the integration of ex-Tuareg rebels in the army, have been delayed.[41] This may explain why the accord was rejected by some Tuareg clans, and tensions between the Tuaregs and the national army is threatening the young democracy.

In Senegal, too, democratization was being accompanied by civil war. Indeed, the entire national army has been mobilized in the Casamance province to contain the awakening of the independentist movement.[42] And a national conference was held to implement democratic reforms in Chad, a country that already experienced twenty years of civil war [43] and whose president, Idriss Deby, was put in power by the French secret services and totally controlled by France.

One can see that France's influence in Africa has led to a plurality of political trajectories. On the one hand, there is a smooth "transition to democracy," as experienced by Benin and Mali and still monitored by France. Then there are "controlled democracies," as those installed in Gabon and Congo and the "manipulated democracies," in those cases where election results were falsified and former dictators returned to power. The restoration of dictatorships, the jailing of opposition leaders, even the instigation of ethnic conflicts, genocide, and civil war have been part of the cost Africans have paid for the protection of French economic and political interests. As a result, in the words of Michel Aurillac, *Ministre de la Coopération* in Chirac's right-wing government from 1986 to 1988:

Today, France can still proclaim world power status because of its possession of independent nuclear power, its seat on the UN Security Council and its continuing presence in sub-saharan Africa.[44]

Aurillac was simply echoing Mitterrand who stated thirty years earlier: "Without Africa, there will be no French history in the twenty-first century."[45]

Despite the introduction of formally democratic institutions and the organization of elections, the interests of the African masses are not represented in the "transition" to democratic rule. Francophone Africa's new democratic leaders do not speak for their constituencies, but are simply the protectors of French interests in the region.[46]

TENSIONS BETWEEN FRANCE AND THE U.S.

The impact of external influences is heightened by the quiet, but aggressive, American penetration of Francophone Africa.[47] The motives behind the U.S. interest in the region are well summarized by George Moose, the State Department Secretary for African Affairs: "We must ensure our access to immense natural resources in Africa. A continent which possesses 78 percent of the world chrome reserves, 89 percent of palatine reserves and 59 percent of cobalt reserves."[48] This U.S. policy shaped French policy during the "democratic transition," as France consistently backed the candidates it considered favorable to its interests, against those suspected of being close to the United States. Tensions between the two countries could be observed at the diplomatic, economic and cultural levels.[49]

Tensions between the United States and France in Francophone Africa surfaced openly after the 1994 massacre in Rwanda. After the death of its ambassador to Zaire, France put a great deal of energy into engineering the political resurrection of Mobuto. Paris intervention allowed Mobuto to reduce the opposition in the Zairian Parliament and create a new majority that chose a pro-Mobuto prime minister, Kendo wa Dondo.[50] France also helped reorganize the Zairian armed forces by supplying them with military counselors and weapons. The same Zairian armed forces were also given weapons taken from the Rwandese governmental troops who had fled from the country after the RPF's military victory.[51]

The French humanitarian operation, "Operation Turkoise," organized to help the Rwandese refugees further contributed to reinforce Mobuto's international stature as he agreed to open Eastern Zaire to the Hutu refugees, humanitarian organizations, and foreign military logistics in the Great Lakes Region. As already mentioned, France's support for Mobuto was instigated by antagonism towards Yuweri Museveni, an Anglophone who was seen as an American ally in central Africa. France felt threatened by the fact that Museveni militarily supported the Sudanese People's Liberation Army (SPLA). In response, France built closer relations with the Sudanese government; its secret services furnished it with photographs taken by French military aircraft based in Bangui detailing the military positions of the SPLA in the south. France also authorized the Sudanese national army to use the Central African Republican territory in order to land at the back of the SPLA. In exchange for these services, France obtained assurances from the Sudanese government that the Jongley Canal would be reopened, and French companies would be the only ones permitted to carry out the construction.[52] Meanwhile, the Sudanese government also retaliated against Museveni's decision to allow the U.S. government to use Ugandan territory to ship weapons to the SPLA by provided assistance to the Senior Liberation Army of Alice Lakwena, which had been resisting Museveni's government since 1989.[53]

The competition between France and the United States in Francophone Africa appears most clearly at the economic level, particularly with regard to the control of oil. The most striking example comes from Congo where the competition between French company Elf Aquitaine, and the American Occidental Petroleum, for Congolese oil, played an important role in the relation between the government of Pascal Lissouba and France. The same type of oil dispute also exploded in Gabon in 1990 where the Anglo-Dutch company Shell was competing with Elf Aquitaine. Following violent demonstrations in Port Gentil after the death of the opposition leader, Joseph ReNdjambe, France evacuated all of its citizens and stopped its oil production in the country, while Shell only suspended its operations. France's actions were interpreted as a sign of hostility by Omar Bongo, who urged France to resume its activities, for otherwise Elf Gabon would loose its favorable economic status to the advantage of Shell. France took Bongo's threat so seriously that it reversed its decision and continued the exploitation of Gabonese oil. Nonetheless, Shell currently controls a significant part of the largest Gabonese oil field of Rabikounga.

A similar game has been played in Chad. The country was ready to exploit an important oil field in Doba in the south. An agreement signed under President Tombalbaye in the 1970s allowed an American oil company CONOCO to head the country's entire oil production. Later, however, in

1987, CONOCO was excluded by economic negotiation, and the majority of the rights of exploitation fell to Shell-Esso. France at this time did not have any share of the exploitation of this important oil field. President Idriss Deby, put into power by the French Secret Services after the fall of Hissen Habre in 1990, felt obligated to seriously consider the French interests in the country. He personally intervened to pressure Shell-Esso to concede 20 percent of the oil right exploitation to Elf Aquitaine.[54]

These examples are proof of the antagonism between France and the United States in Francophone Africa. Naturally, these conflicts have major social and political consequences for African countries, contributing to shape their political future during the democratization process. Tensions between the United States and France can also be found at the cultural level although they are far less visible than those at the political and economic level. Exemplary here is France's intervention in the conflict between Nigeria and Cameroon on the island of Bakassi in 1994; when France aided the Cameroonian government against Nigeria, justifying its assistance as means to protect a largely Francophone country, presumably threatened by an Anglophone one, even though at the basis of the dispute was the ownership of the island oil resource. France's support of the Cameroonian government both served to promote a policy of *Franco-phonie* and to boost Biya's power against the Anglophone opposition leader John Nfru Ndi, who was defended by the American Embassy in Yaounde.[55]

Most examples of U.S.-France antagonism and competition could be drawn from Liberia, (in the course of the struggle between Charles Taylor and Economic Community of West African States Monitoring Group (ECOMOG), Togo and again Cameroon. Finally, Mitterrand's proposition at the 1993 *Francophonie* summit in Maurice Island was shaped by this logic, when Paris officially called on all Francophone countries to support its principle of "cultural exception" during the GATT negotiations against Washington and London.

CHALLLENGES TO FRENCH HEGEMONY IN AFRICA

The U.S. growing challenge to French interests, the devaluation of the Franc CFA, and the process of economic globalization are all contributing to undermine France's hegemony, and the nature of colonial pact that has governed French/African relations in Francophone Africa since independence. There are however other factors that have been putting into crisis France's prestige in the region.

France's policy in Francophone Africa has always been dominated by corruption, clientalism, and patrimonialism. But after Mitterrand's shift to the right, when the network of Jacques Foccart, a former de Gaulle African Affairs Secretary and the defender of the "pre-carre," once again became the center in French African policy, France's loss of prestige accelerated. The resentment people in Africa felt vis-à-vis France, particularly during the first cohabitation government in 1986, when Jacques Chirac was prime minister, and the orientation of the French African policy became clearly conservative was officially expressed by Thomas Sankara, the former president of Burkina Faso who openly accused Mitterrand of pursuing a neocolonial policy.[56]

Echoing the frustration of the African masses vis-à-vis French support of a military coup against Prime Minister Joseph Koffigoh, the *Journal Politique Africaine* published an open letter to President Mitterand stating that: "Nous protestons contre une politique faite de louvoiement et d'atermoiements, dont l'opacitzé n'a d'égal que la confusion. Nous demandons l'application de principes simples-clarté et fermeté- au service de la démocratie."[57]

France's loss of prestige and the African masses resentment toward it—which manifested in 1990 by mob attacks and graffiti campaigns against French interests during the democratic upheavals—reached its peak as it became clear that France had a major responsibility for the crisis and massacre in Rwanda.[58] In the period between 1990 and 1993, the French army helped the Rwandan armed forces engage in war against the RPF, massively equipping them with weaponry; participating in local training camps where torture was a daily practice, encouraging the creation of a murderous Hutu militia. Mitterrand himself had closely monitored the evolution of the military situation in Rwanda from the African Affairs Office at the Elysee Palace between 1993 and 1995; and the same was true of Prime Minister Edouard Balladur and Interior Minister Charles Pasqua. Between April and June 1994, while the massacres were carried out, an important part of the French army continued to provide logistical support for the Rwandan Armed Forces. After the massacre, France interened at the United Nations succeeding in preventing the international community from recognizing the genocide of the Tutsi in Rwanda for six weeks; and saved many high-ranking Hutu, who had ordered the massacre of thousands of Tutsi, and who today are still exiled in France though its "Operation Turkoise" that was launched apparently to save Tutsi lives, but in reality mainly to protect former Hutu leaders allowing them to cross the Zairian border.[59]

The decline of French influence in Africa has also been accelerated by the politics of the World Bank and the IMF that have helped open African market to a U.S. offensive.

Since General De Gaulle's presidency, Jacques Foccart had created a network of relationships with newly independent Francophone countries, the objective of which was to maintain French influence in Francophone Africa. This maneuver led to the establishment of client state status type, between France and African leaders,[60] and to a "patrimonial" type of state, where public and private interests were mixed, and corruption, the plundering of raw materials, and sometimes the official financing of political parties, eroded the sense of the state and public service.

The logical consequence of this system was the emergence of a crisis of multiple dimensions in Francophone Africa. Many Francophone countries fell into heavy debt causing a feeling of gridlock.[61] In order to survive, Francophone African countries received public aid from France that was immediately seized by African leaders and "invested" to strengthen their political alliances with the French government.

As the economic situation of Francophone Africa worsened, the solution for many countries was to turn for rescue to the Bretton Woods institutions, in particular, the World Bank, the IMF and the Paris Club. Structural adjustment policies (SAPs) were implemented starting in 1984,[62] which required that these countries reduce state spending and freeze the hiring process, cut education and health care programs, privatize public enterprises, freeze salaries, and eliminate the subsidies for food and medicines. All these measures were presumably introduced to free African countries from their external debt and favor their integration into the world economy.[63]

But as is now well known, the SAPs did not truly provide the results expected, and the anticipated transition of the African economy from predation to production has not materialized.[64] On the contrary, the SAPs have dismantled the entire social network put into place by the postcolonial state that has stabilized the social landscape. In almost every country this was accompanied by revolts. Thus, SAP has only succeeded in worsening the situation of Francophone Africa by weakening its economy and opening the door to a sustained U.S. attack against the French monopoly in the region.

The fact that France was asked by the Bretton Woods institutions in accordance with the GAAT agreement, to devaluate the CFA Franc and to dismantle the Franc zone in Africa,[65] was the *coup de grace*, in this context, for the pact that since independence had tied France and its former African colonies.

A fixed exchange rate between African countries and France was considered an obstacle to free trade.[66] This devaluation, however, was socially devastating. The cost of living doubled in Francophone Africa leading to popular revolts and reprssion in Mali, Gabon, and the Ivory Coast. This devaluation was perceived by the political class as an act of betrayal by France as African countries were thrown into a new economic environment in which they found themselves totally powerless. Yet France accepted this devaluation and asked that the European Economic Community and the international community to share the burden of African economic and social problems.[67] As Tony Chaffer put it, "In the long term, the political and economic union in Europe, while providing possible opportunities for France to share the costs of its African commitment with its European partners, will also tend to limit the possibilities for it to continue to play a distinctive and independent role in Africa in the future."[68]

As the devaluation of the Franc CFA imposed by the World Bank and the IMF is increasingly dismantling the links between France and its former colonies, the patrimonial network of relationships between African leaders and the Elysee Palace is slowly being replaced by relationships imposed by global capitalism.[69] France, the former colonizer, is being replaced by the international community. These changes are creating new conditions with which African societies have to cope if they are to survive in this changing world. Today, for instance, various accords between France and Francophone Africa are being revisited; and France is reorganizing its relations with its former colonies, reducing the amount of financial assistance and the number of its *cooperants* and disbursing its aid to African countries through non governmental organizations.

Is this evolution creating the conditions for the emergence of a genuine African democracy, a democracy in which the will of African people is expressed without outside interferences? The answer cannot be positive. The candidates who have been appointed do not reflect the will of the African people, but are simply continuing to protect French interests which continue to demand that any genuine democratization process be sabotaged. Even the crisis of the patrimonial state in Africa does not hold much of a promise for the future, as its influence is replaced by that of the World Bank and IMF.

NOTES

This chapter was presented as a lecture at the Department of History at Brown University in Providence, Rhode Island.

1. Postcolonial history is also known as "contemporaneousness" and is described in its structure and chronology by Achille Mbembe and Janet Roitman, "Figures of the Subject in the Times of Crisis," in *Public Culture 7* (1995): 323–352; for more details about the postcolony see Achille Mbembe, "Provisional Notes on the Post-colony," in *Africa* 62 (1) (1992): 4–37.

2. This analysis is thoroughly presented by Jean François Bayart in *L'Etat au Cameroon* (Paris: Presses de la Foundation des Sciences Politiques, 1985), and in *L'Etat en Afrique. La politique du ventre* (Paris: Fayart, 1989). See also Jean-François Medard, "L 'Etat patrimonialise," *Politique Africaine* 39 (1990): 25–37, or Michael Schatzberg, *The Dialectics of Oppression in Zaire* (Indiana: Indiana University Press, 1988), 8–30; Sara Berry, *Fathers Work for their Sons: Accumulation, Mobility and Class Formation in an Extended Yoruba Community* (Berkeley: University of California Press, 1985).

3. This concept is developed by Jean François Medard in "L'Etat Patrimonialise." *Politique Africaine* 39 (September 1990): 25–36, and again his "The Underdeveloped State in Tropical Africa: Political Clientelism or No-Patrimonialism," in C. Clap-man, *Private Patronage and Public Power* (London: Frances, Pincer, 1982), 162–192.

4. Dominique Darbon's, "l' Etat predateur," *Politique Africaine* 39 (September 1990), 37–45. This concept is fully debated in D. B. Cruise, J. O'Brien, Dunn, R. Rathbone (eds.), *Contemporary West African States* (Cambridge, England: Cambridge University Press, 1989).

5. Conflicts between these two entities are carefully analyzed by Donald Rothchild and Naomi Chazan in *The Precarious Balance: State and Society in Africa* (Boulder: Westview Press, 1986). The same analysis is conducted by Jean François Bayart, Achille Mbembe, and Comi Toulabor in *Le Politique par les Bas en Afrique* (Paris:

Karthala, 1992), 9–23.

6. This approach is extensively exposed by Patrick Chabal in *Power in Africa, An Essay in Political Interpretation* (New York: St. Martin's Press, 1994). This same argument is carried out by Achille Mbembe, "Democratization and Social Movement in Africa," in *Africa Demos* 1 (1) November 4, 1990.

7. This dramatic political evolution is discussed in the *New York Times*, January 9, 1990.

8. The official French presence in Rwanda was manifested through by the "operation Turkoise." Circumstances which guided the organization of this expedition are discussed by Collette Braekman, "Autopsie d' un genocide planifie au Rwanda," *Le Monde Diplomatique* (March 1995). *See also* Gerard Prunier, *The Rwanda Crisis, History of a Genocide* (New York: Columbia University Press, 1995), 281–305.

9. The chronological account of these events is made by David Gardinier in his *Relations between France and the U.S. in Gabon*, paper presented at the African Studies Association at Orlando, FL., November 3–4, 1994. A deeper analysis of these events appeared in Martin Edzodzomo's *De la Democracy au Gabon: Les fondements d'un renouveau National* (Paris: Karthala, 1993): 6– 20. Also consult Phillipe Leymarie, "La France et le maintien de l'ordre en Afrique," *Le Monde Diplomatique* (June 1994): 28– 29; David Gardinier, *Political Reforms in Gabon in the 1990*, manuscript 10, Westview Press, 1997.

10. *See* Bresser L. C. Pereira, J. M. Maravall, and A. Przworski, *Economic Reforms in New Democracies, A Social-Democratic Approach* (Cambridge, England: Cambridge University Press, 1993). A more dialectic version of global economy is suggested by Michel Albert in *Capitalism Contre Capitalism* (Paris: ed. Seuil, 1991); *see also* Zaki Laidi, *L'ordre mondial relache* (Paris: ed. Seuil, 1992), Arjun Appadurai, "Disjuncture and Difference in the Global Culture Economy," in *Public Culture* 2 (2) (1990): 1–24; Fred Cooper, "Africa and the World Economy," *African Studies Review* 24 (2–3) (1981).

11. These evolutions are thoroughly analyzed by Leymarie, "En Afrique," 26–27, *also see* Prunier, 281–305.

12. *See* Tony Chaffer, "French African Policy: Towards Change," *African Affairs* 91 (1992): 37–51.

13. The global evolution of Mitterrand's African policy is analyzed by Jean François Bayart in *La politique Africaine de François Mitterrand* (Paris: Karthala, 1989).

14. Read Leymarie, "En Afrique," 26–27.

15. This discussion is carried out by A. Mrakussen and J. Yudken in *Dismantling the Cold War Economy* (International Reader's Collection: Harper Collins, 1992), 16, *or see* Gales Stokes, ed., *From Stalinism to Pluralism* (New York: Oxford University Press, 1991), 167.

16. This entire dynamic is analyzed by Jean François Bayart in "La problematique de la Democracy en Afrique noire: La Baule, et puis apres?" *Politique Africaine* 43 (1990): 5–20. This discussion is pursued from a different perspective by P. T. Robinson in "Democratization: Understanding the Relationship between Regime Change and the Culture of Politics," *African Studies Review* 37 (1) (1994): 41, *or see* Robin Luckham, "The Militarization and Democratization in Africa: Survey of Literature and Issues," *African Studies Review* 37 (2) (1994): 13–77.

17. A complete analysis of this conference is made by J. R. Heilbrunn, "Social Origins of National Conference in Benin and Togo" *Journal of Modern African Studies* 31 (2) (1991); 277–279; and Chris Allen et al. (eds.), *Benin, the Congo, Burkina Faso* (London: Pinter, 1989): 206–207. Read Peter Anyang-Nyong'o, "Political Instability

and Prospects for Democracy in Africa," *African Development* 13 (1) (1988): 72; Bernard Caron et al. (eds.), *Democratic Transition in Africa* (Ibadan: CREDU, 1992).

18. This was the date in which Mathieu Kerekou took power by a military coup against Sylvanus Olympio. More details of this particular political shift are contained in Samuel Decalo's, "The Morphology of Radical Military Rule in Africa," *Journal of Africanist Studies* (1985); *see also Military Regimes of Africa* (London: Macmillan, 1986); Gilbert Khadiagala, "The Military in Africa Democratic Transitions: Regional Dimensions," *Africa Today* 42 (1–2) (1995): 66–74; Baffour Agyeman-Duah, "Military Coups, Regime Change and Inter-State Conflicts in West Africa," *Armed Forces and Society* 16 (4) (1990): 547–570.

19. These local contradictions are highlighted by Gally Michel in "Nouvelles demoracy, nouvelles impatiences," in *Le Monde Diplomatique* (August 1994): 10–11; *also read* Moussa Konate, *Mali, Ils ont assassine l'espoir* (Paris: L'Harmattan, 1990); John Wiseman, "Democratic Resurgence in Black Africa, *Contemporary Review* 259 (July 1991): 7–13; Stephen Riley, "The Democratic Transition in Africa: An End to the One-Party State?" *Conflict Studies* 245 (October 1991): 1–36.

20. This idea is suggested by Leymarie, "La France," 28.

21. A culturalist analysis is carried out by Fabien Eboussi Boulaga, *Les conferences nationales en Afriques noire: Une Affaire a suivre*, (Paris: ed. Karthala, 1993); *see also* Catharine Newbury, "Paradoxes of Democratization in Africa," *African Studies Review* 37 (1) (1994): 1–8; an overview of these conferences is conducted by Julius Nyang'oro in "Reforms Politics and the Democratization Process in Africa," *African Studies Review* 37 (1) (1994): 133–151.

22. An analysis of the relationship between National conferences and regime change is made by Robinson, "Democratization," 52. The same analysis is conducted by Julius Nyang'oro and Jennifer Widner, "Two Leadership Styles and Patterns of Political Liberalization," *African Studies Review* 37 (1) (1994): 151–175.

23. *See* "Mourir pour La Baule," *Politique Africaine* (Paris: Karthala, December 1991): 3–4, a general analysis of Mitterrand's African political evolution is proposed by Jean François Bayart, *La politique Africaine de François Mitterrand* (Paris: Karthala, 1989); see also *Discourses on Democracy: Africa in Comparative Perspectives* (Dar es Salaam: Dar es Salaam: University Press, 1995).

24. *See*, J. F. Pochon, "Ajustement et Democratization: l' atypisme du Gabon," *Geopolitique Africaine*, 15 (1) (1992): 59–70. The same criticisms are pursued in Douglas Yates, "The Rentier State in Gabon," *Boston University African Studies Center, Working Paper* No. 196, (1994): 1–21. The reason why these attacks made by the Bongo regime are carried out are thoroughly discussed by Michael Reed, Gabon: A Neo-Colonial Enclave of Enduring French Interest, *The Journal of Modern African Studies* 25 (2) (1987): 283–320.

25. For a dramatic vision of the events *see* Noel Ngwa Nguema, *Choisir de dire la verite*, (Quebec: Anne Sigier, 1991); *see also* Edzodzomo-Ela, *De la democratie*, 71–113, *see* Pierre Pean, *Affaires Africaines* (Paris: Fayart, 1983), or Dady Bouchard, *La longue Marche de la marche de la democratie Gabonaises* (Libreville: ed. GADEDIP, 1992). A more general study is conducted by George Rosberg in *Personal Rule in Black Africa* (Berkeley: University Press of California, 1982), 156–59.

26. Leymarie, "La France," 28.

27. The strange circumstances surrounding the election are analyzed by Gardinier, "Relations," 1–20, or François Gaulme, France Afrique: une crise de cooperation, *Etudes* 380 (January 1994): 41–45; Guy Martin, "Francophone Africa in the Context of Franco-

African Relations," in John Harbeson and Donald Rothchild (eds.), *Africa in World Politics* (Boulder, CO: Westview), 163–188.

28. The entire democratization process is described by John Clark, Elections, Leadership and Democracy in Congo, *Africa Today*, 1, 41-53 (1994): 41-61. *Also see* "Congo's Political Foes Strike an Agreement," *Africa Report*, 38, (5) (1993): 5.

29. This surprising observation of the French vision and of these tensions appears in Pierre Leymarie, "En Afrique Dieu n'est plus Français," *Le Monde Diplomatique*, (May 1995): 26, a more elaborately detailed character of these relations is described by Pean in *Affaires*, 20–45; *also see* Claude Wauthier, "Dures Epreuves pour les Democraties Africaines," *Le Monde Diplomatique* (September 1996): 3.

30. *See* Jacques Champaud, "Cameroon: au bord de l'effondrement," *Politique Africaine* 44 (December 1991): 115–121, Celestin Monga, "L'Emergence de nouveaux modes de production democratique en Afrique noire," *Afrique 2000: Review Africaine de Politique Internationale* (Geneva) 7 (October–December 1990): 11–125; Achille Mbembe, "Le Cameroun apres la mort d'Ahmadou Ahidjo," *Politique Africaine* 37 (1990): 117–123.

31. Read Monga, "Civil Society" 359–379. For a discussion on the rationality of that system, *see* Achille Mbembe's "The Banality of Power and the Aesthetics of Vulgarity in the Postcolony," *Public Culture* 4 (2) (1992): 1–30.

32. Recent cultural tensions between the two linguistic groups are highlighted by Claude Wauthier, Appetits americaines et compromissions françaises, *Le Monde Diplomatique* (October 1994): 10. The domination of the French language is analyzed by Pierre Dumont in Le français langue africaine (Paris: Karthala, 1989).

33. See Bayart, "La problematique," 5–20, and Leymarie, "La France," 28.

34. An interesting analysis is made by Heilbrunn in "Social Origins," 277–299. *See also* Nyang'oro, "Reforms," 138–144. A deep analysis of the Eyadema system is made by Comi Toulabor in *Le Togo sous Eyadema* (Paris: Karthala, 1986).

35. Heilbrunn, 277–299.

36. The recent political crisis in Zaire is analyzed by D. Numengi in "Le mal Zairois," *Le Monde Diplomatique* (November 1995): 20. A more global reflexion is proposed by J. Banga Bane, "Pourquoi la violence? Reflexion sur des moments douloureux de la transition democratique au Zaire," *Zaire-Afrique* 263 (1992): 133–141; *see also* Phillippe Leymarie, "Dinosaure miracule, population naufragee," *Le Monde Diplomatique* (November 1995): 21.

37. These conflicts are analyzed by Wauthier, "Appetits," 10.

38. These responsibilities are established by François Xavier Verschave, "Connivences françaises au Rwanda," *Le Monde Diplomatique* (March 1995): 10; *see* Collette Braekman's, "Autopsie d'un genocide planifie au Rwanda," *Le Monde Diplomatique* (March 1995): 8–9; *also see* the impressive anaysis conducted by Prunier in *The Rwanda Crisis*, 389; and Collette Breackman, *Rwanda, Histoire d'un genocide* (Paris: Fayart, 1994).

39. *See*, Jibrin Ibrahim, "Political Exclusion, Democratization and Dynamics of Ethnicity in Niger," *Africa Today* 41 (3) (1994): 15–39.

40. Ibrahim, "Political," 35; P. Braque, "Nouvelles enlisements des espoirs de paix dans le conflit Touareg au Mali," *Le Monde Diplomatique* (April 1995): 30–31.

41. Ibrahim 35–36.

42. *See* Leymarie, "L'Afrique appauvrie dans la spirale des conflicts," *Le Monde Diplomatique* (September 1994): 10–11.

43. Ibid.

44. *See* Michel Aurillac, *L'Afrique a Coeur* (Berger-Levrault, Paris, 1987), 59.

45. *See* François Mitterrand, *Presence française et Abandon* (Paris: Tribune Libre, (1957): 237.

46. The originality of political dynamics is mentioned by Mbembe, "Diagnostiques," 57–66. A more general analysis is conducted by Karen Remmer, "Democratization in Latin America," in Robert O. Slater, Barry M. Schutz, and Steven R. Dorr, eds., *Global Transformation and the Third World* (London: Adamantine Press, 1993), 91–113.

47. To understand the American infiltration of Francophone Africa, I have relied heavily upon Wauthier, "Appetis," 10; and upon Phillipe Leymarie's, "Anciennes et nouvelles convoitises americaines," *Le Monde Diplomatique* (July 1993): 17; interesting insights are also found in Gerard Prunier, "The Rwanda," 281–305.

48. Leymarie quotes Moose in "Anciennes," 17.

49. *See* Claude Wauthier, 10.

50. Ibid.

51. Ibid.

52. Ibid.

53. The Alice Lakwena movement is analyzed by Heike Behrend, "Violence dans le nord de l'Ouganda: Le mouvement du saint esprit (1986–1987)," *Politique Africaine* 48 (1992): 103–115; *see also* Heike Behrend, "The Holy Spirit Movement and the forces of nature in the North of Uganda (1985–1987)," Michael Twaddle and H. B. Hansen, eds. *Religion and Politics in East Africa since Independence* (London: 1992), 117–245; a more general study concerning the region is conducted by Sharon Hutchinson, *Remembered and Imagined Administration: SPLA and SSIA Civil Policies in the Western Upper Nile, South Sudan, 1985–1996*, paper presented at the 95th annual meeting of the American Anthropological Association, San Francisco, November 20–24, 1996.

54. *See* Claude Wauthier, 10.

55. For the Anglophone interpretation of this conflict, *see* Comi Toulabor, "Declaration de Buea," *Politique Africaine* 51 (1993): 139–52; interesting insights are also contained in Celestin Monga, "La problematique de la legitimite collective en Afrique noire," paper presented at the conference *Droit de la personne et droit des groupes*, Université d'Avigon, France, November 1994.

56. *See* Leymarie, "En Afrique," 26–27.

57. *See* editorial "Mourir pour la Baule" *Politique Africaine* 44, 4. (December 1991).

58. These massacres are described by Vershave, 10.

59. Leymarie, "En Afrique," 26.

60. Read, Medard, "L'Etat patrimonialise," 25–37.

61. The nature of this spirit is analyzed by Jean Pierre Warnier, *L'esprit d' entreprise au Cameroon* (Paris: Kathala, 1993).

62. The limitations of these programs are illustrated by Richard Sandbrook, *The Politics of Africa's Economic Stagnation* (Cambridge. England: Cambridge University Press, 1985); and John Ravenhill, *Africa in Economic Crisis* (London: MacMillan, 1986).

63. J. Sender and S. Smith, *The Development of Capitalism in Africa* (London: Methane, 1987).

64. This transition is discussed by Achille Mbembe in "Comment organizer le sauvetage economique de l'Afrique?" *Le Monde Diplomatique* (November 1990): 18; *see also* Goran Hyden, *No Shortcuts to Progress: African Development, Management and Perspective* (London: Heineman and Los Angeles: University of California Press, 1983).

65. *See* Leymarie, "En Afrique," 26-27.

66. *See* Patrick Chabal, "France and Structural Adjustment in Francophone Africa," *African Affairs* 90 (1991): 292–297.

67. Read De N. Wall, "The Decline of Franc Zone: Monetary Politics in Francophone Africa," *African Affairs* 90 (1991), 383-405.

68. *See* Chaffer, 51.

69. Jean François Bayart, *La reinvention du capitalisme* (Paris: Karthala, 1994).

8

A Vision of the Past as a Beacon for the Future: The Application of Fatimid Ideals in the City of Cairo

Habibeh Rahim

PRELUDE

Described as "maddening, exhausting, endlessly fascinating," contemporary Cairo "juggles the strains of overpopulation with the wealth of a long history in a rich, chaotic mix."[1] More than 3.5 million visitors flock to Egypt every year and a major percentage end up as tourists in Cairo.[2] What is the fascination for this great influx of people? In part the answer lies in the presence of historical sites and artifacts that are several hundred, if not a few thousand, years old. However, with the constant arrival of the indigenous population who come to the city to stay in search of newer economic opportunities and the tourists who come to enjoy the city and then move on, the metropolis appears to require drastic reformulations in housing and the urban environment for this new millennium in order to enhance the services and quality of life offered to its denizens.

Is it possible to reshape and revamp an aging, antiquated megalopolis not only with physical changes of the built environment but also with philosophical and ideological transformations that may facilitate its dynamic participation in world events? Where would the proposed trail for the philosophical and material changes commence? The answer perchance is secured from the analysis of the historical city more than a thousand years old, which forms the nucleus of the contemporary expansive metropolis. Was the original city established and administered with an ideological context which may serve as a beacon for the present restructuring of the mega city? The inquiry that follows the introduction of the historical city deals with quality of life issues which are timeless.

THE HISTORICAL CITY

Cairo, formally the celebrated wall city, *al-qahirah al-mu`izziyah*, the victorious and triumphant, was founded on July 6, 969, under the aegis of the Fatimid commander Jawhar who arriving from north Africa (present Tunisia), conquered Egypt. Strategically situated on the higher ground near the Mukattam Hills, the city was designed as an ideal urban space with spacious gardens and social amenities interspersed within the built environment.[3] Upon its completion three years later, the Fatimid ruler al-Mu`izz arrived in triumph to al-Qahirah[4] from his previous North African capital of Mahdiah near Qayrawan.

At its inception, the Fatimid imperial city of al-Qahirah, delineated a utopian urban order. Very quickly from a royal enclave it emerged as a cosmopolitan center with a diverse civilian population. Within three decades the regal city progressed to a spirited metropolis as the extended sphere of the older city of Fustat-Misr in the south was incorporated to form a larger unit. The symbiotic identification of the two cities became formalized when al-Hakim the grandson of al-Mu`izz patronized the Ibn Tulun masjid in Fustat and lead prayers there. He also built a new masjid in the Rashida area on the outskirts of Fustat, from where he led prayers on occasion.[5] Eulogized as the Mother of the World, *umm al-dunya*, the victorious majestic city al-Qahirah reflected the apogee of the dynasty during the reign of the first five Fatimid rulers (969–1094). Historically, Cairo's situation on the intersection of commercial routes made it a center for the mingling of a range of cultures, thoughts and communities. Over the centuries, the city has become an effective mirror to reflect Africa's contribution to civilization.

In a time long past, visitors to the Fatimid imperial capital were charmed and intrigued by the civic amenities, the aesthetics of the edifices, the cogency of a diverse cultural multitude, the benign rulership. Though its glory was tempered by adverse situations after the eleventh century, it was provided an increased significance by the Mamluks, and even as late as the fourteenth century it was eulogized. In circa 1325 Ibn Batuta wrote with regards to his visit to the city:

[Al-Qahirah] is the metropolis of the country, master of widespread regions and rich areas; it has attained the ultimate possible limits in the size of its population, and is proud of its beauty and brilliance. It is a meeting place for travellers, a station for the weak and the poor. All kinds of men are found there, scholarly or ignorant, diligent or trivial, noble or plebeian, unknown or famous. The number of inhabitants is so great that they seem to move in waves making the city look like a choppy sea. The city is almost too small to hold them in spite of its large area and its capacity.[6]

For two centuries, the megalopolis survived the turmoil of events to remain the center of the Fatimid dynasty until its end in 1124. Thereafter, al-Qahirah was refurbished as the capital of the Ayyubids until the end of the thirteenth century, progressed to become the center of Mamluk rule until early sixteenth century, the Ottoman seat of government in Egypt until 1798, followed as the seat of government for the dynasty of Muhammad `Ali together with the successive hegemony of the French and British, finally it is now Cairo, the distinctive capital of the modern nation state of Egypt, a republic since 1953. Since it was founded, through shifting boundaries and fluctuating circumstances, it has remained an imperial city for more than a thousand years, an honor which is almost unparalleled.

Today amidst altering fortunes, the city retains its central Fatimid core. Over the past two hundred years, it has made a gradual transition from its composed medieval parameters to the modern purposeful infrastructure with highways, sewage, and other municipal amenities, that extend over an area of 220 kilometers. Yet in this physical transition has the city retained the *spirit de corps* inherent in the original structure? Does it project the original singularly humanistic ideal, or is it merely one among many principal cities in the world with a dismal record on quality of life issues? Are considerations of excellence in social amenities deemed pertinent to the universal weal of the citizenry? Can the custodians of modern Cairo garner and incorporate the idealized civic environment of al-Qahirah? The thesis of this chapter deals with the prospects regarding the ethos for the prosperity and the well-being of the citizenry in contemporary Cairo.

THE CONTEMPORARY CITY

The lengthy chapter of contemporary Cairo began during the rule of Muhammad `Ali (1805– 1849), with the first faltering genesis of novel agencies and institutions to industrialize the country and to streamline the bureaucracy.[7] Later for purposes of the origination of town planning, the modern press, and Egyptian nationalism, the reign of Khedive Ismail (1863–1879) may be considered a watershed. With energetic frenzy he appointed special planners to devise and implement a redesigned urban profile. Appurtenances of modern city life such as lighthouses, post offices, schools and hotels were opened by him with great speed in order to embellish the faded luster of Cairo to impress the Europeans who were to arrive for the opening of the Suez Canal, which occurred in November 1869.[8]

The present city of Cairo may chronologically be designated as having made its debut between 1914 and 1926 when the Ottoman religio-political power and domination over Egypt ended and was replaced by a nationalized rule. Egypt became formally independent in February 1922 with a monarchy, albeit Cairo's progression to an environment at par with the most distinguished of modern metropolis was slow and faltering. In 1926 the Cairo Caliphate Congress, established to "modernize" the city, ended in fiasco, essentially because of an isolationist trend, which would preclude the city and the nation from reaching its potential as a defining factor in global politics. The failure here epitomizes the enduring malaise that appears to filter the society as an endemic condition. For most of this century, the city emerges as a mirror which reflects the troubled anguish of Egypt in general. Alternatively described as "a stalled society" with an "appalling cost of stagnation" in human potential and resources, it becomes then a citizenry in transit.

In its socio-economic and cultural matrix, can this metropolis regain an affinity with the idealized city of yore? What are some of the compelling quality of life issues that city custodians require to address in order to stem and reverse the acute social lassitude? Since 1956, the Ministry of Housing has attempted to appraise, replace, and rebuild structures in this ancient city. Several new suburbs and satellite cities have resulted around the early core, the most promising is the Nasr City.[9]

The pertinence of using the idealistic spirit of the Fatimid past as a beacon to shape a viable future for this abiding city shall be discussed with reference to five topics: (1) Urban structure, inclusive of food supply, agriculture, trade and commerce; (2) social welfare and justice; (3) gender perspectives; (4) cross-communal patronage; (5) education, including environmental concerns.

URBAN STRUCTURE

Al-Qahirah originally had two central palaces[10] and a masjid, surrounded by gardens, followed by accommodations for the officers of the state and the soldiers. In time, more masjids and other structures were added. The houses in medieval Cairo were frequently five or six stories tall, and some were even purported to be fourteen floors high, which made the eleventh century traveler Nasir-i Khusraw describe them "as little hills." The construction of buildings incorporated the principles of expedient usage of space with ventilation that provided for the cool north wind, thus translating the urban space into agreeable living accommodations.[11] That urban accommodation was affable and elegant is indicated by a comment from Nasir-i Khusraw, "they have trees planted in tubs on rooftops. Many roofs are gardens and most of what is grown is fruit-producing, such as oranges, pomegranates, apples, quince, roses, herbs, and vegetables. These trees are transplanted in the earth later."[12]

In stark contrast, today in the impoverished sections of Cairo, which comprises the older medieval quarters, instead of fruit trees there are roof-top tenements on highrises where entire families dwell with very little space for seclusion or for much refuge from the elements of nature.[13] Though research indicates that the people who live here may have clean white sheets on beds, and even have plants, this elusive urban space on the roofs of Cairo's highrises is shared with hens, pigeons, and an odd goat. There is some opinion even that the rooftops are a better solution than the slum areas and living on paperbags in the streets.[14] The crudely constructed rooftop clusters of shelters often pose a dangerous situation. For instance, on October 12, 1992, a rare earthquake killed six hundred people and injured another ten thousand. Several thousand people were rendered homeless in the poorer districts of Cairo through the collapse of tenements not constructed properly.[15] These primitive and rough dwellings offering plausible living conditions that seem to entice little more than a passing contemporary nod, perhaps would have received a more negative scrutiny in that bygone period in the ideal city of yore.

But yet the tourists arrive. Michael Korda thus proclaimed:

Our schedule in Cairo was frenetic. . . . We were never bored for a moment. . . . The city itself is at once fascinating and appalling, vast beyond belief, rivaling even Mexico city in sprawl, squalor, traffic density and population, a kind of ultimate urban nightmare in which even the immense cemeteries, the Cities of the Dead, are overpowered by the living as well as the dead.[16]

With a population base of over 6.5 million people, that represents about a tenth of the total 60 to 65 million inhabitants of Egypt, which Cairo cramps in its approximately 215 kilometers, city planners have attempted to provide some coherency to the inhabitants and their living accommodations. As recorded by Janet Abu-Lughd, the organized Fatimid city, over the centuries, accumulated accretions of haphazard structures which converted it into a morass of people, tiny lanes, and built formats.[17] So she queries: "By what process was the finely planned, right-angled palace city of Fatimid al-Qahirah transformed into the maze-like combination of small cells which characterized it in the late medieval period?"[18] In the spirit of the utopian ideal of the city's founders, architects such as Hasan Fathy, interested in lived structures which are "socially and aesthetically satisfying," have strenuously attempted to find indigenous solutions to housing predicaments.[19] At least one of his students Omar Al Farouk has attempted to adhere to traditional aesthetics. In an interview with him Cathy Powers reported that the Fatimid city of al-Qahira, with its organic but unified form, is Farouk's idea of architectural utopia.

Built over 1000 years ago, everything fitted together with a purpose, he explains. He points to the main street, Sharia Muezz Li Din Allah, explaining how it was lined by public buildings, mosques, and caravanserais. The narrow streets branching off not only gave shade to passers-by but provided a new vision at every turn. "These vistas were like musical notes, with the crescendo culminating in the minarets, which acted as guides. You never lost your way," he says.[20]

Vehemently opposed to the "T-square architecture" Farouk adhers to the structural wisdom of yester years. He was instrumental in reviving the *mashrabeya* (window wood screens) industry. In the 1970s, he would find samples of screens in the city's rubbish heaps. He then tracked down the few artisans of the craft and encouraged them to take up their craft again and explains: "I cannot complete my architecture without the help of these artisans." According to him technology and science must be subservient to the human expression, "architecture is meant to endure and to fit humanity."[21] In order to provide the citizens of Cairo with open space, the El-Darrassa Park near Al-Azhar was inaugurated in 1995. This park was bestowed by His Highness Prince Karim Aga Khan IV, the present Imam for Shi`a Nizari Ismailis. He is a direct descendent of the Fatimid rulers, who were from the progeny of Fatimah, the daughter of Prophet Muhammad, and her husband `Ali b. Abi Talib. The Aga Khan Trust for Culture has also made a formal agreement with the government of Egypt to revitalize the old city quarters and to restore the splendid architectural monuments.

The need for urban space and adequate housing is severe indeed. On the eastern margins of the city, the gigantic graveyards with their scattered mausoleums have become the newest suburbs and are now even provided with electricity and water. Do people feel uncomfortable with these quarters? "Despite being the land of the mummies, Egypt tends to associate the dead with blessings rather than curses," wrote Peter Theroux.[22] He also observed that the people who live here tend to be more hushed and quieter. Over the past twenty years, Egypt has resettled more than twenty thousand earthquake victims, shanty town dwellers, and others into "new desert cities" around Cairo. "More often than not, these projects turn out to be soulless apartment blocks, plagued by electrical and water shortages and located in desolate areas far from commercial centers."[23] Bahteen, a relatively new settlement on the northern outskirts of Cairo began to have severe outbreaks of infectious diseases such as typhoid as a result of the breakdown of street pipes. Part of the problem appears to be a result of misgovernment by local officials.[24] In contrast the controversial Dronka project was a "model of population transfer." Replacing the "crowded, squalid neighborhood" burnt in the fire, the army speedily built the New Dronka, consisting of about 8,000 homes, a health and a family planning clinic, a school, paved soccer courts, and reliable power and water lines. Additionally the architectural planning utilized the traditional design whereby the houses are "cool even at noontime in the Upper Egyptian summer."[25] This settlement, especially the efficient utilization of the resources of the army in a pertinent peace time project, is certainly laudable. It is a project that would have gained the admiration of the Fatimids and results in the query as to why would the Egyptian government not repeat the project as a continuing feature of the nation's urban settlement process.

In Cairo, the Ezbekiya area becomes the dividing line between the old and the recent city. Medieval Cairo with narrow alley ways is past Shari` el Khalig, Canal street, over the tramlines. Westward, away from the old city are new settlements of the Gezira, Imbala and Giza areas. Big villas are constructed in Heliopolis on the western bank of the Nile or along the Pyramid road. Most modern hotels and clubs are in the new sections of the sprawling metropolis. The industrial quarter is on the outskirts of the city. Regarding the poverty and the unsatisfactory living conditions of the old city, what James

Aldridge declared in 1969 appears to still persist:

Poverty is an ocean, and the remains of past glories are the romantic archipelagoes of its neglected beauty. But nothing can hide the fact that it is really a large festering slum, however romantically enclosed it is. You have to occasionally tear your eyes away from its exciting streets and look up at the awful old houses. Sometimes five people live in one tiny room in these tipsy tenements, and some people sleep and eat under stairways or in kerosene-tin shacks on the roofs, or they bed down on balconies among the chickens and goats.[26]

He further observed that though there was no real starvation in the poor areas of the city but many people did not get enough to eat, very few owned more than one change of clothing and not many adults could read or write. Again all these remarks unfortunately seem valid almost two decades later. However, there is a cause for celebration. Aldridge also observed:

Yet you can also find tucked away in the strangest corners of these streets dozens of primary and elementary schools. Before the war there were seventy-nine elementary schools in Cairo . . . these fountain schools are still functioning as well as the new ones which the Ministry of Education is opening as fast as thay can get trained teachers for them. Every one of these schools is a discovery in this old city, because one is inclined to forget in the anarchy of all this poverty and street commerce that children here go to school, and that after all, medieval Cairo has in it one of oldest seminaries in the world—the Azhar . . . now a mosque, a religious school and a fully fledged university.[27]

These attempts at providing the citizens with learning institutions would certainly have received the approval of the Fatimids. The issue of education has been discussed in greater detail in the sections which follow.

In any city, municipal functions become essential indicators of the quality of life available to the inhabitants. Unlike the modern availability of water via cisterns, waterpumps and pipes, in the older era water carriers supplied water. With fifty thousand camels and with brass cups and jugs they went into streets which were too narrow for the camels. Also, the merchants were requird to keep jars of water in their stores to help fight fires—a novelty in those times. How adequate is Cairo's water supply and the municipal's fire department? Are they equal to the best in the world?

Another important aspect of urban life is public transportation. During Nasir-i Khusraw's visit, fifty thousand donkeys were available for hire by the citizenry for a small fee. Only the soldiers and militia rode horses.[28] These reports indicate that by the means available the amenities for transportation were more than adequate. However, for any visitor to Cairo, the jumble of the roadways and trams, alleys and bystreets, buses, cars, and donkey carts,[29] definitely require to be urgently remedied. As the rush for modernization continues, hastily executed and rashly planned urban structures proliferate. Frequently, old edifices with their graceful *mashrabiyah* facades are pulled down and replaced with structures which are plain and utilitarian at most. Conservation is extremely selective and inadequate to preserve the historic centuries old structures.[30] As fine cara-vanserais, special markets and graceful old residential homes fall to ruin or become "upscaled" by sky-high structures,[31] intensive intervention is required to preserve this centuries old heritage of the built environment.

Cairo's urban expansion spreads to the formerly isolated industrial zones. A major blight of modern Cairo are the heavy factories in areas such as Al Weili district and the Shubra Al Kheima. Owners generally ignore environmental regulations so that the inhabitants living nearby are exposed to high levels of toxic fumes.[32] This again is an issue which if a solution were to be defined in the Fatimid context, the industries would perchance be removed to the desert city of 10th Ramadan, or heavy penalties be imposed for the noncompliance of environmental regulations or a consorted effort be made for the removal of inhabitants to safer less noxious areas.

Food Supply

In any given society, especially in a major urban center, food supply, victuals, and related provisions, require considerable administrative organization. Overpricing and accumulating food can cause severe hardships. In the original city, during a high Nile year, the harvest would be more bountiful than in a low time. Hence, people bought extra grain as a speculative asset. To preclude the stockpiling of grain, al-Mu`izz discontinued the public announcement of the ebbing Nile.[33] Food resources have been an ancient problem in Egypt as evident even in the biblical story of Joseph. In modern Cairo as well, the distribution and quality control of food is a major governmental concern. The Egyptian Ministry of Health announced in December of 1994 that rotten imported meat had been processed and sold in cans on the street. This announcement caused the domestic meat prices to rise. Many people prefer to only consume freshly cut meat which tends to be more expensive.[34] Additionally, the price of several staples arose and by the end of December, there were chronic shortages in the supply of sugar, tomatoes, and other crops as well. A series of misfortunes had led to this crises. During the preceding summer due to water rationing the Delta's rice crop had been left high and dry, then floods in November of 1994 had "dumped a thick, oozing layer of mud" over prime agricultural land in Upper Egypt, finally parts of the sugarcane fields of Assiut, Qena, and Minya were bulldozed by the governmental armored carriers in pursuit of the militants. This shortage was seen to be amplified as a result of the contention between the small merchants and the Supply Minister Ahmed al-Guweili. Supporters of the minister claim that the traders are hoarding supplies to break the power of the strongest proponent of consumer protection rights in Egypt's history.[35]

Agriculture

Agriculture is the pivotal enterprise that has regulated the civilization of Egypt. Though essentially a rural activity, dependent on water and fertile land, it affects the quality of life in the urban centers. To encourage agriculture, the Fatimids had encouraged a massive canal system to draw the waters of the Nile. The canal-cutting ceremony in Fustat-Misr was an important part of Nasir-i Khusraw's visit to Cairo. Since the agricultural produce was dependent on the level of the Nile waters, taxation was adjusted accordingly. Hence, we are informed that "unless the level goes above eighteen cubits, the sultan's land tax is not levied on the peasantry." We have also been informed:

The water usually rises for forty days until it has risen eighteen cubits. Then it remains at that level for another forty days, neither increasing nor decreasing. Thereupon it gradually decreases for another forty days until it reaches the winter level. When the water begins to recede, the people follow it down, planting as the land is left dry. All their agriculture, both winter and summer, follows this pattern. They need no other source of water.[36]

Our eleventh-century visitor also related that produce was brought to the city from everywhere and sold in the markets. In the middle of winter, he "saw the following fruits and herbs, all in one day: red roses, lilies, narcissi, oranges, citrons, apples, jasmine, basil, quince, pomegranates, pears, melons, eggplants, squash, turnips, radishes, cabbage, fresh beans, cucumbers, green onions, fresh garlic, carrots and beets."[37]

In the years of abundant Nile, grain was stored not only in governmental granaries, but individual citizens were also allowed to own vast storage units. In times of a low Nile, both the imperial and private grain was put at the disposal of the citizens.[38] The Nile has historically been the foundation of Egypt's prosperity. Today, these life-giving waters are threatened from over extension of dams and canals, as well as by pollution caused in an industrial society. Even aquatic produce has suffered as a result of the impure waters.[39]

Presently, overcrowding, food-import dependency and unemployment has made urban and agricultural expansion into the desert a critical aspect of the country's development. For the past fifteen years, the Desert Development Center of the American University in Cairo has been involved in a project to build, farm, and live in the deserts. University graduates are trained in desert farming and many Egyptians are taught how to manage livestock and agricultural farms.[40] This project to make the "desert bloom" is initiated by the Egyptian Ministry of Agriculture and Land Reclamation and cosponsored by the U.S. Agency for International Development. This laudable attempt to vitalize the desert would definitely have been applauded by the Fatimid ancestors of Cairo. There are five of these experimental desert farms, one of which is on the outskirts of Cairo on the Alexandria road.

Trade and Commerce

Economic activities, including trade and commerce is a focal urban occupation. In an urban center, trade and commerce become the life blood of the economy and a major element for the wealth of the proletariate. Wealth from trade was primarily used not for war but for peace time activities by the Fatimids. The government received considerable revenue from customs dues, trade, and taxes. The monetary standard was improved and the dinar in pure gold was sought by the greater Mediterranean and Arab world. A governing agency that protects commerce, becomes a key facilitator of economic efflorescence in the society. Nasir-i Khusraw commented that "the security and welfare of the people have reached a point that the drapers, moneychangers, and jewelers do not even lock their shops—they only lower a net across the front, and no one tempers with anything."[41] He further commented that:

The merchants of Old Cairo are honest in their dealings and if one of them is caught cheating a customer, he is mounted on a camel with a bell in his hand and paraded about the city, ringing the bell and crying out, "I have committed a misdemeanor and am suffering reproach. Whoever tells a lie is rewarded with public disgrace."[42]

At the crossroads of Europe, Asia and Africa, trade and commerce continue to be a major factor of contemporary Egypt's economy. In the early 1970s, Egypt relaxed restrictions and encouraged private sector investments. Referred to as *infitah* or open-door policy, instituted as Law 43 in 1974, attracted foreign banks and oil companies as investors to Egypt but this plan had a mixed result as inflation and imports increased. Many entrepreneurs amassed fortunes while the living standards of the majority of the population remained unchanged.[43] In 1990, the Egyptian work force was about 14 million people, of which 1.5 million were women and about half a million were girls between the ages of six and fifteen.[44] Cairo has concealed unemployment as well. Incalculable damage occurs to the Gross National Product with laxity at the workplace where no vision or zeal prevails. How would the Fatimids have resolved the situation? Perhaps encourage entrepreneurs to open their own places of business—a reasonable expectation from a progressive and solicitous governing body.

A recent trend to encourage small business appears to have gained prominence with lending schemes such as the "Grameen." Modelled on a similar program in Bangladesh, pioneered by Mohammed Younas, the facility allows for seed money to be lent without collateral, essentially for animal raising to village women. People without collateral are organized into groups of five who then guarantee each other's loans. The group is required to select a head, conduct weekly meetings and establish a group savings account, modeled on the *gam'iyya*, an old customary financial cooperative in Egyptian society.[45] By September 1995, within two and a half years, fifty credit officers, program managers and accountants had been trained by the program and more than two thousand beneficiaries serviced.[46] It is hoped that the program endures and remains to be seen how long the zeal of this initiative will remain. In the Cairo of yore the government frequently took initiatives to help the people in their pursuit of livelihood. For instance, we know that the caliph owned twenty thousand stores in Cairo and Old Cairo (Fustat-Misr) which were rented to merchants at low rents for trading purposes. Other public buildings and service amenities such as caravansaries and bathhouses were also owned by the ruler.[47]

Since the eighteenth century, significant changes have occurred in the commercial composition of the city of Cairo as with the other urban centers. With the import of consumer goods from Europe, the services of a great portion of the artisans became unnecessary and as a result these unemployed craftsmen became day laborers. This was a change which heralded the end of the guild system of medieval society. With economic displacement arrived urban violence and a mercantile group that exploited and manipulated resources for its own end. Foreign merchants dominated commercial venues and a free wage labor replaced the older guild system. This change brought with it a massive displacement of traditional lifestyle structures.[48] However, any attempt at industrialization in contemporary Egypt must accommodate the skill of workers together with their socio-cultural requirements.

Presently, in addition to governmental initiatives, an informal economy provides the citizens of Cairo with alternative resources. Among other opportunities, an informal network enables them to find employment, migrate abroad, resist taxation, save through community associations, *jam'iyat*. The use of *wastah*, personal influence, and patronage is regarded as being necessitated by the inefficiency and corruption of the governmental process.[49]

SOCIAL WELFARE AND JUSTICE

In a successful governmental structure, an efficacious public welfare policy together with an equitable system of justice becomes the *sine qua non* of civilized life. The salubrious promotion of humane endeavors by the administration could lead to a heightened sensitivity of moral responsibility at the personal and community levels.

Assistance to the weak and the poor was considered by the Fatimids as an important social responsibility. In many official ceremonies, physically challenged people were favored with special honors, as at the ceremony of the marking of the Nile level, for instance. In early summer when the water level was sufficiently high, a festival marked the breaking of the temporary dams all over the country. These dams released the waters that would inundate the land for purposes of agriculture. At the festival of the opening of the Nile canal in Cairo, which was witnessed by the entire population of the old and the new city, a carnival atmosphere prevailed with "all sorts of sporting events." Nasir-i Khusraw states that on this occasion "the first ship that sails into the canal is filled with deaf-mutes, whom they must consider auspicious. On that day the sultan distributes alms to the people."[50] And he further mentions with regards to the caliph's palace that "if the people of the city make requests on behalf of the suffering, they are given something. Whatever medication is needed in the city is given out from the harem, and there is also no problem in the distribution of other ointments, such as balsam."[51]

In Egypt in 1992, there were a hundred thousand doctors, fifteen thousand dentists, thirty-five thousand pharmacists, ninety-eight thousand other medical personnel. Of the 6,418 treatment units, there were 329 hospitals with 108,425 beds. Most of these facilities are in the larger cities. As the numbers would indicate, the medical facilities are certainly not adequate for over sixty million people. In recent years, several clinics in Cairo have been involved with the controversial transplant of live kidneys, a transaction in which the very indigent frequently indulge in, not for medical reasons, but as a method of earning money. In specific areas there are rooming houses where not only do poor Egyptians live but so do Somalis and Sudanese until they find a match with a potential affluent recipient. Such a trade in human parts would evoke a repulsion in our estimation of what the Fatimid ideals were for the welfare of the citizenry. This practice is perhaps something that the society requires to ponder upon as it moves to the next millennium. Egyptian doctors have tried to limit the practice but have not been very effective.[52] Must there persist this level of abject poverty, with no real opportunities, for people to become compelled to literally give of themselves to survive and to provide an adequate existence for their families?

In the area of Bahteem, on the northern outskirts of Cairo, three thousand citizens contracted typhoid from January to April 1995, as a result of the street pipes which burst on an almost weekly basis and drinking water was tainted with sewage. Too late, the masjids began to warn the local population over loud speakers not to drink water. Shortage of beds at the Imbaba Fever Hospital precluded many of the afflicted from receiving adequate treatment. Vaccines were distributed at the cost of EL8 a shot, which was too expensive for entire families to avail for themselves. Corrupt doctors were selling the shots to private clinics for EL13 each.[53]

However all of Cairo is not this bleak. Glimpses of the spirit of Fatimid regard and concern for the needy is evident in several organizations. The Awladi Orphanage is managed and controlled by volunteers "with a philosophy of understanding." Approximately half of the children are referred to the facility by the Ministry of Public Health. They are sent to the orphanage between the ages of two to six years in age from "nursing mothers" who provided interim care to the children and were paid by the Egyptian government for feeding and raising the children. They arrive at the orphanage sometimes in poor physical and psychological condition. The staff consists mainly of committed volunteers who bring the gift of time and energy to the management of the orphanage.[54]

Similarly, the Mubarrah orphanage is a humanitarian center that was opened in the mid-1980s by the New Woman Society (Gemeat Al Mara al Gedida) which had been founded in 1919 by Hedeya Barakat, a wealthy Muslim prompted by nationalist hope in the aftermath of the first World War and the Egyptian feminist Hoda Sharaawi. Out of the approximately twenty thousand homeless and abandoned children in Cairo, the orphanage takes care of about two hundred girls who are sent to them regularly by the Ministry of Social Affairs. It has been referred to as "an institution which acts as mother, father, teacher, nurse and policeman" to the children.[55]

While this relief is available for the very young—in the absence of a cohesive welfare system and with the erosion and breakdown of family units as people leave traditional structures—the elderly are at times discarded. Abdel Fatah Hassan, head of the Islamic charity association and former deputy minister of Religious Endowments stated: "The Egyptian family used to rotate around care and love [for the elderly] . . . now the word "old" equals the word "useless.". . Whether their need is financial or emotional, any obligation toward an elderly mother has become a burden to the child."[56]

In the mid-1990s, there are fifty-nine homes for seniors. Of this number, fifty-six are for-profit organizations, whereby with a monetary payment, a family may be rid of unwanted elderly relatives; only three institutions cater to the indigent. The pathos and plight of many disinherited parents, especially in major cities such as Cairo, is a sad commentary on a cultural and social community which has traditionally prided itself on its hospitality and generosity. It is indeed ironic that (as reported by the *Middle East Times* correspondent Dalia Salaheldin), sixty-nine-year-old Farida Abdullah was sleeping on the "pavement of downtown Cairo." When the story was printed in July 1995, she had been "kicked out" seven years previously by her daughter and son-in-law. Her life is thus described:

Now Abdullah earns her living selling sweets to school children and hides under a cardboard box to sleep at night. She fears hunger, sickness, and the police who could arrest her for her unlicensed trade. "As much as I fear death," she says, "I cannot hope for a better refuge."[57]

Can no one come to the aid of the Faridas of contemporary Cairo? How would have the Fatimids addressed this issue associated with an industrial urban society? Perhaps give incentives to the relatives to take her in, perhaps set up institutions to address the problems of seniors—but it is certainly conceivable that they would not have allowed society to degenerate to an extent whereby an elderly woman sleeps on a street under a cardboard box. Nasir-i Khusrow remarked in 1047: "What a happy citizenry and a just ruler to have such conditions in their days! What wealth must there be for the ruler not to inflict injustice and for the peasantry not to hide anything!"[58] He also said:

The people are so secure under the sultan's reign that no one fears his agents, and they rely on him neither to inflict injustice not to have designs on anyone's property. I saw such personal wealth there that were I to describe it, the people of Persia would never believe it. I could discover no end or limit to their wealth, and I never saw such ease and comfort anywhere.[59]

Could this eleventh-century visitor perchance have the same comments regarding modern Cairo as it meanders through the current century? In contemporary Egypt, the policy makers in Cairo appear to be dealing with persistent problems of resource allocations, price differentials and governing iniquities as discussed earlier in the section "Commerce."

Justice

Our Fatimid visitor, Nasir-i Khusraw, noted that the chief justice received a monthly stipend of two thousand dinars, and similarly every judge down the line was provided with adequate compensation "so that the people need not fear venality from the bench."[60]

Justice was not merely relegated to the judiciary control of the *qadis*, or judges, but the Fatimid ruler himself actively participated in fostering fair and equitable dispensations of the law. During his reign, the Fatimid caliph Al-Hakim had an intense concern with the religious and communal life of the population. He was frequently approached during his nightly excursions for redress from fellow citizens, and the chamberlain was instructed to grant access to whoever wanted to give him a petition in the palace.[61]

In modern Egypt the transition from the medieval Shari'ah courts to the inception of new legal attitudes regarding personal and collective duties and freedoms gradually occurred in the nineteenth and early twentieth century. With the arrival of Muhammad Ali on the scene and the legal developments instituted by him, led eventually, to the formulation of several judiciary changes. The establishment of mixed courts in 1876 with jurisdiction over both foreign and Egyptian litigants, initiated a new course for the legal system. Following this, the Advocates Law of September 16, 1893, formation of the Bar Association on September 30, 1912, abolition of the *shari'ah* (Islamic) and *millah* (non-Muslim denominational) courts and transference of their jurisdiction to the National courts in 1955 by the revolutionary government of Nasser, have been particularly important stages.[62]

With regard to the responsibility of the judiciary, a very interesting case comes up for discussion in the 1990s contemporary Cairo. Were the justices involved in this controversy deferring to personal grudges or were they intent to pursue justice? On June 14, 1995, Nasser Hamid Abu Zeid, a university professor was declared a non-Muslim and summarily divorced from his wife by an Egyptian court of appeal.[63] His historicist writings on the revealed nature of the Qur'an led to charges of apostasy, and his subsequent treatment would appear to be a travesty of justice indeed. The issue is not resolved and provokes fiery responses.[64] It also brings into focus the issue of freedom of expression, and the responsibilities of the judiciary. Abu Zeid's wife, Ibithal Younis, a University professor as well, bitterly commented about this decision regarding her personal life over which she had no choice, she considered the ruling a "moral violence" agains t her.[65]

GENDER PERSPECTIVES

The question of gender in the context of the Fatimids is a vital topic, as the dynasty was named after Fatimah, the daughter of Prophet Muhammad, who was married to `Ali ibn Abi Talib.[66] The Fatimid patronage of learning was extended to all sections of society, inclusive of women. Books and the acquisition of wisdom was encouraged, and both men and women could come to the *majlis* or scholarly sessions at the Dar al-Hikmah (House of Wisdom). The women in the royal family appeared to participate with great influence in the socio-political affairs of the dynasty as well. For instance, Princess Sitt al-Mulk, al-Hakim's sister, insured that her nephew az-Zahir was proclaimed as the next ruler after his father's demise. This was despite the fact that al-Hakim had proclaimed as successor his cousin Abu al-Qasim `Abd al-Rahman Ilyas who predeceased him. Subsequent to al-Hakim's death, she also reversed some regulations imposed by him to protect women, such as not allowing them to go out of the house.[67]

Cairo's urban space further testifies to the impact made by women in Fatimid society. Numerous secular and religious buildings were built and charitable foundations were established by the women of the dynasty. Sayyida Duruzzan, al-Mu`izz's wife and al-Aziz's mother was an enthusiastic builder. Additionally, several shrines were dedicated to prominent Shi`a women personalities. The *mashhad*s of Sayyida Nafisa, Sayyida Ruqayya and Sayyida `Atiqa have been historically prominent. These Fatimid women appear to have had strong independent personalities, they were also educated and financially affluent. They appear to have used their wealth and intellect wisely and contributed positively to the socio-cultural legacy of the Fatimids. What is the situation in contemporary Cairo and the Republic of Egypt vis-à-vis the opportunities and accomplishments of women?

Currently, a raging debate exists regarding the hijab or hegab, and women's rights in Cairo and by extension in Egypt. Is the purport of the hegab to be simple in dress, or is it merely a token object attached to the head as a means to define one's moral rectitude? This question needs to be answered at an individual level, and the decision to wear or not, depends on the choice of each person. In the July 30–August 5, issue of *Middle East Times*, Mona El Tahawy, interviewed Nawal Al Saadawi who regards herself as a woman activist and a leading feminist in the Arab world. She has authored more than twenty-five books on the subject of women in Egyptian society and does not wear the veil because it detracts from her humanity and her intellectual aptitude. "I judge the power of morality by the degree of free-dom; the freer you are the more responsible you are, and the more moral." And she further proclaims: "Islam also welcomes ijtihad—which means that everybody has his or her own way of interpreting the Qur'an or Hadith or Islam."[68]

How would Sitt al-Mulk have reacted to the views of this contemporary feminist? Increasingly, with confidence, women are declaring the public efficacy of their intellectual capacities which they use for the benefit of the society. Like Huda Sha'rawi, founder of the Egyptian Feminist Union, and Nabawiyah Musaa, a pioneering female educator[69] before her, Nemat Fouad is another woman regarded to be a potent force in Egyptian life. Her thirst for knowledge and heritage has made her a tireless opponent of projects that would in any way ruin or damage Egypt's aesthetic heritage. So she managed to oppose and block the building of a huge stadium overlooking the Pyramids that had been proposed by the Ministry of Culture.[70] Do these women appear as anomalies, or are they a growing aspect of contemporary Egyptian society and the products of Cairo's cosmopolitan heritage? In June 1979, to ameliorate injustice towards women and to protect them in marriage and divorce, Anwar Sadat had instituted amendments in the Personal Status Laws. These laws were challenged in 1985, but reintroduced and passed by Parliament. However, the increased seats in Parliament allocated to women by Sadat's reforms was overturned in 1987.[71]

CROSS-COMMUNAL PATRONAGE

The Fatimid dynasty faced a particularly challenging prospect in harmonious cross-communal existence. Though Shi`a themselves, they governed a Sunni majority population with pockets of Coptic Christians and some Jewish citizens. Whereas Shi`ism was the official persuasion of the Fatimids, the majority of the population both in the immediate administrative vicinity of Cairo, and in the surrounding provincial regions, were Sunni. Additionally, there were significant numbers of inhabitants belonging to other traditions such as the Jewish and the Coptic Christians. This fact makes the socio-cultural and religio-political blend of the ruler and ruled a very interesting composition. The Fatimid state possessed a cosmopolitan egalitarian population which competed for excellence in arts, commerce, education, generally without restrictions based on doctrinal differences. The prosperous nature of the cosmopolitan city attracted people of varying religious affiliations in droves to the metropolis.

Officers of the state belonged to a variety of persuasions, Isma'ili, Sunni, Christian, Jewish. A genuine latitudinarian acceptance of differing creeds became the *sine qua non* of this progressive medieval dynasty. For instance, in 1014 (405 AH) al-Hakim appointed not an Isma'ili but a Hanbali jurist, Ibn Abi'l-'Awwam as chief qadi. The only stipulation required was that in a case that involved the use of Isma'ili law he would ensure the presence of four Isma'ili jurists in his court.[72]

After he successfully quelled the destructive Abu Rakwa revolt, al-Hakim passed several decrees on the official acceptance of non-Shi'a faith. Some harsh measures necessitated for a short time by the crises were also abrogated. Sunni muezzins could include the phrase "hurry to the best of works" or omit it without penalty and instead say "prayer is better than sleep" for the morning prayer. One's conscience and judgment was deemed important to guide each individual for worship and religious practice.[73] The difference in Shi'a-Sunni persuasions also led to the debate in the matter of whether the date for the celebration of the festival that follows Ramadan would be dictated by the astronomical calculation or by simple observation of the new moon . Again personal choice was allowed to prevail.

Al-Hakim provokes considerable interest by the innovative regulatory injunctions in his administration. He instituted the Dar al-Hikmah (House of Wisdom) near the Western Palace with a magnificent library, where a variety of subjects such as theology, philosophy, medicine, together with both Shi'a and Sunni law was taught. Theologians of varied opinions in addition to scholars in a variety of arts and sciences were invited to this learning center. Voluminous scholarly material was published under its aegis on subjects such as medicine, theology, philosophy, grammar. He also constructed a masjid in the Rashidah area outside the city gate of Bab al-Futuh.

Though they were Shi' as themselves, in all the towns and villages, the maintenance of the various masjids (irrespective of denomination) and the required supplies such as lamp oil, carpets, mats and rugs, salaries for custodians, janitors, muezzins, were all provided for by a stipend from the Fatimid rulers.[74] Al-Hakim also purchased the Masjid of Ibn Tulun and several others in Fustat. He sent 814 copies of the Qur'an to the Ibn Tulun masjid and seven chests containing 1,290 Qur'ans to the masjid of 'Amr. He instituted a census which revealed that nearly eight hundred masjids (of differing denominations) had no revenue. So he allocated 9,220 dirhams monthly for their expenses.[75] Thus, sporadic restrictive edicts in an emergency such as at the time of the revolt of Abu Rakwa in 1004, was quickly replaced by edicts that enabled citizens to freely follow their varied religious creeds and conventions as well as to enable them to florish in their socio-economic activities. Commenting on al-Hakim's policies, Paula Sanders states:

This should serve to remind us that, however tempting it may be to emphasize the erratic character of al-Hakim's decrees and behavior, the evidence as a whole points to an overriding concern with urban and communal life that persisted throughout his reign. ... What mattered to al-Hakim was communal life in an urban landscape that he had come to understand as a single ritual city.[76]

Not only was a genuine official attempt made to provide intercommunal co-existence within Islam, but non-Muslims, i.e. *dimmi*s were treated with respect and were provided protection. These *dimmi*s (protected people) had a favored status in the Fatimid empire and were permitted to build houses of worship in the newly established imperial city. Merit and ability, rather than creed and beliefs appear as significant criteria in the selection of officers by the rulers. Ministers of state were frequently non-Shi`as, and in fact were even non-Muslims. The Geniza documents for instance, display a policy of great benevolence toward the Jewish community.[77] Financial support of the Jerusalem Yeshiva is one of many instances of patronage by the Fatimid authorities. Royal support was proffered to churches and monasteries as well, and land was even granted to churches as pious endowments.

Some of this legacy of intercommunal sharing is evident in the continued camaraderie and affinity with minority faiths in contemporary Cairo. The pervasive spirit of cross- religious harmony is apparent not only in Cairo but is visible in other parts of Egypt as well. For instance, in the delta town of Damanhour, despite the general outrage with Israel after 1967; in 1995, as had been for the preceding seventy-eight years, the Jewish community was welcomed for the annual pilgrimage to the tomb of Rabbi Yaakov Abu Hatzira.[78] This festival referred to commonly as the *moulid* has traditionally been attended by Muslims also.

During Fatimid times as well, the population frequently celebrated festivals that crossed the boundaries of opinion, belief and dogma. For centuries the Muslims and Coptic Christians have celebrated the Coptic New Year. According to popular tradition, there is a two-thousand-year-old year old tree near the Matariya metro station on the outskirts of Cairo where the Virgin Mary and baby Jesus is said to have rested. This tree, cherished and protected, has become a site of special visitations especially around Christmastime.[79] The Coptic church of Egypt is one of Christendom's oldest churches with Pope Shenouda III as the 117th patriarch of this church. The Egyptian government deligently strives to foster the weal and welfare of this and other minority communities.

In the realm of cross-communal discourse, the activities of the militant groups have created significant reversals in the nations traditional ideology of civilized demeanor towards all inhabitants. Recently however, people connected to the Gamaa i.e. the Jama`ah al-Islamiyah, have expressed reflections on using the idiom of dialogue, rather than violence, as a constructive means to find solutions and resolutions to socio-political and economic issues. Thus, in an interview in March 1995, Montasser Zayat, a lawyer who represents the Gamaa, but is not a part of the structure, reflected on the role of the pen and the word to change the political status quo and reform society.[80]

The radical groups are particularly potent in urban centers such as Cairo, perhaps as a result of the prevalence of social and economic tensions resulting in dissatisfied civilians. However, the government's harsh security measures have provoked international disapproval. In late May 1993, Amnesty International published a report in which it condemned the "frightening brutality" of the security forces.[81] The gunman who shot at a Coptic crowd outside the Muharraq monastery near Asyut killing five and wounding three, is perhaps a significant breech of the intercommunal etiquette of Fatimid times where diversity of belief was considered an accepted social composition.

For several decades, some groups have perceived that Islamic laws must be made a more integral aspect of Egyptian society and have frequently disagreed with official polices.[82] Many argue that violence towards innocent citizens is not in conformity with the humane concerns embedded in the message of Islam and have disavowed any connections with the bloodshed. Members of militant groups are generally considered to have been a significant cause of strife during the later years of Anwar Sadat's rule and have been deemed responsible for his assassination in 1981.[83] In February 1997, the Egyptian Parliament voted to extend for another three years the emergency law that enables the government to detain militants suspected of violence.[84] How would the Fatimids have dealt with this crises of militancy and strife? We have a vague glimmer from the time of al-Hakim when at the time of the Abu Rakwa crises he imposed a state of curfew, but as soon as it was past, he addressed the concerns of the population with additional leniency towards religious ritual such as the call for prayers.

The city of yore and the administration which governed the land became hence a haven, the core of idealistic principles, where people of varied affili-ations lived and continued to cohabit as neighbors. Over the centuries, historians have typically made evaluations which resound as follows:

Within Egypt, Isma`ili doctrine seems to have been the preserve of a court and esoteric elite. There was little or no pressure on the predominantly Sunni Muslim and Coptic Christian population of Egypt to convert, and Sunni Muslims, Christians and Jews were able to hold office even at the highest levels of the administration. Isma`ili doctrine was syncretistic, and the speculative tolerance of the elite encouraged a cultural efflorescence in Egypt.[85]

As a result of the tolerance by the Fatimids, indicated also by the documents of the Cairo Geniza, Jewish merchants became prominent principals in the Spain-to-India trade route which passed through Qayrawan. Several prominent medieval Jewish scholars such as Isaac Israeli, Nissim and Hananel flourished under Fatimid rule. They were also enabled to maintain their links with their religious academies in Babylon and Palestine. Encouraged by the Fatimids, from the year 1015 onwards, the head of the Jewish community in Qayrawan bore the princely title of *nagid*, which was a valid designation until modern times.

Moving into the next millennium, the administrative legislators of the contemporary megapolis, the capital of a dynamic nation-state, would fare well if the latitudinarian tolerance of their Fatimid forbearers were to be made into a cohesive statement of policy in a world where collective weal and expansive perspective leave space for the enhancement of the human spirit.

EDUCATION

The Fatimid encouragement of learning is legendary and is considered analogous to the efflorescence of erudition and knowledge in eighteenth century Europe. Savants and scholars were honored and treated with generosity. Physicians, philosophers, poets, historians, all flourished; and libraries were celebrated for their resources. Two institutions in particular became famed, the Al-Azhar masjid to which a center of scholarship was added and the Dar al-Hikmah academy. In addition to these two main institutions of higher learning, the congregational masjids of Ibn Tulun and al-Amr in Old Cairo attracted many savants; and we are informed that all through the night the lamps were kept burning as people discussed and studied. The Fatimids supported these institutions by grants for books and lights as well as stipends for the scholars and the students.

A thousand years later, the Al-Azhar is one of the most renowned institutions of learning in the Muslim world. Over the centuries, new additions have been made to the physical structure and new curricular added. In the initial decades of the twentieth century, Jamal al-Din al-Afghani and Muhammad Abduh were particularly instrumental in introducing the study of modern sciences together with the traditional subjects, thereby aiding its transition to a modern scholarly institution. Since the establishment of Egypt as a republic in 1953, the scholarly shaykhs of Al-Azhar have continued to participate in a vibrant intellectual legacy which has survived more than ten centuries. In 1958, President Nasser attended a Ramadan service similar to the Fatimids. In the same year, the Minister of Awqaf lectured at Al-Azhar in honor of United Nations day.[86]

The Bait al-`Ilm, House of Knowledge, subsequently known as Dar al-Hikmah was inaugurated on Saturday, March 24, 1005, with the largest known collection of manuscripts. Access to this superb library was free; pen, paper, and ink were provided gratis for writing. Additionally, the main masjids such as Ibn Tulun became important centers of learning where "there are always teachers and readers of the Qur'an." The structure was supported by four hundred marble columns and white marble *mihrab* on which the Qur'an was written. Nasir-i Khusraw also informs us that it "is the promenade of the city, as there are never less than five thousand people—students, the indigent, scribes who write checks and money drafts, and others."[87]

The Fatimid sponsorship of savants and encouragement of education becomes a beacon for the educational destiny of the contemporary nation state. Presently about 50 percent of Egypt's adult population is illiterate. The education system from elementary to the university level caters to twelve million students with "incredible shortness of resources." In the poorer sections especially, the meager resources tend to compromise the quality of education received by students. Private tutoring has been on the rise with official attempts to discourage the trend.[88] A few years ago students were made to skip a grade, but this caused a problem as seventeen-year-olds became ready for university. Therefore, some consideration was given to adding the deleted year so that the age, once again, was raised to eighteen. Changes were also made in the peer review formulations for promotion of university teachers and in the admintration and requirements of secondary school exam.[89]

There were twelve universities in 1992, inclusive of Al-Azhar. Al-Azhar University has its own primary, preparatory, and secondary school institutions to educate students who intended to enroll there. The Shaikh of Al-Azhar holds a very prestigious position vis-à-vis serious intellectual decisions for the entire Muslim world. The Al-Azhar was originally instituted as a facility where diversity of opinion would be welcomed and where intellectual decisions and resolutions to problems have traditionally been explored. However, increasingly the Sheikhs appear to be mired in hasty decisions and in proclamations that appear to be reactionary. In 1995, for instance, the Shaikh declared female circumcision to be valid because al-Shafi'i had declared it valid several centuries ago. A scholarly, scientific, opinion was not presented based on current medical information nor was the opinion of other schools of Islamic thought taken into consideration. This cultural practice never received official sanction by the Fatimids. How would the Fatimid sages of Al-Azhar addressed the issue in contemporary terms, given the current facts available regarding human biology?

In another instance, the Grand Mufti of Egypt, Sheikh Mohammed Sayed Tantawi, and the Shaikhs of Al-Azhar have been involved in a public dispute regarding the issue of organ transplantation. While Tantawi sanctioned the transplantation of organs from brain-dead patients, thereby accepting clinical death as being dead, the Al-Azhar position is in disagreement to this opinion. This poses a problem, because frequently patients are artificially kept alive by various devices until their organs have been removed. In the case of kidney transplant, the Tantawi ruling was considered significant as the organ shrivels up very fast without blood and becomes useless for transplantation.[90] Must the Sheikhs at Al-Azhar as well as the other jurists take it upon themselves to be educated in biological and relevant natural sciences and technological know-how, so that *fiqh*, Islamic jurisprudence, may be better served with decisions that are suitable to the human condition?

Again, what was the ideal of education for the Fatimids? Would they have mandated scientific training for the religious jurists so that informed decisions could be made by them? Had they been ruling today, would they have mandated compulsory primary and secondary education and ensured that every Egyptian or at least every youngster in Cairo is educated as we live in the twenty-first century? As the patrons of avant guard education a thousand years ago, how would they have fulfilled today's educational needs? How would they have stipulated the educational requirements of the jurists as well as the students? What would they have formulated to ensure that the nations educational institutions gained global academic prestige?

Most industrialized nation states provide basic education to its citizenry up to age 18, and it is very unlikely that the Fatimid administrators, if ruling today, would not have done likewise and perchance even gone beyond. Their interest in the development and nurturing of the human intellect is evident from their patronage of scholars and academic institutions. Presently, in Egypt and hence Cairo as well, free compulsory education is up to the primary level (age six), thereafter secondary and technical education is free,[91] though not mandatory. Thus the basic literacy level in the modern nation is as yet very low. However, evidently the traditional preoccupation with books and learning continues to persist. A few decades ago, the scholar cum traveler Aldridge observed: "The old city is full of Arabic book shops, because in its darkest trashiest days Cairo published a lot. These older Arabic book shops have a special smell and feeling about them which is not lik e a European book shop. They are dry and a little dusty and have a smell of the desert in them." He further reflects: "What is so revealing about an Arabic book shop now is the kind of titles it has on its shelves. Almost every book written now, and the number is becoming quite formidable, is worrying about Egypt's future."[92]

In recent years, another ray of light has emerged which would have indeed made the Fatimids gratified—the introduction of modernized public libraries with the latest in computerized and audiovisual resources, on Cairo's map. The Mubarak public library, housed in a three-story villa on the west bank of the Nile in Giza, charges a nominal annual fee from regular patrons but one-day visitors are welcome. The use of the collection at the Great Cairo Library in the Zamalek area is gratis to the public.[93] However, it becomes necessary that these facilities be emulated by many more institutions in Cairo and in other parts of the country.

Environmental Concerns

In addition to conventional education, the protection of the environment is also an important concern for informed Egyptians. For this purpose the Egyptian government on July 24, 1995, created the Association of Enterprises for Environmental Conservation, which was mandated to work with various businesses to protect the environment. It includes representatives of several major companies and aimed to organize seminars so that industries may seek technology that would cause reduced levels of pollution. This is another initiative that the Fatimids would have cherished. However, as yet the potential of this organization is to be realized as an effective entity.

CONCLUSION

Separated by time and merged in space, Cairo is al-Qahira, the victorious, with a privileged legacy, a legacy which could be emulated from the year 1000 to transfer to the year 2000 and beyond. Is the citizenry willing to take on this challenge? As the Fatimid city provoked a sense of wonder with its urban utopia, would the city of Cairo take on the mandate of consistent idealistic rebuilding and become a global beacon for the next millennium? Not only is Cairo's daily mundane survival important, but the heritage of an exceptional past must become its great hope for the future—a heritage that ought to be sustained, nourished, and transferred to posterity.

There is certainly much expectation from a city which appears as the paradigm of the optimistic and sanguine transformation of urban landscape that beheld the turmoil of fortune for a thousand years—a city to survive and endure with esteem into the next millennium.

NOTES

1. Douglas Jehl, "Maddening, Fascinating Cairo." *The New York Times*, (Sunday) March 23, 1997, XX 14.

2. A typical visitor, Mini Sheraton, "The Savior of Cairo" *The New York Times Magazine. The Sophisticated Traveler*, Part 2/ March 5, 1995, 35–36, 62–65, records her favorite eating places and mentions that she has been visiting Cairo for thirty-five years.

3. The original walled city had a simple plan with squarish dimensions. 1,200 by 1,650 yards of space was enclosed by a wide wall with five or eight gates. Two principal gates were the Bab el-Zuweila on the south side (through which al-Mu'izz entered the city) and the Bab el-Futuh (the gate of succor) to the north. Inside the square enclosure each population group had its own enclosure.

4. According to some accounts this designation for the city was due to the ascendence of the planet Mars, the Martian or the victorious; the prevalent astrological sign at the time of the foundation ceremony. J. Abu Lughod, *Cairo: 1001 Years of the City Victorious*, 1971, 18–19.

5. Ref. Paula Sanders, *Ritual, Politics, and the City in Fatimid Cairo*, 1994, 52 ff. for the ways in which the older city of Fustat to the south was integrated as an extended component of the new al-Qahirah.

6. Gaston Wiet, *Cairo. City of Art and Commerce*, 1964, 73.

7. Afaf Lutfi al-Sayyid-Marsot, *Egypt in the reign of Muhammad Ali*, 1984. The author discusses at length the process by which an Albanian-Ottoman soldier came to become the virtual ruler of Egypt. The European, specifically French and British attempts to politically occupy Egypt and to commercially subjugate the economy.

The powers were also responsible in dismantling the nascent industrialization of the country, so that it be forced to remain an agricultural region that would supply raw materials to be processed in Europe. Muhammad Ali was also earnest in protecting the *fallah*, the peasants who tilled the land. They could make personal appeals to him if the proper channels did not grant them respite from injustice. He even stated: "Egypt has two sovereigns, Sultan Mahmud and the fallah," (110).

8. Abu-Lughod, *Cairo,* 103–107.

9. Ibid., 232–237.

10. The central palace was the place of origin for the processions led by the khalif on important occasions, Sanders, *Ritual, Politics, and the City in Fatimid Cairo,* 50–51.

11. Wiet, *Cairo,* 46.

12. *Naser-e Khosraw's Book of Travels (Safarnama)*, Trans. W. M. Thackston, Jr., 62–63.

13. There is an interesting picture of the roof-top tenements in *The New York Times Magazine,* August 23, 1992, sec. 6, 34–35.

14. Andrew Hammond, "It's better than Shobra, say roof dwellers. There's room at the top," *Middle East Times,* 6–12, 1995, 8.

15. "Rare Quake Shatters Cairo" in *National Geographic,* April 1993, 68. The epicenter for the quake ten miles south of Cairo also damaged several historic masjids.

16. Michael Korda, "The Nile in High Style" in *The New York Times*, (Sunday) February 25, 1996, XX13.

17. Abu-Lughud, *Cairo,* 65–68.

18. Ibid.

19. Hasan Fathy, in *Architecture for the Poor,* 1973, discusses his attempts at providing adequate housing for especially the rural population constructed with native materials and skilled builders and workers. Many of his ideas could be used for the housing shortage in the cities as well. Moreover, with suitable opportunites and amenities in the rural areas, the flow of people to the urban centers would be controlled.

20. Cathy Powers, "Creating spaces fit to love in," *The Middle East Times,* August 13–19, 1995, 13.

21. Ibid.

22. Peter Theroux, "Cairo—Clamorous Heart of Egypt," *National Geographic,* April 1993: 55, 66–67.

23. *Middle East Times,* June 11–17, 1995, 1, 14.

24. Ibid., April 23–29, 1995, 6.

25. Ibid., June 11–17, 1995, 1,14; see also November 20–26, 1994, 1, 16.

26. Aldridge, *Cairo,* 282.

27. Ibid., 284.

28. *Safernama* 55.

29. For a quick overview of the morass of traffic in Cairo, especially the use of donkey carts, see, Doughlas Jehl, "Cairo Has Trucks, but Donkey-Work Goes to, Well, Donkeys" in *The New York Times* International, Sunday, August 11, 1996, 10.

30. Yasmine Abou El Kher, "Shameless erosion of the old world" in the *Middle East Times,* April 30–May 6, 1995, 13, presents this deplorable state of affairs. Barry Iverson, *Comparative Views of Egypt: Cariro One Hundred Years Later,* 1994, presents nineteenth-century photographs of Cairo besides contemporary views of the same sites. In many cases the change is for the worse. For instance on the Al-Ashraf Khalil Street in the

1870s was the location of a "magnificent mausoleum" now is the site of an "ugly apartment block" and an ice cream distribution outlet.

31. Despite governmental regulations, Cairo's historic Khan Al Khalili is a casualty of this intense "modernization" process. See Fariba Nawa, "Modern commerce swallows antique bazaar," *Middle East Times*, January 1–7, 1995, 12.

32. Steve Negus, *Middle East Times*, November 13–19, 1994, 2.

33. Sanders, *Ritual, Politics, and the City in Fatimid Cairo*, 99.

34. *Middle East Times*, December 11–17, 1994, 3.

35. Steve Negus, "Government and Traders blamed for food crises," in *Middle East Times*, December 25–31, 1994, 1. "The sugar crises is an attempt to overthrow the supply minister," Mufid Fawzi, editor of the cultural magazine *Sabah al Kheir* wrote in his weekly column of December 15. Meanwhile, the semiofficial economic digest *Al-Ahram Iqtisadi* depicted a chess piece in Guweili's likeness surrounded by a squad of turbaned, mustachioed merchants, posing the question: "Have the traders put the supply minister in check?" Officials from the Prime Minister Atif Sidki down have lashed out at "corrupt, greedy traders" taking advantage of market fluctuations to drive up prices.

36. *Safernama*, 42.

37. Ibid., 54.

38. Ibid. 56.

39. Peter Theroux, "The Imperiled Nile Delta" *National Geographic*, January 1977, 2–35.

40. Ward Pincus, "Sands of Salvation," *AUC Today (Magazine of the American University in Cairo)*, winter 1996, 19–21.

41. *Safernama*, 57.

42. Ibid., 55.

43. David Butler, in *Cambridge Encyclopedia of the Middle-East and North Africa*, ed. Mostyn T., et al, 1988, 324.

44. Hunter, B., *The Statesman's Year Book*, 132d ed. New York, NY: St. Martin's Press. 1995-1996, 506.

45. The *gam'iyya* has also been mentioned by Jehan Sadat in *A Woman of Egypt*, New York, Pocket Books (Simon and Shuster, Inc.), 1987, 186, 201–209.

46. *Middle East Times*, September 24–30, 1995, 14.

47. *Safernama*, 45.

48. *Islamic Roots of Capitalism: Egypt, 1760–1840*, 1979, 11–33, 23, 32–34, 178–179.

49. An overview of the informal economy and the growth of nongovernmental organizations is provided by Diane Singerman, *Avenues of Participation: Family, Politics, and Networks in Urban Quarters of Cairo*, 1995; though the issue is discussed here as a feature of society that has an enduring context, in *A* Woman of Egypt, Jehan Sadat has mentioned it as something that changed with time during the presidency of her husband, 141–144.

50. *Sfernama*, 51.

51. Ibid., 57.

52. *New York Times*, January 23, 1992, 1.

53. *Middle East Times*, April 23–29, 1995, 6.

54. Ibid., March 5–11, 1995, 12.

55. Ibid., December 18–24, 1994, 6.

56. Dalia Salaheldin, "Elderly women abandoned as Egypt's traditional family values decline," *Middle East Times* , July 9–15, 1995, 3.

57. Ibid.

58. *Safernama,* 56. He also noted regarding the populous port city of Tennis with "good bazaars" and two masjids, which was famous for its production of fine textile and iron tools, that daily a thousand dinars were remitted to the central treasury via the tax collector. "Nothing is taken from anyone by force. The full price is paid for all the linen and *buqalamun* woven for the sultan, so that the people work willingly—not as in some other countries, where the artisans ar e forced to labor for the vizier and sultan!" (.39–40).

59. *Safernama,* 55.

60. Ibid., 58.

61. Sanders, *Ritual, Politics, and the City in Fatimid Cairo,* 60.

62. Farhat J. Ziadeh, *Lawyers, the Rule of Law and Liberalism in Modern Egypt,* 1968, 14–16, 24–25. The solution of the transference of the shari'ah (Islamic-religious) and millah (community) courts to the national courts was not complete. In dealing with personal status issues, national courts continued in the application of the shari'ah for Muslims and the various denominational laws for non-Muslims (ref. 115).

63. Several issues of the *Middle East Times* covered the story as it reached a crisis point, reference: June 25, July 1, 1995; July 2–8, 1995, 3; July 16–22, 1995; August 13–19, 1995, 12. The government is moving to remove the legal loophole that allowed the Cairo appeals court to institute the divorce. Also, in response to the ruling, more than one hundred intellectuals joined to formulate a Committee for the Freedom of Belief and Expression. Under its aegis, over a thousand people signed a statement condemning the decision of the court, and a new magazine *Huriyya* (Freedom) appeared in August–September 1955.

64. *Middle East Times,* July 30, August 5, 1995, 3. That this charge of apostasy should occur is indicative of the strong hold of tradition bound legal jurisdiction. In 1926, Taha Husayn published *Fi al-Shi'r al-Jahili* (*On pre-Islamic Poetry*) for which he was removed from his post as dean and professor in Egyptian University (now Cairo University). The charges had been instituted by the rector of Al-Azhar and other judges. Ref. Ziadeh, *Lawyers, the Rule of Law and Liberalism in Modern Egypt,* 1968, 96–97. In 1980, Anwar Sadat strenuously attempted to curb the radical groups in the society, both Muslim and Coptic, as discussed by J. Sadat in *A Woman of Egypt,* 348–349.

65. *Middle East Times,* July 9–15, 9.

66. Shi'as believe 'Ali b. Abi Talib to be the first Imam, and he is accepted as the fourth caliph by Sunnis.

67. Yaacov Lev, "The Fatimid Princess Sitt al-Mulk," in *Journal of Semitic Studies* 32 (2) 319–328. Later after Nizar, the Fatimid heir to al-Mustansir, had been denied his dominion by the poweful minister al-Afdal who instead placed al-Musta'li on the throne, a crisis arose with the succession to the latters grandson al Tayyib. Queen Sayyidah al-Hurrah Arwa was instrumental in championing the Tayyibi cause in Yemen. The essential Fatimid notions of gender equality had enabled her to assume this influential religio-political position. See, Leila al-Imad, "Women and Religion in the Fatimid Caliphate: The Case of al-Sayyidah al-Hurrah, Queen of Yemen," *Intellectual Studies on Islam: Essays Written in Honor of Martin B. Dickson,* ed. Michael M. Mazzaoui and Vera B. Moreen, 1990.

68. *Middle East Times,* July 30–August 5, 1995, 9.

69. Ref. Margot Badran, *Feminists, Islam and Nation,* 1966, traces women's

involvement in the Egyptian political arena since the 1890s.

70. *Middle East Times*, July 30–August 5, 1995, 13.

71. Sadat, 364, 464–465.

72. Cited by Sanders, *Ritual, Politics, and the City in Fatimid Cairo*, 166, n. 153. Also reference Rhuvon Guest, ed., *The Governors and Judges of Egypt*, 610—612.

73. Sanders, *Ritual, Politics, and the City in Fatimid Cairo*, 57.

74. *Safernama*, 58.

75. Ibid., 62.

76. Sanders, *Ritual, Politics, and the City in Fatimid Cairo*, 63.

77. S. D. Goiten, "Cairo: An Islamic City in the Light of the Geniza Documents," in *Middle Eastern Cities*, ed. Ira Lapidus, 1969, 80–96; also "Formal Friendship in the Medieval Near East," *Proceedings of the American Philosophical Society*, 115 (6) (1971): 484–489.

78. Steve Negus, "Damanhour Welcomes Jews Despite Suit," *Middle East Times* September 17–23, 1995, 2.

79. *Middle East Times*, December 18–24, 1995, 6.

80. Andrew Hammond, "Gamaa go-between urges dialogue" *Middle East Times* March 5–11, 1995, 6.

81. *The Middle-East and North Africa*, 1995, 41st ed. Europa Publications, Ltd., 371.

82. Raymond William Baker, *Sadat and After: Struggle for Egypt's Political Soul*, 1990, a discussion of the Muslim Brotherhood in Chap. 8, "Return to the Future: The Muslim Brothers," 243–270.

83. Hamied Ansari, *Egypt, the Stalled Society*, 1986, Chap.10, "The Political Expediency of Religion," 211–230.

84. Douglas Jehl, "Killings Erode Cairo's Claim to 'Control' Militants," *The New York Times* (*International* section, Sunday) March 15, 1997.

85. Robert Irwin, "Islamic History from 1000 to 1500," in *The Cambridge Encyclopedia of the Middle East and North Africa*, ed. Trevor Mostyn and Albert Hourani, 1988, 63.

86. Bayard Dodge, *Al-Azhar: A Millennium of Muslim Learning*, 1974, 156-157.

87. *Safernama*, 82-83, there seems to be some confusion in his narrative as he refers to apparently the Ibn Tulun masjid when citiing it as the Bab al-Jawine masjid.

88. *Middle East Times*, April 16–22, 1995, 2.

89. Andrew Hammond, "Through the Din of Political Fraticide and More Students Than Ever Before, Can Anyone Hear the School Bell? Chaos and Crises Plague Egypt's Educational System," *Middle East Times*, April 9–15, 6.

90. Andrew Hammond, "Transplants Spark Religious Dispute," *Middle East Times*, August 20–26, 1995, 2. On other occasions also the standoff between the two authorities has been evident. Many would regared this disagreement as vital to the maintenance of sound judgments and the fostering of diverse opinions in order to have a balanced perspective. Reference, Yasime Abu El Kheir, "The Great Fatwa Fight: Tantawi versus Gad Al Haq," *Middle East Times*, November 13–19, 1994, 6.

91. *The Statesman's Yearbook*, 506.

92. Aldridge, *Cairo*, 324.

93. *Middle East Times*, April 23–29, 12.

SELECTED BIBLIOGRAPHY

Abu-Lughod, J. *Cairo. 1001 Years of the City Victorious.* Princeton, NJ: Princeton University Press, 1971.

_____. *A Tale of Two Cities: The Origins of Modern Cairo*, Comparative Studies in Society and History, (July 1965), 429-457.

Aldridge, James. *Cairo.* Boston: Little Brown and Company, 1969.

Ansari, Hamied, *Egypt, The Stalled Society.* New York: State University of New York Press, 1986.

Assaad, Sadik A. *The Reign of al-Hakim bi Amr Allah (386/996-411/1021): A Political Study.* Beirut: Arab Institute for Research, 1974.

Badran, Margot. *Feminists, Islam and Nation: Gender and the Making of Modern Egypt.* Princeton, NJ: Princeton University Press, 1995.

Baker, Raymond William. *Sadat and After: Struggle for Egypt's Political Soul.* Cambridge, MA: Harvard University Press, 1990.

Berque, Jacques. *Egypt: Imperialism and Revolution.* New York: Praeger Publishers, 1972.

Beshir, B. J. "Fatimid Military Organization." *Der Islam* 55 (1978): 37-56.

Bloom, J. M. "Meaning in Early Fatimid Architecture: Islamic Art in North Africa and Egypt in the Fourth Century, A.H. (Tenth Century *A.D.*)" Ph.D. dissertation, Harvard, 1980.

_____. "The Mosque of al-Hakim in Cairo," *Muqarnas* 1 (1982): 15–36.

_____. "Mosque of the Qarafa in Cairo," *Muqarnas* 4 (1987).

Bosworth, C. E. "The Protected Peoples (Christians and Jews) in Medieval Egypt and Syria," *Bulletin of The John Rylands University Bibliography* 62 (1979): 22.

Butler, D. *Cambridge Encyclopedia of the Middle-East and North Africa.* Cambridge, England: Cambridge University Press, 1988.

Cohen, Mark R. *Jewish Self-Government in Medieval Egypt. The Origins of the Office of Head of the Jews, ca. 1065-1126.* Princeton, NJ: Princeton University Press, 1986.

Cohen, Mark R. and Somekh, S. "In the Court of Ya'qub ibn Killis," *Jewish Quarterly Review* 80 (1990): 283–314.

Colloque international sur l'histoire du Caire. Cairo, 1972.

Crabbs, Jack A., Jr. *The Writing of History in Nineteenth-Century Egypt. A Study in National Transformation.* Detroit, Michigan: Wayne State University Press, 1984.

Creswell, K. A. C. *The Muslim Architecture of Egypt: Ikhshids and Fatimids.* Oxford: Clarendon Press, 1952.

Daftary, Farhad. *The Isma`ilis: Their History and Doctrines*, Cambridge, England: Cambridge University Press, 1990.

Dodge, Bayard. *Al-Azhar: A Millenium of Muslim Learning.* Washington, DC: The Middle East Institute, 1974.

Ehrenkreutz, A. S. "Extracts from the Technical Manual on the Ayyubid Mint in Cairo," *Bulletin of the School of Oriental and African Studies* 15 (1953): 423–27.

_____. Contributions to the Knowlege of the Fiscal Administration of Egypt in the Middle Ages," *Bulletin of the School of Oriental and African Studies* 16 (1954): 502-14.

_____. "The Crisis of Dinar in the Egypt of Saladin," *Journal of the American Oriental Society* 71 (1956): 178–84.

_____. "Arabic *Dinars* Struck by the Crusades: A Case of Ignorance or of Economic

Subversion," *Journal of the Economic and Social History of the Orient* 7 (1964): 167–182.

Encyclopedia of Islam, 2 ed. London: Luzac, 1960. See articles on Dar al-Hikma, Fatimids, Fatimid Art, Fustat, Ismailiyya, Kahira.

Fathy, Hassan. *Architecture for the Poor. An Experiment in Rural Egypt.* Chicago: University of Chicago Press, 1973.

Fischel, Walter J. *Jews in the Economic and Political Life of Medieval Islam.* London, 1937.

Fyzee, Asaf A. A. "Qadi an-Nu'man, the Fatimid Jurist and Author," *Journal of the Royal Asiatic Society* (1934): 1–32.

_____. "The Study of the Literature of the Fatimid Da'wa," in *Arabic and Islamic Studies in Honor of Hamilton A. R. Gibb*, ed. G. Makdisi. Cambridge, MA: Harvard University Press, 1965, 232–249.

Gacek, Adam. *Catalog of Arabic Manuscripts in the Library of the Institute of Ismaili Studies.* (1986): 110.

Gershoni, Israel and Jankowski, James P. *Egypt, Islam and the Arabs: The Search for Egyptian Nationhood, 1900-1930*, New York and Oxford: Oxford University Press, 1968.

Goitein, S. D. *A Mediterranean Society: The Jewish Communities of the Arab World as Portrayed in the Documents of the Cairo Geniza* (5 vols.). Berkeley and Los Angeles: 1967-88.

Grabar, Oleg. "Fatimid Art, Precursor or Culmination," in *Ismaili Contributions to Islamic Culture*, ed. Seyyed Hossein Nasr. Tehran, Iran: Imperial Iranian Academy of Philosophy, 1977.

Gran, Peter. *Islamic Roots of Capitalism: Egypt, 1760–1840.* Austin and London: State University of Texas Press, 1979.

Guest, Rhuvon, ed. *The Governors and Judges of Egypt.* London: E. J. Brill, 1912.

Hamarneh, Sami K. "Medicine and Pharmacy under the Fatimids," in *Isma'ili Contributions to Islamic Culture*, ed. Seyyed Hossein Nasr. Tehran, Iran: Imperial Iranian Academy of Philosophy, 1977.

Hamdani, Abbas. "Evolution of the Organizational Structure of the Fatimi Da'wah." *Arabian Studies* 3 (1976): 85–114.

Haswell, C.J.R. "Cairo, Origin and Development. Some Notes on the Influence of the River Nile and its Changes." *Bulletin de la Societe Royale de Geographie d'Egypte* 11 (3 and 4) (December 1922): 171–176.

Ivanow, W. *Ismaili Tradition Concerning the Rise of the Fatimids.* Bombay, 1942.

_____. "The Organization of the Fatimid Propaganda." *Journal of the Bombay Branch of the Royal Asiatic Society*, 15 (1939): 1-35.

Jehl, Douglas, "Cairo Has Trucks, but Donkey-Work Goes to, Well, Donkeys." International *New York Times* Sunday, August 11, 1996, 10.

_____. "Maddening, Fascinating Cairo" *New York Times*, March 23, 1997.

Kay, H. C. "Al-Kahira and Its Gates," *Journal of the Royal Asiatic Society* (1882): 229-45.

Kedourie, Elie, and Haim, Sylvia G. eds. *Modern Egypt. Studies in Politics and Society.* Totowa, NJ: F. Cass, 1980.

Korda, Michael. "The Nile in High Style." *New York Times*, February 25, 1996, XX, 13–14.

Lane-Poole, Stanley. *The Story of Cairo*, London: J. M. Dent & Co., 1906.

_____. *A History of Egypt in the Middle Ages.* London, England, 1925.

Lev, Yaacov. "The Fatimid Princess Sitt al-Mulk," *Journal of Semitic Studies*, 32, 2 (Autumn 1987): 319-328.

Mahfouz, Nagib. *Cairo Trilogy*. Cairo, 1952.

_____. *Children of the Alley, Cairo*, 1959.

_____. *Middle East Times*, Cairo.

Mostyn, Trevor and Hourani, Albert, Eds. *The Cambridge Encyclopedia of the Middle East and North Africa*. Cambridge, 1988.

Nanji, Azim. "Between Metaphor and Context: The Nature of the Fatimid Ismaili Discourse on Justice and Injustice," *Arabica*, 37 (1990): 234–239.

Nasir-i Khusraw. *Naser-e Khosraw's Book of Travels (Safernamah)*, translated with an introduction and annotation, W. M. Thackston, Jr. New York: Bibliotheca Persica, 1986.

Nasr, S. H. *Isma`ili Contributions to Islamic Culture*. Tehran, Iran: Imperial Iranian Academy of Philosophy, 1977.

Pincus, Ward. "Sands of Salvation," *AUC Today (Magazine of the American University in Cairo)* (Winter 1996): 19–21.

Poonawala, Ismail. *Biobibliography of Ismaili Literature*. Malibu, CA, 1977.

"Rare Quake Shatters Cairo," *National Geographic* (April 1993): 68-69.

Sadat, Jehan. *A Woman of Egypt*. New York: Simon and Schuster, 1987.

Safran, Nadav. *Egypt in Search of Political Community*. Cambridge, MA: Harvard University Press, 1961.

Sanders, Paula. *Ritual, Politics, and the City in Fatimid Cairo*. New York: State University of New York Press, 1994.

al-Sayyid Marsot, Afaf Lutfi. *Egypt in the Reign of Muhammad Ali*. Cambridge: Cambridge University Press, 1984

Sheraton, Mimi. "The Savor of Cairo," *The New York Times Magazine*. March 5, 1995, 35–36, 61–65.

Shoshan, Boaz. "Fatimid Grain Policy and the Post of the Muhtasib," *International Journal of Middle East Studies* 13 (1981): 181–189.

_____. *Popular Culture in Medieval Cairo*. Cambridge: Cambridge University Press. 1993.

Singerman, Diane. *Avenues of Participation: Family, Politics, and Networks in Urban Quarters of Cairo*. 1995.

Staffa, Susan Jane. *Conquest and Fusion: The Social Evolution of Cairo A.D. 642–1850*. Leiden, Netherlands: E. J. Brill, 1977.

Statesman's Yearbook. 132d ed. 1995-1996.

Stern, S. M. *Fatimid Decrees: Original Documents from the Fatimid Chancery*. London, England, 1964.

_____. "Cairo as the Center of the Isma`ili Movement," *Studies in Early Isma`ilism*. Jerusalem: Leiden, 1983, 234-56.

_____. *Cities of the World: Cairo*. London: Phoenix House, 1965.

Stewart, Desmond Stirling. *Cairo, 5500 Years*. 1968.

_____. *Great Cairo: Mother of the World, Egypt*, The American University in Cairo Press. 1981.

Stillman, N. A. *The Jews of Arab Lands*. 1979.

_____. "Charity and Social Service in Medieval Islam," *Societas* 5 (1975): 105-115.

The Nile Still Flows. Directed by Mohammed Fadel, screenwriter Mahfouz Abdel Rahman, funded by Ministry of Information (didactic serial drama on Egypt's population problems). 1995.

Theroux, Peter. "Cairo—Clamourous Heart of Egypt," *National Geographic* (April 1993): 38–67.

_____. "The Imperiled Nile Delta," *National Geographic* (January 1977): 2–35.

Vatikiotis, P. J. *The History of Egypt.* Baltimore, MD: Johns Hopkins University Press, 1988.

_____. *The Fatimid Theory of State.* Lahore, Pakistan: Orientalia Publishers, 1957.

Watson, Andrew, "A Medieval Green Revolution: New Crops and Farming Techniques in the Early Islamic World," in A. L. Udovitch, ed., *The Islamic Middle East, 700– 1900. Studies in Economic and Social History,* Princeton, NJ: Darwin Press, 1981, 20-50.

Wiet, Gaston. *Cairo. City of Art and Commerce.* Norman, University of Oklahoma Press. 1964.

Williams, Caroline. "The Cult of 'Alid Saints in the Fatimid Monuments of Cairo," *Muqarnas* 1 (1983): 37–52; 3 (1985): 39–60.

_____. *Islamic Monuments in Cairo. A Practical Guide.* Cairo: The American University in Cairo Press, 1993.

Ziadeh, Farhat J. *Lawyers, the Rule of Law and Liberalism in Modern Egypt.* California: Stanford University. (1968).

9

Women, AIDS and the Female Condom: Preventing HIV in Southern Africa

Ida Susser

This chapter focuses on suggestions that have emerged from research in southern Africa—in Durban, Natal in 1992 and 1995 and in Namibia in 1996 and 1997— concerning the possibilities for women to negotiate safe sex in terms of AIDS.

In considering resources available to women in different political and economic circumstances, I analyze women's perceptions of the female condom. This provides one window for the unraveling of the complex interaction between economic independence, political mobilization, and women's ability to address sexual issues in public and private settings.

Women's access to political power and forms of mobilization have affected their knowledge of sexuality and the construction of femininity. This research challenges stereotypes of female sexuality as uniformly passive and static and demonstrates changes in women's ability to promote preventive methods in the face of the HIV epidemic.

In all societies the requirements of safe sex interfere with the role of women as bearers of children which in turn affects women's status and opportunities (Stein 1990). Thus, studies of HIV prevention and community mobilization are directly concerned with the politics of reproduction and the changing roles of women in development. We need to examine the access women have to sexual negotiation and the resources they can draw on to protect themselves in sexual interactions (Schoepf 1992; Farmer, Lindenbaum and Good 1993; Gupta and Weiss 1994; Susser and Kreniske 1997).

Women's views of their own sexuality and reproduction as well as their representation by others vary by class, cultural identity and local experience but also change over time (Stoler 1991; Martin 1987; Ginsburg and Rapp 1991; Gallagher and Laqueur 1987; Susser 1991). This work traces possible changes in concepts of femininity and female sexuality with respect to HIV prevention and, specifically, with respect to the development and distribution of methods women can use (see Elias et al., 1996). The chapter considers these issues in the following three areas in southern Africa: (1) In two sites in the emerging state of the new South Africa, an agricultural village out-side the city of Durban, in the KwaZulu (Zulu kingdom) section of Natal as well as a squatter settlement on the outskirts of Durban on the borders of Kwa Zulu; (2) in two sites in Northern Namibia, one in Ovamboland and the other in Rundu, along the Okavango River; (3) among the Ju'/hoansi people in the villages around Tsumkwe, on the Namibian side of the border.

In each of these settings the issue of HIV prevention and female sexuality were addressed in different ways. The data indicate variations in the way women perceive the issues of sexuality in relation to forms of political mobilization. Each case documents continuing struggles over the construction of gender and sexuality.

In 1992, in Natal I worked with Quaraisha Abdool Karim, Nkosazane Zuma, Eleanor Preston-Whyte, and Zena Stein under the sponsorship and connection of the African National Congress (ANC). Political leaders of the ANC provided us with access to community groups in Durban and an outlying village.

In 1995, Eleanor Preston-Whyte and I went back to the informal settlements outside Durban. We were unable to revisit the rural village of the 1992 visit because of the intensity of the political violence in the region at this time.

In the summers of 1996 and 1997, the anthropologist, Richard Lee, and I initiated a program to work with students and public health workers in Namibia to develop local social-cultural research around AIDS. As part of this research project, we traveled to northern Namibia and to the Kalahari and conducted informal interviews with men and women in the rural areas about their knowledge and perceptions of AIDS, and the possibilities for the negotiation of safe sex.

HIV/AIDS IN AFRICA

In 1996, it was estimated that 9.2 million people in sub-Saharan Africa were infected with HIV, and this constituted 63 percent of the people in the world who were estimated to be HIV positive. In sub-Saharan Africa, the virus is mostly spread through heterosexual contact, nowadays more among women than men, and is increasing most rapidly among younger people. The highest rate of infection for women is in the ages from 15 to 19 years and for men, ten years later (Mann and Tarantola 1996).

In 1995 in sub-Saharan Africa, five hundred thousand children were born HIV positive (Mann and Tarantola 1996). In Africa, a higher proportion of babies born to HIV-positive mothers develop AIDS than in the United States, and this has been associated with the prevalence of sexually transmitted diseases (STDs), breastfeeding, and other factors (Le Coeur and Lallemant 1996).

In terms of health care, some people have access to treatment for opportunistic diseases (not decreasing the virus but helping to treat pneumonia, malaria, skin infections, thrush and other diseases that follow the loss of immune functioning). Many drugs were not available or affordable for the general African population at the time of this research, although this is beginning to change. At the present moment, some pregnant mothers in clinical programs in southern Africa are beginning to receive drug treatments that have been shown to reduce the perinatal transmission of HIV.

The messages that have been developed in Southern Africa emphasize "one partner" "love faithfully." However, since many women who contract AIDS have had only one partner, this is not a very useful message for women. Since children contract HIV mostly from their mothers through perinatal transmission and breastfeeding, these messages have little relevance to them either. In fact, there is little available to help women and children from contracting HIV-AIDS and as mentioned above, in Africa, more women than men are HIV positive and the rate of seroconversion is higher.

A brief outline of what can be done in the public health sphere will demonstrate the ways in which anthropological research needs to be integrated with public health to develop effective approaches to prevention and treatment.

As a baseline, it is neccesary to reiterate the public health understanding that caregiving goes in tandem with prevention. As has been clearly articulated since early intervention programs in the African setting (Reid 1997; Schoepf 1992), educating and supporting people with AIDS and caregivers is a crucial step toward the organization of a community for treatment and prevention.

It has recently been established that up to 14 percent of babies born HIV positive in Africa actually contract AIDS through breast-feeding (Le Coeur and Lallemant, 1996). Since it is well known that breast-feeding saves babies from dying of many other infectious diseases, both through reducing the babies' reliance on contaminated water supplies, bottles, and expensive baby formulas, and through the transmission of the mother's immunities in breast milk, this figure raises controversial questions concerning public health policy. Only further research concerning specific social contexts can help states to address these new possibilities for prevention.

In short, appropriate and carefully designed messages about breast-feeding are more useful to women, many of whom are in fact monogamous, in preventing the spread of HIV both among women and their children, than any number of admonitions to "love faithfully" (Reid 1997).

In terms of the broader social context, wars, and social disasters causing population movements and family disintegration are heavily incriminated in the spread of AIDS (Bond, et al. 1997). In southern Africa, wars, internal violence and large scale labor migration are important parameters which have led Namibia and Botswana, the neighboring labor suppliers for South Africa, as well as areas marched over by both the South African army and the fighters for African independence, to be, among the areas with the highest rate of AIDS in the world.

There are two points that emerge dramatically from this research in southern Africa:

1. Under clear threat of the AIDS epidemic, seeing their neighbors die and knowing that they are not that different, not a promiscuous "other," women are demanding methods of prevention and willing to use them.
2. There are approaches which informed communities can develop collectively both to care for people with AIDS and to limit its further spread. We need to provide adequate resources for such mobilization to take place.

The data I present below is derived from interviews in several sites in southern Africa and demonstrates clearly that many women in both rural and urban areas are active, willing and ready to adopt methods which will protect them from the HIV virus. Such methods need to be made available.

The first area was a village about seventy miles outside Durban which was part of the area designated under control of the Zulu King (Kwazulu). The chief in control of this village was also a member of the ANC. The second area was a squatter (informal) settlement on the outskirts of Durban. This African settlement has only existed since the 1980s when the pass laws which restricted freedom of movement for Africans were abolished. In 1992, it was estimated that close to one million people lived in such informal settlements outside Durban.

Rural Village

The village was scattered over a series of hills, a three-hour commute by bus from Durban. Both men and women went to town for work. However, transportation was expensive and difficult, and the common pattern was for men to go to town for the week and return on weekends. Most women participated in a communal-gardening project three days a week when the irrigation was turned on. Although women earned money by selling fruit, vegetables and old clothes, and through child care and domestic work, many relied on contributions from men (Abdool Karim and Morar 1993). At the time when the initial field work was conducted, laundry and personal washing were done in the river at the bottom of the hot dusty hill upon which the mud and ash brick homes were built, and drinking water was carried up by women and children from the same source. Over 1991 to 1992 a public works project was instituted which introduced electricity and running water to the village.

Residents are represented at civic council meetings, and in 1992 all civic council members were men. All members of the tribal court were men and these were many of the same men who represented the village in ANC regional meetings. Although there were 120 organizations among the approximately ten thousand residents of Kwaximba, the women did not often speak publicly. In 1991, the women's branch of the ANC tried to recruit women ANC members to run for office in the village but were unsuccessful. The women were afraid to talk in front of the men.

Through the questionnaires and in public discussions outside the clinic, it became clear that AIDS was associated with witchcraft and attributed to "a disease a man contracts if he sleeps with another man's partner. In addition, at the meetings held by researchers outside the clinic, women scarcely spoke, and the few men on the periphery of the group of women actually attending the clinic, were much more vocal than the women themselves. Field researchers reported that in 1992 women were not expected to speak up in front of men in this rural community under the control of the Zulu king and hereditary chiefdoms.

A survey of two hundred households in the village indicated that the women did not know how to identify sexually transmitted diseases or any names of such diseases. In contrast, the men were very well informed.

It appeared difficult in this setting to involve women in meetings or for women to negotiate safe sex with men or even to talk about their own health issues.

Informal Settlement

The informal settlement north of Durban, consisted of about five thousand homes inhabited by an estimated thirty thousand people. In 1992, no sanitation; running water; or public services, such as garbage collection, roads, or lighting existed in the area. People walked and drove along narrow and precipitous winding dusty footpaths. As a result of the efforts of the women's community organization, seven faucets had been built in scattered locations around the settlement. People could collect water for use in their households from these faucets. Children had to travel to neighboring municipalities to attend school and educational levels were low. Most residents spoke Zulu and many spoke some English. Among this large population of disenfranchised a vibrant economy existed in the informal sector. Bricks were made in the settlement and houses were built. Women made candles, baskets and clothes, and sold them locally or in the markets in Durban.

Although the informal settlements lacked electricity, nearby townships were sources of information and television. It is important to note that people in the area were tied into international media through such networks as CNN. As a result of cable communications and television in general, people in the informal settlements were aware of HIV and other issues, and received international media interpretations of a wide variety of topics.

The researchers made contact with the community through a sewing cooperative organized by and for local women. As noted above, this cooperative had also worked to bring water to the community. They had begun to weave baskets for sale and were concerned with developing ways to tie into the informal economy.

In terms of discussion of sexuality and HIV infection, the women in this cooperative presented a contrasting picture to the women in the rural community of Kwaximba. In 1992, I observed a meeting where members of the research team discussed HIV with the local women. About fifty women and three or four men attended the event. Even before the meeting started the room was in an uproar as the local woman community organizer brought in copies of the ANC constitution translated into Zulu. Dr. Zuma spoke to the group in Zulu about the importance of HIV, and the need for women to protect themselves. Next a representative from the U.S. foundation which funded the research project spoke briefly in English, and then American researchers mentioned the development of the female condom.

At this meeting, the women were very outspoken in front of the men. Women in the audience stood up and argued with the men in the back of the room who claimed that the young girls hanging around the harbor were "asking for it [sex]." Women talked in public about the lack of economic alternatives which lead women to sell sex. One woman explained that when a person has spent the entire day in Durban unsuccessfully looking for work and returns exhausted to the settlement with no money, she might exchange sex for ten dollars to buy sugar for their children that night. The women did not see these situations as being restricted to a group of "sex workers" or "prostitutes" but rather talked about the sale of sex as one last option available to women whose families were in desperate need of money and food.

The women at the meeting were explicit about economic needs and said that the best method they could imagine for preventing HIV in the settlement was to provide work for women. They requested that the project consider funding a candle making factory. They pointed out that since there was no electricity in the settlement, this would be an extremely profitable concern in the informal economy.

When the women were asked if they would use the female condom, they became enthusiastic. They said that they would definitely use something like that, which a woman had control over. They asked when the female condom might be available and requested that the U.S. researchers provide them samples as soon as possible.

Thus, only a few miles removed from their previous existence in the rural areas, women's experiences and their perspectives on sexuality—as well as their willingness to speak in public—dramatically altered.

In 1995, Eleanor Preston-Whyte and I returned to the informal settlement with the community liaison person from the 1992 project. We found women at the meeting which the liaison person convened for us were well aware of the threat which HIV infection holds for them and their children. When asked who was most at risk, they immediately replied that it was women, and commented that this was because their partners had other women, and they, themselves, were dependant on men for support.

As before, they made the point that if they had jobs, they would be able to refuse sex to men who refused to use condoms. The point was also made without prompting that women should be able to avoid unprotected sex with a number of men. Poverty makes us "prostitutes" they said. The connection between sex, and, particularly sex with more than one partner and HIV infection, was reiterated again and again. So was the fact that condom use prevents infection.

While the women at the meeting indicated a knowledge of risk of HIV, and also of the role of male condoms in protection, when we asked if their partners were using male condoms, no woman claimed that they were. When we asked why not, one woman commented, "It is good to have women's groups to help us, but there is no group to support you when you are alone with your husband. . . ." Another woman then said "It might be better if we had a female condom," and this led immediately to an excited discussion of the topic.

The women asked to see a female condom, and when we returned a few days later, we brought a demonstration kit with us. The reaction was immediate and positive. About twenty-five women had collected in the community hall to meet us, and after the demonstration, they eagerly handled the condoms and jokingly practiced using them on the dildo provided by the liaison person. When we cautioned that men might reject their use, as they did the male condom, the women overrode our hesitation. "We can use it and teach other people to use it. It is better that you bring it quickly . . . and that it is free." This opened the way for a discussion once again of the problems which women face in the area—the lack of adequate housing and employment being paramount. One woman said, "In these small two roomed shacks the children can hear everything . . . maybe it will be difficult to talk about this new kind of condom. . . . What we need is better houses." Another noted, "It will be easy to use the female condom if you are working. You just say to your husband that you must not get pregnant or you loose the job. Even a woman can stay alone with her children if she has a job. So we need jobs." Still another commented, "If we have this new condom, we will get our men to use it. . . . It will help us a lot." Finally, a woman said, "We are mostly relying on our husbands because of unemployment. The only way of leaving them is employment. If we earn money, we have power. . . . If we can wear them, we will be free."

Female condoms, although available in some pharmacies in South Africa, are extremely expensive even for relatively wealthy middle-class women. The national AIDS program and the Ministry of Health intended to make them available free through clinic services. However, there was to be a delay of at least three months before such female condoms might become available. (Three years later, at the time of this writing, the program is still facing barriers to implementation). When we relayed this information to the women at the meeting they were indignant. "You must tell the minister [of health] to send us female condoms first. . . . We need them here, and we will show they can work," said one. Another said, "Tell the minister [of health] to bring the female condom quickly. . . . If it should have come before, we would have limited our families more easily."

We ended the meeting by writing a letter to the minister. The women signed their names in an exercise book and spoke into our tape recorder so that "she [the minister] can know that no lies are being told."

Namibia

Women in Namibia also demanded that the female condom be made available to them. The research in Namibia revealed, in some similar and some contrasting ways to the research in South Africa, the interactions between the historical and political situation of women and the strategies they were able to use in the negotiation of sexual issues.

As noted earlier, in 1996, Richard Lee and I visited the University of Namibia in Windhoek, Namibia, to work with Namibian students in social cultural research around HIV (funded by the Fogarty Foundation). Two social science students, a man and a woman from the Ovamba area, accompanied us to their home region, serving as guides, informants, and translators, and, by the end of the project, as interviewers and researchers.

In the Ovamba-speaking region, we interviewed hospital administrators, nurses and doctors, church leaders and counselors, and men and women in their homesteads in the communities along the road North. We visited the homestead of one student, and he introduced us to his mother, his aunt, brothers and sisters and neighbors in the farming area. His father and older brothers were away, working in a town about two days drive distant.

Most of the families in the area relied on the men's work in the towns. Particularly in Windhoek. They travelled seven hundred kilometers home in minibuses on Friday evenings, and they returned in the myriad minibuses and public buses for the drive back to Windhoek on Sunday morning, and this continued all day Sunday.

Families who owned homesteads cultivated the fields surrounding their homes. Men and women who lived in the shanty areas without land might find temporary work as laborers on the land, while the women might also sell homebrewed beer in the little huts which proliferated along the highway, especially at the major bus stops for the journey down to Windhoek.

We learned from hospital administrators that many elite members of the Namibian government and their staff had been cared for with AIDS, but that the government kept this information confidential. Nurses at the hospital said that community members did not believe in AIDS because illnesses were not given that name, and the doctors would say someone died of one of the opportunistic diseases, such as diarrhea or tuberculosis.

The head of the church in the area told us that people did not believe in AIDs because "no one has died of it." He claimed: "You'll never know if somebody died of AIDS, only maybe after somebody is buried it is a rumor," and he added, the church "can't ask what the sickness is, even for your own child. . . . They have codes for sicknesses, one will never find out what the person died of. . . . It is a heterosexual matter, and the church doesn't know how or what to do. . . . It is not discussed because there is not evidence that the person died of AIDS." Like the doctors and nurses, the pastor claimed that people did not talk about AIDS openly or admit to others that they had the disease, even when they might be dying from it.

The pastor also said that he was opposed to the distribution of condoms as that assumed that people did not follow religious rulings of chastity before marriage and monogamy within it. In his words: "Our church does not support the case of condoms to be used, especially by unmarried persons. They are based on the issue of woman and man—a condom, it's like you get rid of principle and breaking it and giving freedom for people to go around." He would not discuss AIDS with his congregation except in such terms of sin and chastity.

Although a progressive force for African freedom, and a strong supporter of the South West African Political Organization (SWAPO) in the war for African independence, the church in Namibia has developed constraining views of family norms which do not directly correspond with the lives of migrant workers, with a history of polygamous homesteads. Many of the Namibian ministers now, including the people we interviewed, have been trained in the United States, and reflect some of the fundamentalist moral trends currently strong among certain sectors of the U.S. population. In some ways, the church contributed to the silence and stigmatization of AIDS, such as in its opposition to the distribution of condoms. AIDS counselors at the hospital said they believed many religious leaders initially opposed the government's program for the distribution of condoms and made effective prevention difficult.

However, as the following cases demonstrate, such ideas were not always expressed by members of church congregations. In one homestead, close to the church grounds, in the midst of harvested fields that resembled desert sands because of the overgrazing in the whole densely populated region, we found women who knew of and talked openly about people with AIDS. Similarly, when we visited a devout church worker and her sister and children in another homestead several miles down the main highway, also surrounded by dusty dry fields with cattle grazing and the homesteads of relatives and friends, we found women concerned and knowledgable about the AIDS epidemic in their midst.

In the middle of a hot dusty day we were brought to the first homestead by our student who had gone to a religious school with one of the daughters. Inside the compound of mud shacks and corrugated iron shanties, we found a woman carrying a small boy and surrounded by many other little children. We began talking to the woman who greeted us, and she then called her sisters in who called their teenage daughters to enter into discussion with us. Although both our students were with us, which meant we were two men and two women, the women did not seem to feel any compunction about discussing topics of contraception or AIDS.

Women in this compound were very aware of the issue of AIDS and also knew people with AIDS. To quote one of the women: "People are very open that there is AIDS, and they talk about it. They are no more hiding it because they know people are getting it. They know people that have AIDS and they talk to them. People are taking care of AIDS victims—but the victim is bleeding and they did not take precautions."

One of the sisters took up the discussion outspokenly and said they were all concerned about AIDS: "Women are very open. They talk to each other about AIDS. . . . Yes, they acknowledge that it is possible they have it. They are very afraid."

They knew AIDS was transmitted sexually, and they wanted their husbands to use condoms but they had no way to insist on this: "It's different. There are some women who ask men to use condoms, but some women don't say it." Later one said, "A husband will not agree to use condoms with his wife. . . . He says he sleeps around but will use condoms outside, but she can't be sure." They said that they were worried that they would get AIDS and die.

Eventually, we showed the women the female condom, and they became animated and said it was what they needed: "We want the female condom today." One woman noted, "It is important that the semen will remain in the woman because men don't like to take the semen out." Another woman said, "You can bring it here."

The women asked where the female condom was available and discussed the expense at the local pharmacy. They were eager to use it and said that although they could not say anything to their husbands, they could use anything they chose. They were definite that it did not matter; that the men could see the female condom. If it was theirs, they had the right to use it: "A woman can make her own decision." Another woman said, "This will be protective from the woman's side." One insisted: "Go to the ministry [of Health] and tell them to order female condoms. . . . Maybe it's better if we have this report [that we said we were writing] and write them a letter."

We next interviewed men and women in the shanties along the edge of the road who said they knew people who had died of AIDS.

However, the next significant interview was with our student's mother and aunt. Since he thought his mother would be more comfortable talking with women, Richard and the male student went to interview a neighbor while the woman student and I stayed to talk with his mother and her sister. Both were women in their forties. They showed us around the homestead. The small buildings were made of mud with straw roofs and separated off by bamboo screens. Each son and daughter over a certain age had their own hut and the entire compound was surrounded by a bamboo wall. Outside the wall were dried out fields and cattle grazing. The student's mother showed us different kinds of beer she had brewed, alcoholic for adults, non-alcoholic for children, and the enclosed but roofless area where she and her sister cooked in huge iron pots over an open fire, using spoons and other instruments made from local material. Four little children dusty and dressed in rags played around our feet as we all sat down on the ground under the trees for the interviews.

However, lest this homestead sound like an unchanged traditional setting, note that the woman's son was a college student (the first), her husband had a civil service job (far away) and in the teenaged son's hut, next to his bed, was a pack of condoms. The mother worked as a liason for the church, helping to identify children with disabilities.

In addition, the University of Namibia student himself had run away as a teenager when the South African army occupied Namibia to join the South West African Political Organization (SWAPO) in Angola and only returned after Namibia had won its independence.

In this "traditional" compound in a rural area in the far north of Namibia, where water had to be fetched a mile away from a faucet along the highway, and most of the food and utensils were prepared from subsistence crops, we found extensive knowledge about AIDS. Both women talked about other people they had known who died of AIDS. A couple who lived across the highway had both recently died, and the wife had asked her neighbor to come visit her explicitly to tell her she had AIDS and to say that others should know.

The two women also told us about a member of their church congregation who had been in the hospital and written a letter to be read during Sunday services. He said he was dying of AIDS and he wanted people to know. He did not want to die in secret but to warn other people of the disease. The women told us that everyone thought that his girlfriend and her baby must have AIDS and that she had left the district and disappeared. They were also wondering whether her later boyfriend, who now had another girlfriend, might be infected.

As this example demonstrates, people were extremely aware of the possibility for heterosexual and perinatal transmission. Although this also sometimes led to stigmatization (which might explain why the girlfriend left the area) it was not through ignorance of the mode of transmission.

Devout respectable churchwomen were explicit that women had no say in an Ovamba bedroom. They could not ask a man to use a condom or comment on any other sexual issue in the bedroom. However, they were extremely enthusiastic about the female condom, saying that this was something women could use. It would be under their control. They said explicitly that they would not be inviting a beating as they would if they were to dare to ask a man to use a condom.

These two cases give a sense of the dynamism within the hierarchy of women and men's roles among the Ovamba. They open up areas for mobilization for care and prevention of HIV and demonstrate the significant agency, open-mindedness, concern, and knowledge to be found among women who might at first appear to be most constrained by church and family.

I will now briefly review a third situation which also suggests the significance of methods women can use in the southern African context.

In July 1997, Richard Lee and I returned to Namibia and Karen Brodkin joined us to interview people along the Okavango River, the Kavanga people, the second-largest northern population. At Rundu, a small town on the Angolan border, we met with health workers and non-governmental organization (NGO) workers and the head of the health district, (an extremely articulate and knowledgeable nurse trained by the community health movement in South Africa), who took us to talk with some women in a sewing cooperative.

The sewing factory, which incorporated about twenty women had been started at the suggestion of NGO workers and was now an active concern run by the women themselves. They worked on their sewing machines at the back of a large shop. Their products were displayed in the front of the store, with no division between the sewers and the customers. We walked into the store and started talking to the women at their sewing machines. Since it was an impromptu meeting, arising partly out of our request to be introduced informally to local women, we did not start talking about HIV/AIDS. We asked the women about their sewing and the materials they used. They asked us what we did and we told them we were concerned with AIDS. The women said they knew about HIV/AIDS. They had been told the modes of transmission by NGO workers. They seemed somewhat bored by the topic. At the end of the conversation I casually mentioned the female condom. Suddenly one of the women listening in a desultory way, turned around and said, "Oh! I've seen one of those in the drugstore here."

Another woman said, "Do you have one, can we see it?" I said I had not brought it with me (it was back at my room) I asked, "Would you use it?" They said, "Yes, yes , tell us about it." I started to talk about the female condom as one method that women could use, and several women left their sewing machines and moved closer to hear what we were saying. After about ten minutes, Karen and I had to go because Richard (who went to interview some-one about local agriculture) was expecting us. But we said we would try to come back and bring a sample with us.

We found Richard, told him we were going to spend the afternoon at the sewing cooperative, and drove back to the rooms for the demonstration materials. When we returned about an hour later, the women were waiting for us. They left their sewing machines, looked at the books and pictures, handed the female condom around and asked us to provide them. I said they would have to get their own government to provide them. They were too expensive for them to buy. I said it would only be possible if they mobilized collectively, as they had for the sewing cooperative, to make this a government priority. They were definite they could use them and they wanted them. The women in the sewing cooperative wanted to make a political demand for women's condoms—almost the identical reaction to the women in the Durban informal settlement who insisted on writing a letter to the minister of health.

Once again it became clear that, given resources, people would act to protect themselves, even if it meant changing sexual mores. Women in the sewing cooperative were familiar with AIDS. They had seen people die. They knew that they or their friends could easily be the next to die. With appropriate resources and support, they said they were ready to act.

When we visited the Ju'/hoansi of the Kalahari desert, we got a different response. Men and women knew about HIV/AIDS. They knew people who had died of the disease. However, the women had a different description of their sexual negotiations. They said "If he won't wear a condom, I won't have sex with him." The women, exhibiting the autonomy of women described by Eleanor Burke Leacock and Richard Lee (1982) said, "He can't control me. I will do what I want, and if he doesn't do what I want, I don't have to have sex."

Apparently, although they hardly hunt and gather anymore (they get food from the government), and although they have settled villages next to bore holes for water dug by the government in contrast to their historic nomadic wanderings in search of water, there seemed to be a dramatic cultural difference between the Ju'/hoansi and the Ovamba, Kavanga and Zulu speaking groups of the Bantu peoples, at least in terms of sexual negotiations. The Ju'/hoansi women had no interest in the female condom. They said they could not see that it had any advantage for them over the male condom.

Questions of cultural difference and historical transformations of the Ju'/hoansi provide an important contrast with our other findings. The differences highlight the significance of the historic moment, as well as the variation in empowerment among women in situations where sexual negotiation is necessary. To conclude, a combination of anthropology and public health is essential in addressing HIV/AIDS in Africa, as well as elsewhere.

Southern Africa has some of the highest rates of HIV/AIDS in the world, but the situation is not hopeless. We have to examine the local context carefully and develop appropriate care and preventive approaches. The data presented suggest that where women mobilize around political issues, they are also more willing to speak out and possibly act concerning issues of sexuality and the negotiation of safe sex. Where women have mobilized around other issues, we found a wealth of grassroots interest and knowledge, willingness to change, and understanding of the necessity to try new methods of sexuality in the face of the HIV/AIDS epidemic.

However, we cannot expect an endless supply of vitality. Women and men at the grass roots level need resources and support. When they allot time to taking care of people and educating others about HIV/AIDS, they take it from other essential tasks. "Resources" does not mean pay alone. Resources mentioned by women we interviewed included training for local women as community health workers, and rotating visiting public health workers who would bring updated information and encouragement. One woman suggested that a goat to feed people at a public assembly where HIV/AIDS could be discussed would be a useful form of community support. Women asked for bicycles to assist in local transportation for community health educators. Local health workers emphasized the necessity for such supports. People are already involved in important community activities. To allow them to adequately care for people with HIV/AIDS and collectively mobilize for prevention, resources have to reach the grassroots.

The female condom is the only method to reduce the risk of HIV infection that is currently available for women to use. Women in the areas we visited, urban South Africa in 1992 and 1995, northern Namibia in 1996 and 1997 were clear and outspoken in their demands that they be given the chance to use this protective device. We promised in each case to make their needs and demands known to governments and other funding agencies. It is clear that women see the female condom as one of the few ways to negotiate safe sex. The male condom is currently more easily available at low or no cost. However, many women explained that they could not ask a man to use a male condom but that they themselves could use a female condom. It is crucial that the female condom be made free and accessible to such women, living at the forefront of the current epidemic, who are willing to use it.

This research demonstrates dramatically the current crisis in preventive strategies, as well as important directions for effective action. Women in the many regions are aware of the risks of AIDS to their families and communities and willing and ready to act when offered appropriate and accessible strategies.

We need to make available methods women can use to protect themselves from HIV/AIDS, such as the female condom and viricides, as soon as possible. We also need to support local communities with the resources to mobilize their own residents to care for people with HIV/AIDs, disseminate information, and distribute and reinforce the use of preventive methods for both women and men.

NOTE

A revised version of this article, which was originally part of the proceedings from the Africa 2000 conference, has been published in the *American Journal of Public Health* (July 2000).

REFERENCES

Abdool Karim, Q., Preston-Whyte, E., and Zuma, N. (1993). Prevention of HIV Infection for Women by Women in Natal, South Africa. Durban: Research Institute for Diseases in a Tropical Environment. Preliminary Findings, International Center for Research on Women. Washington, DC: Women and AIDS Program.

Abdool Karim, Q. and Morar, N. (1993) *Women and AIDS in Natal Kwazulu: Determinants to the Adoption of HIV Protective Behavior.* Report for International Center for Research on Women. Washington, D.C: Women and AIDS Program.

Bond, G., Kreniske, J., Susser I., and Vincent, J. (Eds.) (1997). *AIDS in Africa and the Caribbean.* Boulder, CO: Westview Press.

Elias, C., Heise, L., and Golub, E. (1996). "Women-controlled HIV Prevention Methods." In Mann, Jonathan and Danial Tarantola, (Eds.), *AIDS in the World II.*

New York: Oxford University Press, 196–201.

Farmer, P., Lindenbaum, S., and Good, M. (1993). "Women, Poverty and AIDS: An Introduction." *Culture, Medicine and Psychiatry*, 387–397.

Gallagher, C. and Laqueur T. (Eds.) (1987). *The Making of the Modern Body.* Berkeley: University of California Press.

Ginsburg, F., and Rapp, R. (1991). "The Politics of Reproduction." *Annual Reviews in Anthropology*, 20, 311–344.

Gupta, G., and Weiss, E. (1993). "Women's Lives and Sex: Implications for AIDS Prevention." *Culture, Medicine and Psychiatry*, 17, 399–412.

Gupta, G., Weiss, E., and Whelan, D. (1996). "Women and AIDS: Building a   New HIV Prevention Strategy." In Mann, Jonathan and Daniel Tarantola (Eds.), *Aids in the World II.*. New York: Oxford University Press, 215–229.

Leacock, E., and Lee, R. (Eds.). (1982). *Politics and History in Band Societies.* Cambridge, England: Cambridge University Press.

Le Coeur, S. and Lallemant, M. (1996). "Breastfeeding and HIV/AIDS." In Mann, Jonathan and Daniel Tarantola (Eds.), *Aids in the World II.* New York: Oxford University Press, 273–278.

Lee, R. (1979). *The !Kung San: Men, Women and Work in a Foraging Society.* Cambridge, England: Cambridge University Press.

———. (1993). *The Dobe Ju/'hoansi.* New York: Harcourt Brace.

Mann, Jonathan and Daniel Tarantola (Eds.). (1996). *In Aids in the World II.* New York: Oxford University Press.

Martin, E. (1987). *The Woman in the Body.* Beacon Press: Boston.

Preston-Whyte, E., Susser, I., Abdool Karim, Q., and Zuma, N. "Bring Us the Female Condom: HIV Intervention, Gender and Political Empowerment in Two South African Communities." Unpublished manuscript.

Reid, E. (1997). "Placing Women at the Center of the Analysis." In G. Bond, J. Kreniske, I. Susser, and J. Vincent (Eds.), *AIDS in Africa and the Caribbbean.* Boulder, CO: Westview Press, 159–165.

———. (1992). "The Development Implications of the AIDS Epidemic in Africa." *AIDS in the World*, Mann, J. et al. (Eds.) Harvard University Press.

Schoepf, B. (1992). "Women at Risk: Case Studies from Zaire." In G. Herdt and S. Lindenbaum (Eds.), *The Time of AIDS: Social Analysis, Theory and Method.* Newbury Park, CA: Sage Publications, 259–286.

Shostak, M. (1981). *Nisa: The Life and Words of a !Kung Woman.* Cambridge, MA: Harvard University Press.

Stein, Z. (1990). "HIV Prevention: The Need for Methods Women Can Use." *American Journal of Public Health*, 80, 460–462.

Stoler, A. (1991) "Carnal Knowledge and Imperial Power: Gender, Race and Morality in Colonial Asia." In M. di Leonardo (Ed.), *Gender at the Crossroads of Knowledge.* Berkeley: University of California Press, 51–102.

Susser, I. (1991). "Women as Leaders: An Environmental Health Struggle in Rural Puerto Rico." In Rothstein, Frances and Blim, Michael (Eds.), *The Global Factory: Anthropological Perspectives.* Westport, CT: Bergin and Garvey, 206–220.

Susser, I., and Gonzalez, M., (1991). "Sex, Drugs and Videotape: The Prevention of AIDS in a New York City Shelter for Homeless Men." In Bolton, R. and Singer, M. (Eds.), *Rethinking AIDS Prevention.* Philadelphia, PA: Gordon and Breach Science Publishers, 169–184.

Susser, I. and Kreniske, J. (1997). "Community Organizing Around HIV Prevention in Rural Puerto Rico." In Bond, G., Kreniske, J., Susser , I.., Vincent, J., (Eds.), *AIDS in Africa and the Caribbean*. Boulder, CO: Westview Press.

Part II
Literature, Social Change and Culture

"The Monstrous Instrument"
by
Maina Kīnyattī

A pen
A powerful instrument
One learns soon how it terrifies
Those who fight truth

The other day they came
In my cell number eleven
With clubs and steel whips
Wrecked the place
Looking for this dangerous instrument—
The Pen
They found nothing
The prison boss said:

I must be kept clean
Away from this dangerous instrument
Because I am capable of causing
Irreparable damage
I am mad

After they had gone
I pulled the tiny dangerous instrument
From where I had hidden it
I looked at it awhile
And for
the first time in my life
Realized how powerful
How significant it is

April 2, 1988
Naivasha M. S. Prison

10

African Languages and Global Culture in the Twenty-first Century

Ngũgĩ wa Thiong'o

As we look ahead to the twenty-first century, we also look back on the twentieth century, remembering Du Bois's idea that the twentieth century would be the century of the color line, of race relations; this was prophetically true. One hopes in the twenty-first century to overcome that particular problem and bring our people together. But, in fact, if you look at what is happening and what might happen in the twenty-first century, it is clear that two movements are taking place. One is a movement that is global; a global economy is emerging and a global culture. Whether we like it or not, global culture will continue to emerge through the Internet, faxing, and satellite television.

With these images, there is bound to be a form of global culture, so one movement unites us toward nations and peoples coming together, but there will also be a countermovement. The global phenomenon is a huge phenomenon, and it is likely to be controlled by a number of centers: the Euro-American center with the United States at the center, the European center with Germany at the center, the southeast Asian center with Japan at the center, and so on. But that very phenomenon will probably create a countermovement of localization, a sense of looking for identity and a place in the global community. The question of what, in fact, will link people together becomes important. Is it the wealth of a few connecting a few across the global landscape or is it the poverty of the many linking people across the global landscape?

Traveling around the world, I have observed the terms of poverty; the figure of the beggar has become the connecting link among New York, Nairobi, Johannesburg, London, Paris, and other places, whether in the airport or in the street. The beggar now links the various capitals of the world, with the exception perhaps of a few places. It is important how we organize our economies and cultures to overcome that, making sure there is no beggary or begging in the world. To be linked by a sense of plenty is obviously a challenge for the twenty-first century.

When we talk about Africa, we are talking about the relationship between Africa and the rest of the world. Africa has been part of the emergence of the modern world, though often on a basis of inequality. If you consider the modern world to be emerging from any particular year, say 1492 or 1498, and you think of Columbus and Vasco de Gama, the Portuguese to the east and later other European powers on the entire coast of Africa, you can see that Africa has been an integral part of the modern world.

Although we cannot say that Africa has gained from the modern world, some of the megacenters have developed around North America, Europe, and Japan, and with Africa being divided, we find a situation where Africa continues to play the role of the poor person who always gives to the rich but never really gets anything back. Over the last four hundred years, the era that constitutes modernity for the West, Africa has seen her human beings enslaved, her natural resources looted and her labor power colonized and exploited in the most ruthless of ways.

One of the worst robberies is that of language. In the realm of culture, Africa has been robbed of languages in a most literal and figurative sense so that even today Africa is still defining itself in terms of anglophone, francophone, and lusaphone linguistic zones. In other words, what you see at the close of the twenty-first century is that Europe's virtual linguistic hegemony over Africa is nearly total. The colonization of the means of imagination by way of languages has meant, in a way, that Africa has been alienated from one of the greatest productions of the human mind, that is, languages themselves. Their imprisonment is what I have called the linguistic maximum security prisons of English, French, and Portuguese. Africa was made speechless, and its sons and daughters who should have come back to free the imprisoned tongues came back as prisoners themselves, caught in the capitals of Europe and Africa, holding a dialogue between themselves within the prison walls of their language acquisitions.

In Africa, in the old days when there was no electricity, we depended on fire, and fire was a very important link between the different communities. Fires were what defined neighborhoods. To be able to borrow fire from your neighbor when your fire was out was very important. Imagine a child who is sent by his or her parents to get fire from another house. They cannot cook or do things without the fire, but the child goes there and finds the fire is very warm, and the child sits there and warms himself or herself and forgets having been sent to get the fire and bring it back. But at least the child is there.

To put it in another context, you remember Plato's allegory of the cave. There is the possibility of one or two people coming from the cave, coming into contact with knowledge, with truth, if you like, but it is also their duty as guardians to come back to this particular cave. But you can imagine guardians who do not come back, or, when they come back, they beckon to those who they left behind in tongues that cannot be understood. In other words, they reflect designations in Joseph Conrad's basically racist narrative *Heart of Darkness*, contemptuously, but unfortunately true, what he called reformed Africans. In *Heart of Darkness* where Africa and Africans are seen as just a mass of darkness, the only speech given to the African character is articulated by the boy who announces the death of Kurtz. "Mr. Kurtz, He dead." It is this line that is quoted by one of the major voices of European modernism, T. S. Eliot. He found this particular quote interesting enough to use in his poem *The Wasteland*. One of the early indignities of these reformed Africans, that is those reformed in the linguistic factories of Europe, is their being Kurtz interpreters.

Imagine a peasant, a worker, or any other person for that matter accused of murder in a colonial court of law. His own life is at stake. The judge or magistrate, most likely a white person then, spoke English. The prosecutor spoke English. The defense lawyer, if any, spoke English. The poor peasant accused of murder was entirely dependent upon an interpreter. Fighting for his life, the poor peasant was denied the use of his language. He was like a foreigner in his own country. You can imagine the strain we all feel when we visit a foreign country and have to communicate through an interpreter. Here we are not talking about one or two visits by one or two people. We are talking about the majority of the people turned into foreigners in their own countries.

In the colonial context in most of Africa, Kenya in particular, Africans were divided into two categories: the specialist majority in terms of the language of power and a minority of general interpreters by virtue of their having been to schools and colleges and hence having been trained in English, French, or Portuguese. Here we can note the privileged position of the interpreter. He is in the same linguistic universe as the judge, the prosecutor and the defense lawyer. He can also hear the peasant in the dock. He may develop the illusion that just because he can hear the language of the peasant, he is one with him, that he is actually representing him as well. Again, we can note the position of the peasant or the one accused. He is not in the position to identify with his representation; he is alienated even from his own representation, whether that representation is sympathetic or not. In other words, colonialism as a process produced a class of interpreters, the go-betweens, those who might announce that Mr. Kurtz is dead, Mr. Kurtz is sick, Mr. Kurtz is about to die or Mr. Kurtz should go home, any variation, if you like, of anticolonial nationalism.

That was the colonial era. But the situation has not really changed, and it might be as we go toward the year 2000, the situation will not have changed dramatically. With independence, the interpreters spread out to fill in the vacant places of white judges, prosecutors, defense lawyers, and so on. The peasant, even when pleading the case for his own survival, that is, his economic, political, and cultural survival, is still being denied the use of his tongue to articulate his position and interpret it. He or she can only hear and be heard through the interpreter.

For instance, currently in Africa there is a lot of talk about democracy, but if you listen to that debate and the issues of human rights, they are always being discussed in English and French. The ordinary African person can only negotiate with power through an interpreter or through the process of interpretation. Thus, in Africa today the majority are still aliens in their own territory in the cultural realm. They are ruled by African aliens. Ordinary African persons have to negotiate their way through the marketplaces, through the roads, through the courts of law, through the administration, through this process of interpretation. It does not really matter how sympathetic the interpreter may be to the cause of those for whom he is interpreting. The point still remains the same; the majority negotiate for their space through interpreters.

Can we imagine what this really means for the majority. They are being denied by both the colonial and the postcolonial state their right to name their world. They are still suffering from the total colonization of that entire process and means of imagination. The best example of this at the level of representation, of course, is modern African literature, and since I am a participant in that process, I can talk honestly, or hopefully honestly, about it. I can talk without a sense of a "holier than thou" attitude although some of my critics have not always taken that as an expression of good faith. I have treated that problem in my book *Decolonizing the Mind*, so I do not want to dwell too much on that, but really it is a good example of what I am talking about. If you look at modern African literature in European languages, there has been literally a process of taking *from* African languages and giving to European languages, but you do not get the other process of taking from European languages, European cultures or other cultures of the world and giving to African languages. What has been produced by African languages has been the basis of identity in modern literature in European languages. But African languages are, in a sense, left without those minds to bring something back to those languages. In other words, just as the woking person in Africa produces gold from mines, coffee, and tea leaves, exports to the Western world, in the same way at the level of languages, he or she produces proverbs and songs, drawing upon those songs to create this other identity which is important. However, we do not experience the counter process where the minds produced by Africa roam through the world and get the best that has been thought in the world and bring that back to enrich African literatures and African languages in general.

As we look forward to the year 2000, one of the areas that needs important and urgent attention is the decolonization of that one most basic means of imagination and most basic means of naming the world, that is, languages. We have to insist on redefining our attitudes toward African languages. There is nothing so ridiculous in the world today as to hear about scholars in African history, literature, music, anthropology, politics, theory, and so on who do not know a single word in an African language. Have you ever heard of a professor of French who does not know a single word of French? Imagine an interview for a post—say in German philosophy or history at Hofstra University—and the candidate is asked by those in charge whether he or she knows the language of German, and the answer is "No, I do not know any German, but, nevertheless, I would like to be a professor of German." The interviewers are not likely to be very comfortable no matter how politely they might want to put it. They are likely to let you know that Hofstra is not really for you.

And yet, in fact, schools and colleges in Africa and abroad are peopled by experts, whether sympathetic to the African cause or not, whether progressive or not, who do not have to know African languages. I also want to emphasize that I am talking about the situation in Africa as well. Also, if you look at the United Nations and all its agencies, there is no requirement for an African language, although *all* the other continents are linguistically represented in the United Nations and Europe has the lions share of that situation.

In fact, apart from Arabic, there is no other African language in all of the agencies. Even on the international level, we are still in the days of the Kurtz type peasant of the colonial courtroom—the one that I mentioned before. If you look at the African diaspora, which came into being without our willing participation over the last four hundred years, we have seen Africans in the West lose their names completely. Therefore, identity as human beings is often seen in terms of James or Jones or any other naming system that identifies a person in terms of the Western system even though what the individual may be espousing is counter to that. Names are, in fact, part of a naming system. With the loss of languages, there will be a total loss of our entire naming system. This is what I am concerned about when looking towards the twenty-first century. Unless the trend is reversed, there will be no Africa in the future because Africa will become part of the English system, it will become part of the French system, and it will become part of the Spanish and Portuguese systems—in other words, that which is our identity which makes people say we are this or that. We Africans will be, if you like, willing slaves. We shall sort of go there willingly. In the past we resisted and fought back, but in the area of culture, we shall walk there. There will be no Africa; Africa will be a linguistic extension of Europe. This is why African languages have to fight back until they are no longer aliens in their own land. When I first wrote *Decolonizing the Mind*, some of my most ferocious attacks came from a number of my colleagues who thought I was betraying something. I do not know exactly what I was betraying by insisting on African languages, but then I went through a period of soul searching, and I have come back to the same position that African languages have to fight back—until they are no longer aliens in their own land. They should fight for their space in the world. They must first fight against the colonization of their space by the languages of Europe and, secondly, try to find their place in the global community of tomorrow.

To arrive at another language policy, I think three things are necessary. When I was in Ghana to give the Nkrumah, Du Bois, Padmore Memorial Lecture, I spoke very vehemently about this situation because I felt that those who were our ancestors had done the best they could at the time under those circumstances. I felt that if we were really living up to their memory, we would find a way of speaking to them, and to the people represented in languages that they could understand.

I tried in Ghana to outline a language policy for Africa. To come up with an adequate language policy we need three things. First, we have to get rid of the tyranny of monolingualism and it is not just in Africa. It is everywhere. There is an obsession with monolingualism as seen as a natural form of human intercourse. The Christian era has been for too long haunted by the image of the Tower of Babel. People see many languages as a sin and say, "No, we must have one language." I think it is necessary for Africa to accept the reality of multilingual societies. Of course, there was and there still is a need for an intracommunity language or languages for intraAfrican, diasporic, and inter-continental communication. There is no doubt about that but what would this mean? It would mean that at the national level triglossia or four languages at the minimum would prevail. There would be for every African child a primary language—probably the mother tongue. At the continental and diasporic level, there is a need for a language that would enable continental Africans and diasporic Africans to communicate at the base of their identity while retaining whatever languages they actually have.

Wole Soyinka once suggested Kiswahili as the language of Africa and the African diaspora, and I support that idea. But there is no reason why the choice could not be from among four or so languages that have emerged as the lingua francas of various regions in Africa. In the twenty-first century, English and French will still continue to dominate, and they will be useful tools for intraglobal communication. I am not talking about this as a means of realign-ment or rearrangement for the African child who has to take reality into account. What I am concerned with is that English and French will no longer be used as a primary instrument of our modern cultures.

The art of translation would be highlighted, and the implementation should not be seen on a short term basis where you press a button and there is an answer, but on a long term basis. I also argue that to help in the implementation of such policies, there would have to be rewards associated with the new policy. For instance, there would be no reason why in Africa, passing certain grades in education, getting promotions above certain grades in the civil service or in administration should not be linked to knowledge of African languages.

This will bring a lot of advantages in my view; a whole new area of culture would emerge that is entirely and primarily controlled by Africa. A new scholarly industry in publishing, translation, and interpretation would emerge, and it would also force the new technologies that are emerging to come to terms with the reality of African languages. There is an IBM PC advertisement that uses different languages, but, of course, not a single African language is represented. In other words, this technology, which touches on most languages in the world, does not address Africans talking about PCs in their own languages.

Starting from national and foreign bases, African languages would also have to fight for their space within the international community, particularly the United Nations and all its organs. Currently, all organs of the United Nations are dominated by European languages, and I feel that there should be a change. It should be a matter not only for Africans but for everybody. In matters of academia in Africa and abroad, I believe that qualification in any area or most areas of African scholarship should require a knowledge of an African language, and I was very impressed when I arrived at Hofstra and Professor Robert Leonard actually talked to me in public in Swahili. I said to myself that possibly Hofstra is mapping the way for the future and the liberation of the imagination of our own play in Africa.

I am concerned that eventually there should be dialogue between languages, dialogue between African Asian languages and European languages, but on the basis of equality. I am not talking about isolation; the main challenge is to African scholars and writers. To map out the way to the twenty-first century, we have to change the location of the view of the world to its creative seat among the people, that is, change to where the people are the center in the area of language, literature, and culture and hopefully also in the area of economy and the organization of political power.

11

Hybridity, Neouniversalist Cultural Theory, and the Comparative Study of Black Literatures

F. Odun Balogun

We are living in a momentous, if transistory, period as far as the study of world cultures is concerned. The written literatures by peoples of African descent have matured and gained international reputation with their writers in the last decade predominating in the list of the recipients of the most prestigious award in literature—the Nobel Prize. Eurocentricity is at last on the run and has recently been dealt a significant blow by the Charles Bernheimer Committee of the prestigious and standard-setting American Comparative Literature Association when the latter signaled its intention to make comparative literature truly universal in scope as well as in theoretical and critical practice. We are only too familiar with the notorious subversion of the true meaning of the word *universal* in Eurocentric discourse which had provoked the wrath of black scholars and writers in a spate of counterdiscourse publications nearly three decades ago. Wole Soyinka in *Myth, Literature and the African World* (1976) had among many of the book's wide-ranging project of redemptive poetics of culture, expressed dismay at the exclusion of non-European writing in the literary curricula of British universities. Houston Baker in *Blues, Ideology and Afro-American Literature* (1984) chastised the even more amazing omission of African American writing in official American literary scholarship. Achebe was so outraged that he recommended in the essay on colonialist criticism included in his *Morning, Yet on Creation Day* (1975) a temporary ban on the use of the word *universal* in the discussion of African literature until it was restored fully to its authentic meaning. The collective of black scholars who contributed to Addison Gayle Jr.'s *The Black Aesthetic* (1971) even went so far as to construct a black aesthetic theory to counter the prevailing Eurocentric aesthetic practice. In recent times, to promote multiculturalism and discredit resurgent white conservatism and racism that threaten its gains, black scholars have produced a new wave of publications, informed by modern discoveries in science, genetic biology especially, in which they have initiated a discourse that largely challenges old assumptions in the construction of individuals and cultural identities.

My focus here is on the interventions of four interrelated approaches of black intellectuals to multiculturalism as theorized in the following four representative books: Kwame Anthony Appiah's *In My Father's House: Africa in the Philosophy of Culture* (1992), Paul Gilroy's *The Black Atlantic: Modernity and Double Consciousness* (1993), Molefi Kete Asante's 1989 revised edition of *Afrocentricity,* and Ngũgĩ wa Thiong'o's *Moving the Centre: The Struggle for Cultural Freedoms* (1993). These are works whose complex interrelatedness I have consciously attempted to reflect by conflating their titles to create my own title. My objective is to interrogate the philosophies of the four selected approaches to multiculturalism so as to elucidate their implications for the textual analysis of African and African American literatures as separate entities, but more especially as comparable cultural phenomena as we approach and go beyond the year 2000.

THE INVENTION OF RACE AND THE
HYBRIDITY OF CULTURE

At the center of debate in the four books is the question of how to correctly define black identity with reference to race, ethnicity, nationality, class, gender, and culture, especially as the latter is manifested in language, music, philosophy, and religion. Also of crucial importance is the choice of the appropriate modes of black cultural, economic, and political relationship, cooperation, and development. Appiah submits that the concept of *race* as a mode of classification of people was developed in Europe in stages, with *Hellenistic environmentalism* and *Jewish convenants* as the earliest stages of a process that ultimately developed in nineteenth-century Europe into *racism*. While the Greek and Jewish concepts of identifying differences between people did not necessarily imply the inferiority or superiority of one set of human beings compared with others, *racism*, the later development, was unique in categorizing people of the white race as having heritable characteristics, which make them morally superior to non-whites (11–15). Thus, racism, Appiah submits, is a modern European invention (x, 13, 52) that has now been proved to have no objective foundation in modern biological or genetic sciences (35, 45) and whose sole purpose was exploitation: "The 'whites' invented the Negroes in order to dominate them" (62). Appiah emphatically insists that there is only "one race to which we all belong"—the human race (27).

The view that the biological concept of race is a nineteenth century European invention whose primary purpose was economic exploitation, promoted by the resultant formulation of racist aesthetic principles of beauty, is uniformly shared by Paul Gilroy (8–10, 97), Ngũgĩ wa Thiong'o (116–31), and Molefi Asante. What would surprise any objective scholar on reading the 1989 revised edition of *Afrocentricity* is how much of its basic conceptual assumptions the book shares with the works of Appiah and Gilroy, two of its author's staunchest critics. Molefi Asante, like Appiah and Gilroy, for instance, asserts that "the political concept 'race'" is "an obfuscation of power relations" that "has no biological or anthropological basis" (96).

A second area of conceptual agreement among the four scholars is in the assertion that race, being an artificial invention, cannot be considered a reliable criterion for determining the cultural identity of any people. Their unanimous opinion is that no single culture in the world today has retained a pristine essence that exclusively defines a people. On the contrary, all cultures have borrowed and have been borrowed from; thus, what each people have is essentially a hybrid culture. Affirming that contemporary culture is global, transnational (144) because culturally "we are all already contaminated by each other" (155), Appiah argues that any claim to a uniqueness of cultural identity by any people is as untenable as the illusion of race. Gilroy on his part says that "the syncretic complexity of black expressive cultures alone supplies powerful reasons for resisting the idea that an untouched, pristine Africanity resides inside these forms" (101). Ngũgî recognizes the limitations of negotiating black identity while situated within the reductionist confines of the polarities of race and color; hence, he initiates and consistently pursues his arguments throughout as an "unrepentant universalist" (xvii, 63). Ngũgî rejects the idea of a culture that lives in isolation or one that claims an untainted, pristine ethnic essence because, as he says, "all the dynamic cultures of the world have borrowed from other cultures in a process of mutual fertilization" (22). For Ngũgî, East Africa, and the whole of Africa all the more so, is a "kaleidoscope of colors, cultures, and contours of history" and the region's "cosmopolitan culture" is well reflected in its foods, clothes, music, and composition of the social clubs (161). The concept of cultural hybridity is also a tenet of Afrocentricity, and Asante sees it as exemplified, for instance, in the distinctive speech pattern of America's South which is the result of the union of African and European speech tones (66). Another illustration he cites is the traditional black church whose mode of worship he sees as reflecting a merging of African and European religious forms (75). Even the African American is a being whose blood is a mixture from various ethnic groups including English, Native Americans, Irish, Jewish, Chinese and Gypsy (27), and the Africanity of the African American is itself "a composite of many ancient people, Asante, Efik, Serere, Touculur, Mande, Wolof, Angola, Hausa, Ibo, Yoruba, Dahomean, etc." (67). At the same time, African Americans have created a culture which has a pervasive influence and whose impact "In the areas of clothing, fashions, hairstyles, and expressive behaviors in language . . . has become international, and can be found from Mexico to Japan" (68).

Thus, culture in the afrocentric understanding is not the manifestation of a once-and-for-all-time fixed racial essence; indeed, continual modernization is an immanent part of culture as the following citations show: "Tradition changes; it is not static" (84); "Afrocentricity seeks to modify even African traditions where necessary to meet the demands of modern society" (40); "what our ancestors discovered about herbs, human personality, music, and religion is found to be valid or invalid by afrologists" (61).

MULTICULTURALISM AND ITS DISTINCTIONS

Despite their broad agreements on the issues of race and culture, however, significant differences exist between the four black intellectuals in their methodological approaches to the analysis of cultural phenomena, their notions of what constitutes the black identity, their assessments of black intellectual history, and their perceptions of the future of the black people.

It would be correct to argue that the only distinction between Appiah, Gilroy, Ngũgî, and Asante resides in the difference in their approaches to cultural analysis because all other differences emanate from this central difference. The materials from which Appiah draws sustenance for his discourse belong to high culture—philosophy, literature, intellectual history, religion, art, and music—and his analysis is mostly abstract and distanced from the mundane realities of socioeconomic and political life of black people. Indeed, as the allusion in his book's title to Christ's imagery her's (God's) heavenly kingdom attests, Appiah's analytical methodology is fundamentally fashioned in religious idealism. This is not to deny that in his analysis Appiah has also stretched the symbolic meaning of God's heavenly kingdom (Christ's Father's House) to include this world in which we live. Although Gilroy has been rightly criticized for paying insufficient attention to economic and political questions which have bearing on his subject (Lipsitz 195–199, Williams 184); Gilroy nonetheless tends more than Appiah to show greater involvement with what he calls "the profane realities of black life amidst the debris of deindustrialization" and the "impure world of politics" (99, 102). Also Gilroy periodically reminds readers of the fact that black people today still predominantly live within "the belly of the multinational beast" (105) as victims of what he variously calls "racial capitalism" (37), "scientific racism" (44, 55), "populist racism" (86), and "racial terror" (56, 57). In fact, he draws evidence for his cultural discourse from the material of low culture—popular black music. Both Asante and Ngũgî though belonging to two different ideological persuasions—the former a cultural nationalist, the latter a socialist—adopt a common holistic approach in the selection of analytical materials. They patronize both low and high culture, and their analytical methodology is tooled by class consciousness in that they regard black people as belonging to the class of oppressed peoples. Ngũgî knows that any discussion of culture that is divorced from the economic and political realities that molded it risks reifying itself into mere academism, hence he rightly argues that "the cultural aspects [of society] cannot be seen in total isolation from the economic and political ones" (xv). From this position, Ngũgî carries out a relentlessly rigorous analysis of the nature, methods, and effects of contemporary racism which he identifies as the contemporary cultural and psychological weapon of exploitation by imperialist capitalism (122, 126).

Ngũgĩ elaborately demonstrates how imperialist powers, led by the United States, have so effectively combined the weapon of racism, deployed especially through the subtle medium of imaginative literature, modern communication, and neocolonialist education, with the weapons of economic, political, and psychological manipulation and the control of research, teaching, and publishing, to take over the lives of the people of the Third World in order to ensure their unresisted exploitation. Imperialists, Ngũgĩ believes, would stop at nothing including the use of sabotage, destabilization, assassination, military intervention, and entrenching local dictators so long as these weapons guarantee unhindered access for their multinational companies to exploit their victims who invariably are the impoverished, already overexploited people of the Third World. Ngũgĩ cites the example of his country Kenya where political and cultural repression through bans, arrests, imprisonments, intimidation, arranged accidents, unemployment, exile, and other vicious methods are the regular means of ensuring peace for the operation of the multinationals (88–95, 102). This is why Ngũgĩ, unlike Appiah, lays the blame for the collapse of Third World economies and governmental systems as well as the loss of freedom at the door step of imperialist nations.

Ngũgĩ believes that the only way to end this inhumaneness and restore true humanism, true universalism, is to "move the centre," not in the hegemonic sense of "substituting one centre for the other" (4) but rather by recognizing a plurality of centers and the equality of all people and all cultures:

While there is a need for cultures to reach out to one another and borrow from one another this has to be on the basis of equality and mutual respect. The call for the Western-based new world order should be countered by a continued call for a new, more equitable international economic, political and cultural order within and between nations, a world order that reflects the diversity of world peoples and cultures. (xvi)

Since imperialism is not likely to voluntarily surrender its advantages, one of the several methods that Ngũgĩ sees by which the exploited peoples could liberate themselves from exploitation is to seize the very same weapons of cultural indoctrination with which imperialism has perpetuated its acceptance and to use those weapons to deconstruct, demystify, and expose imperialism. Literature in particular should be used to reeducate exploited people to come to a true understanding of their predicament. To achieve this goal, it is obvious that a writer would have to address his native audience in the language such an audience speaks and understands. This is the logic behind Ngũgĩ's historic switch from English to the use of his native Gikuyu language for his writing, a switch whose objective and efficacy, not surprising, have aroused much controversy.

The main thrust of Ngũgĩ's argument is that the only humane way to arrive at true universalism is through the particular. His illustrations of the truth of this conviction leaves no room for doubts:

We are all human beings but the fact of our being human does not manifest itself in its abstraction but in the particularity of real living human beings of different climes and races. We talk of the human capacity for languages but that capacity manifests itself in real concrete languages as spoken by different peoples of the earth. In other words, we realize language as a universal human phenomenon not in its abstract universality but in its particularity as the different languages of the earth. (26)

Judging by the enormous success of Ngũgĩ's two Gikuyu novels among Kenyan nonelite readers as well as the fact that the novels' negative depiction of imperialist's local and international representatives was sufficiently potent to have aroused the anger of the Arap Moi government, which promptly banned the novels and sought the arrest of their author (157–158), one could safely conclude that Ngũgĩ has successfully demonstrated the viability of the approach to decolonization which he recommends to fellow writers. To say that Ngũgĩ's approach is viable is not to say that it has no limitations. Not every African writer, for instance, possesses the linguistic ability nor the will to write in his or her native African language, and, as frequently pointed out, before translation, an African-language literature is necessarily limited at the beginning to the ethnic group speaking the language in which it is composed. Since these limitations are not insurmountable, they cannot be interpreted as invalidating Ngũgĩ's position which should not be misinterpreted either as denying total relevance to African literatures written in non-African languages. Ngugi's language position is actually about the different levels of the relevance of African literatures written in African and non-African languages, his bias being categorically in favor of the latter.

Gilroy accuses Afrocentricity of being guilty of many sins, including antiracist racism, obsession with origin and myth, romantic idealization of Africa that is based on unsubstantiated revisionist claims of a glorious past, and faulty historicism, which misunderstands the importance of slavery in the formation of both black and white modern identities (188–190). Contrary to this misrepresentation, Asante dissociates himself from the view that "evil was inherent in the white race" by categorically stating that "we know now, of course, that the condition of evil [racial discrimination] in whites is not inherent, but inherited through history and environment" (15)—a point that echoes both Appiah's and Gilroy's observations regarding the European invention of scientific racism which has done much harm to black people since the nineteenth century. Also as Asante insists, Afrocentricity is a concept that "respects and applauds pluralism" (79). Asante acknowledges the diversity of cultures, including diversity within even the black culture: "Unquestionably on the Continent our cultural system is manifested in diverse ways as it is in the Diaspora. We have one African Cultural System manifested in diversities" (2). He carefully explains that the preference afrocentrists show for black culture should not be misinterpreted as a claim to black cultural superiority: "This is not done because we have something against someone else's culture; it is just not ours" (5). More than this, Asante recognizes the individual's right to adopt any culture of his or her choice: "We do not have too many complaints with the person who decides to accept someone else's culture, religion, or ideology, be it Islam, Christianity, or Marxism, if it serves him better than his own" (5–6). "If an African wants to compete in ballet, she must understand that the criteria are not universally derived but culturally specific. She must submit to the rigors of the European view of what ballet is and what it is not" (83).

The restoration of a true humanism, a true universalism, is the primary goal of Afrocentricity. This requires combating racism which manifests itself in the form of a eurocentricity that in turn masquerades as universalism. Asante insists that while institutionalized racism may have ended, "personal racism remains unabated" (35) and he believes that the platform from which to successfully attack it, is cultural nationalism. For Asante, cultural nationalism does not amount to a hegemonic belief in cultural superiority: "There is nothing more sacred about one language than another" although "one language may have special significance to one people more than to others" (4). Also Asante argues that "a nationalist is not necessarily a racist; indeed, the true nationalist is never a racist" (5).

Incidentally, this is a view that is shared by other scholars, notably John Brenkman (1995) who sees Afrocentricity as a response to the despair created by the "excision of racial justice from the national discourse" and the delegitimation of black political participation during the Reagan-Bush era (27, 11–13, 27, 34). Brenkman's analysis shows that today during the Clinton administration, white racism is equally widespread, openly promoted in various guises (including ostensible commitment to "race-neutral" policies) by the New Right in the Republican Party and covertly canvassed by the Civic Liberals and New Democrats (13–36). An objective reading of the components of cultural nationalism in *Afrocentricity* indeed confirms that the ideology is not aimed at putting down the white race, rather it uncompromisingly opposes all manifestations of white racism and their negative effects on blacks. But even more significant is the fact that Afrocentric nationalism is more positively oriented than just fighting white racism. Its major goal is to infuse self-pride and a sense of self-worth in African Americans as antidote to the inferiority complex to which they have been exposed by prolonged racism and exploitation. With strong conviction and passionate religious fervor, Afrocentricity simultaneously asserts the authenticity of African culture, exposes the illogicality of abandoning one's culture for that of another people on the racist pretext that one's culture was inferior, and motivates African Americans to higher achievements by enunciating a set of inspirational tenets of wisdom, morality, and action called *njia, or the way.*

The central thesis that emerges from *Afrocentricity*, therefore, is that there is no universalism that is worthy of the name in its true humanist interpretation that does not recognize the significance, indeed, the equality of all individual cultural identities. In other words, true universalism can be achieved not in abstract generalities, but only through full acknowledgment of the particular.

Thus, while Ngũgî and Asante espouse the cultural concept of multicultural particularism which recognizes the uniqueness as well as the hybridity of every culture, Appiah tends to promote a multicultural philosophy of undifferentiated hybridity that denies identity to individual cultures. On one hand, Appiah denies that Africa has ever had a cultural unity: "The people of Africa have a good deal less culturally in common than is usually assumed" (17); indeed, Africa, he insists, has never at any time had one uniform culture, let alone one that is racially unique or definitive. The rule has consistently been a multiplicity of cultures (chaps. 3 and 4). It naturally follows from all this that Africa has no commonalities of perception and cannot claim a world view, but several world views, each of which is deeply implicated in, that is, "contaminated" by Western worldviews (80, 82, chap. 4).

Not only does Appiah deny cultural unity to Africa, he also denies African cultural particularity to any of the multiple cultures into which he sees Africa as fragmented. What we assume are several African cultures turn out in Appiah's view as hybrids within which the African content is barely existent. Africa, Appiah argues, has no specifically African form of thought, though there are multiplicities of traditional African forms of thought which he defines as ethnophilosophies and none of which, he argues, is particularly unique to an African people (chap. 5). Furthermore, Appiah insists that as a product of a non literate culture, African traditional religious thought lacks the abstract cognitive properties of scientific (that is, Western) thought and is in danger of being marginalized as superstition by the increasing transformation of African culture into literate culture, and the consequent adoption of Western scientific methodology of thought (chap. 6).

Appiah sharply criticizes all those who defend the notion of uniqueness to any aspect of African culture, labeling them "nativists" or "particularists" (56–57). This is the kind of logic with which Appiah transforms the forefathers of Pan-Africanism like Alexander Crummell, Edward W. Blyden, Africanus Horton, and Martin Robinson Delany into antiracist racists. Even more surprising is Appiah's view that urges us to believe that but for the contamination by these Pan-African intellectuals, Africa, in spite of its own direct experience of rabid European racism during slavery and colonialism, would have remained an Eden of purse unracist souls. Thus, Kwame Nkrumah and Leopold Senghor were the creations of Pan-African racism (3–27). Again Appiah omitted to ask why African nationalists like Nkrumah and Senghor went to Europe and America to study in the first place. Perhaps he discounts the fact that Western education was not an end in itself, but a means to end racist exploitation and domination. In any case, any view that lays more weight on influence than on Africans' own firsthand experience of racism as the source of Africa's contamination with racist ideology seems to me to be untenable in view of the horror of the human and systemic devastations caused by slavery and the cruelty of colonialism, particularly the settler type, in Africa. Robin Cohen's recent informative discussion of the character of colonial cruelty is a case in point (43–49).

What Africans share in common for sure, according to Appiah, are historical particularities and the problems that emanated from them. The common history of European domination, the inadequacies of colonial structures, the lack of faith in these structures by Africa's postcolonial governing elite, and the politics of tribalism are some of these common problems, which in addition to the damages caused by mismanagement, drought, wars, and the continuing inequities in the terms of trade with the West, have led to the demise of postcolonial African states. Appiah recommends as solution to these problems the democratization of the state through the empowerment of nongovernmental organizations for community development (chap. 8). In other words, Appiah recommends as solution to Africa's economic woes the very same "democratic" solutions of the structural adjustment programs (SAPs) as were imposed by the International Monetary Funds and the World Bank. These are bodies which most third world scholars have denounced as instruments of multinationals, whose exploitation of Africa has been largely responsible for Africa's economic difficulties and whose limitations Appiah himself partially acknowledges (167–172).

Since "invented histories, invented biologies, invented cultural affinities come with every identity," Appiah is not surprised however that "an African identity is coming into being" (174) despite the falsity of the foundation on which it is currently being built: Africa's supposed racial and cultural uniqueness and shared commonalities. Appiah also recognizes such factual elements as transcontinental African structures and institutions like the Organization of African Unity (OAU), Africa Development Bank, and Economic Community of West African States (ECOWAS) as supporting the claim that "We are Africans already" (177).

Appiah sees his task as an African scholar as truth telling, even when this goes against the common grain, and he insists on this task despite acknowledging at the same time the limitations of academic knowledge: "The real battle is not being fought in the academy." But against this fact he posits a counterbalancing fact: "We cannot change the world simply by evidence and reasoning, but we surely cannot change it without them either" (179). As a philosopher, Appiah should have also recognized the problematic of the concept of truth telling because the obvious question that arises is "Whose truth?" However, Appiah concludes his critique of "nativism" as a strategy for promoting multiculturalism (in other words, genuine universalism) with a personal account of his father's burial which demonstrates the central thesis of his book: African traditional culture which has been the sole basis for the nativists's claim of Africa's racial and cultural uniqueness is fast yielding place to Westernization, a fact that in Appiah's opinion is to be welcomed rather than regretted since it guarantees Africa membership in the world that is fast becoming a global village where all cultures get "mutually contaminated" in a continuous process of becoming hybrids. It does not occur to Appiah to rigorously question, as Ngũgĩ and Asante do, the economic and political terms of the admission of Africa into the hybrid fold of the global culture. This omission constitutes the greatest weakness of Appiah's concept of multiculturalism, for it leaves room for any kind of fascist exploitation and appropriation of one culture and its economic wealth by another culture. This omission is doubly regrettable because its import seems not to be the author's intention.

Similarly like Appiah, Gilroy examines the paradoxical adoption of the European-invented racism by black institutions that were expressly developed to counter racism. But whereas Appiah, in an amazing twist that resembles blaming a victim for the crime, represents the forefathers of Pan-Africanism as black leaders whose principles of action had been tainted by ill-conceived antiracist racism (21), Gilroy paints a picture that depicts the founders of Pan-Africanism as leaders who saw blackness as being more "a matter of politics rather than a common cultural condition" (27). Gilroy shows that Delany, in fact, advocates in his fiction *Blake* an "anti-mystical racial rationalism [which] required that blacks of all shades, classes, and ethnic groups give up the merely accidental differences that served only to mask the deeper unity waiting to be constructed not so much from their African heritage as from the common orientation to the future produced by their militant struggle against slavery" (28).

Furthermore, the later Pan-Africanists like W. E .B Du Bois and Richard Wright are shown to have developed what Gilroy calls the "hermeneutics of suspicion and hermeneutics of memory" both of which "nurtured a redemptive critique" of racism (71). Also Du Bois's concept of double consciousness is not problematicized into a psychologically disabling philosophy as could be expected, but is positively affirmed and adopted by Gilroy as a methodological principle of analysis to reflect all aspects of the modern black experience which "stand simultaneously both inside and outside the western culture" (48–49).

The formulation of the concept of racial and cultural hybridity is the point where Gilroy and Appiah are simultaneously most similar and most dissimilar. The central thesis which constitutes the major contribution of both scholars to contemporary debate and which each of their books elaborately substantiates is the repeated disclaimer of racial purity and the emphatic assertion of hybridity in the composition of racial identity. It is not so much the novelty of the idea of hybridity that is fascinating because, for one thing, cultural borrowing has been a constant factor of human communities from the beginning of times, and for another, George Hutchinson in an *African American Review* article, shows that hybridity as a cultural theory was extensively canvassed at the turn of the century by the journal *The Messenger* in contradistinction to magazines such as *The Crisis* and *Opportunity* which advocated what would today be labeled nativism. What is fascinating is the erudition, analytical rigor, and the wealth of evidence with which the scholars support their views.

However, unlike in the case of Appiah whose antiessentialism mostly sees inevitable surrender and defeat for traditional African culture in the latter's struggle to survive in face of the imperialist aggressiveness of Western culture (Appiah 133–134, epilogue), for Gilroy, the absence of a common black culture, uncontaminated in its pristine Africanity, does not amount to a denial of the existence of distinctively African elements that bring all black cultures of "Africa, America, Europe, and the Caribbean seamlessly together" (95). Drawing examples from the discourse of black music, Gilroy identifies in the current debate on black culture two opposing camps, consisting of the essentialists, on one hand, and the antiessentialists, on the other hand, and voices a powerful critique of both camps from a position that he identifies as "anti-antiessentialist" (102). He says that there is the camp of "those who see the music as the primary means to explore critically and reproduce politically the necessary ethnic essence of blackness and those who would dispute the existence of any such unifying, organic phenomenon" (100, 31–32).

Gilroy follows this critique with an enumeration of some of the distinctively "unifying, organic" African particularities in black music, all of which are associated, first, with the "central place that all these cultures give to music use and music making" and second, to "the ubiquity of antiphonal, social forms that underpin and enclose the plurality of black cultures in the western hemisphere" (200), in other words, the "rituals of performance that provide prima facie evidence of linkage between black cultures" (80–83, 101, 99–110). All of these recall the distinctive features with which Isidore Okpewho differentiates African from European epics (52–62). That even these uniquely African traits "can be taught and learned" (109) by nonblacks does not constitute a denial of their traceability to the African origin; what that fact proves is that cultures constantly intermingle and subsequently mutate into hybrids; hence Gilroy proposes the concept of "a tradition in ceaseless motion—a changing same" (xi, 122); hence he also acknowledges the necessity of the comparative study of black cultures (80–81).

LITERARY IMPLICATIONS

From the analytical approaches employed by the four scholars examined above, two basic methodological implications emerge for the literary critic. Appiah's undeviating employment of strictly abstract and idealist philosophical analytical parameters, which admit no extrinsic factors into consideration in its highbrow discourse, suggests a rather narrow and simplistic approach to literary analysis. On the other hand, Ngûgî's holistic methodological approach, which explodes the false dichotomy between highbrow and lowbrow approach to cultural analysis and which presupposes the compulsory inclusion of economic and political considerations as prerequisite elements of proper cultural discourse, suggests the traditional sociological critical approach which privileges the discussion of both the intrinsic and extrinsic materials of a literary text.

The antipodal philosophical character of Appiah's and Ngûgî's cultural theories encourage two diametrically opposed thematic approaches to the study of literature. Appiah's antiessentialism discourages critical engagement with literature whose preoccupation is race, except if such a preoccupation is the means to discourage claims to racial or cultural exclusivity and all attempts to construct any hierarchy of races. Works that deemphasize race as a subject and which instead show preoccupation with the so-called eternal and universal human questions of love, happiness, suffering, death, and so on will be highly valued. These "universal" questions will be the subject of comparative literary studies rather than the so-called shared cultural elements. Itinerary or hybrid literary elements cannot be traced to any particular cultural home for fear of promoting essentialism. A wholesale critical reevaluation of past writing is a logical development from this theory, and one can predict a rush to a rash ahistorical and decontextualized condemnation of previously praised earlier writers for supposedly perpetuating racial divisiveness.

In an effort to emphasize racial and cultural hybridity, cultural specificities of literatures will be deemphasized when they are not altogether denied as has happened in Sandra Adell's *Double-Consciousness/Double Bind.* Ignoring Ann duCille's assertion in *The Coupling Convention* that American literature is not exclusively white nor is African American literature exclusively black, Adell insists that African American literature in both its thematic and artistic conceptualizations is a Western phenomenon and that efforts like those of Houston Baker in *Blues, Ideology, and Afro-American Literature* and Henry Louis Gates, Jr., in *Signifying Monkey* to trace the unifying national or international threads of the black literary tradition are misdirected. Since African written literature was originally modeled on Western literature, and since even those works written in indigenous African languages have traces of the Western tradition, Africa will soon discover that in spite of winning Nobel Prize awards for literature, it has no literature of its own! At its best, Appiah's model of philosophical and cultural antiessentialism will produce the David Moore type of informed essay on Alex Haley's *Roots*; predominantly, however, it will yield the Adell type of analysis and create a critical tradition that can be sustained only in theoretic abstractions well distanced from reality, but not in concrete textual analyses. In short, antiessentialism's greatest contribution to cultural studies—the theory of hybridity which discourages racism—also holds a dangerous legacy.

Ngûgî's and Asante's universalist particularism which recognizes a hybridity which does not preclude cultural rootedness will promote a literary criticism that frowns on racist literary essentialism at the same time as it encourages a discussion of both hybrid and culturally rooted literary elements not as antipodal but as fluid and coexistent cultural phenomena. For this school, Houston Baker's *Blues* will remain a viable model of national critical scholarship as Gates's *Signifying Monkey* and Soyinka's *Myth, Literature* will continue to be the models for international comparative literary analysis. There will be no shying away from the discussion of any literary subject, least of all racism, if only because the discussion of the latter provides occasion for a moral condemnation and a promotion of what Satya Mohanty calls the "'dignity' or 'intrinsic worth' of every human individual," which is "absolute" and "cannot be traded away" or calculated "in degrees" (116). Indeed, since the understandable negative response to multiculturalism is the intensified effort by racists to stunt its growth, critics of the universalist-particularist persuasion would see the necessity to operate under Cornel West's assumption that still *"race matters,"* and not only as it pertains to the past as Toni Morrison shows in *Playing in the Dark* but also as it relates to the present as was only recently demonstrated by John Brenkman in a *Transition* essay and by Dana Nelson in *The World in Black and White*. Particularities of cultural setting and identity in literary texts will not be avoided but explored fully for their universal values since the universal is only accessible through the particular. In fact, as Leslie Sanders says, "it is only when the particular is most perfectly realized that the universal is most eloquently expressed" (228). In other words, not much would change under the universalist-particularist model except for a continued insistence on the traditional humanist values of pluralism, equality, mutual respect, and tolerance.

Critics who favor Gilroy's "anti-antiessentialism" will adopt his pragmatic philosophy of *strategic essentialism*; thus, on occasions they would be indistinguishable from critics influenced by Ngũgĩ's universalist particularity. For the most part, however, Gilroyists will be antiessentialists who would be indistinguishable from the followers of Appiah, except that they would differ from the latter in that they would welcome both highbrow and popular literatures, while at the same time fastidiously maintaining, like the Appiah scholars, a high-level, abstract discourse in both instances.

REFERENCES

Achebe, Chinua. *Morning, Yet on Creation Day*. London: Heinemann, 1975.

Adell, Sandra. *Double-Consciousness/Double Bind: Theoretical Issues in Twentieth-Century Black Literature*. Urbana: University of Illinois Press, 1994.

Appiah, Kwame Anthony. *In My Father's House: Africa in the Philosophy of Culture*. New York: Oxford University Press, 1992.

Asante, Molefi Kete. *Afrocentricity*, 3 rev. ed. Trenton, NJ: Africa World Press, 1989.

Baker, Houston A, Jr., *Blues, Ideology, and Afro-American Literature: A Vernacular Theory*. Chicago: University of Chicago Press, 1984.

Bernheimer, Charles (Ed.) *Comparative Literature in the Age of Multiculturalism*.

Baltimore and London: John Hopkins University Press, 1995.

Brenkman, John. "Race Politics." *Transition,* 66, *5* (2) (Summer 1995): 4–36.

Cohen, Robin. "Fuzzy Frontiers of Identity: The British Case." *Social Identities: Journal for the Study of Race, Nation and Culture 1* (1) (1995): 35–62.

duCille, Ann. *The Coupling Convention: Sex, Text, and Tradition in Black Women's Fiction.* New York: Oxford University Press, 1993.

Gates, Henry Louis, Jr. *The Signifying Monkey: A Theory of African-American Literary Criticism.* New York: Oxford University Press, 1988.

Gayle, Addison, Jr. (Ed.). *The Black Aesthetic.* New York: Doubleday, 1971.

Gilroy, Paul. *The Black Atlantic: Modernity and Double Consciousness.* Cambridge, MA: Harvard University Press, 1993.

Hutchinson, George. "Mediating 'Race' and 'Nation': The Cultural Politics of *The Messenger.*" *African American Review, 28* (4) (winter 1994): 531–548.

Lipsitz, George. "Review of *Black Atlantic: Modernity and Double Consciousness,* by Paul Gilroy." *Social Identities: Journal for the Study of Race, Nation and Culture, 1* (1) (1995): 193–200.

Mohanty, Satya P. "Colonial Legacies, Multicultural Futures: Relativism, Objectivity, and the Challenge of Otherness." *PMLA, 110* (1) (January 1995): 108–118.

Moore, David Chioni. "Routes: Alex Haley's Roots and the Rhetoric of Genealogy." *Transition, 64* (1994): 4–21.

Morrison, Toni. *Playing in the Dark: Whiteness and the Literary Imagination.* New York: Vintage, 1993.

Nelson, Dana D. *The World in Black and White: Reading "Race" in American Literature, 1638–1867.* New York: Oxford University Press, 1993.

Ngũgĩ wa Thiong'o. *Moving the Centre: The Struggle for Cultural Freedoms.* London: James Currey, 1993.

Okpewho, Isidore. *The Epic in Africa.* New York: Columbia University Press, 1979.

Sanders, Leslie C. *The Development of Black Theater in America: From Shadows to Selves.* Baton Rouge: Louisiana State University Press, 1988.

Soyinka, Wole. *Myth, Literature and the African World.* New York: Cambridge University Press, 1976.

West, Cornel. *Race Matters.* New York: Vintage.

Williams, Brackette F. "Review of *Black Atlantic: Modernity and Double Consciousness,* by Paul Gilroy." *Social Identities: Journal for the Study of Race, Nation and Culture, 1* (1) (1995): 175–192.

12

White Women, Black Revolutionaries: Sex and Politics in Four Novels by Nadine Gordimer

Nancy Topping Bazin

As early as 1959, the white South African novelist, essayist, and short story writer Nadine Gordimer wrote an essay, "Where Do Whites Fit In?" As the black struggle for power intensified and finally achieved its primary goal of black majority rule in 1994, Gordimer continued to reflect upon this question. Her eighth novel, *July's People* (1981), is a psychological and political fable. It celebrates a white woman's readiness to reject the relationships and privileges that bind her to the white world and her readiness to embrace the new South Africa of an emancipated black majority. The novels written before *July's People* focus primarily on a movement away from the remnants of colonial mentality harbored within the white world; the three novels following *July's People* emphasize a radical commitment to the black-dominated social order of the future. *July's People* and nine screenplay versions of the novel (1982–1987) are central to understanding the philosophy that underlies her three later novels—*A Sport of Nature* (1987), *My Son's Story* (1990), and *None to Accompany Me* (1994). Along with the novel and screenplays of *July's People*, these three novels envision possible answers to the question, "Where do whites fit in, in the New Africa?" (Gordimer, "Where Do Whites" 31).

Gordimer pointed out that "belonging to a society implies two factors which are outside reason: The desire to belong . . . and acceptance" ("Where Do Whites" 32). What must white South Africans do to prove themselves worthy of black acceptance? What can possibly persuade blacks to accept whites when "they have had so much of us . . . that all they crave is to have no part of us"? (32). In Gordimer's fictional world, black male leaders are more likely to accept a white woman than a white man. As the power begins to shift among whites and blacks, white females and black males move closer to becoming equals. On the hierarchical ladder, they are the middle levels between white men at the top and black women at the bottom. Furthermore, between white females and black males, sexual attraction, intellectual companionship, and the male's tendency to protect the female can create a bridge. Certainly, in the four novels published between 1981 and 1994, Gordimer's female protagonists look to black males, initially, to gain a sense of belonging and, later, to make possible a sense of independence, rooted in that assurance of belonging. The persistence of this concern with fitting in suggests an increasing preoccupation with personal and political survival as black liberation becomes a reality. Having fought for decades for equality and against apartheid and censorship Gordimer wants blacks to allow whites like her a role in the building of post revolutionary South Africa. She experiments in her fiction with ways that a white female, in particular, might gain this right to participate.

Just after publishing *July's People*, Gordimer wrote an essay, "Living in the Interregnum." In it, she compared the current situation in South Africa to living on a slag heap that, still burning inside, threatens to maim or kill (280). In an earlier essay, she recalls the childhood "thrill of running quickly across a pile of black dust that may at any moment cave in and plunge the adventurer into a bed of incandescent coals" ("South African" 123). The image becomes more powerful when she describes a little girl she knew who had "sunk thigh-deep in living coals and hot ashes" and had been "horribly burned." Despite having seen "the tight-puckered skin of her calves, and the still tighter skin of her hands, which drew up her fingers like claws" (123), Gordimer continued to play on the slag heaps. Moreover, she admired her cousin Roy, who one day "rode a bicycle right to the top of the dump and down the other side, triumphant and unharmed" (123).

So when she describes the period during which she wrote *July's People* as "a place of shifting ground" ("Living" 280) and when she speaks of heroes who take risks, those potent images of the slag heap and her cousin's life-threatening ride come to mind. Her intense admiration for revolutionary heroes is implicit in her later fiction and explicit in her interviews (Bazin and Seymour 121; Gerrard). Although Gordimer says she is not brave enough to be a hero herself, she does take risks (Bazin and Seymour 206). Not surprising, Roland Joffe from Warner Brothers encouraged her to put into her movie of *July's People* "the streak of wildness and adventure I sensed in you as we careered about Africa" (GM B2 November 8, 1984). Her rebellious spirit is even evident in her description of herself as a child: "I was a bolter, from kindergarten age, but unlike most small children rapidly accustoming their soft, round selves to the sharp angles of desks and discipline, I went on running away from school, year after year" ("Bolter" 19). Her admiration for male heroes and her bolting spirit help explain Gordimer's enthusiasm for Maureen's flight from her middle-class responsibilities of husband and children at the end of *July's People*. Maureen is driven to flee by her instinct to survive. Given an untenable position in the white world, the white woman's best option is to bolt across the "color bar" to help blacks create an egalitarian, utopian future. Only there will a white woman who supports black liberation fit in.

In *July's People*, this flight for survival starts as violence erupts with black revolutionaries attacking Johannesburg. For whites, *July's People* represents a nightmare come true. Maureen and Bam Smales support the revolution but, because of their white skins, they are in danger of being killed. Therefore, they and their three children must flee, delivered by their servant July who offers to harbor them in his village. Unexpectedly, their black servant turns out to be, in Gordimer's words, the "frog prince, saviour" (*July's People* 9).

Gordimer's reference to Grimm's fairy tale of the frog prince parallels the transformation of July from servant in the white society to respected male in his African village—from frog to prince. It suggests, too, the symbolic demand of blacks to eat from the whites' golden plates and sleep in their clean beds in exchange for the service blacks have given, in saving the "golden ball"—signifying their lives in the case of Maureen and Bam. All too often whites, like the princess, have not listened to the frog, forgotten the frog, and broken their promises. They have refused the frog's demand to "love" him and be his "companion and playfellow" (Grimm 33). In the fairy tale the princess made these promises to the frog if only he would get her ball out of the well. Yet, afterwards, she assured herself he had only been talking "nonsense," because how could he "possibly be anyone's companion" (33). The next day the frog came to the castle door, so the princess had to tell the king, her father, of her promises. To her chagrin, the king insisted: "That which thou hast promised must thou perform" (34). Therefore, the princess reluctantly let the frog eat from her golden plate; she even took him up to her bedroom. However, when the frog reminded her of her promise to let him sleep in her pretty bed, she angrily threw the frog "with all her strength against the wall" (35). As he fell, the frog turned into "a prince with beautiful kind eyes" (35).

In 1989, Gordimer refers again to this fairy tale in an article in the *New York Review of Books*. She suggests that a prince hidden within a frog ("something monstrous") represents a "psychological loss of self" ("The Gap" 61). Although Grimm's monstrous frog had rescued the Princess's lost ball, sh e still despised him. Only after his recovery of "self" (and hence beauty and respect), will she marry him. Similarly, in *July's People*, the restoration of self occurs for July when he returns to his village where, treated with respect, he regains power and self-confidence; likewise, the black Freedom Fighters gain power and respect when they are able to bring the revolution to the Johannesburg area. Recognizing this and seeking protection, Maureen subtly offers herself first to July and then eventually (one may assume) to one or another of the Freedom Fighters.

In *July's People* Gordimer brilliantly imagines what it would be like to be wrenched away from middle-class comfort and forced to live on a subsistence level. Falling to the bottom of the economic scale had an immediate impact on the Smales's care for and attitudes toward their bodies. They became acutely aware of body odors and bodily functions. Maureen had to use rags for her menstrual periods (67). Their son Royce quickly learned to use a stone in place of toilet paper (35). Deprivation and a lack of privacy greatly diminished Bam and Maureen's sexual desire. In fact, what they learn about the reality of subsistence living reveals that, despite their liberalism, they had understood neither July nor what daily life was like for his "people" (37–38).

Ironically, a nonviolent revolution occurs in July's village while a violent one is occurring in Johannesburg. The black servant, July, assumes power formerly held by the white master, Bam Smales. Since the Smales must hide, July learns to drive and keeps the keys to their bakkie. The lives of Bam and Maureen are totally in his hands. Powerless, Bam can no longer continue his roles as financial supporter, protector, or even lover of his wife. When he fails to fulfill his masculine roles, Maureen feels she owes him nothing. The communal way in which July's people raise children (including her three) undermines her maternal role. Thus, the white couple's interdependency has ended, and Maureen abruptly—and many would say meanly—withdraws her commitment and loyalty to her husband. The outbreak of violence has destroyed both the master-servant relationship and the patriarchal and colonialist male-female relationship. What has happened, as Maureen points out, is "an explosion of roles" (*July's People* 117).

As had happened before in history, the black revolt in the imagined future of *July's People* opens the way for the female revolt. The Smales no longer assume they "know" their servant, July, for *he* is no longer powerless and dependent; *they* are. Maureen and Bam Smales no longer know each other, for they are so powerless in the African village that neither has anything to offer the other. The new situation has shattered their former identities. Like July, Maureen had been in a dependent role. When her love for Bam does not survive his descent from power, she experiences a sense of liberation. At the end of the novel, as she crosses the river—and the "color bar"—she is "born again" (160).

Gordimer's depiction in *July's People* of what it would feel like to crash from middle-class comfort to subsistence living reveals her superb ability to observe detail and imagine the psychological consequences of change. However, like many nightmares and fairy tales, Gordimer's narration of the story raises questions that it leaves unanswered. We accept a tale like "The Frog Prince" as we might a dream that lacks connections, contains contradictions, and asks us to believe the impossible. However, many readers of *July's People* were not so willing to tolerate the unlikely. They felt, in particular, that they were being asked to accept an ending that was hard to believe. Maureen's flight toward the unmarked helicopter seemed both foolhardy and puzzling. When Gordimer rewrote the story as a screenplay, film producer Roland Joffe and other readers of the script asked her to make the story more convincing. She was to clarify Maureen's seemingly cold-hearted abandonment of her husband and especially her children; her evolution from housewife to freedom fighter, and the reasons the men in the helicopter might save Maureen (GM B2 1983–1986C January 14, 1985; December 22, 1986; March 3, 1987). Gordimer's letters to Joffe and her revisions of the screenplay provide answers. Such information about her intentions serves to explain peculiarities in the characters and the plot that mar an otherwise brilliant novel.

The focus in the story on the master, the servant, and, most important, the colonial woman illuminates how colonialism, racism, and sexism intertwine. According to Gordimer, in revolting against the white male, Maureen is rebelling against the colonialist attitudes toward her, which continued in South Africa throughout the years of apartheid. In discussing the screenplay of *July's People* in an October 24, 1986 letter, Gordimer explained the situation of the "colonial white woman":

She is in the doubly powerful position of wielding authority over blacks while at the same time being herself protected, cossetted. Much racist legislation, indeed, is done in her name, for her sake as bearer of future generations of the white race. She is the sacred womb from which only the ruling race must come. Her sexuality must thus be protected from any approach by defiling blacks. (GM B2 1983–1986C)

According to Gordimer, a woman like Maureen is "conditioned to believe she needs protection. A protection which by implication and in practice makes her, her male protector's possession rather than herself' (GM B2 October 24, 1986). When Bam becomes powerless, she is freed from his protection and therefore is no longer his possession. Maureen's first response had been to turn for help to July, who served as her "boy" for fifteen years. She ignores the fact that he has a wife and children and behaves seductively with him (153). But July is too bitter to accept her sexual advances. Therefore, she turns to the other men who have gained power—those carrying guns, the Freedom Fighters.

In becoming involved with the black male, the white woman defies the taboo against black male/white female sexuality that was still illegal when Gordimer wrote the novel. Even lesser forms of intimacy with a black man had once been unthinkable. However, when Maureen tries to offer July equality through intimacy (145–53), equality is not part of his conception of male-female relationships; nor can he forget how working for her, a woman, undermined his manhood psychologically and socially. Furthermore, when he worked closely with Maureen in her house, his sexuality was strictly controlled. As Gordimer stated in an October 24, 1986 letter to Joffe, the black servant is "a eunuch in relation to White Madam." He protects her "at master' s bidding," but to be her protector, the black man must be "emasculated" (GM B2). Any sexual response to her or from her is strictly forbidden. Therefore, Maureen and July revolt against Bam's colonial mentality that denied each of them dignity. As Gordimer says in a March 11,

1987 letter to Joffe, "They destroy Bam, between them; it's their doing. So Bam falls out of the triangle of the power-struggle" (GM B2, 3).

The ending of the novel *July' s People* has evoked considerable controversy. Maureen hears a helicopter landing. The narrator describes it in sexual terms: A high ringing is produced in her ears, her body in its ribcage is thudded with deafening vibration, invaded by a force pumping, jigging in its monstrous orgasm—the helicopter has sprung through the hot brilliant cloud just above them all, its landing gear like spread legs, battling the air with whirling scythes (158).

In "Beyond the Interregnum: A Note on the Ending of *July's People*," Nicholas Visser has pointed out that this image and certain words and phrases at the end of *July's People* echo Yeats's poem "Leda and the Swan," in which Zeus takes the form of the swan and rapes Leda. Leda simultaneously engenders Helen and Clytemnestra, both of whom grow up to be faithless wives. Helen's infidelity in abandoning Menelaus for Paris causes the Trojan War. Agamemnon returns from the war only to discover Clytemnestra's infidelity. Perhaps, then, the emphasis here should be not only, as Visser's was, on "a moment of insemination, from which new possibilities will emerge" (66) but also on the woman's infidelity, made possible by the descending helicopter. The shift in a woman's allegiance alters history in each story. In Gordimer's story, the black revolution and the woman's implied sexual revolt against the colonial husband are interwoven. The echoing of Yeats's use of the myth enhances Gordimer's personal fable about how a white woman can gain acceptance in South Africa. One wonders what Gordimer said to Roland Joffe that made him write to her: "I was very struck by what you said about the white women and black leaders. What you had to say about survival was both optimistic and shocking. I hope the film [*July's People*] will be too. If Maureen's transmutations guide the narrative, I think we'd achieve something remarkable" (GM B2 November 8, 1984, 3).

Nadine Gordimer does not perceive the feminist perspective in her own analysis of the colonial woman. The importance of gender is evident, however, in what she wrote in an October 24, 1986 letter to Joffe: "Of course the feminists will claim Maureen as *the* survivor. But I don't want to make a feminist film, do you?! I could have made my solution-finder, my character capable of *remaking the self*, a man. But I suppose I clearly, if subconsciously, chose a woman because in the situation of the colonial white woman the whole ethos of colonialism, as it distorts the white personality, is epitomized" (GM B2, 2). While emphasizing Maureen's streak of independence, Gordimer also stresses Maureen's dependence on men. She wrote to Joffe on January 24, 1985, "In case the feminists want to claim Maureen, it is to a helicopter *manned*, that she makes her bolt" (GM B2). She specifies that identification with the black women in July's family is not an answer for Maureen. Instead, Gordimer says, Maureen "needs to take the risk of a whole new social order, not take the contemporary version of the 18th century retreat into a convent" (GM B2 October, 24, 1986, 2 #3C). Gordimer's opposition to feminism may have its roots in her girlhood experience of attending a convent school for girls. No more all-female environments for her; having no boys around was not to her liking!

Her outline of the structure for her screenplay is "Stage one, allegiance to Bam. Stage two, shift of allegiance to July. Stage three, rejection of both [Bam and July], and emergence of allegiance to a late and painfully-emerged selfhood" (GM B2 January 24, 1985, *Under the Danger*). If this allegiance to self were persuasive, the feminists might well claim Maureen, but the textual evidence suggests a different story. She flees to a symbol of masculine technological power—the helicopter. In the novel Maureen could not make out the markings on the helicopter and therefore does not know "whether it holds saviours or murderers" (158). However, were she expecting whites to be in the helicopter, she could have taken her husband and children with her. Furthermore, going off with conservative whites would not fit with Maureen's or Gordimer's political ideology or the liberation of the colonial woman Maureen represents.

The story only makes sense if we assume those in the helicopter are black. In an October 1994 interview, Gordimer acknowledged this and said Maureen would "rather take a chance on blacks" (Bazin, "An Interview" 582). In an earlier draft of the novel and in the screenplays of *July's People*, Maureen does identify the helicopter as belonging to the black Freedom Fighters. Yet, in four of the nine versions of the screenplay, the reaction of the Freedom Fighters to Maureen's sudden arrival is still not clarified. In the seventh version, however, Gordimer revises in response to Roland Joffe's desire to know why these Freedom Fighters in the helicopter would be willing to save Maureen. Many readers have not been convinced that black Freedom Fighters would be "saviours" rather than "murderers" for an unknown white woman seeking their help. Thus, the ideological demands on the narrative were in conflict with the behavior one might expect of Freedom Fighters in the midst of a violent conflict with whites. Even if they do not murder her, they are preoccupied with a civil war and can hardly be expected to save her.

Furthermore, as Joffe states in a March 3, 1987 letter, Maureen comes across as "an opportunist" (GM B2, 2). Neither her husband Bam nor July can meet her needs; therefore, she runs toward those who are likely to be the next occupiers of the "Master Bedroom" (Gordimer's symbol for what Bam has lost). Indeed, as she runs, "the smell of boiled potatoes (from a vine indistinguishable to her from others) promises a kitchen, a house just the other side of the next tree" (160). These images, however illusory, suggest a longing to reenter the middle-class lifestyle with the new men in power more than they suggest a willingness to withstand the hardships of the life of a revolutionary. Gordimer may be implying that time spent as a revolutionary would ensure the white woman a place in the postrevolutionary, black-dominated society by the side of a black leader. Maureen's dream is obviously not to live in the new South Africa in a village like July's.

But before Maureen can prove her loyalty during the revolutionary battles, the Freedom Fighters must trust her to be a loyal political ally—one they can rely upon during warfare. They must be able to trust her not to betray the blacks to members of her own race should events turn against the revolutionaries. Thus, acceptance by the black revolutionaries begins with allowing her to depart with them in the helicopter. Upon reading a version of the screenplay that still matched the ending of the novel, Joffe argued that the text was not convincing. Because Maureen had had no previous contact with the Freedom Fighters, they were not likely to trust her or care to save her (GM B2 March 3, 1987, 2 #3). Furthermore, because she had had no prior contact, her solitary run for the helicopter at the end seemed to Joffe "an act of alienation not communion" (GM B2 March 3, 1987, 2 #3).

Joffe suggested that Gordimer prepare the audience for the ending and make it more realistic by building up Maureen's relationship with Daniel, an injured Freedom Fighter staying in July's village until he is healed. Therefore, in the next version of the screenplay, Gordimer has Maureen ride off one day with Daniel and July in Bam's yellow bakkie. Maureen's stated goal is to buy medicine for her son from the Indian store. However, she departs secretly, intentionally not telling Bam, and she knowingly risks her life and the safety of the vehicle. July, Daniel, and Maureen do meet a guerrilla roadblock, and the revolutionaries would have seized the bakkie had July not known one of them since childhood.

Bam is so angry with Maureen when she returns that he slaps her face. He senses her shift of allegiance. When she tells him she can no longer talk to him because the things they used to talk about no longer exist, he says: "Ah, and the children don't exist, I don't exist. You don't exist. We've always trusted each other, and now, here, in this mess—suddenly I can't trust you, either." When she says that at least she has finally seen the Freedom Fighters, he exclaims: "Oh yes, so you know *they* exist, eh" (GM B9 F12, 74).

In this version Maureen becomes more certain that Daniel is a Freedom Fighter when he steals Bam's gun and disappears. Later Daniel comes to Maureen, out of hiding, and she provides him with food and painkillers for another revolutionary. Her actions help confirm her loyalty to the black cause. Thus, at the end when she approaches the helicopter, Daniel vouches for her, offering her safety.

The dialogue in this draft of the screenplay is awkward. However, it clarifies the evolution of thought underlying Gordimer's psychological and political fable about white women and black revolutionaries. One Freedom Fighter from the helicopter asks if she is lost and she replies: "No, found." When he asks, "Where are your people?" she replies: "You are my people. I trust you. I want to be with you. Fight with you. Your women fight with you." When the Freedom Fighter replies "That's impossible, for you," she answers,

"No. Everything else is" (GM B9 F15 insert p. 164 alternate ending). For Maureen, a leap that places her permanently on the other side of the "colour bar" is her only acceptable option. She cannot endure staying in July's village; nor does she want to go back to the white community, where she would have to see blacks as the enemy and blacks would see her as the enemy. She must take the risk of joining the black Freedom Fighters. On March 11, 1987, Gordimer explained to Joffe that Maureen's run is to be "a wild act, a breaking free, a taking of a huge chance." The audience should "fear for her, half-envy her" GM B2, 3). In one of the later versions of the screenplay, Maureen tells Daniel: "I wish I were black. My children were black. You can fight if you're black." When Daniel asks her what she wants to fight for, she replies, "Same things as you" (GM B9 F12, 3). When one of the Freedom Fighters calls Maureen "a mad woman," another defends her by saying, "There were others who worked with us—whites, women—went to jail with us, don't forget. Maybe she's sane, like they were" (GM B9 F15 insert p. 1). In yet a later version when one puzzled comrade asks, "Is she mad?" Daniel replies, "She's with us" (GM B9 F12 rewrite 161-63 scene 250). In that version Maureen helps Daniel move a wounded man into the helicopter and then flies off with these men.

The white woman "fits in" in South Africa by joining the black struggle. That seems the only viable choice she has. These screenplays clarify the fable Gordimer had in mind about how the politically conscious white woman "learns about survival. Not just physical survival, but in the sense of finding a way to go on living, belonging in South Africa" (GM Box 2 October 24, 1986 #3).

Gordimer had begun *July's People* in 1979 and published it in 1981. She worked on the screenplays at least through 1987 and did not abandon the project until 1989 when she received a scriptwriter's revision of her film script and rejected it outright. During these years she published *A Sport of Nature* (1987) and was working on *My Son's Story* (1990). Revising the screenplays, explaining her intentions to Roland Joffe, and envisioning how she would fit into post revolutionary South Africa—all kept the fable she began in the novel *July's People* evolving in her imagination. Thus, in *A Sport of Nature*, *My Son's Story*, and *None to Accompany Me* she creates additional scenarios— attempts to imagine still other ways for the white woman to fit in. The female protagonists in the next three books, Hillela, Hannah, and Vera, are new versions of Maureen. Like Maureen whose instinct to survive turns her into a rebel, they are actively pursuing ways to fit into the process of rapid change in South Africa.

In each of the four novels, the female protagonists are the ones sufficiently dissatisfied with the *status quo* to break away from their families and go off on their own. Each chooses a radical alternative. Like Maureen, the revolt of Hillela in *A Sport of Nature* and Vera in *None to Accompany Me* involves a shift in allegiance from the white world to a black one. Both adopt a new way of life. Hannah in *My Son's Story* has likewise left her family to assist the black liberation movement, but ultimately she goes one step beyond that: she shifts her allegiance from the black male revolutionary to the more radical black female revolutionary. Hannah cuts off her affair with Sonny when she learns that his wife Aila has been charged with terrorism, concealing arms, and acting "as a courier between Umkhonto we Sizwe in neighboring countries and a cell in the Johannesburg area" (233).

In *A Sport of Nature*, Gordimer utilizes sex to facilitate Hillela's rejection of the white world and her acceptance by the black. The absence of Hillela's parents enables her to sever all connections with her own race. Both of her parents had chosen allegiance to a sexual relationship over allegiance to their daughter . Her mother had abandoned her to be with a lover in Mozambique. Her father had chosen to live with his new wife, Billie, rather than Hillela, when he was forced to choose between the two. Then Hillela found herself rejected because of her own sexuality—first, by her Aunt Olga, for associating with a "colored" boy and then, by her Aunt Pauline, for making love with Sasha, who was Pauline's son and Hillela's cousin. However, another sexual relationship enabled Hillela to leave the country, and after she was abandoned by that white man, sexuality became her key to entering the black world.

Like Maureen, Hillela follows her instinct to survive which leads her eventually to the black African male. Hillela becomes the wife of a black revolutionary, Whaila. When she becomes his, his politics become hers. Her political activity is motivated primarily by sex, not politics. She is spurred by her devotion to him, not by her political convictions. Yet, because she is his wife, the black radicals fully trust and accept her, and she plays an active role in the international community of revolutionaries. Her sexuality has served as her key to fitting in.

Later, after Whaila's assassination, Hillela marries Reuel, a black revolutionary leader in another African country, a head of state who is also the chair of the Organization of African Unity. With him she attends the ceremony for the proclamation of the new African state that used to be South Africa. This newly liberated nation is "Whaila's country," the one for which he had given his life. By then Hillela has succeeded so well in "fitting in" that she is one of those toward whom the celebratory fists are lifted "like spores" (354). She is "the wife of the Chairman of the OAU [who] has slowly risen alongside her husband, beside the first black President and Prime Minister, his wife and the other leaders of a new nation and the Presidents, Prime Ministers, party, and union leaders of many others" (354). She fits in with the elite of Africa.

Devoting herself to her black revolutionary lovers, Whaila and Reuel, and their causes, Hillela successfully annihilated her white identity. Even in her first marriage, she had detached herself so totally from her past that she had puzzled Whaila. He had been "dismayed" by "her lack of any identification with her own people" (215). He lived so totally for his people that, for him, when she expressed her indifference, "there was something missing in her . . . like a limb or an organ" (215). Hillela had even been willing to annihilate her body—her whiteness. When she had a baby with Whaila, she was delighted "not to have reproduced herself" (202). She was pleased that her daughter Nomzamo (named for Nomzamo Winnie Mandela) was black like the father. This rejection of her white identity continued with her second black husband, Reuel. She adopted a black African name (Chiemeka) and wore traditional African clothing.

Whaila had seen their black/white "closeness as a sign; the human cause, the human identity that should be possible, once the race and class struggle were won" (215). Her willingness to shed her past identities made this gesture toward a utopian vision possible. Cut off from family, she had been free to strive for this utopian oneness. Until Whaila was assassinated, her dream had been to raise a "rainbow family"; the truest unity would come through the mixing of the races. The ideal of the rainbow family suggests that once everyone is multiracial, racism will disappear. Miscegenation, therefore, seems to be an integral part of Gordimer's utopian vision, along with economic, racial, and sexual equality.

An interracial marriage is an important way for a white woman to make her children fit into the new Africa. Gordimer's two white children chose to leave South Africa. Ironically, Hillela's dark-skinned daughter also deserted her mother's beloved Africa. Nomzamo was an exotic success in the Western, capitalist world as an internationally-known model. Sexual attraction opened Nomzamo's way into the white world just as it had opened her mother's way into the black. The response to racial and sexual difference can be repulsion; sensuality, however, can change that response to love.

In a 1988 interview, Gordimer claimed that "the two greatest drives in people's lives, the two most important things, are sex and politics." She added,

I think there may be a particular connection between sexuality, sensuality, and politics inside South Africa. Because, after all, what is apartheid all about? It's about the body. It's about physical differences. It's about black skin, and it's about woolly hair instead of straight, long blond hair, and black skin instead of white skin. The whole legal structure is based on the physical, so that the body becomes something supremely important. And I think maybe subconsciously that comes into my work too. (Bazin and Seymour 304)

Gordimer's fascination with black-white sexual relationships, which dominates *A Sport of Nature* continues to dominate her next novel *My Son's Story.* In this tenth novel, her white protagonist, Hannah, has an affair with Sonny, a black political activist. Their relationship is both intellectual and sexual. From Sonny, Hannah gains insight into a black revolutionary organization in South Africa; from Hannah, Sonny gains a friend who can listen to and respond to his political concerns.

Whereas Hillela left South Africa to carry on her love affairs and political activities, Hannah comes to Johannesburg from Lesotho. Both women are considerably further along than Maureen in their evolution toward personal independence. In *July's People* Maureen had been a dutiful South African housewife. Not until she was placed in an impossible situation did she become capable of what Gordimer describes in *A Sport of Nature* (279) and *My Son's Story* (215) as "moving on." To survive and to serve a higher cause than oneself, one must retain the freedom to move on, to abandon the known for the unknown. Thus, Maureen had abandoned her family and ran to the helicopter. In response to a series of rejections, Hillela had, in turn, forsaken her country, her family, and her race to move into the future in the company of the black African majority. Hannah has a freer spirit yet, for she is not preoccupied with a need to belong. Her career comes first; she leaves Sonny and Johannesburg because, in Sonny's words, "the common good outside self required this" (224). She left for Addis Ababa (202) to become the United Nations High Commission for Refugees Regional Representative for Africa (201). Hannah is involved in helping Africans not because of Sonny but because of her own political convictions. She was herself first and Sonny's mistress second.

Although Maureen's only thought was for her "lone survival," she had to be saved and was at the mercy of those in the *"manned"* helicopter (GM B2 January, 24, 1985). Hillela relied on men for her survival too; if one man did not help her, another would. She never had only one source of help and undoubtedly could, and often did, survive on her own. Economically independent, Hannah is free to love or not love where and when she chooses. She has what Othello so feared that he became insanely jealous—the power of the female to withdraw her love. Unlike Desdemona, Hannah does, in fact, withdraw her love; Hannah, not Sonny, ends their relationship.

Finally, in Gordimer's eleventh novel, *None to Accompany Me* (1994), Vera Stark, like Maureen, sheds her family and aims to place herself within the new society. Just as Maureen escaped while her husband, suspecting nothing, took the children to the river to fish, Vera waits until her husband, Ben, goes to London to visit their son. Ben admits in London that "she belonged to the reality back there as he himself never had, never could try to, except through her" (322). She owns their house from a prior marriage and so, without consulting him, she sells the house in his absence. Vera goes to live in an "annexe" with separate entrance belonging to Zeph Rapulana (311), a former activist who is now one of the black elite (258). Thus, she is under the protection of a black male; however, this time their relationship is not sexual even though "her whiteness would not be taboo for him, or his blackness for her" (122–23). Vera does consider the possibility of his being interested in her sexually (120-21), but she quickly decides that their relationship is on "a level that was neither sexually intuitive nor that of friendship" (122). Yet, he was very special: "Vera had never before felt—it was more than drawn to— involved in the being of a man to whom she knew no sexual pull. And it was not that she did not find him physically attractive" (123). In his presence, she feels a "reassurance she had not known she no longer found elsewhere with anyone" (123). They have a perfect relationship without sex: "They belonged together as a single sex, a reconciliation of all each had experienced, he as a man, she as a woman" (122). Perhaps more relevant to this than Gordimer recognizes is the fact that Zeph is years younger than Vera.

Vera Stark has reached an age at which she is forced to confront the fact that ultimately each of us is alone. No one else will suffer our particular pains, our illnesses, or our death. Ageing has seemingly led Gordimer to focus in this novel not just on the social condition of her white female protagonist (which can be changed) but also on the human condition (which cannot be changed). Existentially, Vera is alone. Therefore, she chooses to live alone: "To find out about my life. The truth. In the end" (313). In a September 1994 interview, Nicci Gerrard reports that the idea for *None to Accompany Me* came to Gordimer while reading this haiku by the seventeenth-century poet Basho: "None to accompany me on this path: / Nightfall in Autumn." Having used this haiku as an epigraph for her novel, Gordimer told Gerrard: "All the different relationships that people have in life that seem so much to take away the burden of self, in the end it's an illusion and you're alone." In Gordimer's words in her eleventh novel: "The bliss of placing the burden of self on the beloved turns out to be undeliverable. The beloved is unknown at any address, a self, unlike a bed, cannot be shared, and cannot be shed" (121).

Vera is not lonely but she is alone. Her aloneness is made even clearer by a startling surprise near the end of the novel; this encounter makes her seem even more alone precisely because she is sexually irrelevant. This shocking incident begins when a pipe bursts, and Vera hurries into Zeph's house, not to seek help but to borrow his pliers "to turn off the main water control in the yard" (322). Walking quietly in the dark so as not to awaken him, she took the pliers from "the cupboard in the passage between his bedroom and the bathroom" (323). Suddenly, "without any awareness of a shape darker than the darkness she came into contact with a warm soft body" (323).

Through her open jacket this one against her, breasts against breasts, belly against belly. . . . For a few seconds, maybe, she and the girl were tenderly fused in the sap-scent of semen that came from her. Then Vera backed away, and the girl turned and ran on bare feet to his bedroom where the unlatched door let her return without a sound.

Vera came out into the biting ebony-blue of winter air as if she dived into the delicious shock of it. She turned off the tap with the satisfaction of a woman perform-ing a workman-like task. (323)

Oddly enough, no emotional reaction on Vera's part is recorded, but the next generation has obviously replaced her. What goes on in the bedroom belongs to the young. And why not? Vera has her work to do at the Legal Foundation and on a committee writing the new constitution for South Africa (320). She has entered a new stage in life. At times lately she had experienced "an exaltation of solitude. It was connected with something else: A freedom; an attraction between her and a man that had no desire for the usual consummation" (306). Therefore, after walking out of Zeph's house into the garden and looking up at the stars, Vera "took up her way, breath scrolling out, a signature before her" (324).

In short, Maureen has evolved through Hillela and Hannah to become the starkly self-sufficient Vera of *None to Accompany Me*. Vera still needs male protection, but she has chosen a more impersonal source than Ben, her too adoring husband. She has abandoned Ben, "because I cannot live with someone who can't live without me" (310). Yet she has Zeph's house keys as "a precaution Zeph insisted on for her safety; if anything or anyone threatened her, a woman alone, she could come to him" (323). Vera is "working through ... dependencies" (313). She and Zeph have "loyalties but no dependencies" (321). That is why Zeph's nearness, rather than Ben's, better serves her purpose. She now views the personal life as "transitory, it is the political life that is transcendent, like art" (305). The constitution she helps to write will affect many, many lives beyond her own. An atheist, she sees her immortality in what she creates for future generations.

Living not in the main house but, symbolically, in the annexe, Gordimer's protagonist in *None to Accompany Me* has realized Maureen's illusive dream of a politically useful life among the revolutionary elite. However, even Vera is not totally independent, for she remains under the protection of an empowered black male. Although Nadine Gordimer explored black/white sexual relationships in *A Sport of Nature* (1987) and *My Son's Story* (1990), her protagonist, at this later stage in life, rejects not only family, as Maureen did in *July's People*, but also (at least with Zeph) physical intimacy. Still, the bonding between the white woman and the black revolutionary remains a constant in Gordimer's scenarios about the ways a white South African woman might fit into post revolutionary South Africa.

NOTE

I am grateful for the Ball Brothers Foundation Fellowship that provided support for my research in the Lilly Library at Indiana University–Bloomington; and the appointment as a Visiting Scholar at the Institute for Advanced Study at Indiana University during my stay in Bloomington.

In addition, I owe thanks to the Virginia Foundation for the Humanities and Public Policy; I revised this article while a Resident Fellow at The Center for the Humanities in Charlottesville.

REFERENCES

Bazin, Nancy Topping. "An Interview with Nadine Gordimer." *Contemporary Literature,* *36*, (4) (1995): 571–587.

_____ and Marilyn Dallman Seymour (Eds.). *Conversations with Nadine Gordimer.* Jackson, University Press of Mississippi, 1990.

Gerrard, Nicci. "Nadine Gordimer: Chronicler of Apartheid." *The Journal,* September 27, 1994, p. B2.

Gordimer, Nadine. "A Bolter and the Invincible Summer." In *The Essential Gesture: Writing, Politics & Places,* edited by Stephen Clingman, pp. 19-28. New York: Alfred A. Knopf, 1988.

_____. "The Gap between the Writer and the Reader." *The New York Review of Books 36*, (14) (September 28, 1989): 59–61.

_____. *July's People.* 1981. Reprint. New York: Penguin, 1982.

_____. "Living in the Interregnum." In *The Essential Gesture: Writing, Politics & Places,* edited by Stephen Clingman, pp. 261–284. New York: Alfred A. Knopf, 1988.

_____. *My Son's Story.* 1990. New York: Penguin, 1991.

_____. *None to Accompany Me.* New York: Farrar, Straus and Giroux, 1994.

_____. "A South African Childhood: Allusions in a Landscape." *New Yorker,* October 16, 1954: 121–73.

_____. *A Sport of Nature* 1987. Reprint. New York: Penguin, 1988.

_____. "Where Do Whites Fit In?" In *The Essential Gesture: Writing, Politics & Places,* edited by Stephen Clingman, 31–37. New York: Alfred A. Knopf, 1988.

Gordimer Manuscripts (when cited, abbreviated as GM with B for Box). Located at the Lilly Library, Indiana University–Bloomington. I refer to the folders in Box 2 labeled 1-+983–1986 Correspondence; 1987 Correspondence; and 1988–1989 Correspondence; and in Box 9, the folders containing the nine versions of the *July's People* screenplay. The screenplay folders are not filed in the order the versions were written. Listing the folders in chronological order would be, in my judgment, as follows: Folders 8, 13, 9, 16, 10, 11, 15, 12, 14. I have compared openings and endings, handwritten versus typed sections, format, content, and responses to letters and reports to reach that conclusion. Copyright for the screenplay is in Box 9, Folder 14; it reads Felix Licensing BVI 1987. Permission to use the manuscript material in this article was granted by Nadine Gordimer and Russell & Volkening, Inc. .

Grimm Brothers. "The Frog Prince." In *Household Stories from the Collection of the Brothers Grimm* [1886], translated by Lucy Crane, illustrated by Walter Crane, 32–36. New York: McGraw-Hill, 1966.

Visser, Nicholas. "Beyond the Interregnum: A Note on the Ending of *July's People.*" In *Rendering Things Visible: Essays on South African Literary Culture,* edited by Martin Trump, 561–567. Athens: Ohio University Press, 1990.

13

Popular Hausa Drama in Niger and the Politics of Its Appropriation

Ousseina D. Alidou

The primary objective of this chapter is to argue that prior to colonization there were various forms of drama in contemporary Hausa cultures that set the foundations for the modern Hausa popular theater. This chapter also shows that from the precolonial era to the present the Hausa popular drama has been undergoing a restructuring—of language, forms of performance and thematic contents—through the development of new subgenres or the borrowing of new artistic elements from other contact cultures, to reflect the historical and political shifts operating within Hausa society. This restructuring will be illustrated through an examination of the politics of appropriation of Hausa drama in Niger from the precolonial era to the present, and the dramatic genres resulting from the nature of these appropriations.

I will show that in the process of its restructuring, the Hausa traditional drama has lost its most essential feature as a cultural art form that is supposed to represent the voice of the "common" people, as it has been appropriated by the "dominant" classes operating in and out of the country. Thus, unlike what occurs in Latin America, where, according to McCoy (1992: 10), the term *popular theater* (or new theater) "refers to . . . alternative theaters aligned with the 'people'" (marginalized poor, working class, students, etc.) rather than with the "bourgeoisie" who is steeped in European traditions, in Niger "popular" drama unfortunately refers to drama genres that have been deprived of their original capacity to raise the critical consciousness of their performers and audience.

REVIEW OF LITERATURE

Let me begin with the first few scholars who have made a valuable contribution to the study of both the creative and artistic features of Hausa popular drama. At the national level, Dan-Inna Chaibou (1978–1979), a play critic, dramatist and professor of literature at Abdou Moumouni University was the first Nigerien scholar to present a literary critique of Hausa theatrical production in Niger. In his 1979 *Mémoire de Maîtrise*[1] thesis presented at the University d'Abidjan, Dan-Inna provides a taxonomy of Hausa traditional popular drama as performed during both secular and religious ceremonies. Dan-Inna contends that although western culture has unquestionably influenced modern Hausa theatrical performance, through the use of modern technology and the structuring of the staging of performance, it is the authentic resources available in the culture that have set the foundations of modern Hausa popular drama. The result of the incorporation of features from all forms of traditional performance—drumming, singing, oral narrative, ritual mimicking and storytelling—in Hausa theatrical production is what Dan-Inna refers to as "théatrilité" as opposed to the western concept of theater. Dan-Inna's study then raises a question previously addressed in Traoré (1972) regarding the criteria for defining African theater and its realization in different cultures. The issue involved is well stated in David Kerr (1995:1) as follows:

"There has been a heated debate as to whether drama did or did not exist in pre-colonial Africa, and to what extent it could or should be distinguished from rituals. I believe much of this confusion is caused by the use of English words like 'drama,' 'theater,' and 'ritual,' which are loaded with meanings derived from European rather than African culture." Kerr maintains that "drama refers to displays of actions to an audience in which there is an imitation of events in the real or supernatural world and there is an element or story or suspense. . . . Ritual refers to an action that is undertaken to give homage to, obtain assistance from, or in some way intercede with supernatural forces. This may or may not involve dramatic representation. I use the word theater in a very wide sense to cover drama, many forms of ritual, dance, and other performing arts such as acrobatics, mime, semi-dramatized narratives." These definitions of drama and theater are appropriate for the arguments that I develop in this chapter regarding the politics of Hausa theater appropriation in the Republic of Niger.

Janet Beik's (1987) work *Hausa theater. A contemporary Oral Art in Niger* is the second major scholarly study of Hausa popular drama in the Niger Republic. This study is very interesting because it provides in-depth information about the structure of regional Hausa popular drama including the history of theatrical troupe formation, as well as their rehearsal and play performance process. There are, however, some limitations in Beik's study of Hausa theater in Niger as it fails to provide a critical analysis of the history and politics of Nigerian Hausa theatrical production, and to clearly define its cultural essence.

FROM *WASAN KARA-KARA*: TRADITIONAL HAUSA DRAMA DURING THE PRECOLONIAL ERA

Wasan kara-kara, literally meaning "the play of the stake," can be defined as a popular parody or drama typical of traditional Hausa precolonial culture. The essence of *Wasan kara-kara* is what is called *suka* in Hausa. This is a public satire or parody of prominent leaders such as the king and his courtiers, and the religious leaders normally held accountable to the community who elected them. In the precolonial era *Wasan kara-kara* was performed every year to mark the end of a good harvesting season. Its main purpose was to give the common people the opportunity to evaluate the sociopolitical performance of their leaders through parody.

Because of its objective, the themes of this traditional drama included both a satirical denunciation of a leader's misuse of power and corruption, and an appraisal of good leadership. Other social practices not compatible with society's moral code were also thematically targeted in the satire. Thus, like many dramatic performances in other parts of Africa (Baham and Wake 1976), the traditional Hausa drama, *Wasan kara-kara*, was more a purposeful drama than a drama aimed at entertainment, which is the main characteristic of western artistic dramatic performance.

In both the precolonial and preindependence era, the actors in *Wasan kara-kara* were picked not only on the basis of their natural capacity to mimic with humor but, more important, on the basis of their physical appearance, namely their capacity to look like the doubles of the members of the society being parodied. The latter feature was an indispensable requirement of *Wasan kara-kara* performance, because it provided a mirror image of the individuals portrayed and served as a memory to the audience who appreciated the criticism disguised in the performance. Because this feature is essential to the performance of *Wasan kara-kara*, during the 1986 celebration of the International Youth Week, the daily newspaper in Niger publicized the revival of this ancient popular Hausa drama by pointing out that the performance would closely respect the original structure of *Wasan kara-kara*. This meant that the cultural organizers would lead an active search for the doubles of the political figures to be parodied, in order to attract an important audience. The advertisement of the 1986 *Wasan kara-kara* celebration read as follows in the national, government controlled newspaper:

Une première dans notre capitale! Dans le cadre de l'année internationale de la Jeunesse, le très célèbre "*wasan kara-kara*" jeu traditionel populaire de Zinder, aura lieu en 1986 une édition nationale. . . . A l'occasion on pourra voir "les doubles" de presque tous les membres du gouvernments de notre pays dont le chef de l'Etat. Les sosies qu'on pourra voir ne se montreront pas pour banaliser les personnes et les roles qu'elles incarnent: au contraire! C'est simplement du jeu qui, a Niamey, mobilise deja environ 3000 acteurs. Le spectacle promet d'etre une reussite totale. (*Sahel Dimanche* du 12 Janvier 1986: 6)

Never seen before in the capital city! In commemoration of the international youth year, there will be in 1986 a national celebration of the famous Hausa traditional popular play, Wasan kara-kara.... For this occasion, we will see the "doubles," or almost all of the members of the government of our country including the Head of the State. The doubles we will see will not ridicule these fellows nor the functions they fulfill, on the contrary! It is simply a play, which will mobilize about 3000 actors in Niamey. This spectacle promises to be an absolute success.

I will analyze later the content of this advertisement when I discuss the restructuring of *Wasan kara-kara* in the post-independence era.

Structurally, the performance of *Wasan kara-kara* has two components. First, there is the parade, during which various forms of dramatic theatrical performance take place in the form of short dramatic sketches satirically portraying different leaders without any serious commentary. The second part is at the end of the parade where the real *suka's* social satirical criticism takes place in the form of a real drama with denunciation plots. *Wasan kara-kara* is an improvised drama that relies heavily on the actors' instant creativity.

Originally, *filin taro*, "the village square," was the theater where *Wasan kara-kara* was publicly performed. *Filin taro* is an important field because it is the community arena in traditional Hausa society. It is the cultural space where the common people and the leaders of the Hausa aristocracy gathered to debate and make decisions over sociopolitical matters affecting the society's welfare. At the *filin taro*, the audience, spread over a circle, is not passive during the day long performance. It is a participatory audience that contributes by responding to an introductory call thrown at them by the griots, or the actors, in the center stage, in the form of riddles, proverbs and provocative songs. In fact, in most cases, *Wasan kara-kara* first begins with a moment of singing and drumming during the parade, when the griots metaphorically introduce the themes through the lyrics of their songs or the rhythm of their drums. This artistic combination of comic dramatic and verbal performances characterizing Hausa popular drama is what Dan-Inna (1978) refers to as *théatrilité*.

Because of the linguistic homogeneity of the community, only Hausa language is used. However, sometimes, Hausa play languages, mimic speech forms, foreign accents or minimal code-switching are used in the parody of other ethnic groups. Moreover, because Hausa traditional society is characterized by a complex class hierarchy, various speech patterns and styles are used in *Wasan kara-kara* to indicate the sociopolitical classes portrayed in the play. For example, actors portraying the aristocracy use a highly "sophisticated" register; the portrait of a member of the Hausa Islamic clergy involves an excessive or an exaggerated use of Arabic words or phrases, whereas those depicting the common people employ the "regular" speech variety associated with the *paysans*, or sometimes a vulgar language to depict "street" people. This class hierarchy is also reflected in the costumes of the actors and the identification of their houses in the staging of the play.

As Mahamadou (1988) has pointed out, *Wasan kara-kara* is one of the most committed theatrical performance forms, and it clearly indicates the existence of a dialectical structure in precolonial Hausa society, giving room to an open dialogue between the traditional leaders, who were the policy makers, and the common people affected by their policies. *Wasan Kara-kara* was performed in most Hausa regions in precolonial Niger and was tolerated and understood by both the Hausa aristocrats and the common people. It was a "popular" dramatic ethnic art form that instead of objectifying the performers and the audience, engaged both in a subjective way to reflect critically on their sociopolitical condition. Consequently, in the precolonial era, *Wasan kara-kara's* artistic performance was entirely under the control of the common people, and anybody who fulfilled the physical and artistic criteria necessary for it could act in the play without the risk of being reprimanded by the leadership. During that era, censorship of the structure or thematic contents of *Wasan kara-kara suka* by the Hausa leaders was never an issue.

FROM *WASAN KARA KARA* TO *WASAN GUJIYA*: THE MARKING OF COLONIAL HISTORY IN HAUSALAND

During the colonial era, when cash crops harvesting was imposed by France in the colonies, the name of *Wasan kara-kara* was changed to *Wasan gujiya*, meaning "the play of the peanut." This change of name reflected the socio-political condition of Hausa culture under the exploitative rules of colonialism. The name clearly indicated the Hausa people's disapproval of the cash-crop agriculture imposed upon them by the French colonial administration. In Niger, *gujiya* was one of the major cash crops the French imposed on the farmers together with high taxes on their production. Thus, during the colonial era, the targets of the parody shifted from the customary rulers of the Hausa traditional aristocracy to the colonial administrators and their local bootlickers who controlled the production and trading of peanuts in the colonies.

This historical transformation of Hausa society during the colonial era produced other important changes in the structure of *Wasan kara-kara* in addition to the name change. First, because there was no way of finding the double of a white man in Africa who would mimic colonialism and its agents, white masquerades were introduced to mimic the white colonial administrators. However, while in many African cultures concealment of the identity of the actors is an essential component of masquerade performance and dialogue drama (Harding 1996: 59–60), the introduction of white masquerade in Hausa popular drama occurred not for the purpose of disguise, but as a default mechanism. It grossly caricatured the identity of the subject of the satire— the white colonial officers—whose double was not available in the community. In fact, the essence of *Wasan kara-kara,* as a sociopolitical parody, consists in the saritical display of all the characteristics of the characters portrayed during its performance, so that the subjects parodied can properly identify themselves, and the audience can recognize their identity and fairly assess the point of the satire. Because the openness of Hausa traditional society created a safe space for a reflexive dialectical relationship between the performers, the people portrayed in the parody and the audience, secrecy during the performance became a counterproductive feature in *Wasan kara-kara*.

As for the representation of the lackeys of the colonial administration, this called for actors who, in addition to being doubles of the individuals parodied, had to have some knowledge of French or of a broken French called le français des anciens combattants, or "the old combattants French." If the double could not speak either variety of French, then the performance had to make due with the use of Hausa disguised speech forms, that in the ears of the audience sounded like French. Thus, the choice of the language form, that served to show the conflicting power dynamics operating in the society—oppressor/oppressed or colonial/ indigenous—was an important aspect of the creative dimension of this traditional drama.

While the issue of what language to use in the performance of *Wasan kara-kara*, during the precolonial era, arose only as a matter of switch register, to reflect the social classes portrayed, because there was a degree of linguistic homogeneity that allowed for the use of just one (Hausa) language, the shift of the targets of the satire introduced a linguistic change in the original structure of the play. The use of French and broken French in the play, in addition to Hausa, reflected the new power dynamics operating in Hausa society during the colonial era. Each linguistic code marked the social category represented. Hausa represented the voice of the oppressed indigenous population that now included both the *paysans* and their leaders. Actors used French in their portrayal of French colonial administrators, while broken French was used to caricature the indigenous traitors or accomplices of the French. *Wasan kara/gujiya*, originally a popular art form enabling the commoners to portray the internal class dynamics opposing the masses and their traditional leaders, became, during colonization, an art form reflecting the struggle of the natives against the European colonizers, and thus neutralizing the original internal class conflict for a common cause. The struggle for national liberation through the performing arts, eventually trans-formed *Wasan kara-kara*, the ethnic Hausa art form, into a 'popular' national symbol of resistance, particularly in the eastern regions where other ethnic groups also embraced *Wasan kara-kara* as an art form fit for parodying the colonial regime.

The intervention of colonialism in African history had an impact also on the seasonal calendars that determined the calendar of cultural events in Africa. Regarding the colonial attempt to appropriate the celebration of events in Africa, David Kerr (1995: 30–31) pointed out that:

One way in which colonialism attempted this integration was by means of rituals designed to dazzle the indigenous populations with demonstrations of imperial pomp such as coronations, jubilee, military parades, boy scout jamborees, or concerts. They were particularly associated with important festivals and anniversaries of great events in the colonial "mother" country.

Thus, like elsewhere in Africa, the celebration of *Wasan kara-kara*, originally a day long event taking place at the end of a good harvest season, was shifted to match the French colonial calendar. During the colonial era, *Wasan kara-kara* also lost its prominence as the only performing art of the day, due to its militant anticolonial character, and became one of the events in the colonial calendar of celebration. The actors were no longer anybody who wished to participate in the *Wasan kara-kara*. They were now committed Hausa people, aware of the risk they were taking in mocking the French colonial power, and ready to confront European imperialism through their theatrical performance. They were either drawn from the common people (*paysans*), who had never had any direct contact with the French prior to the introduction of forced labor, or from the ranks of the returned *tiralleurs,* who had fought on behalf of France during World War II, but who were disenchanted with the way France had treated them afterward, or from the newly educated élites who attended French colonial schools and were engaged in the struggle for African self-rule.

Thus, unlike the literary drama, whose main producers and performers were people belonging to an educated elite influenced, directly or indirectly, by *William Pointy* dramaturgic school (Baham and Clive 1976, Beik 1987, Graham-White 1976, Kerr 1995) the *Wasan kara-kara* actors, during the late colonial era, included both actors coming from the traditional Hausa dramatic school, and actors from the colonial schools, joined by solidarity against colonial subjugation.

Wasan kara/gujiya became the major artistic means of protest during the colonial era in most Hausa regions. After World War II, a special performance of *Wasan gujiya* took place in Zinder (the first colonial headquarter in a Hausa region to openly resist French domination) to mock colonial rule in Niger during General de Gaulle's visit to the colony. Given the sociopolitical climate of that era, the performance of *Wasan gujiya* was in the hands of nationalist cultural organizers who constituted the new emergent class of leaders in Hausa society.

To sum up, the militant nature of Hausa *Wasan gujiya*, during colonization, had its roots in the precolonial theater form *Wasan kara-kara*, an art form, that in traditional Hausa society, openly parodied the feudal leaders and called for resistance against oppressive ideologies.

FROM *WASAN KARA-KARA* TO *WASAN KWAYKOYO*: THE FORMATION OF A "NATIONAL" POPULAR CULTURE DURING DIORI'S REGIME

In 1960, Niger became independent with the handing over of France's political power to Nigerian nationalists. However, the transfer of power did not come without problems. Prior to the voting for independence there were two competing nationalist parties: the Sawaba party, led by Djibo Bakary, openly antagonistic to the idea of maintaining any bond with France, and the *Rassemblement Democratique Africain* party whose leader Diori Hamani was keen on preserving an alliance with France. Given the *Sawaba* party's rejection of France, the French colonial administration manipulated the election results to appoint Diori as the president of the first republic despite the majority vote in favor of the *Sawaba'* party leader Djibo Bakary. As a result of this situation, there was intense political tension in most of Niger's eastern regions mainly populated by Hausa people who were predominantly pro-*Sawaba*. In these regions the verbal arts—song lyrics, proverbs and riddles—and the performing arts, such as *Wasan kara-kara* and other mimic arts, became important tools for the political opponents of Diori's regime, serving to express their discontent concerning national matters. Often denunciations of the regime's despotism were disguised in these art forms.

In order to prevent the production of radical art forms such as *Wasan kara-kara*, Diori's regime stressed the need to create a national popular culture for the sake of national unity. The regime's cultural policy was to encourage the artistic productions of all ethnic groups, provided they promoted patriotism rather than subversion. Patriotism was understood to mean support for the government and its development programs. Thus, state censorship of art production became a law, and the production of any popular art form was controlled through the creation of youth cultural centers. These centers were opened mainly to cultural organizers or artists affiliated with the regime, or agreeing not to produce political art. In this political climate, singers produced lyrics that praised the regime or its leader, Diori Hamani, often revered in songs as the "father" of the nation. Performing visual arts such as *Wasan kara-kara* were allowed to exist only for their entertaining and comic features, cleansed from any satirical comment concerning national issues. Political satire was seen as counterproductive for the promotion of national unity. The reluctance of *Wasan kara-kara* producers to respect the regime's criteria for national cultural production led to its ban in the 1960s. Consequently, *Wasan kara-kara* lost its status as a national popular symbol of resistance and was relegated to its original ethnic status in Hausa villages.

In order to make the ban on artistic and literary production more effective, Diori's regime developed a youth party organization that controlled and shaped artistic productions according to the government's political agenda. These youth organizations known as *Jeunesse* ("Youth") in French, were a sort of political police whose main task was to assure that political and cultural activities were performed according to the regime's prerogatives. The *Jeunesse* theatrical troupes were composed of both actors accustomed to the traditional understanding of theatrical genres, such as *Wasan kara-kara*, and others who had some knowledge of the western style of theatrical performance, which they had learned through their training in colonial school, or through exposure to western dramatic performances, such as films and colonial drama. The new popular drama genre that emerged, as a result of the syncretism of elements from the indigenous culture and the western culture, is what is referred to in Hausa as *Wasan kway koyo,* or "the game of imitation." On the relationship between *Wasan kara-kara* and the origin of *Wasan kwaykoyo,* Yazi Dogo, Niger's most famous actor and dramatist, commented:

Well before colonization, there existed in Hausaland other forms of theatrical performance from which we modern artists get lots of inspiration. *Wasan kara-kara* is a sort of popular theater played in an open field and well adapted to the humor of Hausa culture. Whenever our plays deal with the customary chiefs, we go back to the tactics of satire of *Wasan kara-kara.* It is really a popular drama. [185]

When asked whether he had produced contemporary *Wasan kwaykoyo* plays inspired by *Wasan kara-kara* Yazi Dogo replied: "Well anytime there is a role that involves a chief/king or an executive, the actors take inspiration from *Wasan kara-kara.* Even if one has to create a play, and present for example scenes with a king, we refer to *Wasan kara-kara.* It is the traditional drama in Niger. *Wasan kara-kara* is all, it is the real drama of the Hausa people."

Yazi's comments indicate the influence of at least the artistic features and, to some extent, the didactic features of *Wasan kara-kara,* evolving from *suka* in the syncretic genre at the structural and comic levels. What is lost, however, with respect to the traditional genre, is the art's power to present a critical image of how citizens respond to their political leaders. *Wasan kwaykoyo* producers developed humoristic propaganda plays that praised Diori, his regime and political programs. Their only goal was to entertain the now powerless audience, the majority of which was illiterate and no longer had the right to question its leaders or protest the production of propaganda art. This resulted from the censorship imposed on all national cultural art production. About the Diori regime's political control on the performing arts, André Salifou, another pioneer of Nigerien drama and a very close colleague of Yazi Dogo, bitterly commented in an interview:

A l'époque quand on se réunissait ici à l'occasion de la Semaine de la Jeunesse, à la fin autour du directeur de la jeunesse, je répétais invariablement donc tous les ans que la sale manie que le pouvoir avait d'imposer des thèmes ne me convenait pas parce que il fallait développer des thèmes susceptibles d'entrer dans les préoccupations du gouvernement. Nous allons louer ce que le gouvernement a fait dans le secteur politique, social, et culturel ou il fallait expliquer ça dans le développement. Moi je considère que ça gène toute création. (André Salifou 1992: 79)

In the old days when we used to meet here during the Youth Celebration Week, in the presence of the Director of the center, I used to rehearse invariably every year, except when the power structure, with its dirty habits, interfered imposing themes that did not suit me because they promoted the government's agenda. We had to praise what the government had accomplished in the social, political, or cultural domains or we had to find a way to explain it in the development of themes. I myself believe that this hinders artistic creativity."

In 1965, when radio was introduced in Niger, all radio programs were controlled by the State. The idea of an improvised radio drama both in Hausa (called *Wasan kwaykoyo na radiyo)* and in other ethnic languages, was developed and strongly promoted under the control of the government. Most of the radio plays produced in the national languages were social commentaries or sheer propaganda plays that praised the government's political course.

Before discussing the restructuring of *Wasan koy koyo* at different stages of Niger's national development, it is important to bear in mind that the emergence of the modern genre of *Wasan koy koyo* in northern Nigeria has followed a different course than in Niger, although they share the same precolonial roots. Because of the difference between the two countries' colonial history, the Hausa theater in northern Nigeria, under the British indirect rule policy, was able to develop primarily as a literary dramatic genre in Hausa, although performances could incorporate improvised oral narratives (Furniss 1996; Tyloch 1985). By contrast, the contemporary popular Hausa plays in Niger have mainly been, and still are, orally improvised, performed and then transcribed depending on their national success. As Yazi Dogo put it (1992: 160), in an interview, when asked whether his plays were written or orally improvised:

Quand on monte une piece, d'abord au debut les pieces ne sont pas ecrites, on prend donc un theme comme ca, on se retrouve, on discute, on donne a chacun les idees qu'il faut developper. On s'entraine, on repete, et le jour ou la piece est bien assise, donc on la presente une fois au public, une, deux, trois fois, a ce moment maintenant elle est bien posée, c'est a ce moment que je prends mon temps pour l'enregistrer sur cassette et la transcrire.

When we compose a play, in the beginning it is not written, we just select a theme, we gather to discuss it, give each one a part to think about for the development of the play. We rehearse it, and once the play is well developed, we present it once, twice, three times to the public. Then, we begin to record it on audio tapes and eventually transcribe it.

While popular Hausa drama in Nigeria currently benefits from the academic support of dramatists from the universities' drama departments or the Center for Nigerian Cultural Studies, (Furniss 1996: 86–88), the Hausa popular drama in Niger has been controlled by both colonial and postcolonial regimes. Both have isolated it from "radical" institutions such as the universities that are perceived as being potentially subversive. Being a member of *francophonie,* the French organ of cultural assimilation and imperialism in France's former colonies, Niger could not have developed a significant drama in any of its national languages. Niger's commitment to *francophonie* was clearly demonstrated by Diori's readiness to host in Niger the first *francophonie* meeting in Africa in 1963.

HAUSA DRAMA DURING THE MILITARY REGIME

In 1974, the military led by Seyni Kountché overthrew Diori and banned any art forms that praised him or his regime in song lyrics, drama or ballets. The new regime also banned the Diori party youth organizations and installed the *Samaria* that, essentially, played the same political propaganda role that *Jeunesse* had played for the previous regime. The *Samaria* were in charge of cultural and artistic productions that, again, had to conform to the military government's agenda. Their dramatic performance often consisted of praises for the government, or the promotion of its development policies.

Under the military regime, the radio drama team benefitted from the building of stage facilities through the development of television broadcasting in Niger in 1978. Like the *Samaria* drama, usually performed during special national events, both Hausa radio drama and television drama weekly air political propaganda plays, or social commentary plays subject to government censorship.

The first television drama that inaugurated the first day of TV broadcasting in Niger, in 1979, was produced by Yazi Dogo's troupe. Later, however, the national radio drama team and the Samaria theatrical troupes became the main producers of TV drama. Radio drama actors, TV actors and actors in Yazi Dogo's troupe all claim that their drama production relies heavily on improvisation. They also reassert the Hausa origin of their art, and claim that their theater, although borrowing some elements from western and other African forms of theatrical performance, owes its performance structures to the Hausa traditional *Wasan kara-kara*.

In the mid 1980s, the Kountché regime, as part of his *retour à l'authenticité* agenda, attempted to revive the spirit of *Wasan kara-kara*, that had been banned in the late 1960s by the Diori regime. What is paradoxical about the military regime's concept of 'return to authenticity,' as far as *Wasan kara-kara* and other forms of traditional dramatic performance are concerned, are the limitations that the government has imposed on the artists' ability to recapture the original essence of the drama. In the case of *Wasan kara-kara*, what the military regime eliminated is the artists' freedom to satirize the political leaders, without their lives and creativity being threatened. Thus, *Wasan kara-kara* from a radical art form has been turned into a comic one, deprived of any capacity to present a satirical critique of society. This essential change is reflected in the ad previously mentioned ("we will see the 'doubles' of almost all the members of the government of our country among whom the Head of the State . . .") whose content assured the leaders that the performance of *Wasan kara-kara*, during the 1986 youth week, would praise rather than satirize the members of the government who were to be the targets of the parody.

The thematic production of the plays of the more contemporary Hausa drama *Wasan koy koyo* was also affected by the takeover by the military whose political philosophy differed from that of the previous regime. The concept of *Société de developpement* ("planned development"), on which the military regime's rule was based, became one of the recurrent themes of most plays in Hausa produced by the competing national theatrical troupes, none of them making any criticism of this political orientation. Thus, the new *Wasan kway koyo* theater, like the other popular theaters appropriated by the dominant class in Africa, performs a propaganda role disguised under the name of "theater for development" (Beik 1987). As the artists are forced to bow to the government's concept of development, their art is stripped of the critical power to raise people's consciousness on social issues affecting their lives. Thus, the essential feature of the Hausa popular drama, under the military regime, whether it be *Wasan kara-kara* or *Wasan kway koyo*, is its distance from the underclass, whose interest it was supposed to protect. An illustration of how the Hausa drama has been newly appropriated to serve the propaganda needs of the postindependence regimes, can be found in the thematic contents of the plays nominated for, or winners of, national festival prizes during Kountché's regime. One of the plays that won the 1980 national competition prize is *Ba Ga Irinta Ba*, also known as *Maman Arrivé*. The plot revolves around the plight of an "irresponsible," "French illiterate," self-made, successful Hausa businessman who confronts his son's school teacher because the latter has severely scolded his son for not being a model student. Throughout the play, what emerges in a dangerously seductive, captivating humor is advocacy for a top-down system of governance within the framework of the *Société de developpment* as defined by the regime. Within this authoritarian framework, the play portrays a social situation where illiteracy in French and nonaffiliation with the regime's *Société de developpement's* local association become synonymous of ignorance and civic disobedience. This is exemplified by the behavior of Maman Arrivé, a citizen who does not hold a membership card of any local political associations. In summing up the scenes of the winning play, Beik (1987: 5) commented:

The scenes form two sets of parallel progression: that of the problems at school reverberating through official channels (from Maman Arrivé's home, to the school, to the inspector's office, to the mayor's office) and that of the resolution of those problems which follow a similar route from Maman's neighborhood's house, to the school, with talk of going to the inspector, to the police station. In this way, the actions demonstrate to the audience not only Maman's growing dilemma (the plot), but also how the government's institutions work and their line of responsibility, power, and authority.

Thus, what is referred to as Hausa "theater for development" in Niger does not allow for the production of plays questioning the failure of government's institutions, like for example, the school system that cannot meet the aspirations of students and parents because it imposes a Francophone type of education that is more subjugating than liberating. Governmental control of the performing arts prevents the production of plays that portray the condition of oppressed people like Maman Arrivé. In this way, the Hausa popular drama has become an important tool of mind control during Kountche's regime.

To sum up, the primary goal of the Hausa popular drama—whether performed on radio or at cultural centers by committed cultural organizations—during both the Diori regime and the military regime, has become the articulation of what Etherton (1982) called the "social rhetoric" of the government. It has served to make the public aware of the government social and political agenda, while avoiding criticism of government's policies even if they harm the nation's welfare.

OTHER AFRICAN EXPERIENCES

What I described in the context of the restructuring of Hausa popular drama is not unique to Niger. The same phenomena have been reported elsewhere in Africa, although with slight structural and functional variations depending on the socio-political and historical circumstances of the given culture. While in Niger nationalist cultural activists leaned on the structure of the traditional, radical performing arts, like *Wasan kara-kara*, to contest the colonial introduction of a cash crop economy, in places like Kenya (Kerr, 1995: 31–32), the British colonial administrators integrated elements of the precolonial performing arts (such as dance, songs, narrative motifs) to create a sort of indigenous theater—often referred to as "theater for development"—that served the colonial agenda. In other words, the British used the indigenous drama as a tool for manipulating the mind of the colonized. Kerr adds that another purpose of the theater for development in the British colonies was to create separatist communities and prevent the emergence of the type of class solidarity between noneducated and educated Africans, that developed in Hausaland. Kerr (1995: 31) argues that the goal of theater for development in the British colonies in Africa was:

to solve a fundamental contradiction in the modes of informal adult education, namely that part of capitalist dynamic was towards creating a 'modern' or 'progressive' class which could achieve the desired agricultural surplus from cashcrop farming, but another part was to suppress those influences which might create 'cheeky natives' who aspired to equality with whites. This contradiction was particularly strong in British colonial policy, with its non-assimilationist ideology of indirect rule.

Religion is another factor that affected the restructuring of the traditional drama resulting from colonial intervention in Nigerien Hausa culture and other African cultures. Kerr (1995) and others have shown how both the French and the British appropriated all forms of precolonial dramatic art in their campaign to convert the indigenous populations to Christianity. Kerr (1995: 33) comments on the emergence of an indigenous Christian theater in Africa as follows:

Particularly in West Africa, the missionaries saw the psychological advantage of employing converted black African auxiliaries as catechists and ministers to promote the Christian faith. They found them particularly skillful in their use of dramatic entertainment of a quasi-indigenous kind to sugarcoat the pill of Christian propaganda.

These "mystery" dramas played an important part in the development of Opera.

The missionaries' appropriation of the traditional performing arts to promote Christianity could not have been possible in Hausaland where a successful cultural and military *Jihad* was led against European colonialism. The rejection of Christianity in Hausaland occurred both in the French and the British territories, although in the latter it figured as an essential element of the peace pact between the Hausa-Fulani Lords in Northern Nigeria and Lord Lugard. Concerning the Muslim Hausa-Fulani strive to preserve their Islamic cultural hegemony during the colonial era, Furniss (1996: 3) noted that:

[t]he descendants of the reform movement of 1804 were faced with the arrival of the British and the French at the end of the century. Lord Lugard's forces inflicted a measure of military defeat upon the northern cities such that a complex pattern of resistance, some withdrawal and more accommodation struck between Lugard and the leaders of the Hausa states involved confirmation, and often reinforcement, of the position of the chief in exchange for allegiance to the crown through acceptance of direction from a local British political officer, the Resident. One important component, in this original deal, was the agreed exclusion from the North of Christian missionaries.

Both the emergence of a nonliterary, modern popular drama in African languages—a genre that combines aesthetic and functional elements drawn from precolonial theatrical forms and western dramaturgic performance (Graham-White 1976; Kerr 1995; Traoré 1972)—and its use by African nationalists as a tool for raising people's consciousness against colonial domination, during the struggle for independence, and in the early post-independence era, were not unique to Hausa culture in Niger. As Idoye writes (1996: 63–64), with regard to the structure of the precolonial African theater in Zambia: "The Africans performed a repertory of plays handed down by their forbearers. The colonialists never recognized the existence of the African theater because it had no resemblance to what the Europeans considered as theater." Idoye also discusses the emergence of the contemporary popular *Chikwakwa* theater from the traditional precolonial African theater, not just as a form of artistic entertainment during the Zambian independence struggle against the white settlers, but as a political medium for raising the Africans' consciousness against white supremacy. One of the main differences between the Hausa and the Zambian colonial and postcolonial theater is that the latter developed both as a literary and an oral-improvised genre, mostly because it was controlled by the university drama department. By contrast, the Hausa popular theater in Niger remains up to date mainly an improvised theater not subjected to any academic control. In the same study, Idoye (1996: 158) argues that although the *Chikwakwa* theater, after independence, was appropriated by the government to promote the national philosophy of "Humanism," which embodied the principle of Zambian national development, it nevertheless managed to maintain its link with the rural communities. This makes the *Chikwakwa* theater more popular than the Hausa theater that has lost its capacity to reflect people's true socio-political realities.

HAUSA DRAMA AND THE PROCESS OF DEMOCRATIZATION IN NIGER

In this chapter I discuss the social-political and historical circumstances that, in Niger, have determined the development of new popular theatrical Hausa genres, that could be characterized as politically committed art forms addressed to the masses. The precolonial *Wasan kara-kara* and *Wasan gujiya*, and the *Wasan kara-kara* performed during the early postindependence era could be considered as revolutionary theater (or "popular" theater as under-stood in the context of Latin American popular theater). During those periods drama was used by both the artists and the masses as a means for social liberation either from the internal dominant class or from the external colonial oppressor. The same, however, cannot be said of the postindependence Hausa drama *Wasan kwaykoyo*, that was appropriated, for propaganda purposes, by the power structure. The aesthetic production and performance of the popular drama during the precolonial and postindependence eras combined both a satire and an undisguised mimesis of the characters portrayed, in order to generate a social dialectic across classes within the society.

My argument is that the democratization of dramatic performance in the precolonial period and during the national struggle, was possible because of the preexisting democratic system that governed social relations in traditional Hausa society. The indigenous understanding of democracy that sustained the production of a liberated art form like *Wasan kara-kara* in the traditional society, was gradually undermined by European colonial power. Although the nationalist drama produced in the Hausa militant anticolonial regions, like Zinder, was also a liberated and revolutionary drama, its survival was quenched by governmental censorship. Consequently, while Latin American popular theaters continue to produce anti-imperialist, mass-oriented plays, the Hausa nationalist theater survived only from 1945 to the early 1960s, when the Diori Hamani regime banned any kind of antigovernment artistic performances.

The new Hausa drama that has emerged with the appropriation of the dramatic troupes and the monopolization of cultural centers by the govern-ment could also be called a politically committed drama. It is often referred to as "development drama" (Beik 1984, 1987). However, unlike the precolonial drama that established a democratic relationship between the elites and the masses, this new drama has become a political tool that objectifies the masses with entertainment and government propaganda.

In order to play an active role in the democratization process, the Hausa drama must regain its traditional "popular/militant" and democratic character and the power to portray in a dialectical manner the sociopolitical and cultural reality of the people. It should return to be a liberated art form engaging both its producers, the masses, and the ruling classes to reflect on the conditions of their cultural struggles, without any control of its social and cultural function.

NOTE

1. *Mémoire de Maîtrise* is the equivalent of a master's thesis.

REFERENCES

Baham, Martin, and Wake, Clive. 1976. *African Theater Today*. London: Pitman Publishing Ltd. .

Beik, Janet. 1987. *Hausa Theater in Niger: A Contemporary Oral Art*. New York: Garland Publishing Inc.

Dan-Inna, Chaibou. 1978–1979. *La Théatralité en Pays Hausa*. Mémoire de Maîtrise, Université Nationale de Côte d'Ivoire.

Dogo, Yazi. 1992. Interview in Penel, Jean. *Literature Nigerienne: Rencontre*, vol. 1. Niamey: Editions du Ténéré.

Etherton, Michael. 1982. *The Development of African Drama*. London: Hutchinson.

Furniss, Graham. 1996. *Poetry, Prose and Popular Culture in Hausa*. Washington, DC: Smithsonian.

Graham-White, Anthony. 1976. *The Drama of Black Africa*. New York: Samuel French.

Harding, Frances. 1996. "Actor and Character in African Masquarade Performance." *Theater Research International, 21* (1): 59–71.

Idoye, Patrick E. 1996. *Theater and Social Change in Zambia: The Chikwakwa Theater*. Lampeter: The Edwin Melle Press.

Kerr, David. 1995. *African Popular Theater: From Precolonial to the Present Day*. London: Studies in African Literature.

Mahamadou, Amadou. 1988. "Le Wasan Kara, Koteba Nigerien?" In *Sahel Dimanche du 22 mai 1988*.

McCoy, Ken. 1992. "Liberating the Latin American Audience: The Conscientizacâo of Enrique Buenaventura and Augusto Boal." *Theater Insight, 14,* 10–16.

Salifou, André. 1992. Interview in Penel, Jean. 1992. *Literature Nigerienne: Rencontre*, vol. 1. Niamey: Editions du Ténéré.

Traoré, Bakary. 1972. *Black African Theater and its Social Functions*. Ibadan: Ibadan University Press.

Tyloch, G. 1985. *Literatures in African Languages: Theoretical Issues and Sample Surveys*, ed. B. W. Andrzejewski, S. Pilaszewicz, W. Tyloch. New York: Cambridge University Press.

14

Developmental Pleasures, Education, Entertainment, and Popular Literacy in South Africa

Loren Kruger

In South Africa today, the clear-cut opposition between the state and its antagonist, the people, which sustained the antiapartheid struggle, has been replaced by many local skirmishes, whose participants largely regard the new people' government, as a remote authority. The unassailable image of *people's culture*, understood as "cultural weapon" (Masakela 1989)—a normative category for mobilization—has at least in part given way to a patchwork of popular cultures—a variety of forms, practices, and habits of consumption—in contradictory relation to ongoing grassroots struggle, regional, national and international mass media, and the pleasures and pitfalls of modernity. This entails, for the majority of South Africans, as for other denizens of the South, the desired, anticipated, and deferred good life of liberation. This desire may focus directly on immediate needs—housing, health, employment—but also encompasses a contradictory sense of modernity—the thrill and threat of the city, the aspiration of individual autonomy and the persistence of dependence.

In this context, which contains in uneasy coexistence and friction, First and Third Worlds, north and south, culture for development has to critically negotiate the dialectic of modernity—as an object of desire and aversion—if it is to avoid the twin temptations of naive developmentalism (the West is best and we have to catch up) and a capitulation to capitalism and consumerism, on the one hand, or of demonizing modernity as mere cultural imperialism on the other. This means, in practical terms, that South African cultural for development cannot simply imitate the influential paradigm of theater for development, from Botswana (Kidd and Byram 1978) and Lesotho (Mda 1993) to Tanzania (Mlama 1991), whose constituents have been predominantly rural and whose mode of transmission almost always oral in explicit or implicit resistance to state manipulation of mass media and literacy dissemination.

I do not wish to slight the achievements of theater for development, especially the projects critical of facile claims for the immediate impact of theater on social change (Mda 1993; Mlama 1991), nor to dismiss the efforts of current projects in South African—such as the AIDS education theater of the Johannesburg Health Department and the African Research and Educational Puppetry Program (Evian 1992; Friedman 1992).

I do want to suggest, however, that an exclusive focus on oral transmission ignores the impact of alternative media at odds with state centralized institutions. It also underestimates the widespread perception of the city as crucible of modernity, a perception that pervades rural as well as urban communities, as well as the part played by visual and linguistic literacy in the making of modernity. Literacy should be understood not merely in terms of acquisition of discrete skills by those allegedly empty of education (Freire 1985: 44) but rather in terms that take into account the perspectives and values of those seeking literacy and its benefits perceived to be associated with skills (Smith 1990: 264), including desired access to modern agency and "reinventing identity" (Bhola 1990: 18).[1]

Conversely, while one should acknowledge that the effects of apartheid schooling for subjection reverberate in the indifference of many young people to the formal discipline of literacy, we should not therefore assume that this discipline is essentially oppressive. As Johannes Fabian has recently argued, literacy should be understood not as an abstract and remote development goal, but rather as a variable ensemble of concrete skills and habits evolving in dynamic interaction in particular contexts (Fabian 1993: 82–83).

The link between the modernity and literacy in English, as twin aspirations has been strong, but not straightforward in recent South African history. In colonial and neocolonial South Africa, English was the medium of instruction for the mission schools that provided the sole opportunity of formal education for Africans. Under apartheid's enforcement of the "tribal" vernaculars, English, continued—at a distance—to signify emancipation. Today, African parents scramble to send their children to "English" schools, while progressive educators caution against overly hasty abandonment of mother-tongue instruction (McKenzie 1994). While debates on the institutionalization of South Africa's ten national languages continues and nationalists from Afrikaner and African (predominantly Zulu) ranks seek to preserve or secure preeminent status, English retains its prestige as well as its historical associations with emancipation. At the same time, English in South Africa has developed its own distinctive character in reaction not only to regional vernaculars but also to the pressures and opportunities of invention and improvisation characteristic of languages in widespread use as a *lingua franca*.

Acknowledging that literacy is multiple and often fractured and that literacy in English involves competence in a range of linguistic and cultural registers and the ability to negotiate the boundaries between registers, teachers, especially those addressing the needs of students on the fringes of formal schooling, the generation whose education was disrupted by a decade and a half of social turmoil since 1976,[2] have turned to media that traverse the boundaries between formal and informal communication, pleasure and instruction, word and image. The comic, or, more precisely, the graphic short story straddles these boundaries and has become in recent years an exemplary means of charting this territory.[3] Because media distribution, outside public broadcasting, remains mostly in the hands of white entrepreneurs, the production and circulation of print media other than newspapers remain relatively limited.

In the 1980s, simple sketches illustrating learning strategies appeared in the education supplements of progressive newspapers such as the *New Nation* and *South*, as well as *Learn and Teach*, a magazine designed for students by the independent organization, South African Council on Higher Education.[4] These short strips were clearly didactic; they made little use of the dramatic techniques and the narrative and visual suspense of comics and avoided the taint of melodrama and romance associated, at least in South Africa, with the more familiar photonovella. Cheaply produced photonovella romances, in grainy black and white, with titles like *Kyk* or *Bona* (*See*) and plots that favor adventure and marriage drama, have circulated widely, especially among first generation city dwellers with primary education, although not on the scale of chapbooks sold at the Onitsha market in Nigeria in the 1950s and 1960s, or comics in Mexico, for instance, where one third of the population typically reads a comic a week (Ross 1988).[5]

Although there is no long-standing production of comics in South Africa (Esterhuysen 1991: 274), at least in format familiar to American readers of comics, mass market or independent, independent educational groups, such as the Storyteller Group (Johannesburg) and Story Circle (Cape Town) in consultation with public institutions such as Witwatersrand University (Wits) and the Medical Research Council, have recently experimented with full-length (over 30 pages, A4 format) graphic short stories for readers, predominantly young adults in their teens and early twenties. Although the graphic short stories incorporate information and guidance on topics such as AIDS and, less directly, gender socialization, they do so within a narrative framework and visual style borrowed from the melodrama and romance conventions of the photonovella, which provide a familiar format and a generic framework more appealing than more overtly educational material.

Story Circle's *Roxy* (1993), for instance, subtitled *Life, Love, and Sex in the Nineties*, employs the photonovella format to portray the lives of coloured and African teenagers in inner city Cape Town, encompassing the sexual and social dilemmas faced by young people, who might be Christian and Moslem, hetero- and homosexual, men or women.[6] The photonovella incorporates potentially explosive social issues such as the roles of women, gay identity, and African machismo, as well as pointed advice on dealing with drugs and alcohol, and condom use, by embedding these topics within scenes of family gossip or peer group teasing, as well as the dynamics of the romance scenario.

These scenes are in turn represented in a visual style that combines the verisimilitude of the photographs with the cartoon character of exaggerated gestures and facial expressions, occasionally off-kilter framing and camera angles, and printed sound effects. This strategy seeks not only to grant legitimate space to taboo topics, but to *naturalize* them as part of everyday life and so make them part of the pleasure of recognizing the everyday and the local as "storied" (Esterhuysen 1991: 276), as amenable, in other words, to legitimate representation as the (often imported narratives of the metropolitan mass media. The popularity of this photonovella among young people in rural kwaZulu, whose linguistic, social, and economic development differs sharply from that of the characters in *Roxy*, suggests that readers' perceptions of legitimate locale and their (self) recognition in this narrative are more flexible processes than health policy might have predicted (Schneider 1994).

Rural readers' reinterpretations and recreations of urban-based narratives is both the subject and the occasion of the Storyteller Group's most recent graphic short story, *Heart to Heart* (1994). Drawing on graphic styles from a variety of sources, including Hergé (*Tintin* in Belgium) and the brothers Hernandez (*Love and Rockets*, USA), this group had produced mostly stories about young urban students. Their best-known works, *99 Sharp Street* (1990), distributed as a series of inserts in the catalog of Sales House, a Johannesburg department store whose clients include white collar workers as well as students, dealt with the lives of young Africans attempting to further their education (Esterhuysen 1991: 274—279). Drawn in a clear-line style reminiscent of Hergé (by a Portuguese-South African, Carlos Carvalho), the stories were situated in Hillbrow, an integrated but unsettled inner-city neighborhood and the language combined Std 8 (Grade 10) English in the text-blocks with city and township slang in the bubbles, written in large part by the young playwright, Nhanhala Sicelo; the title alludes to "sharp, sharp," response to the greeting "Heyta Ngwenya?" (or "Eita Da! Hoezit?", roughly "Yo! What's happenin'?").

Although produced for urban readers, *99 Sharp Street* proved popular enough with students in rural schools to encourage the production of a local story. *Heart to Heart* (1994), a graphic romance in two versions, *Dream Love* and *True Love*, and a metacommentary identified as "the students' story," was produced by the Storyteller Group on the basis of videotaped workshops with students from Magwagwaza High School in Timbavati in the Eastern Transvaal in 1991 and 1993. While the story, the wooing of a student, Tintswalo, by Magezi, an older, relatively well-off store owner in the village, and the pictured environment of half-built schools and improvised dwellings, depict the reality of rural poverty in what was then the Gazankulu reserve, the production of the graphic story mediates this reality in a number of ways. *Dream Love* offers a happy ending of sorts, with the marriage of Magezi and Tintswalo, which nonetheless dodges the question of his womanizing and her abandoned schooling in favor of their child, as well as the gender and economic basis of his status, is clearly mediated by metropolitan mass cultural prototypes, radio series in the vernacular alongside TV soap operas from the United States. The alternative scenario of *True Love*, in which Tintswalo asserts herself against Magezi's double standard, leaving the romance open-ended, conforms primarily to the wishes of the facilitators. Finally, the entire project, though staged in the rural periphery, is necessarily sustained by the resources of the center, from Liberty Life's sponsorship of Applied English Language Studies at Wits in Johannesburg to the Wits Rural Facility (WRF) near Acornhoek, a village that has become a kind of commercial center thanks to capital generated, directly or indirectly, by the presence of WRF.

Student reaction to this occasion suggests an awareness of ambiguities in the dialectic between agency and dependence. According to project coordinator, Patricia Watson (1994), students responded enthusiastically to the prospect of creating a story of their own, but remained wary that researchers from Johannesburg or WRF, Johannesburg's surrogate in the Mhala Mhala district, were just "playing with them." They and their community also expected something in return for the students' labor. Compensation, which took the form of food and transportation during workshops and English teaching during a local teachers' strike (with their permission) against the Bantustan administration, had symbolic rather than economic significance but was essential to the success of the project in a community where many—mostly migrant laborers and their under-employed families—receive little from metropolitan capital—financial or cultural. Furthermore, the authority of the coordinator, an unmarried urban white woman not much older than the students, had continually to be negotiated as a permissible exception to local gender relations that pitted the informal, but considerable power of older matriarchs against the fractured prestige of migrant men (Ngwenya 1994).

This dialectic of agency and dependence, modernization and traditional *habitus*, should not be seen as merely background, since it not only provided material for workshops and the published story, but also determined the distinct character of each encounter. In the first case, in 1991, students met in WRF, which they and the facilitators identified as a kind of "Egoli" (place of gold) in the periphery.[7] They based this workshop on scenes from *99 Sharp Street*, which reinforced the prestige of Egoli, even if reenactments were interrupted and redirected following the simultaneous dramaturgy of Augusto Boal (Boal 1979:132). The use of *99 Sharp Street* encouraged students to speak in English, thus initially favoring those with greater facility in the language, but discussions about social mores tended often to slip into Tsonga (Watson 1994). *Dream Love*, the result of the first workshop, is certainly situated in Timbavati Village but the representation of local lives is shaped by the inexorable pressure of the romance logic on the narrative generated by the students— Tintswalo marries Magezi, despite his womanizing and his mother's disapproval of a woman she calls a *xitlakati* (used rag)—and on the graphic style chosen by the Storyteller artist, Justin Wells, which offers glamorous portraits in close-up with everyday village detail in the background). Although not as self-referential, these images recall the representation of the fictional Central American village of Palomar in Gilbert Hernandez's *Heartbreak Soup* and *Chelo's Burden* in the *Love and Rockets* collection, from the voluptuous and determined women to the decidedly unbucolic village.

Rather than dispense with glamorous pictures, which intellectuals might consider un-African, but African youth still enjoy (Ngwenya 1994), the team gave voice and image to their doubts in the "students' story" that bridges the two romances. Watson's concerns about the sexist aspects of *Dream Love*, not only sexual coercion and the reinforcement of female domesticity rather than autonomy, but also the pressures on young men to make up for their economic dependence on women by physically abusing them, became the point of departure for workshops to reenact and revise *Dream Love*. Using a light sketchy quality reminiscent of *99 Sharp Street*, rather than the lush images of *Dream Love*, the "students' story" recalls the educational directives of the earlier graphic, as well as the improvised feel of its narrative. *True Love*, on the other hand, returns to the seductive pictures along with the narrative frame of the rural romance. This version begins with the same first page and apparent preparations for the wedding, only to deconstruct this idyll as a daydream. Thereafter, it continually juxtaposes elements of the "dream" script and romantic images with Tintswalo's skeptical reactions and, in lieu of a conclusion, displays the disjunction between romantic lush images and angular and ironic metagraphic, as creators are figured inspecting their handiwork.

The reactions of target readers—students and young people in urban and periurban, as well as rural areas—suggest that the foregrounding of the process of production, and the multiplicity of potential stories made available a discourse about process and reflection that had not been readily accessible. To be sure, participants in focus groups (conducted in the relevant vernaculars, including English, by local facilitators) read *Dream* and *True Love* literally, in that they interpreted these stories as indications of actual behavior patterns, as well as normatively, as instructions for better modes of behavior (Storytellers Group 1994: 4, 6, 8). Reactions to the "student's story," however, reflect an interest in the process of creating narrative and meaning—"It's got more ideas in it"; "I think we can do a continuation of the Students' Story"; "the actors saw their mistakes and changed them" (1994:8). This attention to process, as well as to the ways in which a story about a particular rural place might nonetheless resonate in other places (both urban and rural) suggests the development of creative agency in shaping the story (11) rather than merely obeying its instructions.

Heart to Heart's significance for culture and development lies in the way in which the graphic story and the different accounts of its creation make visible the tension between manipulation and communication, critical intervention and outside imposition, that troubles—and animates—not only this particular project, but the staging of conscientization more generally, which, as Zakes Mda's dissection of culture for development aspirations reminds us, is not an automatic product of certain forms or practices (Mda 1993: 186). What it can do is provide a stage for enacting the dialectic between fiction and daily practice, or, in Raymond Williams's words, between "subjunctive" and "indicative" action (Williams 1981: 219, 224), a place and occasion that might be called a "virtual public sphere," a discursive and social field within which alternative representations of potential action can be entertained before they are tested in practice (Kruger 1994: 117). To be sure, this field occupies a small space in an education system that still relies heavily on rote and corporal punishment to discipline overflowing classes of unevenly prepared students, but nonetheless offers the terrain for alternative scenarios, whose constituent elements may be local but whose resonance, as in the case of *Roxy* and *Heart to Heart*, is potentially national—even international—in scope.[8]

The work of the Storyteller Group and Story Circle are part of a growing variety of projects in South Africa that depart in a number of ways from the culture for development paradigm. They respect the specific concerns of rural and urban communities but also showing their necessary and productive interaction; they draw on modes of oral transmission and live performance but stress the value of appropriating mass mediation from print to video, and they recognize the ambiguous impact of national and international capital—Liberty Life, Shell Oil, and so on—alongside state subsidy, while demonstrating how this capital may be put to use. They acknowledge, moreover, that the lives of their audiences and interlocutors, even in areas like the former Bantustans, are shaped, in positve as well as negative ways, by the pleasures of mass mediated representations of popular recreation, as well as those of local recreation. The achievement of these local projects is grounded in their capacity to *entertain* these pleasures in dialogue with but not in subservience to the pressure of immediate need.

NOTES

1. Bhola's overview of literacy in Africa (in recognition of the International Year of Literacy, 1990) takes no account of conditions in South Africa. While this is not surprising from a practical point of view, (South Africa's effective exclusion from the United Nations led to the exclusion of UN agencies from South Africa), the legacy of this isolation is the perpetuation of a sort of South African exceptionalism.

2. The school boycotts of the 1970s and 1980s have led to an increase in the number of young adults attempting to earn a living in the city, while trying to finish their secondary school education in mostly commercial "cram colleges," rather than formal, but often dysfunctional schools in the townships.

3. I use the term *graphic short story* first to acknowledge the term used by African members of pilot groups organized by the Storytellers Group and secondly to distinguish the relatively unfamiliar illustrated format from the more familiar photo-novella or photocomic.

4. At the time of writing, *New Nation* and *South* are floundering as nongovern-mental organization funding that used to target antiapartheid ventures now goes to the

postapartheid government. *Learn and Teach* also recently suspended publication.

5. Esterhuysen uses these examples as points of comparison for the popular *aspirations* of the Storyteller Group, rather than as a quantitative measure of their impact. Since the stories here are designed to change prevailing social habits, the notion of popular culture that they embody departs from that represented by the Onitsha chapbooks, which tended to be socially conservative in their celebration of fantasies about fame and fortune in the city, as well as unequal gender relations; however, much their informality—in production and distribution as well as language and format— suggested popular resilience (Barber 1987: 38–39, 48–53). Closer to home, the success in its 1950s heyday of *Drum* magazine among literature and marginally literate urban South Africans, should not make us forget that it was run by white mining capital, which determined the subjects (and omissions) of its famous exposés.

6. My usage here is the conventional one, which acknowledges the ongoing relevance of cultural and ethnic difference in a nonracial polity: "African" refers to people who have historically spoken Bantu languages, whether or not they continue to identify themselves as members of a tribe or practitioners of animist custom; "Colored" refers to people of mixed descent, who have historically spoken Afrikaans and, more recently, English, and whose religious affiliation tends to be Christian or Moslem, but not animist. Colored inhabitants of the Western Cape ports, especially Cape Town, (the earliest urban settlement in the country) have for various reasons—among them, cosmopolitan contact, and the disassociation with the patriarchal nationalism of African and Afrikaner persuasion—tended to be more tolerant of overt homosexual identification than other sectors of South Afrian society (Gevisser 1994: 28), a tendency reflected in *Roxy*.

7. Egoli (or eGoli) is the Nguni (Zulu/ Xhosa) name for Johannesburg, place of gold, also used as a borrowing in Tsonga, the community language of the area and now one of South Africa's national languages. It also signifies, in more general terms, a site that defines prestige for those far away. Indeed, students in Timbavati village are likely to be more aware of goings-on in and about Johannesburg than in the neighboring districts.

8. *Heart to Heart* is already circulating in Zimbabwe and will be distributed in West Africa, in French translation by Bayard (Watson 1994).

REFERENCES

Barber, Karen. 1987. "Popular Arts in Africa," *African Studies Review, 30* (3), 1–78.
Bhola, H. S. 1990. "Overview of Literacy in Sub-Saharan Africa." *African Studies Review, 33* (3), 5–20. (Special issue on the International Year of Literacy).
Boal, Augusto. 1979. *Theater of the Oppressed.* Trans. Charles and Marla-Odilia Leal McBride. New York: Urizen.
Esterhuysen, Peter. 1991. " 'Heyta Ngwenya'. 'Sharp, sharp'. Popular Visual Literature and a New Pedagogy." In *Media Matters in South Africa*, ed. Bob Ferguson. Durban: University of Natal. 274–279.
Evian, Clive. 1992. "Community Theater and AIDS Education in South Africa. *Progress* (spring/ summer): 34–37.
Fabian, Johannes. 1993. "Keep Listening. Ethnography and Reading." In *The Ethnography of Reading*, ed. Jonathan Boyarim. Berkeley: University of California Press. 80–97.

Freire, Paulo. 1985. *The Politics of Education, Culture, Power and Liberation*. Trans. Donaldo Macedo. South Hadlēy, MA: Bergin and Garvey.

Friedman, Gary. 1992. "Puppetry and AIDS Education." *Progress* (spring/ summer): 38–40.

Gevisser, Mark. 1994. "A Different Fight For Freedom. A History of Gay and Lesbian Lives in South Africa." Introduction to *Defiant Desire*. Johannesburg: Ravan. 14– 56.

Kidd, Ross, and Byram, Martin. 1978. *Popular Theater and Participation in Development*. Gaborone: Bosele Tshwaraganang Publications.

Kruger, Loren. 1994. "Placing 'New Africans' in the 'Old' South Africa. Drama, Modernity and Racial Identities in Johannesburg, ca. 1935." *Modernism and Modernity, 1* (2), 113–131.

Masakela, Barbara. 1989. Keynote Address. *Culture in another South Africa*. Willem Campschreur and Joost Divendal, eds. New York: Olive Branch Press.

McKenzie, Judith. 1994. Interview, Wits [Witwatersrand University] Rural Facility, Acornhoek, 15 November.

Mda, Zakes. 1993. *When People Play People. Development Communication through Theater*. Johannesburg: Witwatersrand University Press.

Mlama, Penina. 1991. *Culture and Development. The Popular Theater Approach in Africa*. Uppsala: Nordiska Afrikainstitutet.

Ngwenya, Shirley. 1994. Interview, Health Services Development Unit, Tintswalo Hospital, Acornhoek, 15 November.

Ross, J. 1988. *Hot-selling "minis" vanquish the home grown super-heroes*. Gemini News Service.

Schneider, Helene. 1994. Interview, Centre for Health Policy, Johannesburg, 1 November.

Smith, David. 1990. "The Anthropology of Literacy Acquisition." In *The Acquisition of Literacy: Ethnographic Perspectives*. Bambi Shiffelin and Perry Gilmore, eds. Norwood, NJ : Ablex. 260–275.

Storyteller Group. 1994. *Does "Heart to Heart" work as an effective resource in sexuality education? A Preliminary Research Report*. Johannesburg: Storyteller Group.

Watson, Patricia. 1994. Interview, Johannesburg, 28 November.

Williams, Raymond. 1981. "Beyond Brecht." In *Politics and Letters. Interviews with New Left Review*. Raymond Williams, ed., London: New Left Books. 214– 234.

15

Socialist-Oriented Literature in Postcolonial Africa: Retrospective and Prospective

Alamin M. Mazrui

This chapter is intended to be a broad reflection on where socialist-inspired writing in post-colonial Africa might be going as we approach the year 2000; but in the process, I also discuss some of the foundations of this literature. Following Emmanuel Ngara, socialist literature can be defined as one that reflects "the class structure of society and presents social struggles from the point of view of class and promote the ideal of socialism" (1985: 17). The existence of a socialist-inspired literature in Africa shall be taken for granted for the purposes of this essay since the socialist thrust of many of the texts discussed here has already been the subject of analysis in the works of a number of literary critics, including Emmanuel Ngara (1985), George Gugelberger (1985), Chidi Amuta (1986, 1989) and Udenta O. Udenta (1993).

Of more direct concern for us here are two seemingly conflicting predictions on the destiny of socialist inspired literature in Africa. We have, on the one hand, the position of Udenta to the effect that "The most significant direction of the African literary process is the revolutionary direction, sustained in virtually all parts of the continent" (1993: xxi). This revolutionary direction is projected in terms of Marxist dialectical materialism, and African literature is deemed to be on a progressive path from its apologist beginnings, through intermediate liberalist, negationist and critical stages, to a final revolutionary, Marxist peak.

On the other hand, there is the position of Ogembo who, based on his observations of the developments in Kenya's literary scene, concludes—at least with regard to this East African nation—that what he calls "post-Ngũgĩ" fiction—that is, the radical fiction of revolutionary commitment—is increasingly moving away from the kinds of political concerns that would normally sustain the growth of a socialist-inspired literature (1995: 97–98).

In Ogembo's opinion, the thematic shift is toward issues with a narrower social agenda like corruption, the rural-urban tension, and the cultural conflict between "tradition" and "modernity," without any radical ideological underpinnings.

Udenta's views are somewhat impressionistic and not based on any empirical work. Ogembo's, on the other hand, are a product of a survey of Kenya's literary output over the last few years. Which of these two positions, then, is likely to be vindicated by events in Africa by the year 2000? Perhaps there is some justification for both predictions. The short-term picture may indeed be in conformity with Ogembo's views; but in the long run, the situation is likely to tilt more towards Udenta's projection. Present political considerations may seem to favor Ogembo, while the trend of economic development may ultimately vindicate Udenta.[1]

But before we can look at where socialist-inspired literature in Africa might be going, we must first consider where it is coming from.

BACKGROUND

Many political observers have noted that the history of socialism in twentieth-century Africa has strong links with the ideology of nationalism. In the words of Edmond Keller, for example:

Socialist ideals have appealed to African political leaders since the earliest stages of the nationalist period. Socialist thought ranging from indigenous African notions of socialism to Owen, Saint-Simon, Fourier, Engels, Marx, Lenin and Mao, all informed (and in some cases shaped) the notions many African leaders had of the ills that afflicted their respective societies and provided them with the vision of a framework for their liberation. (1987:1)[2]

National leaders, from Ahmad Ben Bella of Algeria to Modibo Keita of Mali, from Sekou Toure of Guinea-Conakry to Robert Mugabe of Zimbabwe, all invoked socialist ideas of one form or another to popularize their movements against European colonial rule.

The nationalist foundation of socialism in Africa is as true of the continent's politics as it is of its literature. In "Lusophone Africa," in particular, socialist literature emerged as a direct product of the nationalist struggles against colonialism. Luandino Vieira's novella, *The Real Life of Domingos Xavier*, for example, written in 1961, a few months after the Popular Movement for the Liberation of Angola (MPLA) launched its first military attack against the Portuguese administration, seeks to emphasize the idea that the struggle to liberate Angola is ultimately a class struggle rather than a racial one. Mussunda, the tailor, tells his young friend, Chico, "that there was not white, nor black, nor mulatto, but only poor and rich and that the rich was the enemy of the poor because he wanted the other to remain poor," and that without the exploitation of the poor, the money of the rich could not yield more money (1978: 27–28). This kind of thematic thrust that regards the struggle to establish socialism as an aspect of the nationalist struggle against colonialism, is clearly noticeable in Africa's Lusophone literary experience.

Socialist-inspired literature in "Anglophone Africa," on the other hand, was precipitated more by *postcolonial* than by colonial conditions. For most writers in Anglophone Africa, their anticolonial nationalism was informed by the false premise that the liberation of Africa was predicated only on the demise of (direct) European/white control of the continent. And the emergence of independent regimes beginning with countries like Egypt and Ghana became a source of great hope prompting imaginative writing inspired by nationalist sentiments.

But the euphoria of independence was soon replaced with disillusionment as it became increasingly clear that the end of colonial racism, looting and oppression had only paved the way for the rise of ethnocratic, keleptocratic, and autocratic African regimes. The principles of democracy and liberty had been sacrificed at the alter of personal power and greed. Dictatorship had become the pillar of a leadership bent on turning the state into lucrative means of self-aggrandizement. Some civilian regimes began to capitulate to those who were better placed to command, to those who wielded the gun as a matter of professional requirement. Things had certainly fallen apart, and the literature of national hope began to give way to the literature of political disillusionment.

From this point on, the *nationalist* imagination took different directions in the quest for an explanation for the seeming "rot" of this political situation. Some writers simply fell into a state of literary hibernation, perhaps digging deep in search of answers. Others personalized Africa's autocracy problem, seeing it as a direct product of an inept and degenerate political leadership. Others still attributed this politicoeconomic malaise to a deformation of Africa's political cultures wrought by the destruction of local institutions and the imposition of alien ones. But there still remained a group of writers who continued to see the white people, although in alliance with a local bourgeoisie, as the root cause of Africa's political and economic under-development, as the perpetrators of a new form of colonialism sometimes referred to as *neocolonialism*.

Kwame Nkrumah once described neocolonialism as the highest stage of imperialism; and Lenin before him regarded imperialism as the highest stage of capitalism. Like colonialism, then, neocolonialism could still be regarded as essentially a product of capitalism through this Nkrumahist-Leninist equation. And just as colonialism, by virtue of its association with capitalism, sometimes prompted a socialist inspired nationalism, neocolonialism now gave rise to its "natural" antithesis, to a *neonationalism* with a socialist garb.

In the literary domain, in much of "Anglophone Africa,"[3] the presence of socialist themes has been more of a response to neocolonialism than to colonialism. The neonationalist ideology that emerged against this post-colonial form of imperialism in turn gave rise to at least three different socialist currents in African literature. One was inspired by a *socialism of utopia*,[4] the other by a *socialism of nostalgia*, and the third by the *socialism of Tanzania*. What are the characteristics of these socialisms and how have they manifested themselves in African literature?

The literature inspired by the socialism of utopia is usually Marxist based, and tends to locate the possibility of radical change in Africa within the context of specific class tensions. These tensions are situated in the political economy of capitalism within the nation-state, but are linked, at the same time, to global capitalism in a dependency, center-periphery relationship. The strategy chosen for revolutionary change is often the mass uprising of the proletariat or the peasantry, or the petty bourgeoisie, or some alliance(s) between these classes against the exploitative practices of neocolonial capitalism. And the revolutionary society envisioned is inspired by Marxian scientific socialism. This kind of Marxist neonationalist literature can be found in both the English language—in the works of Ngũgĩ wa Thiong'o like *Petals of Blood* (1977), of Femi Osofison like *Once Upon Four Robbers* (1991), of Alex La Guma like *In the Fog of the Season's End* (1972)—as well as in more indigenous languages—as in the Kiswahili novels of Katama Mkangi *Mafuta* (Greese) (1984), Rocha Chimerah *Nyongo Mkalia Ini* (Pancreas, Oppressor of the Liver) (1995), and Said A. Mohamed *Kiza Katika Nuru* (Shadows in the Midst of Light) (1988).

This link between neonationalism and the socialism of utopia is particularly evident in some of the writings of Ngũgĩ wa Thiong'o. In the *Devil on the Cross* (1982), for example, Ngũgĩ explicitly reaffirms the inviolability of the colonial boundaries of African nations when one of his leading characters, Gatuiria, proclaims:

We all come from the same womb, the common womb of Kenya. The blood shed for our freedom has washed away the differences between that clan and this one. Today there is no Luo, Gikuyu, Kamba, Giriama, Luhya, Maasai, Meru, Kalenjin or Turkana. We are all children of one mother. Our mother is Kenya, the mother of all Kenyan people. (1982: 234–235)

It is in this womb of Kenya that the struggle unfolds between those of its offspring seeking a change toward a new, socialist order, and those determined to maintain the state of capitalism of the periphery.

In virtually all of Ngũgĩ's novels that are Marxist inspired—including *Petals of Blood, Devil on the Cross*, and *Matigari* (1987)—there is a constant reference not to the struggle of the international proletariat, but to the betrayal of the nationalist Mau Mau movement for the liberation of Kenya as a nation from the clutches of imperialism. It is true that in some instances Ngũgĩ wa Thiong'o recognizes the internationalism of the proletariat by describing it as a class that belongs everywhere and nowhere (1977:291). But nowhere in the text is this internationalism seen to transcend nationalist terms of reference.

In addition, the neocolonial phase of imperialism is predicated upon dependency relations, with Euro-American conglomerates behind the scenes determining the politico economic destiny of Kenya as a nation. An impression is thus created that should there be any exploitation of the multifarious resources of the country, it ought to be by the Kenyan nationals themselves. This is the position represented by Mwireri wa Mukiraai in *Devil on the Cross*, a potential member of the national bourgeoisie otherwise thwarted by his country's dependency ties with the West. Mwireri too likens the nation to a mother and proceeds to tell foreign investors: "Go back home and rape your own mothers, and leave me to toy with my mother's thighs" (1982: 168).

In the opening note to the reader/listener of *Matigari*, Ngũgĩ claims, of course, that:

> This story is imaginary.
> The actions are imaginary.
> The characters are imaginary.
> The country is imaginary—it has no place even.
> Readers/listeners: May the story take place in the country of your choice!

Yet *Matigari* is so heavily centered on Kenya's *concrete* experiences under President Daniel Arap Moi's misrule since about 1980, that its national boundaries are unmistakable. If the story appears somewhat grotesque, it is partly because the Kenyan political reality under Moi was sometimes more fantastic than fiction.

In short, then, in spite of his Marxist-Leninist leanings, Ngũgĩ's works betray a strong neonationalist stand. As Paul Tiyambe Zeleza has suggested, Ngũgĩ's conception of labor operates only within the colonial boundaries, and the general thrust of his narrative does not challenge "the identity and the nation" wrought by independence from colonial rule. In fact, it seeks to constitute it (1994:9). His socialism, in other words, is informed by an underlying neonationalist ideology, and his socialist vision is utopian in the proper sense of the word.

The literature inspired by the socialism of nostalgia, on the other hand, has greater affinity with Negritude than with Marxism, and is best exemplified by some of the works of Ayi Kwei Armah, the noted Ghanaian writer. Armah himself objects to the claim that scientific thinking about socialism and socialist revolutions is an exclusive preserve of Marxism and western thought in general. He contends that there have been numerous revolutionary movements in various parts of the world, from Africa to the Americas, from Asia to Australia. And wherever in the world they occur, such movements tend to be communistic when the revolutionary momentum they generate is married to the ideal of universal justice. Phenomena and ideals of revolution and communism are both of ancient lineage; and the thinking about them in the past was not always chaotic, primitive, unsystematic, unscientific. Nineteenth century European claims of having discovered or pioneered scientific thinking about revolution and communism deserve to be received with humor, as charming instances of Chutzpah. (1984: 39)

Armah's socialist inspiration, then, is derived not from the "futurism" of Marxist thought, but from the past of African experience. He espouses a socialism of nostalgia seeking the recovery of supposedly indigenous, precolonial African social relations with their emphasis on egalitarianism without the mediating institutions of royalty and chieftancy.

In his *Two Thousand Seasons* (1973), Armah further suggests that, in Africa, social stratification itself is a product of external forces. The novel is a yearning for the primordial African social ethos symbolically described as "the way" which, over the centuries, had been destroyed by Arab, and later western imperialism. Socialist revolution in this context implies the reconstruction of "the way," the restoration of the socioeconomic value system destroyed by successive waves of imperialists.

This reconstruction is conceived of as a healing process; and this is the subject matter of Armah's next novel, *The Healers* (1978). Part of the destruction of "the way" brought about by imperialism was the scattering and balkanization of Africa, setting its people in perpetual conflict against each other. One of the revolutionary functions of the healers, therefore, is to reunite the black people of Africa. From *The Healers*, then, one gets the sense that the neonationalism that inspires the socialist thrust in Armah's works is not based on the narrow geographical boundaries created by colonialism and its aftermath, but is more pan-African in nature.

This pan-African thrust of Armah's quest for a more egalitarian Africa takes on a transcontinental dimension in his *Osiris Rising* (1995), as Ast, an African American professor in search of her roots plays the protagonist. Her continental African male friend, Asar, is a member of a "secret society seeking to establish a society without established hierarchies, privileges, handicaps" (1995: 131), a society which, under the present neocolonial circumstances, can only be achieved through revolutionary means. In Asar's opinion, change that would qualify as revolutionary is the type that results in a just society. Aspiring Afro-Marxist regimes in Africa—with Zimbabwe, Angola, Mozambique, and Guinea being singled out or specific mention—are considered nonrevolutionary precisely because they have remained structured in hierarchical and socially unjust ways (1995: 116).

Interestingly enough, Ngûgî too seems to have been inspired to some degree by a socialism of nostalgia in his *Matigari*. At one point, Matigari reminisces over his precolonial society that was bound by mutual love and sharing:

Great love I saw there,
Among the women and the children.
We shared even the single bean
That fell upon the ground. (1987: 6)

Matigari is Ngũgĩ's only novel written in exile. Situated in the belly of a capitalist, European society, could Ngũgĩ's nostalgia for home have resulted in the idealization of the egalitarian foundations of precolonial Africa?

In spite of the differences in their ideological orientation, both the socialism of utopia and the socialism of nostalgia are essentially reactions to neocolonial capitalism and its attendant effects in many African nations. The opposition to neocolonialism has also entailed the rejection of its capitalist face, resulting in a neonationalist response with a socialist thrust. The socialist-inspired literature of these neonationalists, therefore, has tended to be more of a critique of colonial and neocolonial capitalist relations than an articulation of a socialist vision. It is a literature that seems intended to expose the present evils of neocolonial capitalism more than the future benefits of socialism.

A different body of literature that concerns us here is the type inspired by the socialism of Tanzania. As the name implies, this kind of literature is found mainly in Tanzania and virtually all of it is in Kiswahili. The background to Tanzania's socialist literature is the country's move toward the populist socialism of *Ujamaa* after the Arusha declaration of July 1967. In contradistinction to Marxism-Leninism, *Ujamaa* can be described as populist partly because it revolved around a charismatic leader who invoked moral arguments for its justification and sought to mobilize, not just the proletariat, but the entire "people" through a political campaign. This type socialism too, however, had national roots as it sought to promote national self-reliance in the politico economic, social, and cultural spheres. The intellectual stimulation generated by this move to the left expectedly had its impact on the Kiswahili literature of postcolonial Tanzania.

But we do need to distinguish between the socialist literature of *mainland* Tanzania (or what was known as Tanganyika before its union with Zanzibar in 1964) and that of *island* Tanzania (encompassing the islands of what was once the independent nation of Zanzibar). The socialist literature of mainland Tanzania seems to have been more explicit inspired by the living experience of the *Ujamaa* villages. Much of this literature supports the ideals of *Ujamaa*, and is intended to demonstrate the socioeconomic and moral superiority of *Ujamaa* village life.

We have, for example, K. K. Kahigi's and A. A. Ngerema's *Mwanzo Wa Tufani* (The Beginning of a Storm) (1976), in which the domestic worker, Kazimoto, who is exploited and abused by his employers, gains the sympathy and love of their daughter, Tereza; the two finally run away and find refuge and support in a socialist village. In John Ngomoi's *Ndoto Ya Ndaria* (Ndaria's Dream) (1976), the leading character, Ndaria, is a rich farmer who uses every means at his disposal to prevent the introduction of *Ujamaa* in his village of Ranzi. But once he notices how flourishing a neighboring *Ujamaa* village had become in a few years time, he becomes guilt ridden, and subsequently does his utmost to turn Ranzi into an *Ujamaa* village.

Along the same lines, in the socialist literature of mainland Tanzania, we find writings that again support the ideals of *Ujamaa* but that are critical of the excesses of some of the leaders involved in the formation and management of the *Ujamaa* villages. These excesses include forced villagization, administrative mismanagement and corruption. Some of this literature also highlights more practical problems of socialism, and of the socialist construction of *Ujamaa* villages without, however, questioning the validity of the *Ujamaa* ideals and claims. Examples of texts belonging to this category of critical *Ujamaa* literature include *Kijiji Chetu* (Our Village) by Ngalimecha Ngahyoma (1975), *Nyota ya Huzuni* (The Star of Grief) (1980) by George Liwenga, and *Dunia Uwanja wa Fujo* (The World is a Stadium of Confusion) (1975) by Euphrase Kezilahabi.

On a somewhat different trajectory is the socialist oriented literature from Zanzibar. The island of Zanzibar, that is part of the Federal Union of Tanzania, over the years, has also experimented with *Ujamaa* and the creation of *Ujamaa* villages. But, unlike the socialist literature of mainland Tanzania, the socialist literature of island Tanzania has not drawn much inspiration from the living experiences of *Ujamaa*. Rather, its inspiration seems to have been derived from what came to be known as the Zanzibar Revolution.

Within a couple of months after gaining independence from British colonial rule, an attempted revolution erupted on the island on January 11, 1964. In essence, this was the first class-based revolutionary attempt of its kind in postcolonial Africa. It was an initiative intended to bring to an end class privileges in a multiracial society through the establishment of a socialist order. If all had gone according to plan, revolutionary Zanzibar was to be Africa's Cuba. But matters did not go according to plan, and the uprising turned out to be extremely violent and bloody. At the end of the day, however, the independence government of the Zanzibar Nationalist party had been effectively overthrown and a new political order had been put in place.

It was in the immediate aftermath of this revolution that Tanganyika and Zanzibar agreed on a political merger to form the federation of Tanzania. When *Ujamaa* was finally promulgated as the economic policy of the nation in 1967, then, Zanzibar was already in the thick of a revolutionary socialist mood, misguided as it was in some of its agendas. The revolutionary momentum in Zanzibar was so strong, in fact, that Amrit Wilson (1989) has suggested that the union of Tanganyika and Zanzibar was itself conceived by the then president of Tanganyika, Julius Nyerere, in liason with American and British governments, as a way of preempting the island's complete move towards communism.

Whatever the case, the important point to bear in mind here is that the road to *Ujamaa* in mainland Tanzania, though pursued bureaucratically rather than democratically, was ultimately peaceful, enjoying much popular goodwill and meeting no militant opposition from antisocialist interest groups. The road to socialism in island Tanzania, on the other hand, was marked by a tremendous amount of violence. For historical reasons connected with "race" relations on the island, and due to the fear of a counterrevolution, Zanzibar experienced an undue amount of bloodshed in its quest for socialist transformation.

Against the backdrop sketched above, therefore, the socialist imagination in island Tanzania became virtually entrapped in a discourse of rationalization. Socialist-inspired writers of island Tanzania seemed to be under moral pressure to justify or explain the basis of the Zanzibar revolution. They have sought to highlight the feudal/capitalist relations of exploitation and the inhuman conditions of the life of the underprivileged classes in prerevolutionary Zanzibar. The impression is thus created that the magnitude of exploitation and oppression in prerevolutionary Zanzibar was bound to trigger a violent revolutionary upsurge with socialist aims. Mohamed S. Mohamed's *Nyota Ya Rehema* (1976), Shafi Adam Shafi's *Kasri ya Mwinyi Fuad* (1978), Said Ahmed Mohamed's *Dunia Mti Mkavu* (1980), all betray this rationalizing tendency in Zanzibar's socialist-inspired literature.

In spite of the differences between the socialist-inspired literature of mainland Tanzania and that of island Tanzania, the two have been united by their omission of any reference to neocolonial capitalism and dependency. This relative absence of a critique of neocolonialism distinguishes the socialist-inspired literature of Tanzania (mainland and island) and that of the rest of Anglophone Africa. The focus on the home-grown system of *Ujamaa* in mainland Tanzania, and on the locally induced revolution at the dawn of independence in Zanzibar— both taking place before a full awareness of the workings of neocolonialism in the nation had developed—tended to relegate neocolonialism to the preiphery of the Tanzanian literary imagination.

In recapitulation, then, different political factors and forces gave rise to somewhat different expressions of socialist inspired literature in Anglophone Africa. Within Tanzania, the mainland socialist-inspired literature (both critical and uncritical) has tended to be moralistic partly because it has been a response to the living experiences of *Ujamaa*. The island socialist-inspired literature, on the other hand, has tended to be more revolutionary partly because it has been a response to the circumstances that led to the Zanzibar Revolution of 1964. Outside Tanzania there have also been two streams of socialist-inspired literature. The stream of nostalgia and the stream of utopia. But, unlike the socialist-inspired literature of Tanzania, the socialist-inspired literature outside Tanzania has not been prompted by any living socialist experience. Rather, both streams have been neonationalist responses to the kind of capitalism that has been part and parcel of the neocolonial condition.

Given the background of socialist-inspired literature in Africa, then, what is likely to be its direction in the decades to come? Will it follow the direction predicted by Udenta, or will it be more in line with Ogembo's observations based on the Kenyan experience?

THE WAY AHEAD

There are several political developments currently taking place in Africa which may seem to support Ogembo's thesis. In the first place, the ideology of neonationalism that prompted the different types of socialism and socialist-inspired writings over the decades is itself on the decline. This trend has been particularly strong since the beginning of the 1990s when local and international pressure against dictatorial regimes in Africa picked up momentum. Western nations that had once been accused of neocolonialism are now being embraced as friends, partners and leaders in the struggle for Africa's liberation against internal tyranny. In Kenya, for instance, the now retired American Ambassador, Smith Hempstone, and his German counterpart, received glowing tributes from the country's opposition for their "support" of democratic change before, and in the immediate aftermath of, the nation's 1992 multiparty elections. This decline of anti-imperialist neonationalism against the West, then, could conceivably put the socialist agenda on hold.

The policy shift in the west from its traditional support of tyrants to its more recent push for democratic reforms has been precipitated in part, of course, by the collapse of the Soviet Union and the dissolution of the Warsaw Pact. But this end of the cold war also constitutes the second political development which may affect the destiny of socialist-inspired literature in Africa. While it lasted, the cold war probably affected African writers much more than it affected African writing. Superpower rivalries helped to radicalize some writers while making right-wing governments more intolerant. A few writers even received direct logistical assistance from the Soviet Union for some of their creative ventures. The question, then, is whether left-wing African writers in general will be eclipsed as a result of the collapse of the socialist world.

Third we see the rise of angry democratic movements demanding greater political accountability, economic honesty and more equitable representation virtually throughout the continent. And to the extent that many of the socialist regimes in the eastern bloc were regarded as authoritarian, the prodemocracy mood in Africa may also tend to be somewhat suspicious of socialism. To take Kenya again as an example, even opposition parties which have a relatively high concentration of intellectuals once associated with socialist thinking, have avoided any reference to socialism or socialist reforms in their manifestos. In addition we now witness intellectuals, including a number of creative writers, who had hitherto espoused conflicting political ideologies, working together in newly formed opposition political parties. And there seems to be almost a silent agreement between these different ideological "factions " that, at this stage of the game, energies ought to be concentrated on political democratization rather than on political economic revolution. Socialist inspired writing, then, may again be in danger of being pushed to the periphery by this immediate concern with political reforms.

The final political development of concern to us here is more national and refers to Tanzania's virtual abandonment of the ideology of *Ujamaa* and self-reliance—which had once served as an important inspiration for socialist-inclined literature in the country—and its seeming ideological capitulation to the dictates of world capitalism. The country has opened itself up to private enterprise, foreign investments and International Monetary Fund (IMF) conditionalities to a point that it has begun to relax on some of its important nationalist cultural policies like the expansion of the role of Kiswahili as a medium of instruction. The decline in anti-western sentiments that is taking place in much of Africa is also noticeable in this East African country that was regarded as a model of self-reliance and independence from the West. The future of socialist-inspired literature in Tanzania too, therefore, appears to be somewhat bleak.

If the above political developments in Africa do not seem to be in favor of socialist inspired literature, however, their effect may be short lived. This proposition is based on the observation that there is a class dynamic in Africa that, in the long run, may promote a more organic development of socialist-inspired literature. Much of the socialist inspired (written) literature so far has been produced by writers coming from the ranks of the petty bourgeoisie and, in particular, by members of the educated elite. But now there is evidence that while the petty bourgeoisie is expanding, there is a large section of it that is rapidly becoming "proletarianized." An increasing number of educated Africans with university degrees, some relatively exposed to Marxism and other radical ideas, is being pushed to the fringes of society as a result of the economic hardships precipitated by peripheral capitalism, IMF conditionalities and other such factors. The ministry of education in Kenya, for example, once guaranteed jobs for all educated graduates; this has now ceased to be the case as a result of IMF/World Bank pressures on the government to cut down on civil service employment. Many of these unemployed graduates have now ended up in the slum areas of cities like Nairobi and have to struggle with the implications of being unemployed. The majority seem to be graduates in the liberal arts and humanities, fields in which political issues are more likely covered. The same socioeconomic pattern of development is evident in many other African countries. Indeed, in places like Nigeria, there is growing concern that the professional middle class in public institutions is itself being sacrificed at the alter of international capitalist agendas of one sort or another.

The formation of an educated "underclass," then, with living underclass experiences, may eventually give rise to a more organic crop of socialist-inspired African writers. Ogembo may be right when he claims that there is a shift away from socialist concerns in Kenya's literature in English. But in the heart of the Kibera slum in Nairobi, there is perhaps a sign of the trend to come. An informal group of unemployed high school graduates, under the leadership and direction of young Chris Owino, is struggling to produce a dramatized version of one of Ngũgî wa Thiong'o's overtly Marxist novels, *Devil on the Cross*. In spite of the seeming threat to socialist literature caused by certain political events, therefore, there is a counterdynamic operating at the economic level leading to the increasing proletarianization and pauper-ization of society and promising that literatue may have a more organic growth in the long run.

But in which linguistic medium—European or African—is this socialist-inspired literature of the future likely to be rendered? The writer who has been associated most consistently with the campaign for the linguistic indigeni-zation of African literature is Ngũgî wa Thiong'o. One dimension of Ngũgî's campaign derives from his neonationalism. This is the idea that literature is African only if created in an African language. The other dimension of his linguistic campaign is more a product of his socialism. Committed writers must address "the people" in the language(s) of "the people." Are developments in Africa likely to consolidate this union between the people's (socialist) mesage and the people's (linguistic) medium as envisioned by Ngũgî?

As indicated earlier, the struggle for political pluralism in Africa is leading to the decline of neonationalism. At the same time, however, that struggle seems to be leading to rising ethnonationalism. This ethnic focus in the politics of pluralism may, in turn, promote a greater use of indigenous African languages in African literature, including socialist inspired literature. There is already a proliferation of journalistic and other types of projects in ethnic-bound languages in several African countries that can be correlated with the democratic tide since the beginning of the 1990s.

On the other hand, precisely because this ethnonationalism is a reaction to the perceived internal state of ethnocracy, it is not likely to undermine the development of European languages on the African soil. On the contrary, English, in particular, seems to be consolidating itself, especially in the urban areas—the fertile ground of socialist inspired literature. And given that anti-Western neonationalism is not likely to constitute the foundation of this future socialist literature, socialist inspired writers may not at all be inclined to shun the use of English.

English is getting increasingly "Africanized." An increasing number of Africans is acquiring English as a first language, and peculiarly African brands of English are emerging. In the process, the language is beginning to demonstrate its potential as the medium of the "educated underclass" from whose ranks a new socialist-inspired literature may eventually arise.

In other words, economic realities in Africa seem to be leading to both *social restratification* and *linguistic restratification*, and ultimately they are bound to affect both the *message* and the *medium* of African literature in the decades to come.

NOTES

1. One limitation of the literary survey for this essay is that it has been based exclusively on the novel. It is possible that a broader transgenre survey will reveal other socialist trends not discussed here.

2. The link between socialism and nationalism is perhaps quite in conformity with Lenin's analysis of imperialism as the highest stage of capitalism. Despite the fact that Marx saw colonialism as a product of the "vilest interests" of Europe, he regarded it, at the same time, as a kind of necessary evil that would eventually lead to the evolution of the conditions required for a socialist revolution. It was Lenin who articulated most extensively the opposite argument: that colonialism itself is just a product of capitalism. And it was this Leninist assertion that perhaps came to influence some African nationalists. If capitalism was an ally of colonialism, then, naturally socialism would be the ally of the nationalist struggle against colonialism.

3. The distinction among "Anglophone," Francophone," and "Lusophone" Africa, apart from its obvious racial and class bias—giving prominence to languages inherited from the colonial tradition, that are still spoken by a minority from the ranks of the elite—masks the great similarities in the literatures of these regions. In fact, there is much greater thematic and stylistic difference between the literatures in European languages in Africa and those in the indigenous languages than between the literatures in the various ex-colonial languages. Any difference between the literatures of Kenya and Mozambique, therefore, ought not to be located in their Euro-linguisitic differences, but in the specificity of their historical conditions.

4. The term *utopia* here is *not* used in Engel's sense; rather, it is taken more loosely to refer to any "future" society even if achieved by "scientific" social developments.

REFERENCES

Amuta, Chidi. *The Theory of African Literature: Implications for Practical Criticism.* London: Zed Books Limited, 1989.

_____. *Towards A Sociology of African Literature.* Oguta (Nigeria): Zim Pan African Publishers, 1986.

Armah, Ayi Kwei. *The Healers.* London: Heinemann, 1978.

_____ "Masks and Marx." In *Presence Africaine, 139* (1984), 37–45.

_____. *Osiris Rising.* Popenguine (Senegal): Per Ankl, 1995.

_____. *Two Thousand Seasons.* Nairobi: East African Publishing House, 1973.

Chimerah, Rocha. *Nyongo Mkalia Ini.* Nairobi: Oxford University Press, 1995.

Gugelberger, George (Ed.). *Marxism and African Literature.* Trenton, NJ: Africa World Press, 1985.

Kahigi, K.K. and Ngerema, A.A. *Mwanzo wa Tufani.* Dar es Salaam: Tanzania Publishing House, 1976.

Keller, Edmond J. and Rothchild, Donald. *Afro-Marxist Regimes: Ideology and Public Policy.* Boulder, CO: Lynne Rienner, 1987.

Kezilahabi, Euphrase. *Dunia Uwanja wa Fujo.* Dar es Salaam/Nairobi/Kampala: East African Literature Bureau, 1975.

La Guma, Alex. *In the Fog of the Season's End.* London: Heinemann, 1972.

Liwenga, George. *Nyota ya Huzuni.* Dar es Salaam: Tanzania Publishing House, 1980.

Mkangi, Katama. *Mafuta*. Nairobi: East African Educational Publishers, 1984.

Mohamed, Said Amhed. *Kiza Katika Nuru*. Nairobi: Oxford University Press, 1988.

———. *Dunia Mti Mkavu*. Nairobi: Longman, 1980.

Mohamed, Mohamed S. *Nyota ya Rehema*. Nairobi: Oxford University Press, 1976.

Moser, Gerald. "The Lusophone Literatures of Africa since Independence." In Donald Burness (Ed.), *Critical Perspectives on Lusophone African Literature*. Washington, DC: Three Continents Press, 1981. 31–44.

Ngahyoma, Ngalimecha. *Kijiji Chetu*. Dar es Salaam: Tanzania Publishing House, 1975.

Ngara, Emmanuel. *Art and Ideology in the African Novel: A Study of the Influence of Marxism on African Writing*. London: Heinemann, 1985.

Ngomoi, John. *Ndoto ya Ndaria*. Dar es Salaam: Tanzania Publishing House, 1976.

Ngũgĩ wa Thiong'o. *Devil on the Cross*. London: Heinmann, 1982.

———. *Matigari*. London: Heinemann, 1987.

———. *Petals of Blood*. London: Heinemann, 1977.

Ogembo, Jack O. "The Language of Post-Ngũgĩ Fiction." In Kwadzo Senamu and Dril Williams (Eds.), *Creative Use of Language in Kenya*. Nairobi: Jomo Kenyatta Foundation, 1995. 24–33.

Osofison, Femi. *Once Upon Four Robbers*. Ibadan: Heinemann, 1991.

Shafi, Shafi Adam. *Kasri ya Mwinyi Fuad*. Dar es Salaam: Tanzania Publishing House, 1978.

Udenta, Udenta O. *Revolutionary Aesthetics and the African Literary Process*. Enugu (Nigeria): Fourth Dimension, 1993.

Vieira, Luandino. *The Real Life of Domingos Xavier*. London: Heinemann, 1978.

Wilson, Amrit. *U.S. Foreign Policy and Revolution: The Creation of Tanzania*. London: Pluto Press, 1989.

Zeleza, Paul Tiyambe. "Visions of Democracy in Post-Colonial African Literature." Unpublished paper presented at the Center for African Studies, Ohio State University, Columbus, January 14, 1994.

Zolberg, Aristide R. *Creating Political Order: The Party States of West Africa*. Chicago: Rand McNally, 1966.

16

The Nigerian Novel in English:
Trends and Prospects

Joseph McLaren

Since the 1950s, Nigerian novelists writing in English have produced a considerable body of fiction published in Nigeria and the West. Instrumental in shaping modern and postmodern African literature, their works reflect varied trends and prospects for the Nigerian novel in the twenty-first century. Nigerian novels have dealt with a wide range of political themes, among them colonial reassessments, the neocolonial state, military regimes, and gender issues. Nigerian novelists have contributed to the stylistics of the African novel by using Western structures as well as devices from the oral tradition and so-called magic realism. For reasons related to literary production—maintaining audience, publishing opportunities, and censorship—these writers have often had to choose between remaining at home and voluntary or forced exile in the West.

The political situation when Nigeria was controlled by the military presented a challenge for writers who were politically committed and resided in Nigeria. Direct protest, whether in literary art, journalistic writing, or political action, might have resulted in arrest, detention, or execution, as in the case of Ken Saro-Wiwa, a leading writer and activist for the Ogoni cause, hanged on November 10, 1995, as a result of a much disputed verdict handed down by a government tribunal. Politically committed writers have often chosen exile, exemplified by Nobel laureate Wole Soyinka, who has resided in both the United States and England. (Soyinka's *The Open Sore of a Continent: A Personal Narrative of the Nigerian Crisis* [1996] not only proposes definitions of nationhood but addresses the tragedy of Saro-Wiwa's execution. Soyinka's play *The Beatification of Area Boy* [1996] was a commentary on Nigeria's military regime). The dilemma of exile is certainly not restricted to Nigeria; imprisonment of writers is a worldwide concern, evidenced by the interventions of Amnesty International. During and after the 1960s, the South African liberation struggle generated a significant number of detainees and literary exiles. TransAfrica, which addressed the Nigerian dilemma of military rule, had been actively involved in the South African situation.

Publishing opportunities and "audience" are two concerns of Nigerian novelists, such as Chinua Achebe, Buchi Emecheta, and Ben Okri, all of whom who have been well received by Western readers. These writers reside outside of Nigeria for political, economic, or personal reasons and have been published by prominent publishing houses in England and the United States. Certain Nigerian novelists who have remained in Nigeria have directed their works to an indigenous audience, although these authors should not be considered provincial writers since many of them have been published by local and international presses. Two such writers, Femi Osofisan and the late Ken Saro-Wiwa, exemplify the challenges of literary production that differ from those encountered by writers who primarily receive Western sponsorship. Limited publishing outlets and censorship are two of these realities. However, such conditions have not silenced writers who, as in the case of both Osofisan and Saro-Wiwa, have used serialized fiction in the popular press as a way of publishing longer works. Another mode, the television drama, was used by Saro-Wiwa to create an audience that was later receptive to a novel derived from the television series *Basi and Co.*

For popular Nigerian writers, literary survival is dependent on accessibility to the broadest audience, which primarily seeks entertainment through popular themes. Furthermore, those writers producing novels in English further limit their readership based on language because of the variable literacy rates in English and the prevalence of pidgin and indigenous languages. Cyprian Ekwensi, whose *Jagua Nana* (1961) is a classic, chose English as linguistic medium and entertaining as a primary goal, although his writings also contain social commentary. One category of politically relevant popular writing in Nigeria is the war novel of the Biafran conflict, exemplified by such works as Aniebo's *The Anonymity of Sacrifice* (1974), Iroh's *Forty-Eight Guns for the General* (1976), Okpewho's *The Last Duty* (1976), and Saro-Wiwa's *Sozaboy* (1985). Festus Iyai's *Violence* (1979) is another example of clearly political popular fiction.

Despite alternative and innovative forms of disseminating novels, the availability of conventional publishing is of primary importance to the future of the Nigerian novel. Production and distribution are conditioned by internal economic and political conditions as during the Babangida years, when there was a decline in book publishing. The publication of romance novels was part of a popular trend, suggesting an attempt to "create a literature that is not as highbrow." Malthouse Press, associated with Malthouse Publishing in England and based in Lagos, produced a series of titles in the late 1980s. Fagbamigbe Press, which specialized in producing popular literature primarily for entertainment, ceased operations in 1983 (Osofisan, personal interview, 23 July). Spectrum is yet another publishing operation in Nigeria, as is Fourth Dimension Press in Enugu. Many of Osofisan's plays were published by New

Horn Press, Ibadan. Nigerian writers themselves have established their own publishing outlets: Saro-Wiwa's Saros International Publishers, which brought out his works in the 1980s, and Flora Nwapa's Tana Press, which has struggled to survive since her death. The maintenance of local presses is a continual challenge, and the degree to which they remain productive and politically relevant is conditioned as well by the economics of publishing.

In reality, the impact of the structural adjustment program in Nigeria, as a result of policies introduced by the World Bank and the International Monetary Fund, (IMF) has severely limited the availability of funds necessary to publish books as well as purchase them. As documented by the Committee for Academic Freedom in Africa, the undermining of cultural production in Africa will have consequences for successive generations. As expressed by Nigerian poet Niyi Osundare in tribute to Saro-Wiwa, "'the subversion of the democratic ideal invariably precipitates a disruption of cultural space,'" hampering the literary impulse, "'one of the finest manifestations of the soul and collective imagination of a people'" (9).

Although more than forty booksellers and publishers have been identified in Nigeria, many of them attached to universities, the productivity of these presses is questionable. The decline in book publishing in the 1980s and 1990s was exacerbated by problems of infrastructure, distribution, high tariffs on equipment, and investment dilemmas.[1] Western based presses such as Heinemann, Longman, and Macmillan (Pacesetters Series) have had outlets in Nigeria, though the viability of international outlets diminishes during periods of instability (Osofisan, Personal interview, July 23, 1993). Furthermore, it is important to develop internal publishing because "an agenda set from outside the continent ultimately denies Africa the right to speak for itself" (Jay). Organizations such as African Books Collective (ABC) and African Publishers' Network (APNET) have attempted to address some of the publishing obstacles on the continent.

The internal publishing dilemma contrasts with the situation of those writers who reside outside of Nigeria, such as Achebe, Emecheta, and Okri, who have been promoted by such publishers as Doubleday and Heinemann. These writers, unconstrained by the threat of censorship or detention, have addressed national issues, gender, and alternative narrative modes, such as so-called magic realism, which, in many respects, is a return to narrative stylistics found in the oral tradition.

Two of the persistent themes voiced by Achebe are the political situation in Nigeria and the relationship of the writer to the state. A longtime social critic, Achebe has supported politically committed literary activity. In *The Trouble with Nigeria* (1984), he identifies the crisis in leadership, an issue relevant to Nigeria's political past: "The Nigerian problem is the unwillingness or inability of its leaders to rise to the responsibility, to the challenge of personal example which are the hallmarks of true leadership" (Achebe, *Trouble* 1). The relationship of the writer to national politics has been voiced

as well by Kenyan writer Ngũgĩ wa Thiong'o, who experienced both detention and exile. In *Writers in Politics* (1981), Ngũgĩ argues that "the product
of a writer's pen both reflects reality and also attempts to persuade us to take
a certain attitude to that reality" (Ngũgĩ 7). That writers should be catalysts
of social change is also voiced by Adewale Maja-Pearce, who observes that
those writers who maintain a commitment to political issues are "the continent's only hope of salvation" (xiii).

Achebe's *Anthills of the Savannah* (1987) suggests that the writer who
challenges political power will be silenced, imprisoned, and, ultimately,
eliminated, an ironic foreshadowing of the fate of Ken Saro-Wiwa. Achebe's
novel is a richly textured work, which questions the writer's role as an
agent of protest. The state in *Anthills* is a military one under the
leadership of "His Excellency"; the portrayal of His Excellency and the
machinery of government in the fictional Kangan—an obvious parallel to
Nigeria when it was under military rule—is handled with a sharp satiric style.

With Chris, Commissioner of Information, as narrator, Achebe achieves an
ironic view of the inner workings of Kangan's cabinet. Chris sees himself as
occupying a "silly observation post" from where he makes "farcical entries
in the crazy log-book of this our ship of state" (Achebe, *Anthills* 2). In
addition to the development of Chris as a strong central character, Achebe
also uses Beatrice, Chris's mate, as a primary element of the narrative, suggesting
that Achebe answered certain of his critics who considered his earlier works
to be ineffective in their treatment of women characters.

Somali writer Nuruddin Farah points out that, in many respects, Beatrice
is given "a lioness's share in the telling of the story itself" (1831). The
traditional ceremony of naming is modified when it becomes a collective act
initiated by Beatrice, whose decision to give a male name to the female
child of Ikem and Elewa demonstrates a certain level of power and leadership.
Beatrice and the remaining survivors of the group, which had included Chris
and Ikem, signify a future coalition based on a new consciousness that
recognizes tradition but goes beyond its proscriptive rituals. Achebe intentionally
elevates Beatrice, though it has been argued by Florence Stratton that Beatrice
is "allowed to exercise power only within certain limited boundaries, which
confirm the separate sphere of the sexes" (Stratton 168).

Gender issues, breaking the silences of women's voices, are political in
their own right, though they have parallels to questions of power and the state.
Buchi Emecheta, hailed by Western feminists since the 1970s, has been
primarily concerned with voicing the dilemmas faced by Igbo women, who
she portrays as struggling to address traditional boundaries in order to liberate
themselves from the patriarchal limitations of marriage and motherhood.
Although Emecheta does not identify herself as a "feminist," her writings are
obviously about the liberation of women. Molara Ogundipe-Leslie attributes
Emecheta's denial of the feminist label to the "successful intimidation of
African women by men over the issues of women's liberation and feminism"

(Ogundipe-Leslie 64). Emecheta's status as an expatriate writer whose portrayal of Igbo women has been challenged by African women critics raises issues of the national identity of the writer who resides permanently in the West. Emecheta's universalism and her position as a world writer effects, to a certain extent, her identity as a Nigerian author. Though her focus, for the most part, is still on Nigerian characters, she considers herself to be a "citizen of the world" (Jussawalla and Dasenbrock 97).

Emecheta's interrogation of gender has followed an autobiographical track; her own experiences as a transplanted Igbo woman in London have been repeatedly explored. *Second-Class Citizen* (1975) addresses these circumstances as do *The Family* (1990) and *Kehinde* (1994). One of the recurring themes is the adaptation of the family to the social conditions of London. As Carole Boyce Davies notes, *Second-Class Citizen* is "well-recognized for engaging the British welfare system" as well as "cultural/familial practices which attempt to subordinate women" (Davies 112).

Kehinde, which examines the return to traditional society of a "been to" woman and her family, establishes London as a signifier of liberation in the Anglo-African Diaspora; the assimilation of the Okolo family occurs over a period of years. One of the primary tensions of the novel involves gender politics and reproduction. Albert, Kehinde's husband, forces her to have an abortion. The paradox is that in the traditional Ibuza context, there is a valorization of childbirth as Emecheta dramatically explores in *The Joys of Motherhood*. In the West, the decision to abort has been associated with the woman's right to choose, but in *Kehinde* it becomes another extension of Albert's dominance. Furthermore, Kehinde's liberation is connected to residence in London, often presented as a site of problematic assimilation for Africans, but in Emecheta's work, there is an ambivalence in her presentation of London. The ultimate return of Kehinde to London, her rejection of her status in Nigeria, valorizes the economic mobility signified by the West.

Another of Emecheta's thematic interests has been bridging the African Diaspora. *The Family* (1989), also titled *Gwendolen*, not only depicts Nigerians and Ghanaians residing in England but is substantially about Jamaican life. The novel, which shows Emecheta's experimentation with Caribbean English, is dedicated "to that woman in the Diaspora who refused to sever her umbilical cord with Africa" (Emecheta, *The Family* n. pag.). Despite the tragic sexual abuse of Gwendolen, Emecheta sees this novel as "'a book of hope and triumph'" (Washington 50). Although there is an emphasis on gender politics in her novels, Emecheta is similar to many African male writers in her "views on colonialism and on Nigerian politicians." Perhaps the common political interests of both groups of writers may lead to a needed reduction in "the level of antagonism in the politics of gender" (Stratton 132, 176).

Like Emecheta, Ben Okri resides in London and has been primarily recognized by Western audiences. His writing in a style that has been classified by Western critics as magic realism suggests how Nigerian novels can incorporate traditional elements and pursue plot structures that are different from the Western model. Okri, representing the third generation of post-independence African writers, draws on cultural traditions that he has learned from literary progenitors such as Soyinka, reflecting interethnic influence inasmuch as Okri's ethnic background is Urhobo rather than Yoruba. Okri's literary production has been varied and continually experimental in narrative possibilities. *The Famished Road* (1991), which won the Booker Prize, Britain's most prestigious literary award, suggests alternate directions in plot structure and characterization. Okri has produced four other novels, *Flowers and Shadows* (1980), *The Landscapes Within* (1981), *Songs of Enchantment* (1993)—a sequel to *The Famished Road*—*Dangerous Love* (1996), as well as two short–story collections, *Incidents at the Shrine* (1987) and *Stars of the New Curfew* (1989).

The Famished Road and its sequel, *Songs of Enchantment*, use a Yoruba world view and a literary style that departs from the linear structures of the Western novel. These novels somewhat resemble the style of D. O. Fagunwa's *Ogboju Ode Ninu Igbo Irunwale* (*Forest of a Thousand Daemons*), translated by Soyinka, and Amos Tutuola's works, such as *The Palm-Wine Drinkard* (1952). (Tutuola was one of the first Nigerian novelists to publish in English). Henry Louis Gates Jr., commenting on the relative youth of the "black African novel in English," recognizes Okri's blending of Western stylistics with traditional African storytelling, as found in Soyinka's dramas (Gates 3, 20).

In *The Famished Road*, the landscape of Azaro's imagination becomes setting and texture. Okri achieves a unique portrayal of traditional culture and the social historical by exploring character through what postmodernists call magic realism, a literary style found in the works of such writers as Márquez and Morrison. However, magical elements have been a consistent feature of traditional African storytelling, which predates Western magic realism; Okri owes as much to African sources as he does to Western influences. His novel can also be read for its political and social critique, the tensions between rural village life and urbanism.

The dominant metaphor in *The Famished Road* is the "road" itself, which has numerous metaphorical and political implications, echoing Soyinka's title in his play *The Road* (1965), a treatment of political themes interwoven with Yoruba cosmological implications. For Okri, the road represents a conduit of experience, one that reemerges in the consciousness of Azaro as a world in transition. There is also political context in the portrayal of the Party's attempt to dominate Azaro's community. Azaro's father becomes a voice of political resistance when he objects to the Party's collecting of funds. Dad's initiation of his own political agenda is connected as well to the metaphor of the road. His "political declaration" links him to the outcasts, who resemble the marginalized characters in Sembene Ousmane's 1974 novel, *Xala* (Okri 419).

Okri's style contrasts sharply with the direct popular style of novels written for consumption within Nigeria. The example of Femi Osofisan and Ken Saro-Wiwa, multigenre writers who have also produced novels, shows how those authors who mainly address indigenous audiences use disguise, humor, and satire to address political issues. Both Osofisan and Saro-Wiwa rely on the linear sequencing of events crucial in serialized works or television dramas; straightforward sequencing of episodes is a way of maintaining audience interest.

Osofisan, who also writes under the pen name Okinba Launko, is primarily known as a dramatist though he has produced award-winning poetry—*Minted Coins* (1987). A prolific author of over a dozen plays, including *The Oriki of a Grasshopper* (1986), *Esu and the Vagabond Minstrels* (1991), and *Aringindin and the Nightwatchmen* (1992), he has been a consistent observer of the political scene. In his preface to *Aringindin and the Nightwatchmen*, he comments on political transitions: "When the military fails us, we promptly ask for another coup d'etat! Whereas all we need is to seize the power ourselves, and distribute it among ourselves, among the people" (Osofisan, Preface viii).

Osofisan's *Cordelia* (1989), a novel originally serialized for twenty-seven weeks in the *Guardian*, a prominent Nigerian newspaper considered moderately independent, presents both political and social issues. The work depicts student unrest, a military coup, and the resulting dilemmas faced by a university professor. The depiction of the military is a clear mockery of oppressive forces in Nigeria during the Babangida era; however, the novel also treats marital relations, a popular theme for Nigerian readers. The story's serialization was a way to both reach and develop a wider audience; the episodes were encouraged by the audience, whose demands for continuance forced the author to create new segments.

Osofisan produced other serialized fictional works: *Ma'aami* (Mother), which was written in half-page segments for the *Guardian* and ran seven weeks; *Wuraola* (Forever), which ran for twenty-seven weeks, and *Abigail*, which continued in the *Sunday Times* for thirty-five weeks (Osofisan, Personal interview, 21 June 1995). The novelist as journalist, however, is a tenuous status; writers employed by certain newspapers are discouraged from writing fictionalized works that contain political content.

Publishing serialized novels in the popular press has parallels to dramatic television programs in that both are alternatives to traditional publishing formats. Ken Saro-Wiwa, who wrote popular and historical fiction, is known for *Basi and Company*, the successful Nigerian television comedy series that ran from 1985–1990 and later became the subject for a novel of the same name. Saro-Wiwa's other novels include *Sozaboy* (1985)—called a "work of rare artistic power" by Abiola Irele—*Prisoners of Jebs* (1988), a satire of the Nigerian judicial system serialized in *Vanguard* for fifty-three weeks in 1986–1987, and *Pita Dumbrok's Prison* (1991), a sequel to *Prisoners of Jebs*, in which a Professor represents a voice of the nation, a parallel to Soyinka's Professor in *The Road* and perhaps to Soyinka himself. A prolific writer, Saro-Wiwa authored plays, radio scripts and a short-story collection, *A Forest of Flowers*

(1986) (Irele 14; Saro-Wiwa, "Author's Note," *Prisoners;* Thorpe 524). Saro-Wiwa, who became increasingly political after 1990, recognized the connection between political critique and the oral tradition among the Ogoni for whom the "relationship between literature and nonviolent struggle is an old and acknowledged one." The Ogoni "sang to satirize or praise or to cleanse society of some ill" (Saro-Wiwa, Acceptance Speech 18).

Detained in 1992, the beginning of a series of detentions culminating in his arrest in May 1994 allegedly for incitement to murder, Saro-Wiwa was imprisoned for a year and then executed along with eight other Ogoni activists at Port Harcourt on November 10, 1995, as a result of the verdict of a "specially convened tribunal" (Boyd xii–xiii; Saro-Wiwa, "Author's Note," *Prisoners*). Saro-Wiwa exemplifies how writers who become critical of the state can become targets of political oppression, as in Achebe's *Anthills of the Savannah*. In Saro-Wiwa's case, his leadership of Movement for the Survival of the Ogoni People (MOSOP), whose mission was to deter "environmental pollution by multinational oil companies," led to his demise ("Writers in Prison" 22–23). Saro-Wiwa re-created the events surrounding his detention in *A Month and a Day: A Detention Diary* (1995), which chronicles in narrative format his arrest and treatment by Nigerian officials; in may ways, the work is a testament to the "close relationship between the Ogoni people and their environment" (Saro-Wiwa, *Month* 2). For Soyinka, Saro-Wiwa's execution may have "sounded the death-knell" of the old Nigeria (Soyinka 153).

Saro-Wiwa's political concerns are reflected in a diverse group of novels. *Basi and Company* resembles an African folktale, avoiding, for the most part, the "flashbacks" and "psychological analysis" associated with the Western novel (Saro-Wiwa, "Author's Note," *Basi*). Like Okri's "road" invention, Saro-Wiwa uses Adetola Street in Lagos as focal point for this novel, although Saro-Wiwa avoids so-called magic realism. Adetola Street is the domain of Basi, Mr. B., whose main intention is to earn a million dollars. In one chapter of the novel, "A Shipload of Rice," a potential rice boon is equated with a "plot to enrich a few people and take the nation's oil money away to America"—an ironic foreshadowing of the author's campaign against oil pollution (Saro-Wiwa, *Basi* 54).

Saro-Wiwa addressed historical issues in *Sozaboy*, which not only examines the Biafran War but valorizes pidgin as a literary style. The novel, sympathetic to those unwittingly drawn into the conflict, follows through on Saro-Wiwa's opposition to the Biafran cause. (He had worked for the federal government during the war, a curious past for one who ultimately supported ethnic self-determination). Also in a political vein, *Prisoners of Jebs* foreshadows Saro-Wiwa's own fate. Though the mythical Jebs prison is a creation of the Organization of African Unity (OAU), implying a broader critique of continental duplicity, locating the prison in Nigeria facilitates a satire of Nigerian society, especially of those figures represented in newspaper articles.

Although based on "the stuff of Nigerian life," the incidents in *Prisoners of*

Jebs, which includes a range of characters—politicians, smugglers, bureaucrats, judges, politicians, and professors—would have caused some to be fearful of repercussions. However, Saro-Wiwa believed, as did the editor of *Vanguard*, that since the situations were based on "facts and opinions already published in various newspapers" and there were no references to "the government of the day," that there was no need to fear reprisals. Pita Dumbrok, one of the main characters, resembles the Nigerian journalist Dele Giwa, killed not long after he appeared on a 1987 *Sixty Minutes* broadcast (Saro-Wiwa, "Author's Note," *Prisoners;* Nwankwo 762). Saro-Wiwa's execution exemplifies the tragic outcome of political commitment beyond the literary enterprise.

The varied literary intentions of Saro-Wiwa, Achebe, Emecheta, Okri, and Osofisan suggest prospects for the Nigerian novel produced by writers living in the West or those who reside in Nigeria. If they choose to, those writers living in the West can be effective critics of the state during periods of national instability. Novelists who chose to remain in Nigeria when it was under oppressive military rule weighed the benefits of direct political critique against the silencing of imprisonment or execution.

Because the internal production of novels is more difficult during repressive periods and severe economic conditions, writers and publishers concerned with political issues should continue to use alternative modes, including serialized fiction, film, video, television, and live drama as ways of generating audiences that can become receptive to the published text. Novelists will undoubtedly continue to write in mother tongues, expanding production in indigenous languages. Achieving a balance between popular fiction, the purpose of which is primarily entertainment, and works that present substantive issues of ethnicity, national identity, state politics, and gender is a challenge facing Nigerian novelists. Women's issues should not be considered secondary to national politics because they are directly related to the transformation of the state.

Ultimately, the internal production of novels in English will depend on the maintenance of publishing houses and the viability of an audience receptive to texts in English. Troubling economic conditions and censorship by the state both deter the production of politically committed writing. Publishing houses in the West can be effective in promoting Nigerian writers if these houses are willing to take the risks associated with literary production in Nigeria and if they expand their publication of works by Nigerian writers in the West and elsewhere. Publishing houses in England and the United States can assist Nigerian presses in producing novels that continue the oral tradition, as writers both inside and outside pursue the mission of the storyteller, the seer-critic, at the crossroads of the new millennium.

NOTE

1. In the mid-nineties, numerous small presses were identified in Nigeria, including New Horn Press, Ibadan University Press, Obafemi Awolowo University Press, Sankore

Publishers, University of Lagos Press, University of Nigeria Press, University of Maiduguri Press, University of Port Harcourt Press, Ahmadu Bello University Press, Cross Continents Press, Hudahuda Publishing Company, Onibonoje Press, Gbemi Sodipo Press, and others. See *African Literature Association Bulletin* 22. 1 (Winter 1996): 29–31. Also African Books Collective has identified Nigerian publishers. Mary Jay, "African Books Collective: Its Contribution to African Publishing," reprint from *Africa Bibliography 1992. Works on Africa Published During 1992*. Edinburgh: Edinburgh University Press (for International African Institute), 1994.

REFERENCES

Achebe, Chinua. *Anthills of the Savannah*. New York: Doubleday, 1987.

————. *The Trouble with Nigeria*. London: Heinemann, 1984.

Aniebo, I.N.C. *The Anonymity of Sacrifice:* London: Heinemann, 1974.

Boyd, William. Introduction. *A Month and a Day: A Detention Diary*, by Ken Saro-Wiwa. New York: Penguin, 1995. vii–xv.

Davies, Carole Boyce. *Black Women, Writing and Identity: Migrations of the Subject*. London: Routledge, 1994.

Ekwensi, Cyprian. *Jagua Nana*. London: Hutchinson, 1961.

Emecheta, Buchi. *The Family*. New York: George Braziller, 1990.

————. *Kehinde*. London: Heinemann, 1994.

————. *Second-Class Citizen*. New York: George Braziller, 1975.

Fagunwa, D. O. *Forest of a Thousand Daemons*. Trans. Wole Soyinka. New York: Random House, 1982.

Farah, Nuruddin. "A Tale of Tyranny." Review of *Anthills of the Savannah*, by Chinua Achebe. *West Africa* 21 Sept. 1987: 1828–1831.

Gates, Henry Louis, Jr. "Between the Living and the Unborn." Review of *The Famished Road*, by Ben Okri. *New York Times Book Review* 28 June 1992: 3+.

Irele, Abiola. Review of *Sozaboy*, by Ken Saro-Wiwa. Quoted in *Everything about Basi & Co*. Lagos: Saros International, n.d. 14.

Iroh, Eddie. *Forty-Eight Guns for the General*. Portsmouth, NH: Heinemann, 1976.

Iyai, Festus. *Violence*. Harlow, England: Longman, 1979.

Jay, Mary. "African Books Collective: Its Contribution to African Publishing." *Africa Bibliography 1992*. Edinburgh: Edinburgh University Press, 1994. n. pag.

Jussawalla, Feroza, and Reed Way Dasenbrock, eds. *Interviews with Writers of the Post-Colonial World*. Jackson: University Press of Mississippi, 1992.

Maja-Pearce, Adewale. *Who's Afraid of Wole Soyinka?: Essays on Censorship*. Portsmouth, NH: Heinemann, 1991.

Ngũgĩ wa Thiong'o. *Writers in Politics*. London: Heinemann, 1981.

Nwankwo, Chimalum. Review of *Pita Dumbrok's Prison*, by Ken Saro-Wiwa. *World Literature Today* 66.4 (Autumn 1992): 762.

Ogundipe-Leslie, Molara. *Re-creating Ourselves: African Women & Critical Trans-formations*. Trenton, NJ: Africa World Press, 1994.

Okpewho, Isidore. *The Last Duty*. Harlow, England: Longman, 1976.

Okri, Ben. *Dangerous Love*. London: Phoenix House, 1996.

————. *The Famished Road*. London: Vintage, 1991.

————. *Flowers and Shadows*. Harlow, England: Longman, 1980.

————. *Incidents at the Shrine*. Boston: Faber and Faber, 1986.

_____. *The Landscapes Within.* Harlow, England: Longman, 1981.

_____. *Songs of Enchantment.* New York: Talese/Doubleday, 1993.

_____. *Stars of the New Curfew.* New York: Viking, 1989.

Osofisan, Femi. *Esu and the Vagabond Minstrels.* Ibadan, Nigeria: New Horn, 1991.

_____. *Minted Coins.* Ibadan, Nigeria: Heinemann, 1987.

_____. *The Oriki of a Grasshopper. Two One-Act Plays.* Ibadan, Nigeria: New Horn, 1986.

_____. Personal interview. July 23, 1993.

_____. Personal interview. June 21, 1995.

_____. Preface. *Aringindin and the Nightwatchmen.* Ibadan, Nigeria: Heinemann, 1992. viii–ix.

Osundare, Niyi. "The Longest Day." *African Literature Association Bulletin* 23.1 (Winter 1997): 7–10.

Saro-Wiwa, Ken. Acceptance Speech, 1994 Fonlon-Nichols Laureate, *African Literature Association Bulletin* 20.2 (Spring 1994): 17–21.

_____. *Basi and Company: A Modern African Folktale.* Port Harcourt: Saros International, 1987.

_____. *A Month and a Day: A Detention Diary.* New York: Penguin, 1995.

_____. *Prisoners of Jebs.* Port Harcourt: Saros International, 1988.

_____. *Sozaboy.* Port Harcourt: Saros International, 1985.

Soyinka, Wole. *The Open Sore of a Continent: A Personal Essay of the Nigerian Crisis.* New York: Oxford University Press, 1996.

_____. *The Road.* London: Oxford, 1965.

Stratton, Florence. *Contemporary African Literature and the Politics of Gender.* London: Routledge, 1994.

Thorpe, Michael. Review of *Prisoners of Jebs*, by Ken Saro-Wiwa. *World Literature Today* 63.3 (1989): 524.

Tutuola, Amos. *The Palm-Wine Drinkard.* London: Faber and Faber, 1952.

Washington, Else B. "Buchi Emecheta: The Secrets of Black Women." *Essence* August 1990: 50.

"Writers in Prison." *African Literature Association Bulletin* 20.3 (Summer 1994): 22–23.

17

Writing In and Out of Algeria, Writing Algeria, Today

Soraya Mekerta

What does it mean, today, to write in Algeria? Never before, in the history of Algeria, has the question been charged with such serious consequences as the loss of one's life, the threat of losing one's life, being condemned to death (and not always knowing it), or living in forced exile. All of this creates a climate of total fear and uncertainty. Thus, one may wonder why; why would any one continue to write?

Writing in Algeria today raises acutely, and appropriately, the question of implications. It is absolutely impossible not to implicate oneself in the unfolding of current events, and dissociate that from writing. Clearly, when the very act of writing means that one might, with more certainty than probability, lose one's life, it becomes all the more filled with an overtone of seriousness, one which carries a sense of urgency, a heavy weight: that of the hundreds and thousands of bodies . . . , fallen bodies, bodies torn, and tortured, and raped, and blown in so many pieces, that they become nameless, nameless bodies. . . .

"Le silence c'est la mort, et toi si tu te tais tu meurs, et si tu parles tu meurs, alors dis et tu meurs" (Silence is death, and if you keep quiet, you die, and if you speak you die, so speak and you die), explains Assia, one of the characters in *Algérie en éclats*.[1] One of the poignant elements of the play is the fact that the characters keep on rehearsing the play, knowing perfectly well how ludicrous it is, since it will never be enacted.[2] In spite of this, they rehearse, defying both silence and death as they report current events, denounce daily atrocities, and dare remember passages from books, and articles from newspapers, as they immortalize their authors.[3] Ludicrous? Perhaps not, if one considers the power of words, in this case, even of one's words to oneself. For, there are such things as the unbearable, and the unspeakable, and more so then, than ever, the ability to enunciate the unbearable and the unspeakable becomes, to a certain degree, affirming and liberating, if one can say that, when considering the case of Algeria and the

Algerian people, today.

Many authors emphasize this latter point. Afsa Zinaï-Koudil links her writing, and in particular her recent novel, *Sans voix*[4] (*Voiceless*), to the impossibility of escaping reality, and to the impossibility of separating her writing from the struggle of Algerian women in Algeria, or in France, where she lives in exile since April 1995,[5] and to the impossibility of healing. "La réalité est toujours là, et je n'ai pas pu mettre la distanciation entre toutes ces femmes, qu'elles soient là-bas ou ici, je n'ai pas pu guérir de ça" (Reality is always there, and I could not put any distance between all these women, whether they are over there or over here, I could not heal from that), she asserts.[6] And, as she attempts to explain further, it becomes clear that she cannot separate writing from reality precisely because "c'est encore brûlant, c'est encore chaud, c'est là, [. . .] çame triture de jour et de nuit." ("It is still burning, it is still hot, it is there, [. . .] it pulls me apart, day and night.") Thus, not surprisingly, the immense pain she has witnessed and experienced in Algeria, and continues to feel, is inseparable from the act of writing. *Sans voix* is punctuated by the call to Aïcha to keep on writing: "Écris, Aïcha, ècris! [. . .] Mais il faut dire avant de mourir. Écrïs Aicha!"[7] (Write, Aïcha, write! [. . .] You must speak before you die. Write Aïcha!). Indeed, sometimes writing becomes the sole reason for living. Letifa Ben Mansour, in *La Prière de la peur*[8] (*The prayer of fear*) depicts a character who, once mutilated after a bomb exploded in Algiers airport, finds the strength to go on, that is, to continue to live, only because she hopes to write a book.

Equally, the writing of the pain, and the pain of writing, propel authors and readers into the world of the imaginary, which is not so disconnected from the 'real' world,[9] a world where pain and suffering take such horrible proportions, that one would indeed believe that it simply cannot be 'real,' sort of like a bad dream, rather, a terrifying nightmare, out of which one awakens confused, and not knowing for a second or two, what was real and what was not. In fact, even when one figures out that it was 'just a nightmare,' one is still astonished before the sensation that it felt so 'real,' with still in mind vivid pictures, and detailed memory of 'what happened.' This situation, or particular moment of not knowing for sure, creates a conflict between wanting to remember the exact events which have caused such fear and panic on the one hand, because the state of fear and panic is experienced as 'real,' and needing to erase those events, either because they are so atrocious that they become unbearable, or because one manages to convince oneself that they must not have occurred, because they could not have occurred, since it was, after all, a 'nightmare,' on the other hand. However, when reality is a nightmare, or the nightmare *is* real, clearly, there is no exit, nor escape. It is then precisely the very moment of ambiguity, anxiety, and tension described above, which becomes central, as it is prolonged, and repeated.

Aïssa Khelladi explores the role of the imaginary in Algerian people today, as he seeks to understand fear.[10] The question which interests him is not so much why Algerian people are afraid, but rather, what are the mechanics of fear? In other words, how does fear operate? For him, the moment of ambiguity is pivotal in coming to an understanding of fear. The ambiguity resides in the fact that in Algeria today, the entire population is kept hostage to the interpretation, and misinterpretation of anyone and everyone else, to the extent that hardly anyone can trust anyone else.[11] Under these circumstances, people tend to operate on the basis of assumption, perception, and fear, more so than on anything else that would be more reliable or tangible. Hafsa Zinai-Koudil has one of the characters explain: "L'horrible peur de la peur meserrait le ventre, et dans le noir, elle devenait insupportable, lourde, oppressante."[12] (The horrible fear of fear would tighten my belly and in the dark it would become unbearable, heavy and oppressing). This has far reaching consequences, and penetrates the core of Algerian society which is group based, and family or community centered. In *Peurs et mensonges*, the main character, Amin Touati, is a journalist who is held responsible and found guilty by a judge. Politically, he is found guilty because he wrote an article. Furthermore, and most importantly, he is held responsible and found guilty of "the fear of others," of "the fear which others have of him," and of the "supposed fear which others feel toward him."[13] Why? Because as a journalist he has access to speech, he has a voice, and he can write. Worst of all, he has an audience. In other words, he is seen as a (potential) threat. Not surprisingly, he is the target of both the fundamentalists and the government.[14] However, the author is quick to remind us of a disturbing factor: the fundamentalists and the government come from somewhere, and indeed, they are our neighbors, they are a part of us, and sometimes they are in our families. According to Aïssa Khelladi, the Algerian imaginary is "traumatized" by the fear of one brother assassinating another.[15] This fear is all the more real in that the catastrophic event is known to have occurred several times. Such is the case in *Sans voix* when Hafsa Zenai-Koudil depicts the murder of an Algerian policeman by his younger brother in front of their mother at the breaking of the fast during Ramadan.[16] Thus, Algerian society is then destabilized at its very core: the family unit, even if only at the level of a "traumatized" imaginary. In an environment where fear takes such proportions, this latter point can neither be ignored nor minimized.

When one looks further into the mechanics of fear, it is obvious that an impossible situation is created. As pointed out, it consists of being held responsible and presumed guilty for the feelings of others, which operate essentially at the level of anticipated fear. It must be noted then, that under these conditions everything can potentially be distorted, look suspicious, and become abnormal, justifying in turn, the abnormal. How else could one explain the slaughter? That is why Aïssa Khelladi insists that the emphasis be on the naming of fear, with the goal to identify it with precision, to look deep into it, to dissect it, and to understand it, in order to overcome it, eventually. Therefore, this investigative gesture of uncovering is essential. Not only does the author indicate that one can find strength in it, but also, he seems to suggest that the beginning of an answer to the Algerian situation might lie just *there*. However, given the particular circumstances, the task of "demystifying" fear is certainly not an easy one. For one thing, it takes time, and in the meantime, catastrophies do occur. Nevertheless, the main character in *Peurs et mensonges* decides to attempt just that, in spite of his being caught in an impossible situation between the Fundamentalists and the Government: two forces out of touch with the 'real' issues, and blinded by one another.

One of the main obstacles to any sort of resolution, is when the abnormal and the massacre become part of the day to day life and somewhat normal. The real danger does not rely in the slaughter or massacre per sé (although obviously people do die, and that is a very serious matter), but in being so out of touch with one's fear (even though clearly it is there), that the slaughter and the massacre become acceptable. This fact is a source of great concern to Latifa Ben Mansour, in *La Prière de la peur*. Starting with the title of her book, it must be noted that the "prayer of fear" does exist. It refers to a specific Surah of the *Qur'an*. Interestingly enough, the prayer of fear appears in the Surah on women, which happens to be the longest Surah. It is said that even when one prays one must be on one's guard, for fear of dying, or causing the death of someone, especially if that someone is a believer (meaning a practicing Muslim).[17] Also, it is known in the legend that the prophet himself was afraid, (this latter point is confirmed by the fact that he himself often insisted that he was just another human being). Subsequently, Latifa Ben Mansour is appalled by those who purport to belong to Islam solely to serve their own purposes through means which are fundamentally anti-Islamic, precisely because they murder, and participate in mass-murders "*without* fear, nor regrets, nor remorse."[18] In this sense, *La Prière de la peur* serves as a reminder that today's wrongdoings are the loudest indication that this bloodbath has nothing to do with Islam, that is, with true Islam, as revealed to the prophet Muhammad. Halen's name, which means "gentleness" in Arabic, stands as an excellent reminder that in spite of all the brutality, one can still conceive of "gentleness." Also, *La Prière de la peur* serves as an assertion that nothing can destroy, nor effectively come in the way of the rich history and tradition of Algeria and the Algerian people. From that standpoint, the book is a wonderful testimony of the past and the present because it depicts the Algeria of yesterday, with its stories, legends, and traditions, and the one of today with its ugly face, and yet, with its longstanding tradition of resisting. Therefore, the book also serves as a warning that evil forces and actions will not succeed in destroying the spirit of Algerian people. This is portrayed by Halen, the mutilated female character of the book, because in spite of great personal loss, and catastrophic current events, she is determined to celebrate life. *La Prière de la peur* gives a clear indication that Algeria will be born again, even if it must be from its own ashes: "Par le serment de nos femmes [. . .] par le serment des femmes [. . .] De tes cendres, tu renaîtras, Algerie."[19] (By the oath of our women, [. . .] by the oath of women [. . .] from your ashes you will be born again Algeria."

The question of course is which Algeria? It would be difficult to imagine any Algerian who does not have an opinion on the subject. In fact, it would not be presumptuous to say that just about any Algerian can be very specific on the topic. Without doubt, this question is threatening to those involved in the current leadership, and those seeking the leadership of Algeria. It is at the source of the political and social impasse of today. It is charged with the lives and deaths of the Algerian people. It has become the justification for the slaughter (and not just for the two sides mentioned previously, because there have been so many disagreements that there are many subdivisions and groups involved). Essentially, the question is two-faceted: It has a political dimension (including political/ religious), and a cultural dimension (including cultural/religious). In the various debates one does not always dissociate easily the political from the religious or the cultural dimensions. That is because to "do" politics, religion, or culture "Algerian style," it is practically impossible to consider one without the others.

Certainly, at the political level the battle centers around which type of government should preside over the Algerian people, a secular government with its emphasis on democracy and individuals (as separate entities), or a government which does not dissociate the state from the religion, and thus one which emphasizes the group over the individuals? The answer to this question is key to the future of Algeria, and not just to its future politically. However, it seems to me that the real question is hardly ever discussed. That is, is Algeria ready and willing to acknowledge the fact that it is a pluralistic society, and is its leadership willing to protect the rights of all its citizens? Progressively, Algeria has been trapped in the vicious cycle of intolerance/dictatorship, with a few concessions here and there (some of which remain a puzzle to the Algerian population), and back to rigidity. In fact, it seems that one of the problems has been the lack of consistency on the part of the Algerian government, starting with not respecting some of the principles followed during the War of Independence (whatever happened to the right to self-determination, being one),[20] corruption (not just at the political and economical level, but with all kinds of "favoritisms" and "punishments" at the cultural level),[21] and the question of women, and more particularly, the place of women in Algerian society, with the institution of the Code de la Famille (family law) in 1984 which places women in a subordinate position to men.[22]

The undeniable fact that Algeria *is* a pluralistic society is indeed, troublesome to many. In fact, the debate goes far beyond the borders of the country, although it has not taken the same proportion. Having said that the Maghreb is pluralistic,[23] one must also point to the Diaspora of Maghrebian people, and perhaps more toward France, where large numbers of Maghrebian people live, with their descendants, born in France.[24] Unless one takes this plural identity into account, accepts it, deals with it, and why not, celebrates it, Algeria will continue along the path of civil war, and suicide. This means that Algeria, and all factions of Algerian society must come to terms with the past, and in particular with French colonization,[25] and of course, in the future, it will have to come to terms with the present.[26]

In the context of the current disastrous situation, it is absolutely courageous to keep on standing up, to speak and shout, to write, to create, to organize, to protest, to denounce, to dare, to hope, to imagine, and to live. To do so, in spite of the horrific reality, gives a new kind of purpose to one's life: one which cannot be measured but by life itself, and the love of life. Khalida Messaoudi, an activist who still lives in Algeria in spite of her condemnation to death by the Groupe Islamiste Armé (Armed Islamist Group or GIA), continues to be outspoken, and to organize protests for a free and democratic Algeria, which respects all its citizens, and which protects the rights of women. This message is highlighted in *Une Algérienne debout*[27] (*An Algerian woman standing*). One should not be mislead by the title of the book, for it is not about one Algerian woman who stands, or remains standing, but about one among several, many Algerian women. The author makes it clear that for Algerian women standing is a deeply rooted tradition, inscribed in the fibers of a plural original identity, and a pluralistic society. Thus, the mere fact of standing is a way of "saying" the Algerian identity. It is a way of writing it.

Finally, just like any attempt to go back in time renders this plural identity undeniable, any attempt to go forward moves us in the direction of multiplicity, inclusion, and acceptance. That is, . . . if Algeria overcomes this nightmare, and truly means to live in peace. In the meantime, Algeria will continue to draw incredible strength and courage from those who mark the way as they stand, and as they die. The bodies of those who stand or die serve as marks, that is, as evidence that an important activity is going on and consists in writing in and out of Algeria, writing Algeria.

NOTES

1. *Algérie en éclats*, adapted by Catherine Levy-Mariée. The play was originally published by Editions des Amandiers, Paris: 1995. It was produced recently in Paris, at Le Théatre de Petit Hebertot, in March 1997. Catherine Levy-Mariée attributes these words to Azzedine Menasra whom she reports to have said that on the occasion of the death of renowned author and journalist Tahar Djaout. A possible translation of the title of the play could be *"Algeria blown-up"* or *"Algeria Fragmented."*

2. "Reste-t-il encore une place pour le théâtre dans ce pays?" (Is there still a place for theater in this country?), wonders one of the characters in *Algérie en éclats*.

3. About half of the play is made of quotes which Catherine Levy-Mariée takes directly from many Algerian authors and many different sources. Primarily she uses excerpts from books, poems, and newspaper articles from current authors, film makers, and journalists.

4. *Sans Voix*, Hafsa Zinaï-Koudil, Paris: Editions Plon, 1997.

5. Hafsa Zinaï-Koudil was forced into exile in April 1995 when the GIA (Groups Islamiste Armé, or Armed Islamist Group) condemned her to death for her film *Le Démon au Féminin* (could be translated as *"The Demon Feminine Style"* or *"The Demon Personified as a Woman"*). In the film, Salima—a young, determined, intelligent woman who also describes herself as a "faithful spouse and a believer" (i.e., a practicing Muslim)— "dares" argue with her mother (who is completely veiled) over the fact that she refuses to wear the hijab, in spite of her husband's numerous requests and threats. Steadfastly and

angrily, she explains: "I like getting dressed, putting on some make-up. I love living. I do not want to be buried alive." Too daring, and certainly not a role model for the viewers, in the eyes of the GIA. Furthermore, and most importantly perhaps, the film offers a strong criticism of anyone who utilizes Islam as a means of justification of what he or she does for personal, self-serving, and/or political reasons.

6. In a televised interview with Bernard Pivot. See "Bouillon de Culture," France 2, April 19, 1997. Realization: Elisabeth Preschey.

7. *Sans voix*, Hafsa Zinai-Koudil, 24.

8. Letifa Ben Mansour, *La Prière de la peur*, Editions La Différence, 1997.

9. It is perhaps in the works of such artists as humorist Slim (see for example his cartoons in *Recueil d'Hahuristan*, Editions du Seuil), or drawings by Camel Yayaoui (especially *Le voyage des exilés* with poems by renowned Algerian author Nabile Farés to illustrate the drawings, Editions Salamandre) that one can find examples of this.

10. Aïssa Khelladi is an Algerian journalist and author who lives in exile in France, since the end of 1994. His book *Peur et mensonges (Fear and Lies)* was published recently by Paris: Editions du Seuil, April 1997.

11. I borrow this idea that the Algerian population is kept hostage from the very rich and in-depth study of the complexity of the Algerian situation made by the group "Reporters sans Frontières," and which was published by Editions de la Découverte (1996), under the title *Le Drame Algérien, Un peuple en otage*.

12. *Sans voix*, Hafsa Zinai-Koudil, 42.

13. "Il est coupable . . . etre coupable de la peur des autres ou de la peur qu'on éprouve face aux autres, et de la peur supposée face au personnage, qui est donc journaliste, et qui a accès à la parole, et qui écrit, " explains Aïssa Khelladi in "Bouillon de Culture."

14. Unfortunately, that has been the case for many people. In particular, two years ago that was the case for Lounès Matoub, famous Berber singer (who sings in Berber language) when a policeman shot him five times at close range and when the GIA kept him in captivity for two weeks. Both groups have come to consider Berber culture and language as a main threat to the Algerian National Identity. See his book, *Rebelle*, Editions Stock, 1995. In the book, Lounès Matoub talks about his fear. Forcibly, the fear of dying (as he wonders which death will be his: shot, slaughtered, etc.), but also the fear for Berber identity and its future.

15. "Bouillon de Culture," April 19, 1997, France 2.

16. *Sans voix*, Hafsa Zinai-Koudil, 14.

17. See specifically Surah IV: 102, 92, and 93. Although Muhammad Marmaduke Pickthaill's text and explanatory translation of *The Glorious Qur'an* which includes both the Arabic and English translation pays more attention to details, I use for the purpose of this translation the more commonly known version presented by N. J. Dawood, in *The Koran* (Penguin Classics, 1983 edition). Surah IV: 102 reads in part: "When you (Prophet), are with the faithful, conducting their prayers, let one party of them rise up to pray with you, armed with their weapons. After making their prostrations, let them withdraw to the rear and let another party who have not prayed come forward and pray with you; and let these also be on their guard, armed with their weapons" (p. 377). Surah IV: 92 reads in part: "It is unlawful for a believer to kill another believer except by accident" (p. 376). Surah IV: 93 reads: "He that kills a believer by design shall burn in Hell forever. He shall incur the wrath of Allah, who will lay His curse on him and prepare for him a woeful scourge" (p. 376).

18. Refer to "Bouillon de Culture" previously mentioned.

19. Latifa ben Monsour *La Prière de la peur*, 380.

20. There were major Kabyle protests in 1980.

21. Included in the cultural question is that of languages, particularly French language, but certainly not limited to it. It must be said that although it is true that those who write in French are more frequently targeted with death sentences, and many journalists, authors, and intellectuals have been killed because of that, those who write or sing in other languages have been targeted as well, including arabophone authors. Thus, it is correct to say that it is the sum of the specific ideas which the various languages carry that is condemned, more so than the languages in which they are expressed.

The Algerian population, and in particular young people, reached such a degree of dissatisfaction and frustration with the economical and cultural situation of the country that it lead to the well publicized massive protest of October 1988, during which several hundred people were killed by the army.

22. Subsequently, within a few years, Algerian women organized themselves in some twenty associations. On March 8, 1990, almost every association was represented at a Festival of Women in Algiers.

23. For more details on this point, refer to Moroccan author and theoretician, Abdelkebir Khatiby's magnificant book: *Maghreb Pluriel*, Denoël, 1983.

24. Kadour Zouilaï makes a thought provoking suggestion in "L'individu Algérien: une invention à faire," in *Algérie 30 ans, les enfants de l'indépendance*, Paris: Editions Autrement, 1992. It reads: "Il faudrait recenser toute la culture algérienne qui est née et qui a fleuri à l'extérieur de l'Algérie. Culture d'une grande richesse. Il en est d'ailleurs de même pour l'ensemble du monde Arabe. Curieux paradoxe quand même: une cultutre du monde arabe hors du monde arabe. Inconnue du monde arabe" (p. 153). "It would be necessary to account for the Algerian culture which is born and which has flourished outside Algeria. A culture of great wealth. It is, in fact, the same for the entire Arab World. A curious paradox, nevertheless: A culture of the Arab World outside the Arab World. Unknown to the Arab World."

25. As contemporary French historian Benjamin Stora has pointed out, the French are struggling with the same issue. They have not resolved the Algerian question.

26. This will be no easy task for the enemies of yesterday were foreigners, and Algeria has not quite come to terms with that part of its past, and the enemies of today are from within. Can Algeria heal from these self-inflicted wounds?

27. *Une Algérienne Debout*, Editions Flammarion, 1995.

18

Post Apartheid Drama

Donald M. Morales

In Esiaba Irobi's play, *Gold, Frankincense and Myrrh* (1989), the Nigerian playwright turns the long-standing debate on Wole Soyinka's linguistic complexity into high comedy. The setting is an African Writer's convention at Ibadan's University Staff Club where Soyinka is on trial for "crimes" of "private obscurantism," and "gratuitous conundrums" (25). To underscore these charges, Irobi gives Soyinka, "Ogun" in the play, an interpreter to paraphrase his remarks for an attending audience of writers and scholars.[1] However, in the midst of this comic debate, a South African woman proffers a sobering thought, "Do you think all this howling about elitist and traditional literature would arise if you were in South Africa? If you were suffering the abject negation of man" (44).

Such a literary debate and satiric play would seem improbable in South Africa—at least in the South Africa of apartheid. Apartheid has etched such an indelible mark over South African life that it serves as a palimpsest over which writers try to fashion new ideas. Athol Fugard's drama, *A Road to Mecca*, for example, contrasts two Afrikaner women who stand on opposite poles of social conformity and rebellion, yet apartheid's presence is never absent. One brief meeting of a dispossessed black woman[2] and child in the Karoo desert reinforces the *ideas of desolation and moral censorship placed on the Afrikaner women.*

Writing in South Africa has not been able to escape the assumption of politics. Fugard observed "if you're a black person in South Africa, and an opportunity comes up to tell a story on stage, any real separation of arts and politics is impossible. The black person's sense of silence, of not having had a voice, is colossal" (Engstrom 22). Thus, without a means of redress through the political process, the South African artist becomes, willingly or unwillingly, the artist/politician. "Culture is," playwright Matsemela Manaka comments, "one of the last weapons we have to mobilize society for change" (Horn vii). But as South Africa adjusts to a new democratization, what happens to the nature of a theater that relies so heavily on political metaphor? As the remnants of apartheid are buried deeper into the palimpsest, in what direction does South African theater move for black and white playwrights?

Very little writing has come out of South Africa since the February 11, 1990, release of Nelson Mandela. There seems to be an unconscious literary moratorium awaiting the outcome of South Africa's political quagmire. It would be pure speculation to predict the nature of future writing. Breyten Breytenback's travelogue, *Return to Paradise* (1993), warns "To my mind only a fool would pretend to understand comprehensively what South Africa is really about, or be objective and farsighted enough to glimpse its future course" (xviii).

But based on what little has emerged, plays like Fugard's *Playland* (1992), Duma Ndlovu's *Black Codes from the Underground* (1993), Tug Yourgrau's *Song of Jacob Zulu* (1993), Mbongeni Ngema's *Sheila's Day* (1993), Hilary Blecher's *Daughter of Nebo* (1993) and comments from artists familiar with the South African situation, one can at least venture into possibilities. Surely there will be a sense of negotiation in the plays, an awareness by artists of the datedness of past themes. Afrikaner writing is understandably paranoiac, guilt-ridden, and conciliatory—when the Afrikaner woman in *A Road to Mecca* offers the nomadic black a ride, it is offered culpably and not with a sense of wanting to effect change. Dennis Brutus recently commented that reconciliation is "part of the national psyche and part of the process of creating a new South Africa" (Personal Interview). If this national psyche is explored honestly, it can lead to great drama and not drama that has become predictable and static.

Writing by black South Africans may move into a more self-revelatory mode, casting off overt political writing since apartheid may no longer be an obvious target. Irobi's play is an in-house investigation of Nigerian writing. And although politics is and has always been a vital ingredient in Nigerian life, it is in the background of this play, a play where cultural choices move to the forefront. Percy Mtwa's *Bopha* produced in 1986 and turned into a 1993 film, and Ngema's new drama *Magic at Four AM* move slowly away from straight political theater and more into self disclosure.

Coleen Angove in a constructive essay, "Alternative Theatre: Reflecting a Multi Racial South African Society?" observed South African drama from the Grahamstown Festival and considered whether the society on stage reflected a South Africa moving towards unification or polarization. She witnessed recent theater falling into three classes: an Afrikaner drama preoccupied with white fears over a black controlled government; a black theater that primarily aired black grievances aimed at black audiences; and an alternative theater that rejected polarization while attempting to graft a distinct South Africa, a theater of reconciliation. Her analysis might be a good starting point to a project a future theater.

The first class of plays she comments on is from 1988 to 1989 and they capture a conservative Afrikaner mindset. Norman Coombs's *Snake in the Grass* (February 1988) depicts elderly whites living in a colonial-style hotel. The heavily symbolic play uses a melancholic and nostalgic setting that signals the end of white control in Africa. The age of the characters and hoary setting projects a death watch for whites in Africa. *Scorched Earth* (April 1988) by Pieter Dirk Uys tackles the homeland question. An Afrikaner family's ownership of an estate given them for their service to the English is threatened by the new postapartheid black government (41). These plays illustrate the paranoiac fears of a black-centered government and the diminished role whites may play. They are agitprop types geared obviously to a very specific white conservative clientele with an iron resolve to relinquish little.

A more problematic class is the theater of reconciliation, liberal Afrikaner writing that runs across racial barriers with varying levels of communication. Each character is allowed "a voice, an opinion, an indulgence" (43). Here Angove uses the March 1989 Market Theater production of Pieter Dirk Uys's *Just Like Home*. It is a play of exiles: Cathy September, a black domestic who travels to London with her South African employers; Hector Price, a white political exile and Trevor Juries, a nephew of the domestic in London fighting for the revolution. Cathy, after twelve years in London, decides to return to South Africa for nonpolitical reasons and finds herself justifying her return to both Hector and Trevor (43). The final irony is that South Africa unites each character because in the end it is home to all.

The multifaceted Uys occasionally approaches apartheid from an absurdist position. His 1987 play *Panorama*, recently produced by the Africa Arts Theater Company in New York (April 1994), is one example. Two Afrikaner women who live on a penal island working as teachers reluctantly house the daughter of one of the inmates; this one-night stay is forceably arranged by local authorities. Uys uses the visit to create a black woman who embodies everything the Afrikaner women want to become: fearless, rational, committed and sexually secure. Uys paints a picture of Afrikaners imprisoned in their own land.

What is troubling with this type of theater is the facile treatment of an endemic South African problem. Because apartheid separates society so conclusively, there is very little opportunity for authentic exchange, more so for whites, and this can become a problem when Afrikaner dramatists voice black aspirations or delineate black characters. Sibi, the black woman of Uys's *Panorama*, is projected as "everywoman"—intelligent, caring, pregnant with the child of a white lover.

The Afrikaner playwright often writes from the perspective of an outsider, leading, in some cases, to political stereotypes that lack human dimension or plays that contain misleading desires of its black characters. A play that

comes to mind is *The Song of Jacob Zulu* which opened at Chicago's Steppenwolf Theater in late 1992. Tug Yourgrau, a white South African documentary
filmmaker and television producer who came to the United States when he
was ten, conceived the musical. It was originally a courtroom teleplay based on
the 1985 bombing of a shopping center near Durban that killed five people
and injured fifty. The accused, Andrew Zondo, a nineteen-year-old son of a
black minister, was convicted and hanged (Waites 25). Yourgrau examines this
transformation from a bright and quiet religious man to an African National
Congress (ANC) member turned terrorist.

The play ruminated for some five years before it was reconceived for the
Steppenwolf Theater in 1990. Yourgrau collaborated with Ladysmith Black
Mambazo, the nine male member acappella group known for Isicathamiya, a
folk form that combines traditional Zulu, varied gospel, R & B, doo-wop with
stomping dance movements (Pareles 1). The playwright uses Ladysmith as a
Greek chorus to comment on the action of the play, but the group, led by
Joseph Shabalala, becomes instead the heart and soul of the drama which in
turn exposes Yourgrau's bare and polemical script. Frank Rich of the *New
York Times* wrote that the antiapartheid drama "lack [ed] the poetic texture,
eloquence, surprises and deep feeling—in short, the voice—of its music"
(Rich "Sad Song" 17). There is a level of arrogation of Ladysmith because
Yourgrau, of necessity, writes from the vantage point of an interloper. Rich
lauds the mining camp origins of the music but is not as generous with
Yourgrau's writing which he describes as "utilitarian" and "pedagogical"
(17). Yourgrau's comment about Ladysmith's inclusion is telling: "I think
it (Ladysmith) made a difference, I think Ladysmith was our trump card"
(Waites 25). The character of Jacob Zulu is never illuminated but regresses into
a blurry metaphor for South African injustice. Mr. Yourgrau's distance from
his subjects produces a static work that does not move beyond cliché.

The most prominent of the Afrikaner playwrights is Athol Fugard. He is
at once committed to change yet ambivalent about this commitment. After a
career of antiapartheid plays that subtly attacked the way he envisioned
apartheid affected blacks—*Bloodknot* (1961), *Boesman and Lena* (1969),
Statements (1972), *Sizwe Banzi Is Dead* and *The Island* (1973)—Fugard
changed perspective. *A Lesson from Aloes* (1980) portrayed the effects of the
growing South African violence upon an Afrikaner family. *Master Harold and
the Boys* (1982), largely autobiographical, recounted the growing chasm that
inevitably occurs between master and servant. *The Road to Mecca* (1984)
focused almost exclusively on the isolation of two Afrikaner women. Most
surprising, *A Place with the Pigs* (1987), described as a personal parable of
a Russian deserter in self-imposed exile for forty-one years, was set outside
of South Africa.

When questioned about this change he responded, "obviously politics is one
of the elements in my playwriting . . . (but) sometimes create (s) a wrong
anticipation on the part of critics and audiences who wait for a certain sort

of thing when I'm doing something else" (Engstrom 22). Politics often forces an individual to take positions that compromise ideals. In Fugard's case he was castigating his own sense of identity. Living in South Africa under apartheid created for him a "monumental guilt trip . . . by being white, by being an Afrikaner . . . circumstances have made me harshly judge South Africa, and I am judging something I love. I am judging my own people" (Freedman 1). In writing *Boesman and Lena*, Fugard reflected, "Can I align myself with a future, a possibility, which I believe in (hope for) but of which I have no image" (*Notebooks* 179). In his *Notebooks* he questioned his commitment to a changing South Africa "Could it (change) be sooner if I chose to sacrifice. But I can't" (161).

Fugard's *My Children, My Africa* (1989), which Ms. Angove includes in her theater of reconciliation, seemingly returns to the political front—the 1984 school boycotts. A black schoolteacher and student trade political differences but stationed between the two is a young Afrikaner student whose debating team is brought in from a private boarding school as an experiment meant to lift the shadow of ignorance between the races. Young Isabel has virtually no contact with blacks accept for an "auntie" and boy who delivers medicine for her chemist father. She initially views her relationship with Thami, the black student, as a great liberal experiment, but during the course of the drama, her character grows as she realizes "there is a whole world without [her] imprint." The play is essentially an argument where Fugard's persona, the black school teacher, debates education over politics. Fugard, like Yourgrau, is writing as an observer and imposing his vision of reality over something very distant from him. This distance sometimes questions the credibility of his plays, especially among black observers. Producer/playwright Duma Ndlovu points out that Fugard writes what he thinks is a political priority for blacks. Ndlovu looks at the themes of *Bloodknot, Boesman and Lena* and *Master Harold* as integrative priorities low on the political agenda for blacks (Personal Interview).

A drama that has emerged from Fugard since Mandela's release is *Playland*, originally produced at the Market Theater in July, 1992. *Playland* is set in a traveling amusement park bordering a Karoo town in South Africa. The time is New Year's Eve 1989, several weeks before the February 11, 1990, release of Nelson Mandela. Its two characters, a black night watchman and a white Defense Force soldier, pass the evening attempting to hide the sins of their pasts: Martinus Zoeloe, the watchman, killed an Afrikaner for raping the woman he loved while Gideon Le Roux gunned down dozens of black rebels in his border confrontation with the Southwest Africa Peoples Organization (SWAPO) while in the South African Defense Force. Fugard spreads the guilt equally so that their confrontation can end in optimism, an optimism Fugard would like to extend to a new South Africa.

One New York critic, complained that Fugard has been writing the same play since *Bloodknot* in 1961 (Simon 71). The criticism suggests that since South

Africa has changed, should not there be changing themes in Fugard's writing? So many of his plays investigate an existential landscape using Port Elizabeth as backdrop; there is not the writing of an engaged artist fully aware of the full-bodiness of its black characters. He has always been more concerned with man's isolation in an alien universe than with the volatile political predicament in South Africa. South African poet/activist Dennis Brutus has always sensed a degree of dishonesty in Fugard's "committed" theater, "I always felt that there was an element of exploitation in his work, that he really was, in a sense, writing about the predicament of blacks without completely supporting them so we've had various disagreements about various plays of his" (Personal Interview). Similar attacks are leveled at his most recent drama, *My People*, a metaplay using the voices of young women.

The ambiguity an Afrikaner faces when working under the burden of apartheid is overwhelming. *Playland* wishes the problem away through good will on both sides. Rich commented that the play is "reductivist to a fault . . . almost fanatically tidy. It's as if Mr. Fugard felt he could contain his society's messy, careening history and even more miraculously, push it to a hopeful denouement by maintaining rigid control over everything that happens on a patch of stage" ("Boiled" C15). Martinus and Gideon are metaphors of defined positions, not fully drawn characters with unequaled histories. The one-act work reveals a South African playwright searching for an image of himself in an alien environment.

Fugard is more credible when he details an Afrikaner sensibility. His film, *The Guest*, confirms this. Fugard plays Eugene Marais (1871–1936), a South African poet and naturalist who exposes political corruption working as a newspaper editor. Marais' stay on a farm run by an Afrikaner family poignantly unveils the nuances of their stark Calvinistic existence. The strictures within the farm family, the unbending resolve of a fixed moral code and the uncompromising nature of an Afrikaner people are clearly evident. This film illustrates that Fugard is better served in defining the Afrikaner sensibility than projecting a black world view unless, of course, it is done in a collaboration as was the case with *Sizwe Banzi Is Dead* and *The Island*[5] where actors John Kani and Winston Ntshona improvised their own limitations under apartheid before the scenes were finally put down on paper. Interestingly, Fugard's latest work *My Life* (1995), returns to the collaborative form where he presents five women—two blacks, one white, Indian, and colored—pantomining excerpts from their own diaries.

Society can never dictate to an artist what he or she should write. But as a new order comes into being, new terrain needs to be examined dramatically by the Afrikaner: The Dutch Reform Church's support of apartheid on biblical grounds, the existence of an Afrikaner Broederbond set up in 1918 to "prevent the disappearance of the Afrikaner volk as a separate political, language, social and cultural entity"; the Afrikaner of 1948 caught between the rich, educated Englishman and the black South African; the psychological impact on Afrikaners over changing symbols—flags, anthems, holidays—as a new South Africa develops; growing world audience needs to understand the thinking of the Afrikaner that pushed him into such an untenable racial predicament. The Afrikaner theater of postapartheid South Africa will have to exorcise demons and not lobby for political justice for its black future citizens out of a sense of guilt.

Angove's description of black plays developed at the Grahamstown festival— *Kuyase Africa* (People's Cultural organization), *Kuma* (Fuda Centre, Soweto October 1988), *Ababhemi* (Darlington and Mnembe Black Sun October 1988), *Dankie Auntie* (Mda), *Kode Kubeneni* (M. Memela Makhanya), *Kagoos* (January 1989) (42)—fall under the umbrella of urban ills created by apartheid. They are not unlike the 1986 Woza Afrika theater festival that introduced a New York audience to township plays—Maishe Maponya's *Gangsters*, Matsemela Manaka's *Children of Asazi*, Mbongeni Ngema's *Asinamali!*, Percy Mtwa's *Bopha*. Township theater is revelatory and message oriented; it is as Mponya said "theater of the fist," a theater born of political repression. It would be senseless to argue aesthetics when a theater's aim is to effect political change. But as the landscape changes, it is up to the artist to find new ground to accommodate a new social order.

Some voices in South Africa who see a new South African emerging argue that art not be so tied to politics. Albie Sachs, a former member of the legal department of the ANC, said back in 1966 (*The Jail Diary of Albie Sachs*) and most recently at the New Nation Conference that the arts should not become a prisoner of the struggle and ignore themes of the human condition (Chapman 2). Nadime Gordimer has warned "Agitprop binds the artist with the means by which it aims to free minds of the people. It licenses a phony subart" (137). Njabulo Ndebele at the 1986 Second Stockholm Conference for African Writers "Refining Relevance" said, "Post-protest literature . . . should probe beyond the observable facts, to reveal new worlds where it was previously thought they did not exist" (Gray 25). Zwelakhe Sisulu (New Nation Writers Conference, Wits University, December 1991) spoke of reconstructing South Africa anew through literature. This kind of thinking, however, is on a theoretical level for it has yet to surface in the drama written by black South Africans since Mandela's release.

Thuli Dumakude's *Buya Africa* has run intermittently at various locations in New York over the past two years. Ms. Dumakude, the lead vocalist in *Cry Freedom*, served as the vocal coach to the young actors in *Sarafina*. *Buya Africa* is a series of dramatic monologues accompanied by songs that recount her growing up and coming of age in South Africa. Her eclectic style draws from traditional, South African, gospel and contemporary music. In *Buya Africa*, the content is overtly political—a teacher witnessing her students striking, forced removals. Julius Novick of *Newsday* commented, "Dumakude's heart is in the right place, but her political analyses does not get much beyond 'Apartheid no! Freedom yes!' " The playwright's call for communal song at the play's end begs empathy but does little in the way of creating an effective drama. It cries of 1960s participatory theater.

Duma Ndlovu and Layding Kaliba collaborated on *Black Codes from the Underground* that ran at Barbara Ann Teer's Harlem-based National Black Theater during the summer of 1993. This is Ndlovu's second play where he synthesizes South African and American experiences in an attempt to find parallels in oppression. In *Codes* there are several men awaiting execution for terrorist acts in the United States during the sixties. Each recounts, in monologue, his reason for being there. The South African prisoner, in the midst of his story, finds parallels in the sixties' Civil Rights battles with that of Steve Biko's black consciousness movement and this is Ndlovu's input since he was intimately a part of that movement before coming to the United States in 1977. The American monologues are predictable and Biko's invocation forced.

A more developed work is *Sheila's Day*. The musical was work-shopped for an eight-week period in 1989 by Ngema, Ndlovu, and Dumakude who choreographed the work; later, Americans Ruby Lee and Ebony Jo-Ann created the American element. The play is a celebration of domestic workers both in South Africa and the United States who are, as Ndlovu states, the "spiritual center of the African continuum . . . the keepers of tradition and the intercessors with the ancestral spirits" (BAM Program Note). The title is a reference to the name white employers give workers whose names they refuse to learn; the name is also a reference to Thursday, the traditional day off for South African domestic workers. Ndlovu says the day is additionally a gathering day for women who come together in prayer, song, and testimony to heal and renew themselves (Note). Metaphorically they are the liberating force within Africa and throughout the African Diaspora.

The twelve-woman musical is also based on the deaths of two men: Jimmy Lee Jackson who, in 1965 Alabama, died at the hands of the police while protecting his mother from police attack, and Mthuli KaShezi who was beaten and pushed in front of a moving train while defending domestic workers harassed by white men in Johannesburg South Africa. The four authors point out that both men were refused treatment at local hospitals and later their tombstones desecrated. The authors contend the deaths changed "the collective consciousness of their nations" (Note).

Song and dance are the play's force as the women make use of traditional Zulu chants, tribal anthems, gospel/Pentecostal screams and the blues. The American and South African women's stories are told chronologically and sequentially. The Civil Rights and antiapartheid movements are juxtaposed through dramatic monologue and music. The women are not heroic but merely in the way of historic boycotts and protests; they are rather humble people who simply want to work and eat but are caught up in the sweeping history of the moment. Once caught up, however, they quickly fall in step with their American and South African acappella choruses and become part of the struggle.

Sheila's Day has undergone subtle changes since its workshop period and was last performed at the Grahamstown Theater Festival in Grahamstown, South Africa by the Crossroads Theater Company in the summer of 1993 (July 6–11)—the first Actor's Equity organization to perform in South Africa in thirty years. The reaction varied according to audience age. Older white South Africans resented an American company coming to South Africa to interpret the situation in their own country. Dumakude anticipated this reaction because she understands how sensitive South Africans are about being analyzed from abroad. But she adds South African writing is no longer subject to the kind of censorship as in previous years where actors memorized parts so scripts could not not be judged by censors, although that's how *Sheila's Day* started out (i. e., guerrilla theater). Now situations have changed. "South Africans aren't speaking between the lines anymore. . . . [There are] no more double meanings to get a point across," she says (Collins). The critical reception was mixed. Terry Herbst of the *Eastern Province Herald* commented: "I can't remember when I last saw a theatrical event so richly deserving of this ultimate accolade." Barry Ronge of *Cue* voiced doubts about the plot's credibility: "This plot device is . . . contrived . . . barely believable, even allowing for the suspension of disbelief, that two women could, between them, stumble into every major civil rights event that occurred on two different continents."

Although the music is riveting, the *Sheila's Day* collaboration is along the lines of *Codes*. It does not break new ground dramatically and really is a reshuffling of old themes—a modern-day Civil Rights pageant. There is high energy and musical prowess in the piece, but as theater, it does not rise above the mundane.

The Crossroads' visit to South Africa was more than the presentation of a play, however. It offered a further view into South African theater. Patreshettarlina Adams, the Crossroads' stage manager, was able to sample several other works including a South African cast performing Ntozake Shange's *Colored Girls*. Much of the program of black South African plays revolved around life in the townships, hostels or mines, similar to what Angove observed at the festival several years before. Ms. Adams recalled one play, however, that moved in another direction. *Daughter of Nebo* is a Hilary Blecher, Victor N'toni and Rashid Lanie music theater collaboration based on a documentary made by Sara Blecher and James Mthoba. The story is a traditional tale of village people who place communal responsibility high on their list of priorities. In the drama, a young girl is murdered and it is incumbent upon the village to find out what happened and act upon it. They discover the murderer is the father who claims that he was possessed by demons. He is given over to the white government who do not sentence him to death. Ms . Adams indicated the play's theme is that black South Africans have created their own communal laws and must believe and fight for them. Accordingly, the father is sentenced to death by the village. What surprised Ms. Adams was the apolitical nature of the play, the absence of anger or shock that is so common with agitprop theater. *Nebo* was subsequently brought to the United States by the Brooklyn Academy of Music (BAM) for a short, spring 1994 run and received favorable reviews.

Ms. Adams thinks straight political theater is limiting and sees so many other possibilities available to playwrights. "You know intellectually as well as emotionally there are so many stories that should be told; they've only begun to realize that they have the power to tell them" (Personal Interview). In this context she mentioned Ngema's new work, *Magic at Four A.M.*, a play about men gathering in the ungodly hour of 4 A.M. to watch a Muhammad Ali title match. The men see Ali's heroic qualities in themselves and become the magic at 4 A. M. The two plays, *Magic* and *Daughter* are plays Ms. Adams sees as moving towards the internal concerns of black South Africans without reference to the white antagonist that has dominated their lives.

Bill Keller, the present *New York Times* correspondent in South Africa, writes of the paucity of real images about the South Africa he covers and knows. And although he is talking primarily about films like *Bopha*, *The Power of One* (1992), *A Dry White Season* (1989), *Cry Freedom* and *Sarafina*, what he says applies to the theater as well. Keller quotes Barry Ronge, the cultural voice of South Africa, who accuses American directors of coming to South Africa with "imaginations paralyzed by apartheid" (13). Plots must revolve around attacks on apartheid and are "immobilized by a reverence for the struggle" (13).

Another journalist, Michael Clough, in a review of David Ottaway's *Chained Together: Mandela, de Klerk and the Struggle to Remake South Africa*, writes, "The grand struggle is over. Stark contrasts between good and evil have blurred. The ennobling challenge of ending apartheid has been replaced by a host of more mundane tasks. Many of the heroes have been tarnished. Most of the old villains seem less evil and less menacing" (3). Ottaway, who was the *Washington Post's* correspondent in South Africa from 1990 to 1992, finds Mandela a rather mundane politician whose view of the world belongs to another generation. This gray hue of the present is what confronts the writer of postapartheid South Africa. The fixed targets of the past are no longer there. The truth of the matter is that "The South African Play" has yet to be written. "The South African Play" must develop from cultural and psychological roots, not from a sense of angst or political vendettas.

Breyten Breytenbach is an example of what becomes of a writer so consumed by politics. He has not lived in South Africa since 1959 and spent seven years in a South African prison from 1975 to 1982, two in solitary confinement. During that period he felt abandoned by the African National Congress (ANC) who saw him as a romantic militant. This bitterness with South Africa penetrates almost every page of *Return to Paradise*. Toward the conclusion, his South African host accuses him of being a "poseur, a misery sponge, a bird of doom come here for the satisfaction of high and holy moral indignation to spew disgust over the assembly, flying off to lick imagined wounds in 'exile'" (215).

Now that South Africa approaches a new period, Bryetenbach cautions like some punch-drunk boxer, "the war is invisible" (Finnegan 3). He searches for new illusions to insure his survival, the "psychological necessity" of this. Of politics and writing he sees them as coming out of the same source: "They both use the same means of deception, the same words, the same concepts, dreams" (Finnegan 3). A writer's function for Breytenback is to "contest" ideas, to make uncomfortable the comfortable. This frame of reference places him outside any idea of reconciliation: "I (forfeit) the repose of belonging to 'my country' with 'my own people', I (deform) my past and (destroy) my future." It is because politics is "voracious, deadening all else" (*Paradise* 218).

Dennis Brutus's comments at an October 1993 poetry reading might begin to round out this discussion. He alluded to the 1991 New Nations Conference at Wits University where a suggestion, maybe even a prescription for future South African writing was made. First, there should be no writing about suffering of the past, that new writing should only focus on the creation of a new society. Brutus's response was that he found it "troubling that some people (are) trying to prescribe to the writers what their themes should be in the future" (Personal Interview). He hastily rejects this literary censorship to "buy" a peaceful South Africa. "You cannot," Brutus warns, "come to grips with the present if you pretend that the past doesn't exist" (Personal Interview).

Somewhere there has to be compromise or politics will consume all of South Africa along with its artists. Their record of literature will be of period works that mark a decade but do not reveal a generation or a culture. Nigerain playwright Femi Osofisan has warned of the writer's limitation, "It is not the writer who will correct (in his case) Nigeria's . . . situation. The writer can help diagnose and increase awareness; he can protest, and move others to protest; he cannot cure or heal" (Dunton 68). There are so many virulent dramas to be written about South Africa. Perhaps a work like Irobi's *Gold, Frankincense and Myrrh* is one of them.

NOTES

1. Among the participants are Chinua Achebe (Achibiri), Awi Kwei Armah (Baako), J. P. Clark (Clerk), Femi Osofisan (Osofolo), Ngũgî Wa Thiong'o (Kariuka), Chinweizu (Chekwas).

2. The play's original title—*My English Name Is Patience*—is a reference to this black woman who has been widowed and forced to move on (O'Quinn 43).

Redress through the political process, the South African artist becomes, willingly or unwillingly, the artist/politician. "Culture is," playwright Matsemela Manaka comments, "one of the last weapons we have to mobilize society for change" (Horn vii). But as South Africa heads in the direction of an excruciatingly slow democratization, what happens to the nature of a theater that relies so heavily on political metaphor? As the remnants of apartheid are buried deeper into the palimpsest, in what direction does South African theater move for black and white playwrights?

3. Actors John Kani and Winston Ntshona improvised their own limitations under apartheid before the scenes were finally put down on paper; flags, anthems, holidays—as a new South Africa develops. A growing world audience needs to understand the thinking of the Afrikaner that pushed him into such an untenable racial predicament. The Afrikaner theater of postapartheid South Africa will have to exorcise demons and not lobby for political justice for its black future citizens out of a sense of guilt.

REFERENCES

Angove, Coleen. "Alternative Theatre: Reflecting a Multi Racial SA Society? *Theatre Research International* 17 (spring 1992): 39–45.

Breytenbach, Breyten. *Return to Paradise.* New York: Harcourt Brace, 1993.

Brutus, Dennis. Personal Interview. October 8, 1993. (Poetry Reading: Artists Ilse Schreiber and Dennis Brutus, MJS Books and Graphics, 9 E. 82d Street).

Chapman, Michael. "The Critic in a State of Emergency: Towards a Theory of Reconstruction (after February 2)." *On Shifting Sands: New Art and Literature from South Africa.* Ed. Kirsten Holst Petersen and Anna Rutherford. Portsmouth: Heinemann, 1991. 1–13.

Clough, Michael. "Now What? A Reporter Ponders Life after Apartheid in South Africa." *New York Times Book Review*, December 1993: 3+.

Collins, Karyn D. "*Sheila's Day' Heads Back to Spiritual Home.*" Ashbury Park Press. June 10, 1993. (New Jersey Clipping Service).

Dunton, Chris. *Make Man Talk True: Nigerian Drama in English since 1970.* London: Hans Zell, 1992.

Engstrom, John. "A 'Lesson' from Athol Fugard." *New York Times,* November 16, 1980, Arts and Leisure: 3+.

Finnegan, William. "The Post-Apartheid Power Scramble: Return to Paradise" *New York Times Book Review,* November 28, 1993: 3+.

Freedman, Samuel G. "Fugard Traces a Dark Parallel on Film." *New York Times,* June 10, 1984, Arts and Leisure: 1+.

Fugard, Athol. *Notebooks 1960/1977 Athol Fugard.* Ed. Mary Benson. London: Faber and Faber, 1983.

Gordimer, Nadime. *Essential Gesture.* New York: Alfred A. Knopf, 1988.

Gray, Stephen. "An Author's Agenda: Revisioning Past and Present for a Future South Africa." *On Shifting Sands: New Art and Literature from South Africa.* Ed. Kirsten Holst Petersen and Anna Rutherford. Portsmouth: Heinemann, 1991. 23–31.

Herbst, Terry. "Stirring Stuff by US Equity Group" *Eastern Province Herald* July 8, 1993: N. pag. (New Jersey Clipping Service).

Horn, Andrew. Introduction. In *The Plays of Zakes Mda* by Zakes Mda. Johannesburg: Raven Press, 1990: Vii–Liv.

Irobi, Esiaba. *Gold, Frankincense and Myrrh.* Enugu: ABIC Books, 1989.

James, Caryn. "Around Town with Breyten Breytenbach: Writing in English, Crying in Afrikaans." *New York Times,* November 25, 1993: C1+.

Keller, Bill. "Is That Really South Africa?" *New York Times,* October 10, 1993, Arts and Leisure: 13+.

Ndlovu, Duma. Personal Interview. December 9, 1986.

Novick, Julius. "South African Songs Sung True." *Newsday,* May 28, 1993, 74..

Oberhelman, Harley D., Ed. *Gabriel Garcia Marquez: A Study of the Short Fiction.* Boston: Twayne, 1991.

O'Quinn, Jim. "Theater: Human Highway" *Seven Days,* April 20, 1988: 43.

Ottaway, Marina. *South Africa: The Struggle for a New Order.* Washington, DC: The Brookings Institution, 1993.

Pareles, Jon. "Ladysmith Raises Its Voice on Broadway" *New York Times,* March 21, 1993, Arts and Leisure: 1.

Patreshettarlina, Adams. Personal Interview. September 17, 1993.

Program Notes. *Sheila's Day.* BAM, June 2–6, 1993.

Rich, Frank. "A Sad Song of Grief, Violence and Apartheid." *New York Times,* March 25, 1993: C17+.

_____. "South Africa's Conflict, Boiled Down to 2 Men." *New York Times,* June 9, 1993: C15.

Ronge, Barry. "Sheila's Heyday." Cue July 7, 1993: N. pag. (New Jersey Clipping Service).

Simon, John. "Invasion of the One-Actors" *New York,* 26, 25 (June 21, 1993): 71.

Sisulu, Zwelakhe, Ed. *New Nation Writers Conference December 1–6, 1991.* DJ Du Plessis Centre, Wits University, 1991.

Waites, James. "A Whole Generation Sacrificed to History. "*ABC Radio 24 Hours* n.d.: 24–25.

Index

ABOUT THE EDITORS AND CONTRIBUTORS

OUSSEINA D. ALIDOU is from the Niger Republic (West Africa). She is currently Assistant Professor in French and Francophone Literature in the Department of Modern Languages at Cleveland State University. Her main areas of teaching and research are Francophone Studies, Hausa language, and African literature. She is a co-ordinator of the Committee for Academic Freedom in Africa. Her works include: *A Thousand Flowers. Structural Adjustment and the Struggle for Education in Africa* (2000) of which she is a co-editor.

F. ODUN BALOGUN is a writer and a scholar. He teaches at Delaware State University and has published extensively, including two books of literary studies, *Tradition and Modernity in the African Short Story* (Greenwood, 1991) and *Ngũgĩ and African Postcolonial Narrative: The Novel as Oral Narrative in Multigenre Performance* (1997). In addition to his award-winning short-story collection *Adjusted Lives* (1995, his fiction has appeared in anthologies in English, French, German, Swedish and other languages. The essay published here is from his book in progress *The Geography of the Ego: Self, Place and Identity Narration in Black Literature*. He recently completed his first novel *Immigrant Story: The Call of the West* (1999).

NANCY TOPPING BAZIN is an eminent scholar and professor of English at Old Dominion University in Norfolk, Virginia. She has directed three women's studies programs (Rutgers, Pittsburgh, and Old Dominion) and, from 1985 to 1989, chaired the Old Dominion English Department. Dr. Bazin has published two books—*Virginia Woolf and the Androgynous Vision* (1973) and *Conversations with Nadine Gordimer* (1990)—and forty articles. In addition to essays on Margaret Atwood, Edith Wharton, Marge Piercy, Anita

Desai, Flora Nwapa, Mariama Ba, and Athol Fugard, her articles have been primarily on curriculum transformation and writers Doris Lessing, Buchi Emecheta, Bessie Head, Virginia Woolf, and Nadine Gordimer. Dr. Bazin has been a visiting scholar at the Institute for Advanced Study at Indiana University–Bloomington and at the Virginia Center for the Humanities. She has participated in faculty development projects in Postcolonial Literature, Third World Studies (with trips to the Ivory Coast, Tanzania, and Morocco), and East Asian Studies (with a trip in 1989 to Japan and China). In 1994, Dr. Bazin was one of eleven in the Commonwealth of Virginia to be honored with an Outstanding Faculty Award. In 1996, she received The Charles O. and Elizabeth Burgess Faculty Research and Creativity Award.

DENNIS BRUTUS was born in Zimbabwe, formerly Rhodesia, but grew up in South Africa. He was a teacher until 1962 when, as a result of his political activism, notably his protest against all white South African sports, he was arrested, wounded as he tried to escape, and imprisoned in the infamous Robin Island. He went into exile in 1966. His testimony concerning *apartheid* helped win support for the ban against South Africa's participation in the 1970s Olympics. Since then, he has taught at American universities—Northwestern University until 1985 and the University of Pittsburgh, where he currently teaches in the Department of African Studies. Dennis Brutus is also known worldwide for his poetry that reflects his prison experiences, his struggle for justice, and the agony of political exile. Notable among his publications are *Salutes and Censures* (1982); *Stubborn Hope* (1975); *A Simple Lust: Collected Poems of South African Jail and Exile including Letters to Martha* (1973); *China Poems* (1975).

C. GEORGE CAFFENTZIS has taught at the University of Calabar (Nigeria); he is now Associate Professor of Philosophy at the University of Southern Maine. His research is in the field of political philosophy and philosophy of money. His publications include: *Abused Words, Clipped Coins and Civil Government: John Locke's Philosophy of Money* (1989), and *Exciting The Industry of Mankind: George Berkeley's Philosophy of Money* (forthcoming), the first two volumes of a trilogy on the British empiricists' philosophy of money and the construction of colonial theory. He is the co-editor of *A Thousand Flowers. Structural Adjustment and the Struggle for Education in Africa* (2000). He is a co-ordinator of the Committee for Academic Freedom in Africa.

DIANE CIEKAWY is Associate Professor of Anthropology at Ohio University. She has conducted research with Mijikenda people of the Kenya coast since 1982. Her articles on politics, law, human rights and religion appear in *Humanity and Society, Political and Legal Anthropology Review, Women's Studies International Forum and African Studies Review*. She is currently completing an ethnography of Kajiwe's Uganga wa Kuvoyera Movement in Coastal Kenya.

STEVEN COLATRELLA is currently Visiting Assistant Professor of Sociology at Bard College in Annadale-on-Hudson (New York). He has also taught sociology in Rome (Italy) at the American University of Rome and Loyola University's Rome Center. His research work is in the area of world migration, development, and social movements. His works include: *Workers of the World: African and Asian Migrants in Italy* (forthcoming); *Midnight Oil: Work, Energy, War 1973–1992* (1992 (co-edited). He is a member of the Midnight Notes journal collective.

SILVIA FEDERICI is Associate Professor of International Studies and Political Philosophy at New College of Hofstra University. Her research work has been in the fields of womens' studies and multicultural studies. She has written essays on feminist theory, education, and multiculturalism. Her works include: *Il Grande Calibano. Storia del Corpo Sociale Ribelle Nella Prima Fase del Capitale* (1984) (co-authored) *(The Great Caliban. History of the Rebel Social Body in the First Phase of Capitalism); Enduring Western Civilization: The Construction of the Concept of Western Civilization and Its "Others"* (1995) (edited); *A Thousand Flowers. Structural Adjustment and the Struggle For Education in Africa* (2000) (co-edited). She is a co-ordinator of the Committee for Academic Freedom in Africa.

KARIM F. HIRJI was born and grew up in Tanzania. He has taught at the University of Dar es Salaam, the National Institute of Transport in Tanzania, and the University of California at Los Angeles. His research interests have covered development of statistical methods, biomedical data analysis, and the history and contemporary problems of education in Tanzania. He has published over fifty papers in a variety of journals and is an internationally recognized expert on the analysis of small sample data. He is also a recipient of the Snedecor Award for Best Publication in Biometry from the American Statistical Association and the International Biometrics Society. His current research focus is on the ethics of health research in Africa and the Third World.

MAINA WA KĪNYATTĪ is one of Keyna's most progressive historians. In June 1982 he was arrested by the Kenyan authoritarian regime, charged with possession of seditious literature and imprisoned. He suffered for six-and-a-half years in the hands of his captors. He was repeatedly held in solitary confinement and was constantly insulted and beaten. But he remained defiant, his courage and spirit unbroken. He is most renowned for his historical work on the Mau Mau struggle. His works include: *Thunder from the Mountains* (1980); *Kenya Freedom Struggle* (1987); *Mau Mau: A Revolution Betrayed*

(1992); *A Season of Blood: Poems from Kenya Prisons* (1995); *Kenya: A Prison Notebook* (1996).

LOREN KRUGER is Professor of English, Comparative Literature, and African Studies at the University of Chicago. She is the author of *The Drama of South Africa: Plays, Pageants and Publics Since 1910* (Routledge, 1999) and "Theatre for Development or TV Nation?" published in *Research in African Literatures* (1999).

ALAMIN M. MAZRUI is Associate Professor at the Department of American and African Studies at Ohio State University at Columbus. He has published widely on the politics of language and on African literature and politics. He is the co-author, with Ibrahim Shariff, of *The Swahili: Idiom and Identity* (1994), and (with Ali Mazrui) of *The Tower of Babel: Language and Governance in the African Experience* (1998). He has also published two plays: *Kilio Cha Haki* (1982) and *Shadows of the Moon* (1992).

JOSEPH McLAREN, is Associate Professor of English at Hofstra University, specializes in African American literature and African literature in English. He has written numerous articles on black literature and culture. His writings have appeared in the *Popular Culture Review, Masterpieces of African American Literature, The African American Encyclopedia, The Cyclopedia of World Authors*, the *Langston Hughes Review,* and the *Journal of Black Studies*. Dr. McLaren has presented papers at national and international conferences of the Popular Culture Association and the African Literature Association. Among his other interests are jazz studies and contemporary African American cinema. He is the author of *Langston Hughes: Folk Dramatist in the Protest Tradition, 1921–1943* (Greenwood, 1997) and co-editor of *Migrating Words and Worlds: Pan-Africanism Updated* (Africa World Press, 1999).

SORAYA MEKERTA is Assistant Professor of French and Francophone studies at Spelman College. She has developed several courses in Francophone Studies (literature and film) and has taught courses on the African Diaspora and the world. Her scholarly research and interests are interdisciplinary and focus on the intersections of literature, culture, and politics for a diversity of Francophone communities, including the north African Diaspora. She is a native of Algeria.

DONALD M. MORALES is Associate Professor of literature at Mercy College, Westchester, New York with a specialization in African and African American drama. Publications include "Black Arts and Radical South African Theater: A Comparative View," *The Literary Griot*, (fall 1989), "Post-

Apartheid Theater," *1994 African Literature Association Annual* Selected Papers (1994); "The African Image in Gabriel Garcia Marquez' Fiction," *Journal of Afro-Latin American Studies and Literatures* (1998); and "Do Black Theater Institutions Translate into Great Drama?" *African American Review* (winter 1997). In 1987–1989, Dr. Morales served with Leslie Lee as Drama judges for the NEC's playwriting contest.

CHERYL B. MWARIA, is Associate Professor of Anthropology at Hofstra University where she is currently the Director of Africana Studies. Among her recent works are "Biomedical Ethics, Gender and Ethnicity: Implications for Black Feminist Anthropology" in Irma McClaurin (ed.), *Black Feminist Anthropology: Theory, Praxis, Politics and Poetics* (forthcoming); Diversity in the Context of Medical Anthropology: A New Look at the Curriculum. Book chapter in Ida Susser & Tom Patterson, (eds.), *Cultural Diversity in the U.S.: A Critical Reader* (forthcoming); "Physican-Assisted Suicide: An Anthropological Perspective" in *Fordham Urban Law Journal*, vol. xxiv, no. 4 (1997). As a medical anthropoligist, she has conducted research in Africa, the Middle East, and the Caribbean. She has written on childbirth and child rearing in Kenya, biomedical ethics, women's health and race relations. Currently, her research focuses on issues pertaining to disability.

FRANÇOIS NGOLET is Assistant Professor of History at the College of Staten Island of the City University of New York. His interest on research lie on migrations and cultural changes in the Ogooué River Basin. He is presently analyzing problems of ethnicity in colonial and postcolonial Gabon. Professor Ngolet has published many articles in scholarly journals such as the *Journal of African History, Africa Today* and the *Revue Française d'Histoire d'Outre-Mer*. He is currently working on a book length manuscript focusing on the invention of ethnic identity in central Gabon.

NGŨGĨ WA THIONG'O is one of the most important contemporary writers from the African continent. He wrote his first novels and plays in English. His novels include *Weep Not, Child, The River Between, A Grain of Wheat* and *Petals of Blood.* He has also written several plays including *The Trial of Dedan Kimathi* and essays on literature and language, such as *Barrel of a Pen: Resistance to Repression in Neo-Colonial Kenya* (1983) and *Decolonising the Mind. The Politics of Language in African Literature* (1986).

HABIBEH RAHIM is currently Assistant Professor in the Department of Theological and Religious Studies at St. John's University, Jamaica, New York. She received her doctorate from Harvard University in the Department of Near Eastern Languages and Civilizations. Her research interests include Islamic Studies, Comparative Spirituality, Religion and Literature, and Art. In

1996, she directed an international conference and simultaneously curated an exhibition, both entitled: Inscription as Art in the World of Islam: Unity in Diversity at Hofstra University, Hempstead, New York.

IDA SUSSER is Professor of Anthropology at Hunter College and the Graduate Center of the City University of New York. She is the author of *Norman Street: Poverty and Politics in an Urban Neighborhood* (1982), co-author of Medical Anthropology in the World System (Bergin and Garvey, 1997) and co-editor of *AIDS in Africa and the Caribbean* (1997). She has conducted research in the United States, Puerto Rico and Southern Africa and has published numerous articles concerning inequality, health and gender.